THE ISLAND RACE

Rooted in a period of vigorous exploration and colonialism, *The Island Race: Englishness, Empire and Gender in the Eighteenth Century* is an innovative study of the issues of nation, gender and identity.

In the rapidly expanding eighteenth-century world, English perceptions of origin and heritage became altered – the question of national identity emerging as a particularly troubled and ambiguous issue. Wilson bases her analysis on a wide range of case studies drawn both from Britain and across the Atlantic and Pacific worlds. Creating a colorful and original colonial landscape, she considers topics such as sodomy, theater, masculinity, the symbolism of Britannia and the role of women in war. Wilson shows the far-reaching implications that colonial power and expansion had upon the English people's sense of self, and argues that the vaunted singularity of English culture was in fact constituted by the bodies, practices and exchanges of peoples across the globe. Theoretically rigorous and highly readable, *The Island Race* will become a seminal text for understanding the pressing issues that it confronts.

Kathleen Wilson is Associate Professor of History at the State University of New York at Stony Brook. She has written widely on empire and the politics of culture in eighteenth-century Britain, including *The Sense of the People: Politics, Culture and Imperialism in England 1715–1785*, winner of the 1995 Whitfield Prize for British History, Royal Historical Society, and the 1996 John Ben Snow Prize of the North American Conference on British Studies.

THE ISLAND RACE

Englishness, empire and gender in the eighteenth century

Kathleen Wilson

London and New York

First published 2003
by Routledge
11 New Fetter Lane, London EC4P 4EE

Simultaneously published in the USA and Canada
by Routledge
29 West 35th Street, New York, NY 10001

Routledge is an imprint of the Taylor & Francis Group

© 2003 Kathleen Wilson

Typeset in Goudy by
Keystroke, Jacaranda Lodge, Wolverhampton
Printed and bound in Great Britain by
St Edmundsbury Press, Bury St Edmunds, Suffolk

British Library Cataloguing in Publication Data
A catalogue record for this book is available from the British Library

Library of Congress Cataloging in Publication Data
A catalog record for this book has been requested

ISBN 0–415–15895–8 (hbk)
ISBN 0–415–15896–6 (pbk)

FOR NICK AND HANNAH

CONTENTS

FIGURES AND MAPS

Figures

PREFACE AND
ACKNOWLEDGMENTS

This book, to my mind, is a monograph masquerading as a book of essays. It is written by a single author, and it pursues the same set of ideas through a variety of historical and geographical terrains. Its overarching theme is the heterogeneous and unstable nature of national identity in eighteenth-century Britain and its first empire; its subtopics explore the impact of empire and gender on productions of national identity and its failures. It is a new kind of history book, in that it is both archivally based and attempts to engage with historical issues and theoretical debates emanating from a more cross-disciplinary arena than history alone. Hopefully it will intrigue scholars of whatever disciplines interested in the processual, embedded nature of identity in historical settings. One more caveat should be stressed from the outset. The argument here is presented through a series of case studies that allows the reader to range widely across the globe, but it does not pretend to be comprehensive. Rather, the focus is on some of the cultural sites of "nation-ness" within England and the colonies that reveal how islands and empire converged to structure eighteenth-century Britons' beliefs about their national character and destiny. Needless to say, there are other ways to address these questions, some of which are on display in recent studies of nationalism. The significance of the growing presence of the British in India as well as British forays into North and West Africa, the Middle and Far East, and the Arctic could all be addressed with profit through the analytic I develop here, and I hope to be able to extend my geographical scope further in a future study. Nevertheless, readers interested by these topics and locations may also want to read this book, because its concepts, problems and questions are all equally imbricated in the dynamic and interconnected network of transculture, commodities and identities forged by eighteenth-century empires.

Since the start of my academic career, I have been asked by British students and senior scholars alike why I, as an American, am interested in British history. The question never fails to produce in me two contradictory responses, one of which I consciously reject, and one of which I embrace. The first response attempts to mobilize my claims to the eighteenth-century British past in terms of my own genealogy. Some of my maternal progenitors were Puritans who immigrated from Bedfordshire and Nottinghamshire to New England in 1629; their descendants in the 1700s played prominent roles in colonial Connecticut politics (as both British loyalists and radicals during the beginning of the troubles in the 1760s) and in the Atlantic trade. My great-great-uncle, a famous atheist and political activist of the later nineteenth century, also maintained assiduous personal and familial ties with a transatlantic community interested in metaphysical and moral issues and human rights. Hence, my "stake" in British history: I was, as it were, British and colonial in the eighteenth century, historical filiations which were continued by other means into the next! But such a defense, if made almost automatic by centuries of indoctrination by nation-states, is politically retrograde. It assumes that some people have more of a claim on their pasts than others, that the histories of nations have a natural constituency and a logical progression, both of which unfold within well-defined territorial frontiers, and that the cultural and mental boundaries of national belonging cannot be crossed save by claims of "blood." And indeed, although the family history I outline above is "true," like all genealogies it is also a political mystification that, in my case, deliberately obscures the wonderfully hybrid peoples and circumstances that also are part of my background, embracing Swedish, Scottish and German as well as (statistically likely) Native American and African-American forebears. I am thus much more comfortable with my second response, which is to declare I've as much a right to reinterpret the British past as any other denizen of the modern world. Indeed, if we are to take seriously the much-trumpeted discovery of the past two decades that national identities are fictions and nation-states invented, then we must also embrace the idea that we share a collective and entangled set of histories to which each of us, regardless of national, gender or ethnic origin, has equal "rights." More particularly, only the dead now inhabit the eighteenth century, so any bid for exclusive ownership is hamstrung from the start. Yet we all live and wrestle with their legacies, which we must claim, contest or refute for ourselves. "The past is an emergency," Walter Benjamin once wrote, by which he meant that history is too important to be allowed to "speak for itself" and must instead be seized upon and made to give up its possibilities for critique, challenge and transformation. The geographical and temporal location of such an emergency is identified by every historian. In my case, it is located firmly in an eighteenth-century British and colonial past, exhilarating in its multiplicities, its complex and transoceanic configurations of cultural, political and demographic movement, and its refusal to settle down into tidy, complacent narratives.

This book has been several years in the making, and I am pleased to be able to acknowledge the many institutions and people who have helped bring it to completion. A University Fellowship from the National Endowment for the Humanities and a Newberry-National Endowment for the Humanities Fellowship from The Newberry Library provided me with two years of research that laid the groundwork for this study. This is not the book either institution thought it was funding, but hopefully they may find it acceptable nonetheless. Other support came from semesters or summers of research funded by the Nuala Drescher Fund at the State University of New York, Individual Development Awards from the United University Professions Union, the Department of History, State University of New York, Stony Brook, the Henry E. Huntington Library, the British Academy, and the Humanities Research Centre, Australian National University. Archivists and librarians at the British Library, British Museum Department of Prints and Drawings, the Public Record Office, the Theatre Museum (V & A), the Bedfordshire Record Office, the Norwich and Norfolk Record Office, the American Antiquarian Society, The Huntington Library, The Newberry Library, The John Carter Brown Library, Houghton Library of Harvard University, Beinecke Library of Yale University, Columbia University Library, the University of Wisconsin-Madison Library, the Special Collections and Interlibrary Loan at Melville Library, SUNY-Stony Brook, and the National Library of Australia were unfailing in their assistance, advice and tireless efforts to find me what I needed. To all, my sincere and humble thanks.

Individuals and groups have listened to every one of the chapters in this book with varying amounts of attention and appreciation, and I have benefited from the comments I have received in all cases. Versions were given as papers to: The Center for Literary and Cultural Studies, Harvard University, the Berkshire Conference of Women Historians, the Columbia University Atlantic World Seminar, the CUNY Graduate Center, the Mid-West American Society for Eighteenth Century Studies, the University of Delaware, the annual conferences of the North American Conference on British Studies, the American Society for Eighteenth Century Studies, and the American Historical Association, conferences of the Feminism and Enlightenment Project at the University of Warwick and the University of London, the Huntington Library, the Yale Center for British Art and the Center for Eighteenth Century Studies at York. I would like to thank the participants at all of these forums for their lively interest and astute questions. The ideas in this book were first tried out in successive gatherings of my graduate seminar, 'Histories, Empires, Identities', at the State University of New York at Stony Brook. All of the students deserve plaudits for gamely working through its changing and overly ambitious intellectual agenda. I would like to thank in particular Dr. Judith Travers, Dr. William Barnhart, Dr. Diane Robinson-Dunn, Dr. James Genova and Jenise DePinto for their insights. The History Department Faculty Colloquium series provided encouragement and enthusiasm for the project throughout; the caliber and verve of the outstanding intellectual community within the History Department and the University help keep the insularity of Long Island at bay. Finally, I was very fortunate to be able to prepare the final version of this manuscript while a Visiting Fellow at the Humanities Research Center, Australian National University. The Introduction and Chapter 5 have consequently benefited from informed discussion offered by participants of the Work in Progress Seminar, HRC, the Libertine Enlightenment Conference, University of Queensland, and the English and Cultural Studies seminar at Melbourne University.

An earlier version of Chapter 1 appeared in *Eighteenth Century Studies*, vol. 29 (1995–6), 69–96. Some of the materials in Chapter 2 were first published in "The

Island Race: Captain Cook, Evangelicalism and English National Identity, 1760–1820," Tony Claydon and Ian McBride, eds., *Protestantism and National Identity 1760–1820* (Cambridge: Cambridge University Press, 1998), 265–90; and in "Pacific Modernity: Theatre, Englishness and the Arts of Discovery," Colin Jones and Dror Wahrman (eds), *The Age of Cultural Revolutions* (Berkeley and Los Angeles: University of California Press, 2001). Thanks to the publishers for republication permission.

Other friends and colleagues upon whose support, criticisms, suggestions, competing interpretations and good humor I have relied include: Jan Albers, John Brewer, Michèle Cohen, Young-Sun Hong, Margaret Hunt, Joanna Innes, Lawrence Klein, Ned Landsman, Iona Man-Cheong, Gary Marker and Rachel Weil. John Brewer's cogent comments on the penultimate draft of the manuscript sharpened and clarified its arguments at several points, as did the remarks of Catherine Hall and Felicity Nussbaum. Dror Wahrman debated ideas about eighteenth-century identities with me, to the benefit of my subsequent thinking on the subject. Michael Dobson confirmed my early and somewhat inchoate convictions about the centrality of theater in English culture. Dian Kriz kindly pointed me to the Edwards MS held at the John Carter Brown Library. Sacha Mirzoeff first alerted me to Kingston Deverill "Save the Stones!" campaign, and passed on relevant literature. The late Michael Sprinter gave effusive support for this project in its embryonic stage. Above all, Nicholas Mirzoeff shared ideas and interpretations with his typical generosity and intellectual acumen, and read more drafts of the manuscript than I care to recall: of his brilliance (and fortitude) I remain in awe. At Routledge, Heather McCallum, and, more recently, Victoria Peters provided models of engaged editorial support and expertise, and I am grateful to them both. Pamela Cohen of Australian National University provided invaluable assistance with the notes. And I would be extremely remiss if I did not thank at the start all the scholars, formally acknowledged within, upon whose territory I am impinging in this exploration, and from whose work I have learned an immense amount. Their collective efforts have done nothing less than refashion my intellectual vistas and my sense of possibilities. I should add that they are in no way responsible for the (mis) use I have made of their findings.

Finally, I want to thank all my friends and family for continuing to put up with me. Special commendations go to my parents-in-laws, Judith and Eddie Mirzoeff, without whose heroic levels of hospitality and childcare this book could not have been written. My mother, Alice Wilson, has urged me on despite the travails of infancy and toddlerhood (my own, as well as my daughter's). My nephews, Michael Wilson and Alex Wilson, have always been fonts of energy and happiness for me. Most of all, I must thank my husband, Nicholas Mirzoeff, and my daughter, Hannah Mirzoeff, for being the joys of my life. This book is dedicated to them, in Hannah's year 6, for all the right reasons.

Stony Brook, Long Island, USA   Canberra, ACT, Australia

ABBREVIATIONS

AHR	*American Historical Review*
AR	*Annual Register*
Cook	J. C. Beaglehole, *The Journals of Captain Cook*, 3 vols. (Cambridge: Cambridge University Press for the Hakluyt Society, 1955–65)
	I *Voyage of the Endeavour* (1955)
	II *Voyage of the Resolution and Adventure* (1961)
	III *Voyage of the Resolution and Discovery* (1965)
BL	British Library
BM	British Museum, Dept. of Prints and Drawings
DNB	*Dictionary of National Biography*
ECS	*Eighteenth Century Studies*
HJ	*Historical Journal*
HL	Huntington Library
JBS	*Journal of British Studies*
JCB	John Carter Brown Library
Long	Edward Long, *The History of Jamaica*, 3 vols. (London, 1774, reprt., London: Frank Cass, 1970)
OHBE	*The Oxford History of the British Empire* ser. ed. William Roger Louis (Oxford: Oxford University Press, 1998)
	I Nicholas Canny, ed., *The Origins of Empire*
	II Peter Marshall, ed., *The Eighteenth Century*
P & P	*Past and Present*
PRO	Public Record Office
TRHS	*Transactions of the Royal Historical Society*
WMQ	*William and Mary Quarterly*

Note: In the references, publishers are given for printed archival materials whenever traceable; when not, the date alone appears. For manuscript as well as printed sources, Old Style dates have not been changed, but the year has been taken to begin on January 1.

No man is an *Island*, entire of it self; every man is a piece of the *Continent*, a part of the main . . .

John Donne, *Meditation XVII* (1624)

The English are a People not only separated from the rest of the world by Situation, but different also from other Nations as well in the Complexion and Temperament of the Natural Body, as in the Constitution of our Body Politick.

George Farquhar, A *Discourse on Comedy* (1702)

Nations are for the most part so blended by war, by commerce or by other means that vain would be the attempt to trace out an original character in any cultivated nation . . . The nations that may be the most relied on for an original character, are Islanders at a distance from the continent and from each other.

Henry Home, Lord Kames, *Sketches of the History of Man* (1778)

When Great Britain was first visited by the Phoenicians, the inhabitants were painted savages, much less civilized than those of Tongataboo, or Otaheite; and it is not impossible, but that our late voyages may, in process of time, spread the blessings of civilization amongst the numerous islanders of the South Pacific Ocean, and be the means of abolishing their abominable repasts, and almost equally abominable sacrifices.

James Cook and James King, A *Voyage to the Pacific Ocean* (1784)

INTRODUCTION: NATIONS, EMPIRES AND IDENTITIES IN THE EIGHTEENTH CENTURY

... As Self-Love is an Instinct planted in us for the Good and Safety of each particular Person, the Love of our Country is impress'd on our Minds for the Happiness and Preservation of the Community. This Instinct is so remarkable, that we find Examples of it in those who are born in the most uncomfortable Climates, or the worst of Governments. ... We have an Instance ... among the very *Hottentots*. One of these Savages was brought into *England*, taught our Language, and in a great Measure polish'd out of his natural Barbarity: But upon being carry'd back to the Cape of *Good Hope* (where it was thought he been of Advantage to our *English* Traders) he mix'd in a kind of Transport with his Country-men, brutaliz'd with 'em in their Habit and Manners, and wou'd never again return to his foreign Acquaintance ... the Love of one's Country is natural to every Man.
> Joseph Addison, *The Freeholder*, January 6, 1716

Ever since the French got a good footing in North America, Great Britain, in my humble opinion, should no longer have considered herself as an island; ... While our northern colonies are surrounded on the *North* and *West* by the French settlements, we must ... consider *Britain*, in some measure, as a continental state. She owes protection to those colonies, as being now her chief support, and they cannot be effectually protected but by well-disciplined troops and experienced officers.
> *Newcastle General Magazine*, 1757

JOHNSON: You may remember an officer at Fort Augustus, who had served in America, told us of a woman they were obliged to *bind*, in order to get her back from the savage life.
BOSWELL: She must have been an animal, a beast.
JOHNSON: Sir, she was a speaking cat.
> *Life of Johnson*, 1778

What is identity? Scholars of eighteenth-century Britain aren't sure, but they think they know it when they see it. Although the past decade has seen a proliferation of studies focusing on early modern Britain and Europe that are concerned with questions of identity – of nation, gender, empire, class, politics and race – the concept of identity itself, and its usefulness as an analytic or descriptive category in historical work, has received surprisingly little attention.[1] Part of the problem, of course, is that historians have not been able to agree exactly on what "identity" means in premodern societies. Is it voluntary, or is it imposed? Is it as applicable to the individual as the collectivity, in an age when people took their status from family, region, occupation, religion and connections?[2] I argue here that it is. Certainly in some ways, the notion of identity in its modern psychological sense may have been anachronistic: for much of the period, Georgian people, or at least those to whom we have access, tended to assess themselves less through their internal lives (although their state of virtue, sin and morality was important to many) than through their behavior, social position and reputation. Nevertheless, as we have discovered in our studies of class, gender, sexuality and politics, anachronism can be productive in interpreting the past, not least by disrupting our own sense of inevitable progress: indeed, history itself is but a higher form of anachronism. Further, as a host of distinguished historians and postcolonial critics have observed, a politics of identity has been in place since the beginnings of colonization and slavery, even if it has not been acknowledged as such.[3] From this perspective, although identity functions as an analytic or interpretive concept, it also could radically configure historical experience. Hence to look for the grounds of identity-formation in the eighteenth century may also cast a searching light on the instability and unpredictability of those intersections of history, culture and agency where people group themselves, as well as where they are grouped.

Yet identity was in fact a concept used in scientific and philosophical discussion in the eighteenth century to describe the presumed fact that a person or thing is itself and not something else. "Of all relations the most universal is that of identity, being common to every being, whose existence has any duration," Hume remarked in his *Treatise on Human Nature* (1739),[4] thereby rekindling debates on identity, consciousness and the laws of psychology swirling since Locke. Hume's conceptualization of identity as the idea of being the same over time – i.e., that the self has "invariable and uninterrupted existence through the whole course of our lives" – would come under increasing scrutiny over the century, as the emphasis on the individual's interior life as central to social progress was naturalized by the growth of print culture, the cult of sensibility and new psycho-physiological paradigms.[5] Moreover, backed by Adam Smith's moral theory that envisaged the self as a public performance, Georgian people explored the possibilities of social masquerade in allowing them to be "in some degree whatever character we choose," as James Boswell asserted, so that personal identity could seem for some to be as much a product of choice as of birth.[6] Yet these new technologies of the self also *required* class, gender, sexual and national identifications, and marked a shift in the meaning of identity from the state of being the same, to the state of being different. In this study, the conceptualization of identity is, unusually, indebted to Hume, Smith and their postmodern critics, for it defines identity as a *relation*, and a *mode of differentiation*, emerging through dialogic engagement with the social, that is the product

of both agency and coercion. To put it another way, identity results from the negotiation between where one is placed and where one places oneself within social
networks, working through what is possible as well as what is forbidden.[7] Existing
in time as neither a "stable, unchanging and continuous fram[e] of reference" nor
a fact of the past waiting to be recovered, identity is a historical process, "a matter
of 'becoming' as well as of 'being,'" as Stuart Hall has evocatively put it, that
produces and is produced by people's positioning in the narratives of the past.[8]

As a historical process, identity is tentative, multiple and contingent, and its
modalities change over time. In the eighteenth century, the relations of individuals
and collectives to each other were rendered through religion, politics, geography,
sociability, politeness and "stage" of civilization, among other things, and these
relations, or identities, could be expressed through verbal, textual, kinesthetic and
visual forms. But however actualized, identities were, and are, inextricably bound
to a historical social order and both concretized and challenged through practices
of everyday life. As Thomas Holt has eloquently argued, "One of the primordial
ways in which the self is knowable or realized . . . is through its interactions with
everyday life, where other entities and other selves are encountered." History
is crucial to this process of both personal and collective identity and memory –
"To think 'I am' requires 'I was' which needs in turn a narrative of 'they' and/or 'we'
. . . A self is knowable . . . only in terms of its history."[9] And although identity was
in part performative – that is, a citational social practice that *constitutes* "the very
subject it is purported to express"[10] – it nevertheless could pose, as Hume suggests,
as both universal and irreducible, an essence of the individual or national character.
Therein lay its complexities and its dangers.

If Hume's definition provides one of the poles against which identity is
understood in this study, then Samuel Johnson's definition of the "national" as
public performance poses the other. Defining "nation" as "a people distinguished
from another people; generally by language, original [*sic*] or government," the
"national," according to his *Dictionary*, is "publick, general; not private, not
particular," the public expression or acts of a people.[11] As Johnson intimates,
national identity, too, was performed through group and individual interactions in
the matrix of everyday relations, where the public and the domestic, the personal
and the historical intersected, and social performance was paramount in defining
the relations between self and world. But one further aspect in the production of
a "national identity" needs to be stressed at the outset: although never automatic,
national identity, like other identities, depended upon the ability of individuals to
insert themselves into the weft of collective narratives, and to identify themselves
with experiences that are shared through representation. As such, identification
with the nation is a "phantasmatic staging," an event that takes place in the
imaginary,[12] a psychic as well as social production that certain kinds of sources, such
as diaries and memoirs, may allow us to track with some care.[13] Approaching
national identity as a historical process rather than an outcome, and as an individual as well as collective mode of consciousness, shifts the grounds of historical
interpretation, enabling us to track how contending ideas about difference and the

terms of national, ethnic and imperial belonging were proliferated across varied social terrains and performed crucial ideological work in eighteenth-century notions of self, polity and collectivity. Such a perspective also encourages us to aim to write histories of identity through representation, examining the ways in which people "were positioned and subject-ed in the dominant regimes of representation . . . [as] critical exercises of cultural power and normalization," rather than histories of the representation of identity. As Homi Bhabha has noted, nations, "like narratives, lose their origins in the myths of time and only fully realize their horizons in the mind's eye."[14]

With these conceptual issues in mind, this book undertakes to examine the episodic and unstable nature of national identities in eighteenth-century Britain. It begins by recognizing identity as a problem, rather than an automatic auxiliary of state expansion, colonization and the ideologies of nation. Its chapters explore the divergent meanings of modernity for eighteenth-century Britons, the construction of English ethnicity through the figure of Captain Cook, the impact of warfare on women's identities as citizens, the serial self-inventions of an English courtesan turned Jamaican émigré, and the role of gender misrecognition on the Cook voyages in producing late Enlightenment categories of difference. Throughout the analysis attempts to probe the range of historical meanings and consequences of eighteenth-century understandings of identity as national belonging, citizenship and difference. In the process, national identity emerges as a fragmented and fragmenting process – that "structuring presence of alterity in the formulation of the we," to paraphrase Judith Butler – that promises, but can never deliver, a full and final recognition.[15] At the same time, the ideologies of nation both invented and performed social and historical difference[16] – and those differences invariably have not only distinguished *the* nation from other nations, but have also divided the citizens within its own boundaries. As historical productions whose cultural and political meanings change over time, Britishness and Englishness were not immutable and eternal formations, but sites of struggle whose tropes of representation are specific to particular periods. In the early modern period, within the "nation" mapped out by territorial, linguistic or patrilineal ties, national identities were understood, performed and consumed in a variety of ways by different groups, depending upon the gender, class and ethnicity of their members and hence upon these groups' and individuals' (unequal) access to the resources of the nation-state. The histories of these multiple and heterogeneous experiences of national identification and disavowal cannot be reduced to histories of "nationalism(s)" per se, but must be recovered instead through the analysis of the fragmentary and often paradoxical modes and meanings of cultural expression that constructed identities themselves, and the analysis of representational and material practices as well as policies.[17] "Englishness" from this perspective appears to be less a stable and eternal entity (revolving, for example, around the supposed perennial fixities of Protestantism, King, Parliament, Liberty and Englishmen's birthrights) than a continually contested terrain, a "sign of difference" the specific meanings of which depended upon the contexts of its articulations.[18] Whose nation, then, was it? Who was imagining it, and what was it imagined to consist of? If the imagined community of the nation was imagined as *fraternal* community, as many scholars have suggested, then how did its cultural representations address, mobilize and influence the desires and aspirations of *all* of its citizens and subjects? Could the terms of national belonging be rendered capacious enough to accommodate all of the "others" within? Or does belonging depend upon exclusion?

However, in attempting to give historical specificity and grounding to competing abstractions about the English nation, this study deliberately expands the boundaries of "English culture" beyond its traditional ones. "The English are not less divided from the rest of the world by the circumfluent seas," Oliver Goldsmith wrote in 1760, the year after the *annus mirabilis* had cemented Britain's hold on the North American empire, "than differing from them in their manners, dispositions, and turn of thinking."[19] This view of the relationship between national topography and national character continues to be a hallowed article of Englishness to this day. In the early modern period, the myth of the island as solitary and singular – "this blessed plot" – and as harborer of distinctive, marvelous or endangered forms of life cast a powerful spell over the European and English imagination. At the same time, islands' importance as generators of colonization, capitalist production and ecological thinking alike became increasingly pronounced.[20] But as Caribbeanists have stressed for some time, islands can be said to exist only in relation to other things, such as seas, continents and other islands, and so they are not "insular" but vibrant entrepots in oceanic networks linking people, goods and cultures.[21] England itself, of course, had never been an island. But a convergence of developments leads to the re-discovery of island-ness as a formative force within British and English history. Indeed, at the precise moment when England was *less* an island than ever before – when the reach of British trade, arms, colonies and claims transected several seas in an increasingly global grasp; when an explosion of travel literature disseminated images of tropical island paradises to force a re-thinking of Britain's own pasts; when voyaging and exploration took on new psychological significance as mental and moral as well as political and commercial activities; and when the labor, movement, commodities and cultures of foreign and colonial peoples were underwriting English prosperity and "character" – English people were most eager to stress the ways in which their nation was unique, culturally as well as topographically. The trope of the island, in other words, although long powerful in imaginary literature and material policies, began to serve not only as metaphor but also as explanation for English dominance and superiority in arts and arms. And as islands became important devices in the examination of self, society and species, they also served as the engines for new ways of thinking about nation, race and gender. Hence, reaching far beyond the Atlantic archipelago to transoceanic settings where both old and new theaters of exploration and colonization exerted their centripetal pull, English culture and epistemology was being made in the eighteenth century from the "outside" as well as in. The multiplicities and divergences of national experience and national identification within specific sites of the broader imperium thus provide both our point of departure and our itinerary.

The Race of Nation

The quotations with which the chapter began point one way in to eighteenth-century British thinking about national identity. Addison's remarks on the "Instinct" for love of country locates nationality in both nature and nurture: impressed onto the blank slate of the infant through experience, national identity becomes inextricable from the self, an essence of distinctiveness as universal as human nature, and as ineradicable as climate and geography. Not even a "Hottentot" could escape its force, and as such it becomes part of an individual and collective inheritance.[22] More implicit in Addison's rumination was the role played by empire and expansion in the thinking about national identity, a role the writer for the *Newcastle Magazine* made explicit. From this perspective, Britain's growing imperial possessions had to force changes in the way that national identity was conceived, understood and defended and that "Britain" and England were thought about as discrete entities, for the relationship between mother country and filial colonies required more expansive frontiers and an ever-sterner masculine military protection. Johnson and Boswell's discussion of the English woman who went native succinctly captures the ambivalence of the inscription of nationality for women and the dangers that could await them in colonization itself: with culture as the unstable gloss on their more rudimentary nature, they were less able to withstand the lure of the exotic, bestial or sensual: they, unlike the Hottentot, could too easily forget their own culture.[23] All three quotations share some obvious assumptions about the relation of gender and descent to patriotism and nationality, to which we shall return. Perhaps less obviously, all three also exhibit conundrums at the heart of British Enlightenment thinking about national identity and difference, familiar to the thinkers themselves and to their historians: the tenuous nature of the opposition between nature and society,[24] the innate and the acquired, or, to put it another way, the distressing tendency for supposedly "natural" characteristics to degenerate into their opposites: Englishness into savagery, masculinity into effeminacy, femininity into vulgarity. The difficulties generated by these oppositions and their always imminent collapse permeated British conceptions of national belonging throughout most of the eighteenth century; they are never resolved within the discourses of difference available to Enlightenment thinkers and writers, and, indeed, may have yet to be resolved.[25] Emerging through and between the century's authoritative assertions about the "sexed mind" or the "savage's" capacity for progress, the poles of an essentialized Nature and a capricious Evironment exerted their contrary pulls through ideas that linger in ghostly forms in our own efforts at theorizing the period. In the 1700s, they mobilized not only confident assertions about the superiority of English culture and political institutions, but also protracted, recurrent and obsessive fears about the fungibility of the national identity and the virtue of the national character. They also, most crucially, gave notions of national identity their almost magical power to *make what is acquired seem innate*. In the rest of this introduction, I shall sketch in the productive conflicts that arise from eighteenth-century notions of national identity as essence and as simulacrum, and relate these conflicts to equivalent indeterminacies in historical and historiographic constructions of empire, race and gender.

Although there can be little doubt that the nation was coming to be the most accepted and convenient category through which to organize knowledge and consciousness in the eighteenth century, there were still significant differences in the conceptualization of the nascent nations of early modern Europe and our own day. The idea of "nation" once referred to a breed, stock or race; and, although the idea of nation as a political entity was gaining ascendancy, the more restrictive racial sense remained embedded in its use.[26] In the eighteenth century, nation as a political-territorial entity continued to compete with older Biblical and juridical concepts of nation as a people, located in a relatively fixed spatial and cultural terrain, that was conceived of geographically and ethnographically (as well as ethnocentrically). In this context, dividing the human species up into nations was arguably the most widely used category of difference in the period, and nation served to map, literally and metaphorically, the moral, philosophical, theological and historical debates over human diversity, human nature, and the impact of climate, government, language and laws on both.[27] The belief that different nations had different moral, intellectual and perhaps even physical characteristics, of course, dated from ancient times.[28] But these were given renewed force by eighteenth-century explorations of the boundaries of self and world, and by the proliferation of printed and performed material that enumerated the distinctive characters of the different nations of the globe.[29] As the work of intellectuals from John Locke to John Millar suggests, Britons of the period never tired of investigating how humanity's common descent and "universal" nature resulted in the marvelous cultural, linguistic and physical multiplicity of the modern world. But the interest in the explanation of national and human difference was never confined to philosophers and scientists: it occupied the attention of a range of writers, artists and social performers, from clergymen, journalists, painters, actors, travelers, novelists, playwrights and memoirists to ordinary men and women; was conceptualized and understood in a variety of competing and not always compatible ways; and aligned to modes of understanding in the natural and political as well as social and cultural realms. Overall, of course, few doubted that in the assessment of "the common arts of life," as Millar called them, Britain enjoyed superior advantages. "Hail Britain, happiest of countries! Happy in thy climate, fertility, situation and commerce; but still happier in the peculiar nature of thy laws and government," Goldsmith extolled.[30] "Nation," then, provided an essential principle of social organization and taxonomy in eighteenth-century Britain, a way of imagining community that tied people together *less* by physical characteristics (although these played a significant role) than by customs, descent and "blood" – that mysterious if "common substance passed on through heterosexual relations and birth," as Tessie Liu has argued in another context.[31]

The idea of the national character, rendered through political aggregation, is intimately linked to this ethnographic idea of nation. "Where a number of men are

7

united into one political body," Hume surmised, "the occasions of their intercourse must be so frequent, for defense, commerce and government, that, together with the same speech or language, they must acquire a resemblance in their manners, and have a common or national character, as well as a personal one, peculiar to each individual." Lord Kames preferred the term "manners" to character, but still grounded shared national attributes on shared institutions and morality: "Such peculiarities in a whole nation, by which it differs from other nations or from itself at different periods, are termed *the manners of that nation*. Manners therefore signify a mode of behaviour peculiar to a certain person, or to a certain nation."[32] Although both of these philosophers would sow as much dissent as unanimity with many of their controversial opinions, their ideas about the existence and nature of national character were not seriously disputed. Whether the product of moral causes (as Hume and Kames would have it), or climatic exigencies (as Goldsmith, William Falconer and many others contended), national characters were believed to result from the universal human propensity for mimesis and conformity, making propinquity as important as institutions in producing the fact of difference. Throughout the century, however, the conception of national character as contingent – based on proximity and shared language, laws, government and social organization – was interpenetrated with more absolutist notions of national character as something inherited – an essence that could not otherwise be acquired – and at moments of crisis the more absolutist version of national belonging gained the ascendant. In the 1790s, Edmund Burke could proclaim, in the midst of an antirevolutionary diatribe, "Nation is a moral essence, not a geographical arrangement, or a denomination of the nomenclator."[33] The incongruity of the Irishman speaking authoritatively about the essential nature of Englishness did not lessen his ideas' impact on conservative nationalist culture; indeed, as we shall see, Scots, Irish, French and other "non-English" spokespeople took leading roles in ascertaining and verifying the peculiarities of the English in this period. The question becomes, how, when and why did the idea of nation travel from one mode to the other?

The following essays suggest that although the capacity for "nation" to be understood in quasi-essentialist terms was always present, empire, exploration and the reconfiguration of time, space and history had crucial roles to play in validating more absolutist notions of national community. The rise of stadial theory and the often circuitous routes taken by so-called conjectural historians to narrativize the story of human progress and degradation has recently undergone extensive scholarly re-examination, often with illuminating results.[34] But the uses to which stadial theory was put by writers, explorers and ordinary English people in constructing and naturalizing ideas about national belonging and exclusion require more detailed examination. Arguably, one of the most significant revolutions in the "age of revolutions" lay in the transformation of the timeless inventory of Creation – "the purely architectonic, static, and spatial order of categories" – into a "historical, inconstant, and changing" one, in which transition and movement were accepted as dominant modes of human life.[35] These changes, intellectually, took place on many fronts, but here we pay particular attention to two. By the mid eighteenth century, History itself had emerged as a primary vehicle of national self-understanding and identity as well as philosophical reflection, promoting a cosmopolitan perspective and a deeply grounded sense of national specificity. Didactic and rhetorical, embracing "facts" instead of "fables," History aimed to engage the reader's imagination and reason in the spectacle of the past, to encourage the exercise of ethical and aesthetic choices, and to make evident "the interplay of likeness and difference within the family of Christian churches and nations."[36] Even the mythical state of nature came to be thought of in historical terms, and savage nations became evidence that could be used to plot the development of humanity. The "American nations" provided the raw material "to complete the history of the human mind, and to attain a perfect knowledge of its nature and operations," William Robertson asserted; for by following them in the "progress through the different stages of society . . . from the infant state of civil life towards its maturity and decline," we can observe "how the faculties of [the] understanding unfold."[37] However, it was an axiom of Enlightenment historians that savage nations themselves had no history, none, that is, until their "discovery" and documentation by literate Europeans made possible the production of "evidence" and the examples of civility and morality that could lead them into modern time. Hence History in its enlightened mode both reflected and extended ideas about the evolution of progress in the material, scientific and intellectual, as well as civil, realms, and the possibilities for degradation and decline.

At the same time, ideas about natural and historical time were changing over the century in a number of ways. Natural history had led to the emergence of notions of "deep time," that required the adjustment of humanity's cosmological, social and biological location.[38] As social scientists consequently came under greater pressure to found the study of human society upon a firm empirical base, voyagers, travelers and explorers alike eagerly embraced the new national mission to describe and explain differences among the peoples of the world. The voyages of Captain Cook, in particular, were widely heralded as providing the "facts" about new nations and races of peoples that would allow natural historians "to establish permanent truths in the history of Man." This new history of humanity melded time and space to generalize and extend History to encompass the globe, and relationships between parts of the world became conceptualized as temporal ones.[39] Hence, the unfolding array of peoples in the South Pacific not only allowed naturalists such as Johann Forster to invent new theories of the ways in which the different island nations developed in relation to climate and "race," and new ways to define "race" through migration and language; they also provided British observers with living examples of the vagaries of social transition. Indeed, the idea of transition becomes crucial to establishing temporal and social hierarchy, as empire provided a panorama in which the progress of modernity could, ideally, unfold before the observer's eyes. As James King put it in the introduction to the Admiralty volume on the third voyage to the South Pacific, "Some rays of light must have darted on the Friendly, Society and Sandwich Islands, by our repeated intercourse with them . . . Convinced, by comparing themselves to their English visitors, of their extreme inferiority, they will probably endeavour to emerge from it, to rise nearer to a level with those, who left behind them so many proofs of their generosity and humanity."[40] Travel through the space-time continuum of the globe thus held out the possibilities for self-realization for explorers and explored alike. More perniciously, the evidence provided by the proliferation of material on indigenous peoples led philosophers and non-intellectuals to believe that man's progression from his earliest state was not inevitable, but the product of agency, hard work and struggle. As a number of writers argued, some groups, such as Africans, Eskimos and Native Americans, clearly preferred freedom over refinement and their own traditions over progress. Mimesis failed as a form of knowledge production, because of the deficiencies of their own natures.[41]

As noted above, the universalism of stadial theorists and historians, philosophers and playwrights, was founded on a belief in an essential human nature.[42] But, as we shall see in the chapters below, History, climate, mode of subsistence and the capacity for progress all seemed to have made human nature so varied and so malleable as to raise the question, what is the essential stuff here? As a result, national character is never convincingly described as entirely the product of nature or nurture, of "physical" or "moral" causes; and, by the last quarter of the century, commentators were plumping for *moral* difference as both cause and effect of national difference, a difference that could be eradicated, if at all, only with glacial slowness. "We see every country capable only of a gradual improvement, as well with regard to its natural qualities, as to the moral character of its inhabitants," Goldsmith asserted in 1760. Lord Kames saw it even more absolutely: "The principles of morality are little understood among savages: and if they arrive at maturity among enlightened nations, it is by slow degrees." Adam Smith observed that "virtue requires habit and resolution of mind, as well as delicacy of sentiment."[43]

Certainly, as Colin Kidd has recently reminded us, the challenge in the seventeenth and for much of the eighteenth century was to explain unity in the face of difference and so uphold Christian orthodoxy. The secular strands of Enlightenment social science confirmed this quest by making history provide evidence of the universal laws of human development that were identified as "natural" and common to all societies. But the radical implications of the same theories threatened to dissolve their own premises, as explorers and social scientists observed that what was held to be most "natural" to humanity (for example, a fondness for family, affection between partners, virtue) was found to be product of historical socialization rather than innate propensity.[44] The arts of "discovery," in the New and old Worlds of the South Seas, America, Africa and India, confirmed and expanded the growing belief that God or Nature had produced some nasty, unthinking brutes whose difference from Europeans could not be more marked. In the wake of the American war especially, as the empire in North America contracted and that in the East and the Pacific began to expand, English observers from all social levels began to articulate less geographically expansive notions of the nation and narrower definitions of national belonging. The force of these notions was such that antislavery advocates were at pains to challenge them by arguing for the need for reformation "throughout our Islands" across the world. Nevertheless, in the eyes of increasing numbers of English observers, the empire of the seas, once idealized as the domain of free white British peoples, had become the imperium of palpably alien colonial subjects, and the nation was confined increasingly to the island of Great Britain itself; even Ireland was excluded.[45]

Yet it is *not* the purpose here to argue that this was the "moment" when modern notions of "race" first took their pernicious hold. As a number of scholars have recently argued, "race" in the eighteenth century referred not to "scientific sets of physical characteristics but to bloodline and lineage."[46] The "savages" who provided the ground zero point for the analysis of progress and assessment of "civilization" were nevertheless seen as more culturally than racially different from Europeans, and color was just one signifier that could be trumped by culture – as the celebrations of African princes and Indian kings in popular culture and imaginative literature showed.[47] But, following the leads of historians of science,[48] some of the same writers have also identified a shift in thinking about diversity in the 1770s that brings to the fore recognizably "modern" ideas about race as fixed, inherent difference, articulated through and signified primarily by physical appearance and the "science of surfaces." Historians of abolitionism and antislavery have also seen the "age of democratic revolutions" bringing about a new grammar of difference and belonging, as the political rhetoric of liberty and equality undermined class as a basis of social hierarchy, and shifted the foundation to "race."[49]

The above analysis seems in many ways to be extremely compelling, and even beyond dispute. The problems arise when one realizes that scholars working in other periods are just as confident that they have discovered the appearance of notions of "race" that do the same ideological work as modern ones. Recent classical, medieval and early modern scholarship has argued, respectively, that recognizably biological notions of "race" existed in ancient times, discourses of religious difference and "blood" produced impassable cultural boundaries, and skin color functioned as a signifier of morality, virtue and unnaturalizable alterity.[50] Alternatively, historians and critics of Victorian culture and politics have shown that biology and science were merely components in the construction of difference in their period: culture, gender, religion, sexual customs, morality and family structure, to name a few, were just as important as physical features in categorizing humanity into races.[51] "Race," it seems, like gender and ethnicity, was a historically contingent construction that did not describe empirical, static or absolute conditions in societies, but positional relationships made and unmade in historical circumstances and manipulated in the pursuit of power. In the eighteenth century, "race" as a line of descent or group was identified and signified through religion, custom, language, climate, aesthetics and historical time as much as physiognomy and skin color (although certainly the latter two played important, if contested, roles). And "race" and "nation" bore intertwined as well as competing systems of meaning, used interchangeably in much of the cultural, political, scientific and travel literature of the day.[52] The search for the originary moment in the production of modern notions of race or ethnicity may, then, in the end, lead us to ignore this very political history, and to efface the ways in which the most "traditional" discourses – of religion, history, community, and descent – could be just as pernicious and essentializing, and create symbolic barriers just as impassable as any scientific or biological ones, in the early modern period and today.[53]

Further, these racialized notions of nation were put to work in the colonies to define the grounds for inclusion in the local community: religion, descent and language were the primary, and skin color secondary, requirements to qualify as "British" in Jamaican law; and antimiscegenation laws aimed at discouraging cultural, as much as sexual, mixing and contagion.[54] In their battles with Parliament, the American colonists were wont to stress that they were not "a compound mongrel mixture of *English, Indian* and *Negro,* but . . . freeborn *British white* subjects" and so deserving of the same liberties and privileges as Englishmen at home – thus denying the obvious truth in favor of a racialized version of Britishness recognized in the metropole as well as the colonies.[55] Similarly, cultural articulations of race, posted as "natural," could be just as essentializing as the most reductionist physiological theory. Traditional languages of natural philosophy, for example, "though not predicated on a modern concept of race . . . nevertheless generated statements that helped to create a racial definition of humanity," as Joyce Chaplin has persuasively argued.[56] From early colonization, bodies were the sites for constructing identities of insiders and outsiders. Well-established notions about the inheritance of a "national complexion" led the New England colonists to claim that their complexion was unchanged from that of their English forebears: and "as it is for the outward complexion, so it is for the inward constitution."[57] As Benjamin Franklin put it, a "true Briton" remained one even in the colonial setting, largely thanks to this inheritance:

> Great Numbers of our own People are of the BRITISH RACE . . . Our Neighbours of New-England afford the World a Convincing Proof that BRITONS, tho' a Hundred Years transplanted, and to the remotest Part of the Earth, may yet retain, even to the third or fourth Descent, that Zeal for the "Public Good," that "military Prowess," and that "undaunted Spirit," have we likewise of "those brave People," whose Fathers in the last Age made so glorious a stand for our Religion and Liberties.[58]

Both cultural ideas about race and racialized notions of nation, then, identified a juncture where rationality, nationality and physical difference become intertwined, and where acquired cultural characteristics are transformed into innate ones, the intangible inheritance of "blood." This alchemy of national identity is manifested from the early decades of the century. Conversely, as we shall see, at conjunctures when national identity and character are being defined and defended in narrower and less inclusive terms, the social typologies that in part shaped and were also shaped by these definitions were revealed to be insufficient. The Pacific discoveries of Cook and his men and their attempts to map Oceanic social and sexual practices through Enlightenment typologies, in particular, made palpable the fictive nature and irresolvable tensions within emerging "modern" categories of difference.

In and through these strategies, Englishness itself had emerged by the 1760s and 1770s as a nascent ethnicity that, although certainly defined through government, institutions and language, and sharing important features with European and Celtic cultures, still had within it what we would recognize as racialized assumptions, which ranged from the superior capacity of English people for rational thought to the greater aesthetic beauty of the "pink and white complexion." Recognition of shared roots in a Gothic past could not abrogate the centuries of historical differentiation that had shaped the different governments, religions, polities and characters of peoples, even within the British Isles. From this perspective, although there certainly were other "island races" in the British archipelago, there was clearly only one superior Island Race. As Goldsmith remarked of the "native Irish," "The manners of the original inhabitants, which they to this day preserve unvaried, are entirely different from those of the English, and partake somewhat of the ancient Scythian, and modern Spanish customs, as described by travelers and historians, for from these two nations the country was at different periods inhabited."[59] The English national character, in all its wonderful diversity, rested upon this commitment to the formative and exclusionary nature of historical experience (however much that experience simultaneously registered degrees of consanguinity), and a particularized history could be an effective shield against all sorts of foreigners' claims. The contention that English people did not organize their consciousness through skin color – that they discovered their "whiteness" only on the multiracial frontiers of empire – seems to me to be untenable, evidenced, to choose just two examples, by the centuries of disparagement of the "native Irish," and the recurrent hostility towards black British immigration that dated from Elizabethan times. Instead, the Georgian period reveals the rhetorical strategies and practices through which ideas of nation and national belonging become systematically linked to ideas about ethnic difference whose features are not naturalizable, and to a racialized understanding of community – real and imagined – that grouped some people together, and irrevocably separated others.

Colonies provided an important test case for the examination and verification of national character as a production of climate, environment, stage of civilization and human agency, as we shall see. Hume maintained that the "same set of manners will follow a nation, and adhere to them over the whole globe, as well as the same laws and language."[60] However, the experiences of colonists and travelers suggested otherwise: it seemed that the national character, acquired through propinquity, could when removed from the structures of civilized life quickly give way. Commenting on how the Dutch at Batavia forgot their national abstemiousness and adopted "all the luxurious manners of the Asiatics," Goldsmith remarked that "After two or three generations at farthest, the blood loses its primitive qualities, and those of the climate manifest themselves in men, animals and plants."[61] English historians of the Indian subcontinent agreed that Mughal warriors had lost their martial edge and become sensual and effeminate owing to their contact with and subordination to Indians.[62] On the other hand, if savages could never, at least not in real time, become English, English people could degenerate into savagery, as soldiers on the frontiers of empire, female sexual adventurers in the metropolis and planters in tropical outposts clearly showed: hence eighteenth-century ideas about history involving inevitable progress and degeneration distinguish its evolutionary thinking from its Victorian successors. The impact of these experiences was to provide the substance for the analysis of how supposedly "natural" features changed into their opposites, as nationality was transmuted into a degraded copy. Lewis Grant, Scottish colonist in Jamaica, wrote in 1742:

> I look upon us Europeans in this part of the World to be in the Same Condition with West Indian Planters when carry'd to Briton, if they are carefully kept in Greenhouses the heat of the Sun doubl'd upon them in Summer and kept warm with fires in winter, they will doe tollearbly weall, but when expos'd to the inclemency of our air in the open fields they quickly decay and dye, it is just soe with us hear, if we can afford the Convenancy's of Life and use them temporarily we may does prittie weall but if we are obliged to march or Labor in the heat of the day, and Lye out in the night it is certain death.[63]

Grant's assessment stands, on the one hand, as a perfect example of the longevity of natural philosophy's neoclassical explanation of human difference in environmental and climactic terms. But it also expresses an idea about national identity and difference that, if produced by climate, was also grounded on physiological attributes, and turned "West Indians" and "Europeans" into quite different creatures. Edward Long would use the most advanced physiological and climatic theory of the day to show how this cultural movement produced *physical* changes that would then get transmitted through reproduction, and his ideas about the differential productions of *whiteness* were more influential than many eighteenth-century historians would like to believe.[64] In the same way that the products of empire raised fears about initiating a move towards luxury and degeneration "at home," so colonial settlers' examples of cultural regression on the frontiers of empire swelled anxieties about the tentative and contingent nature of Englishness abroad. Hence the Earl of Shaftesbury's famous remark could stand for the perils of colonization as well as consumption: "Our Relish or *Taste* must of necessity grow barbarous, whilst *Barbarian Customs, Savage* Manners, *Indian* Wars and Wonders of the *Terra Incognita* employ our leisure Hours."[65]

The essays in this volume, then, suggest how particular articulations of national belonging and character become predicated upon notions of community and identity that were both labile and difficult, if not impossible, to acquire or naturalize. This aspect of thinking about "nation-ness" is both implicitly and explicitly developed in eighteenth-century discourse, cultural practice and official

14

policy, and it may betray more than the shared etymological roots of Nation and Race. As Etienne Balibar has argued, the nation as a historical product was aligned almost inevitably with a notion of race structured on patrimonial prerogatives and inheritance.[66] Through such a connection, "nation" was capable of staking out a terrain of practically incommensurable differences in eighteenth-century culture. Nation and race thus formed (to borrow a phrase from Laurence Sterne) one of those "unhappy association of ideas, which have no connection in nature . . . Which strange combination of ideas, the sagacious Locke . . . affirms to have produced more wry actions than all other sources of prejudice whatsoever."[67]

Networks of Empire

As the discussion above suggests, this study proceeds from what was once thought to be a perverse assumption: that empire mattered to ordinary people in eighteenth-century England. In the last decade, the proliferation of studies on the impact and meanings of empire in the Hanoverian period has made it unnecessary to defend this position.[68] The eighteenth-century British "empire of the sea" – of trading "outposts" and maritime colonies – mercantilist, old-fashioned, commercial and increasingly territorial as it was, was also a generator for ideas about nationality, race, ethnicity and difference that impacted metropolitan culture and categories of knowledge in profound and quotidian ways. As such it was central to the broader social and political transformations of the eighteenth century. What still requires attention, however, is the multiplicity of visions, aspirations and experience at work in eighteenth-century imperial settings, and the heterogeneous, contingent and conflictual characteristics of the processes of empire and colonization themselves. As Peter Marshall has remarked, in a sympathetic moment, "empire could be interpreted in a wide diversity of ways. There were many imperial projects."[69] Rather than assuming that the politics and agendas of these projects and the attitudes of Britons towards them are self-evident, it is necessary instead to examine the specificities of the national and colonial communities in which imperial power and its refusal was negotiated and lived through, the instabilities of categories taken to be given, such as "colonizers" and "colonized," "white" and "black," and the modes of representation that played upon and legitimized bonds of consanguinity and difference among peoples. Within imperial and colonial settings, colonial intentions, both formal and informal, were incompletely and ambiguously realized; historical actors were defined in multiple ways; and different genders, classes, ethnicities and races all participated, albeit in varied and unequal measure, in the creation of their history. The movement of peoples and goods, the clash of cultures and experience and the imperial contexts of everyday life forged the many links that connected men and women living on both sides of the Atlantic and across the Indian and Pacific oceans. No singular British system or idea of Englishness or indeed of empire emerged from the process of imperial expansion in the seventeenth and eighteenth centuries, but many systems and ideas, linked to each other through often disparate bonds of identity, experience and practice.[70]

The essays in this book attempt to track some of the ways in which the fact or possibility of British imperial power shaped the practices, aspirations and identities of men and women, for whom empire, nation and difference were understood in unexpected and discontinuous ways. In the process, the analysis suggests that the shifting parameters of British imperial power over the century sustained a circuitry of identity, alterity, exchange and transformation that disrupted the polarities of metropole–colony and destabilized notions of the "national character." Certainly, as a number of studies have argued, empire provided an arena in which a united national policy could be invented and inscribed, overlaying social and political tensions of the domestic polity. But even the most confident narratives of national identity and imperial power were haunted by anxieties. As Kate Teltscher has argued, "the assumption of colonial power marks the emergence of a much more precarious sense of self."[71] Generating conflicts, ambiguities, pleasures and desires, the products of empire – its people, commodities, routes and cultures – challenged the quasi-essentialist categories of nation described above. Roxanne Wheeler has recently argued in her suggestive study of racialist thinking that "ideas about human differences developed at a different pace in England than in the colonies, and they had different histories in the West Indies, North America, Australia, New Zealand and the East Indies." That the definitions of nation and race looked differently in different colonial contexts is indisputable, an observation also borne out by the recent distinguished analyses contained in the multivolume *Oxford History of the British Empire*. And it is important to identify the conjunctures where political, social and geographical regimes of difference collided to re-define the so-called center.[72] But the separation between what went on "out there" and "in here" could not and cannot be so easily maintained. As a number of studies have demonstrated, national and regional boundaries were easily transgressed by the systemic, if not systematic, nature of empire itself.[73] Despite the lack of coherence in central policy, the eighteenth-century "empire of the sea" and the wars that threatened, maintained and extended it created a *network* that, halting and imperfect, was also remarkably efficient in allowing people, gossip, connections, ideas and identity to travel and be transformed.[74] Indeed the idea of the "network" as a nexus of communication linking up disparate but interrelated centers is crucial to the following analysis. It allows us to treat the metropole and colonies as inter-connected analytical fields – which is emphatically to say *not* that the two are "the same," but that each provides a local translation of a wider imperial circuit that impacted the forms of labor, consumption, servitude, freedom and belonging in specific ways. In these complex historical locations, identity was situational and commodified, bestowed, adopted, marketed or appropriated as an entitlement, an avenue to freedom, or a marker distinguishing who was protected by British "rights and liberties" and who was not. Hence the Barbadoes assembly's claim in an address to Cromwell that they were "Englishmen of as clear and pure extract as any" and thus entitled to "enjoy . . . liberty and freedome equal with the rest of our countrymen" was echoed over one hundred years later, when Jamaican Assemblymen insisted in their legislation that to be "called English meant to be

... free from all taint of the Negroe race" and Londoners complained about the likelihood of the capital taking on "the appearance of an Ethiopian colony" if black immigration was not stopped.[75] Conversely, enslaved Africans, Native Americans and Pacific islanders could also challenge, contest and reconfigure the categories of identity retailed by governors, settlers, merchants and explorers alike. As we shall see, practices and identities circulated across and beyond an Atlantic and increasingly transoceanic world that did not begin or end at national borders.

Attending to the circuitry of empire in the eighteenth century also reveals the cultural intermixing that was, paradoxically, an instrument of national self-fashioning and definition. Empire was, in a very real sense, the frontier of the nation, the place where, under the pressure of contact and exchange, boundaries deemed crucial to national identity – white and black, civilized and savage, law and vengeance – were blurred, dissolved or rendered impossible to uphold. One of the most important contributions of the renewed attention to the imperial frame of eighteenth-century British history has been the revelation of that "middle ground" that empire produced, a space disrupting comfortable binary oppositions about insiders and outsiders posted by eighteenth-century European intellectuals to make sense of the wider world. West/Orient, white/black, free/slave, masculine/effeminate, parents/children, social/natural, home/abroad, are some of the oppositions that are visibly undone by the products of empire itself: the mulatto, the free black and the Eurasian, the indentured servant and the imported or extirpated "native," the Creole and the métis as much as sugar and tobacco give embodied form to the permeability and instability of national and hemispheric boundaries and to the fact of cultural miscegenation. As the Englishness of the British empire, in terms of personnel, began to diminish, and "Scots and Irish came to dominate emigration from the British Isles at every level from indentured servant to colonial governor," the cultural Anglophilia of expatriated planters, merchants and traders significantly expanded. Englishness became a performance of non-English and even non-British peoples, a trope of white civilization, maintained through social and theatricalized practices and displays at all levels, that attempted to set off its performers from "indigenous" savagery. Yet at the same time, the "savages" or "natives" in question initiated performances that significantly undermined "white" claims to distinctiveness, originality or superior under-standing.[76] Hence in a period when the nation was attempting to superimpose its orthodoxies and myths of homogenous culture on its heterogeneous subjects, the practices of everyday life in the colonies demonstrated the contradictions and incoherencies of the ideology of nation by offering up their own "routinely hybridized, collectively-created forms."[77]

"Transculture" was the analytical term coined by Cuban anthropologist Fernando Ortiz to convey the dynamic of encounter, loss and transformation in the colonization of the Caribbean.[78] Unlike the term "hybridity," which describes the result of encounter, "transculture" gives us a sense of the confrontational dynamic of the process and the creativity of the consequent production. Indeed, Ortiz has shown how the constitution of the modern world has entailed, as

Fernando Coronil has summarized, "the clash and disarticulation of peoples and civilizations together with the production of images of integrated cultures, bounded identities, and inexorable progress." Through the analysis of the interplay of cultural forms and material conditions, and the "social identities" of colonial products, his counterpoint of cultures also brought into focus the violence, the riskiness and the work of desire in the sensibilities and epistemologies forged by colonial projects.[79] As such, his neologism of transculture has purchase for historians of empire, who are confronted with colonial communities so much like, and so unlike, those "at home." Formed and transformed through the dynamic processes of transculturation, the modernity of the eighteenth century, to its denizens and to us, should be understood in relation to the *conditions of possibility* created by the changing geopolitics, and chronopolitics, of empire. Not only people – transculturated Africans, Jews, French, English, Spanish, Dutch and East Asian, to name a few – but also commodities contributed to these conditions of possibility: sugar itself, for example, a native to Asia Minor, was transplanted to the Caribbean where its own fabrication from brown to white was part of the larger processes through which "natural" attributes were transformed by human agency and capitalist productive relations.[80] Clearly, the "empire of the seas" generated social, cultural and epistemological networks as well as profoundly political and economic ones. Our attention to them underscores the vital place of everyday life in forging the many links that connected men, women and children living across the oceans, registering degrees of both consanguinity and difference.

Engendering Nations

This conceptualization of empire as a network and of nation and identity as processes also sheds new light on our study of gender in the metropole and colonies. Until lately, the importance of gender to nation and empire building has not received its share of attention.[81] The study of the differential masculinities and femininities at play in the period is flourishing, and a spate of recent important work is doing no less than recasting our knowledge and assumptions about the expectations and experience of men and women living in Georgian England.[82] But the vibrant and wide-ranging studies of empire, gender and culture undertaken by Tudor-Stuart and Victorian scholars have only begun to find parallels for the Georgian period.[83] The essays in this volume make a small contribution to furthering this project, by engaging with the complex entanglements of gender, nation and empire in shaping the aspirations and identities of men and women living in England and some of its possessions. In the process, gender, like national, identity, emerges itself as an uneven, ambiguous and more troubled process than is usually supposed – marked by indeterminacies rather than radical departures, and refusals as well as affirmations. Further, men and women's variegated roles in the imperial projects of the day molded not only ideas about national belonging and exclusion, but quotidian social and political relations "at home," in the act of colonization and the arts of discovery. In other words, the nation and the empire were gendered, as well as racialized locations that shaped the understanding of difference in the metropole, traveling, transforming and being transformed through the networks of empire.[84]

The masculinities and femininities at play in colonial settings were as heterogeneous as in England, and this study makes no claim to approaching them all. Nevertheless, we can discern some of the idealizations of gender that were mobilized at moments of national anxiety and complacency. As I have argued elsewhere, gender provided powerful metaphors and images through which changing relations between Britain and the empire could be articulated. The idea of empire as a free and prosperous extension of a free and prosperous Britain did not only reveal the formative impact of overseas dominions on English political culture; it also highlighted salient constructions of masculinity and femininity within the polity. Conceptualized as an antidote to perceived national effeminacy and corruption, empire could be imagined as the territorial and mental space where an austere, forceful, disciplined and martial manliness could restore national spirit and power.[85] But these notions of manliness and of empire were not static, and could be reshaped by the exigencies of imperial power abroad and social and cultural initiatives within England. In the wake of the Seven Years War, as the triumphalism evidenced in *The Triumph of Britannia* (1762) (Fig. 1) gave way to self-critique, Britain's possession of an extensive and diverse imperial polity and tolerance of a variety of humanitarian abuses within it galvanized not only campaigns for political and social reform and antislavery, but also new requirements for imperial leaders. Captain Cook became the exemplar of both this new imperialism and a new masculinity, combining expertise, humanitarianism and compassion in equal measure. Both borrowing from and recasting the cult of sensibility of the day, this new inquiring masculinity was striated with national, class and gender prejudices and ideals, but it was, in the 1770s and 1780s, as eagerly embraced by sailors, servants and slaves as well as by officers engaged in the arts of discovery, even as its tenets and goals conspicuously failed.[86]

Women's symbolic and empirical fortunes roles in the national and imperial projects of the day also fluctuated over the course of the century. Within metropolitan culture, women's bodies served as symbols of national virtue, superiority and martial potency (as *The Triumph of Britannia* evinces). Real-life women's superior capacities for civility, refinement and sensibility were put to work within public and private arenas of sociability and philanthropy, even as their actual and symbolic propensities for excessive consumption (of goods, men, fashion) and luxury meant that they had to be well regulated and kept from unnatural exercises of authority. Further, constructions of female identity played innovative roles in articulating contending relationships between Britain and the colonies. In the 1740s and 1750s, women were seen as both emblematic and symptomatic of the forces of dangerous luxury and degeneration that threatened to overtake the national polity, and women were accordingly urged to curtail their "natural" inclinations towards fripperies and emotionalism for the greater national good. Yet by the 1770s, women's role in empire and patriotism was being presented as more beneficial if less

Figure 1 Simon Ravenet, after Francis Hayman, *The Triumph of Britannia* (1762). Courtesy of the National Maritime Museum. Britannia, holding a portrait of George III, rides proudly in a sea-borne chariot driven by Neptune, as nereids from the four continents cavort with images of the leading admirals of the Seven Year's War. In the distance is a view of Admiral Hawkes's 1759 victory over the French at Quiberon Bay. Hayman's painting, displayed to much acclaim at Vauxhall Gardens, articulated the nationalist triumphalism of the day.

direct, when their capacity for domestic virtue was promoted as a source of virtue in the national polity writ large. This much-vaunted moral, and moralizing, influence of English women, rooted in their superior domestic and emotional authority, saturated colonial reform iniatives such as antislavery, which enjoined English women to bring their feminine compassion and sympathy to bear on the practices of consumption that perpetuated the cruelties of slavery.[87] Hence the moral standing and superiority of Englishness itself came to rest in no small part on English women's capacity for, and exhibition of, domestic virtue and refinement. Women's engagement with the processes of war, imperial expansion and national aggrandizement both reflected and shaped these concerns, while also influencing their aspirations and identities in novel and unexpected ways, illuminating, for the historian, new avenues in the analysis of Georgian women's personal and sexual desires.

Within the empire, women were equally enjoined to bring their special qualities to bear on the arts of war, colonization and discovery. Indeed, the movement of gender ideologies across colonial networks demonstrated how culture and identities could travel and be transformed. Women, as wives and mothers, were meant to exert complementary domesticating influences on the front and the colonial frontier, in order to nurture the seeds of civilization and ensure the reproduction of the national culture and stock far from home. As Edward Long asserted, lamenting the miscegenating consequences of black concubinage on Jamaica, the moralizing influence of proper English women would render the island

> more populous, and residence in it more eligible, . . . banish ignorance from the rising generation, restrain numbers from seeking these improvements, at hazard of life, in other countries, and from unnaturally reviling a place which they would love and prefer, if they could enjoy in it that necessary culture, without which life and property lose their relish to those who are born, not only to inherit, but to adorn, a fortune.[88]

Yet empire provided a means of escape not just for impecunious younger sons but also for unconventional women, who would try their luck abroad and take advantages of the opportunities dislocation from the metropole offered for self re-invention. Women who refused to take on conventional roles, on the frontier or at the heart of the metropole – and, as we shall see, even some who did – were marginalized, ostracized or denigrated, and their characters and nationality suspected. Further, in the British plantation colonies of the Caribbean, although European women of various social and ethnic backgrounds could do very well, Creole women could still be perceived as contaminated by their environments, failed imitations of real English ladies. And while New World plantation systems depended upon the myth of white women's superiority and inviolability compared to the allegedly debased femininities and sexualities of the enslaved, women of color also exploited available networks of social power to secure positions of property and influence within Caribbean societies.[89] In other words, a range of opportunities and disadvantages presented themselves to women in the empire, which could have unexpected social and symbolic consequences for metropolitan and colonial culture. Certainly white women held comparatively privileged positions within the British Atlantic world, but these positions were heterogeneous and fluid, dependent upon the shifting requirements of nationality and gender. Women's central task in colonial island settings was to mark and regulate sexuality, deemed crucial to the maintenance of the boundaries setting off colonizers and colonized, free-born Briton and enslaved. Here, where the codes of domestic femininity were called upon to bolster the differences between black and white, miscegenation was considered to be a social problem that could quickly amount to a crisis, for its products – both biological and cultural – made such boundaries increasingly difficult to maintain. In these ways and more, women's access to empire had the potential to threaten the security and stability of the national order, and so continued to be a source of concern and anxiety as well as solace.

Conversely, in settings where European women were absent, such as the South Pacific prior to the late 1780s, gender and sexual practices provided crucial, but extremely unstable and mutable markers of identity, alterity and dispossession for European men and Oceanic men and women alike. Much has been made in recent studies of eighteenth-century sexualities of the "gender revolution," whereby advances in anatomical science and the intellectual victory of an oppositional "two-sex model" in the later decades produced more fixed and essential notions of gender difference that inaugurated the "modern" regime of compulsory heterosexuality.[90] Yet as with the comparable discovery of newly essentialist notions of race in the same period, the timing and suddenness of this emergence may be overdrawn. The automatic, one-to-one correspondence between sexual practice, object choice and gender identity seems to me to be very debatable over the century. The issue is not only that, as a number of gender and queer theorists have reminded us, sexual identity is not solely determined by object choice, and gender historically is not produced by sexual practice alone.[91] It is also that eighteenth-century discourses and conventions produced uneasy alliances between so-called "natural" distinctions between the sexes, and gender practices and roles.

Take for example the recently much-examined problem of the eighteenth-century understanding of "effeminacy." Randolph Trumbach has famously argued that the notion of effeminacy came to be seen by the middle third of the century as the product of same-sex desire or relations, and effeminates associated more or less exclusively with the demeanor and practices of the molly. Yet (leaving aside the identification of the "modern sexual regime" *tout court* with *male* sexuality) "effeminacy" was a complex notion in this period that appeared in a range of political, cultural and satirical as well as sexual discourses.[92] Designating, according to Johnson's *Dictionary*, both "the admission of the qualities of a woman, softness, unmanly delicacy" as well as "addiction to women," effeminates were men who resembled women, or who excessively desired them. Effeminacy, in other words, demarcated "that ambiguous realm where gender boundaries were blurred and sexual difference affirmed," as Michèle Cohen has recently argued.[93] But the fear of effeminacy also expressed the recurrent fears of eighteenth-century observers and moralists about the distressing tendency of uncontrolled mimesis to corrupt or debase "natural" social distinctions: in this case, for masculinity, the cultural expression of male sexual difference, to degenerate into its opposite – not femininity but effeminacy. This gender regime does not meet in any one-to-one correspondence with the sexual regime described by Trumbach, but exists in an asymmetrical relation. This is not to argue that there were no powerful initiatives to anchor gender distinctions more aggressively to unchangeable biological bodies or essences at different junctures, particularly in the later part of the century: as John Tosh has suggested, the greater security for the "natural" differences between the sexes from the 1790s onwards may explain why "effeminacy" was so much less a concern of Victorians than Georgians.[94] But the later eighteenth century was as notable for its ambiguities and irresolvabilities as for its brave new beginnings. In the arts of discovery deployed by Cook and his men on their South Pacific voyages, the attribution of sodomitical desires to Oceanic people clearly flagged the fears of difference and social exile attached to such desire in England; but suspect desire or practices could disrupt and certainly could not "prove" essentialized sexual identities such as that of the sodomite. Although Britain's manly and enlightened explorers clearly carried with them the freight of cultural initiatives and anxieties within England, their encounters drew them into a more tangled, confusing circuitry of gender identification and alterity that were impossible to translate into clear-cut definitions of self and other, still less in a one-to-one relationship between sexual identity and object choice. In this as in other ways, empire and exploration could unsettle metropolitan categories of being and becoming.

Before turning to the essays, two final points must be made about the relations between nation, empire and gender in this period. First, eighteenth-century thinking about gender and sexual difference, like the varieties of masculinities and femininities performed and practiced, exhibited circuitous and even contradictory logics that foundered on the irresolvability of gender's status as natural or ascribed.[95] Certainly women's improved treatment and condition in such "advanced" commercial societies as eighteenth-century Britain was a common self-congratulatory trope of Enlightenment social theory. "That women are indebted to the refinements of polished manners for a happy change in their state, is a point which can admit of no doubt," William Robertson asserted; "To despise and to degrade the female sex, is the characteristic of the savage state in every part of the globe."[96] William Alexander found women to be even more exact barometers of historical progress, arguing in his *History of Women* that "the rank . . . and condition, in which we find women in any country, mark out to us with the greatest precision, the exact point in the scale of civil society, to which the people of such country have arrived." In the discourses of politeness and sensibility, as in conjectural history, women were also placed in the center of "society" and its progress, key to the refinement, elevation, polish and support of their men.[97]

Moreover, the English and, depending on the writer, the British and their progenitors were held to have been particularly advanced in the good treatment of women. William Alexander, William Falconer, Adam Ferguson, Lord Kames and others argued that the German tribes, "even in their native forest paid a kind of devotion to the female sex,"[98] providing evidence of the distance between savage and modern nations even in archaic time. In modern space-time, English and British women were emblems of the leading place their society held among advanced nations. William Russell could flatter his numerous female readers by reminding them that

> in this age, in this island . . . [we have] women who would have done honour to any age or country; who join a refined taste and cultivated understanding to a feeling heart, and who adorn their talents and their sensibility with sentiments of virtue, honour and humanity. We have women who could have reasoned with Locke, who might have disputed the laurel with Pope, and to whom Addison would have listened with pleasure.[99]

Gender and sexual relations clearly provided a dominant idiom through which differences in the national manners of humanity could be articulated and ranked. Such theories did no less than link "changes in sexual authority, wage relations and forms of state power in one overarching historical process."[100]

But on the subject of the generic differences between the sexes, British writers were much less flattering to women. Although observers agreed that men and women shared an equality of rational souls, most also thought that there were "natural," fundamental differences between the sexes that suited them for the very different social roles and responsibilities. "I do not mean it an injury to women," wrote Steele in the Tatler, "when I say there is a sort of sex in souls." "If those Speeches and Actions, which in their own Nature are indifferent, appear ridiculous when they proceed from a wrong Sex, the Faults and Imperfections of one Sex transplanted into another, appear black and monstrous," Addison elaborated in the Spectator.[101] These ideas were not displaced by stadial theory or the scientific scrutiny of the diversity of human manners – although, as already noted, the understanding of the consequences of these "natural" differences between the sexes was changing. "With regard to the outlines, whether of internal disposition or of external figure, men and women are the same," Kames wrote; "Nature, however, intending them for mates, has given them dispositions different but concordant, so as to produce together delicious harmony."[102] Hannah More agreed that "the mind in each sex has some natural kind of bias, which constitutes a distinction of character" suiting them for their respective roles, and which women would do well to accept. "On the whole, . . . is it not better to succeed as women, than to fail as men?" she railed in presciently postfeminist fashion.[103] Even John Millar, who explicitly moved the theoretical anchor of social development from government to domestic relations, remained committed to the idea that women's "nature" itself

24

did not change much historically; it was only men's appreciation of women's special qualities that evolved. As he put it,

> When men begin to disuse their ancient barbarous practices, when their attention is not wholly engrossed by the pursuit of military reputation, when they have made some progress in the arts, and have attained to a proportional degree of refinement, they are necessarily led to set a value upon those female accomplishments and virtues which have so much influence upon every species of improvement, and which contribute in so many ways to multiply the comforts of life.[104]

Women, like primitive peoples of past and present, remained somewhat outside of History, although their centrality to the levels of virtue and domestic comforts in a society continued to be emphasized by feminist and conservative commentators alike into the 1790s. Hence the arguments that ensued over "the sex" and their roles in progress had to do with whether nature or education could be the most important in shaping the manners of women, and how the potential for corruption increased in nations where women had too much power or too little chastity. Culture and nature get irredeemably entangled here, as when Enlightenment theorists prescribed women's status in civilized society as her only "natural" position, while also regarding their "progress" as consisting less in *their* improvement than in the increased estimation which men have for apparently invariant feminine sensibilities and abilities.[105]

Of course, "nature" itself was never enough to guarantee gender difference, but had to be regulated by social codes and the progress of civilization to keep it from degenerating into its opposite. The fragility of female virtue, emphasized by male and female writers, was a theme also taken up by colonial projectors and apologists, who urged that special care must be taken to prevent the dissolution of English women's morals in colonial settings.[106] Moreover, at home and abroad, women's sexed minds and bodies and the emphasis on maternity and romantic love never entirely displace the older notion that every female is at heart a rake – if it did, there would be no need for the endless insistence, most fashionably by Rousseau but also by scores of English writers, that female education and environment indoctrinate gender difference, "prepare women's heart and mind to love home," as Hannah More demanded, and thereby not obliterate the "natural difference between the sexes."[107] Hence, if the sapphist had no broader social role in this period (which I think can be contested),[108] it is because "manliness" was not conceived of as the antithesis of femininity, but *vulgarity* was – that is, the commonness, impropriety, licentiousness and depravity that femininity is liable to degenerate into in its lowest and most savage state. And this repugnance to the vulgar provides one source of the "hegemonic gender identity" that seemed to have some Georgian women in its grip from the beginning to the end of the century.[109] Female chafing at and exceeding the bounds of a supposedly natural feminine propriety is a recurrent theme in letters by women in all decades, as is the embrace of and retreat to the

same feature by these women at other times. Proper women were not supposed to
have extramarital sex, and its occurrence was frequently seen as a sign of aristocratic
excess – just as sodomy was for men. Women who ignored these rules paid prices
for it even as they simultaneously claimed some greater freedom for themselves.
The socially and intellectually compromising nature of sexual passion for women
was a fear voiced by courtesans at the beginning of the period as by respectable
dissenters, male novelists and female moralists at the end, for it not only clouded
the judgment and ruined the reputation, but it threatened to transform femininity
into its antithesis – vulgarity. The domestic space of the home, though certainly
not private in our sense, was the place where exclusivity promised to promote
civility and the derogation of vulgarity, and passion, if any, was kept within its
proper bounds. The recurrent stress on female propriety and domesticity, recently
emphasized by Amanda Vickery, can thus be seen as part of the effort to keep
female nature from degenerating into the licentiousness and savagery largely by
keeping the passions in check.[110] As Johnson's cautionary tale of the woman who
"went native" on the frontiers of empire suggests, women's "nature" had a politics
that reverberated across the networks of nation and empire, and so became a source
of contestation as well as inspiration for men and women over the century.

Finally, the attempt to analyze the relations between identity, nationality, gender
and discovery confronts the historian with the need to speak from silences – of
English, British, enslaved and indigenous peoples alike. Although Chapters 1 and
2 address articulations of hegemonic national identities and their consequences,
and Chapters 3–5 of appropriations and resistances to them, the sources used
throughout include many that would be deemed both unreliable and unverifiable
within traditional historiography: day books filled in by servants, women's memoirs
and testimonies brokered and edited by men, life stories fleshed out by gossip, and
"first contacts" recorded and filtered by European witnesses alone. In other words,
many of the historical subjects pursued in these chapters are, from the point of
view of the discipline of History, subaltern. As postcolonial scholars have
demonstrated, the kinds of knowledge valorized by traditional historical sources
are of privileged subjects and their concerns, who belong and circulate in
"particularistic networks" of kinship, class, gender and power.[111] The purpose here
is not to somehow "document" or speak for the lives lived beyond the so-called
centers – not least because subaltern or indigenous historical thinking was not
necessarily defined around the same events and chronologies as elite European
narratives. Rather, it is to delve into a history of national and colonial inter-
penetration that identifies failures, uncertainties and impasses in "the record," and
the lacunae which attempted to disallow certain groups or individuals to speak or
record.[112] Outcast women, South Sea "princes," enslaved or displaced Africans
and Oceanic actors make their presence known and felt through practices and
performances that could not but be noticed by those who believed themselves to
be in charge of History. The record that comes back to us as a confrontation of
modernity and tradition or respectability and opprobrium can thus be interrogated
and probed at its pressure points to offer up both challenges to nationalist

historiographies, and resonant vestiges of marginalized individuals and peoples' being and becoming. As Gyan Prakash has argued, although "[t]he possibility of retrieval . . . is also a sign of its impossibility," historians have "no alternative but to inhabit the discipline . . . and push at the limits of historical knowledge to turn its contradictions, ambivalences and gaps into grounds for its rewriting."[113] These essays are offered as a small contribution to such a historical emergency.

The Voyage Out

The following chapters engage with the range of conceptual issues outlined above in order to ask new kinds of questions about identity, national belonging and the consequences of empire for English culture. They also try to raise fresh queries about myths of origins, causality and "evidence," the role of representation in accessing historical experience, and the nature of the archive. Certainly these questions have been at play in literary, film, media and cultural studies for some time, and with fruitful results. Within the increasingly disciplinary confines of history, however – and despite some notable exceptions – probing at the politics of historical knowledge has led to a sort of recidivist stonewalling, an insistence that some things just cannot be known because there are no reliable sources, or, alternatively, that some archives do provide us with splendid access to "history as it really was." The attention here on the performativity of identities – collective as well as individual – and the struggle to formulate and maintain them, is thus an effort to draw us back to the importance of *social practice*, and to the complex visual, kinesthetic and textual ways in which social practice is historically recorded, transmitted, transformed and rendered meaningful, to those in the past and to ourselves. In the process, it is hoped that the eighteenth century emerges as both stranger, and a little more familiar, than when we set out.

Over the course of the eighteenth century, protracted wars, invasion scares, colonial expansion and commercial conquest all produced intense if recurrent anxieties about the nature and worth of the national character that was articulated by village shopkeepers, bluestockings and colonial émigrés alike. In this setting, when national boundaries seemed permeable and the capacity for national self-definition unstable, women, laborers, slaves and other immigrant groups, from Jews to French Protestants, "foreign" visitors and colonials joined war heroes, explorers and aristocrats in producing gendered and racialized notions of the British and English national identity. Moreover, empire and war could confound efforts to imagine the British nation as a supposed unity of people, state and territory, for state aggrandizement and colonies, and their often clashing productions of ideas, commodities and cultures highlighted the disarticulation between these con-stitutive elements. Empire, its imagined forms and seemingly limitless possibilities, its dangers and its contradictions brought into sharp relief for many participants the fissures produced by national imaginings in the face of domestic and imperial diversity and difference, the palpable gulfs between the people and the state, the state and the nation, the English and the British, "natives" and "foreigners." Empire also, however, made clear, to anyone who cared to look, that the much-vaunted singularity of English culture was performed and constituted by the bodies, practices, exchanges and movements of peoples across the globe. It is to a few of these performances that we will now turn.

1

CITIZENSHIP, EMPIRE AND MODERNITY IN THE ENGLISH PROVINCES

Now, by our country, considered in itself, we shall (I conceive) most rationally understand, not barely a certain tract of land, which makes up the external appearance of it; but chiefly, the collective body of its inhabitants, with their public and joint interests.

> Rev. George Fothergill, *The Duty, Objects and Offices of the Love of Country*, Restoration Day sermon, 1758

In faith, my friend, the present time is rather *comique* – Ireland almost in as true a state of rebellion as America – Admirals quarrelling in the West-Indies – and at home Admirals that do not chuse to fight – The British Empire mouldering away in the West, annihilated in the North – . . . and England fast asleep . . . – for my part, it's nothing to me, as I am only a lodger, and hardly that.

> Ignatius Sancho, *Letters*, 1779[1]

Historicism contents itself with establishing a causal connection between various moments in history. But no fact that is a cause is for that very reason historical. It became historical posthumously, as it were, through events that may be separated from it by thousands of years. A historian who takes this as his point of departure stops telling the sequence of events like the beads of a rosary. Instead, he grasps the constellation which his own era has formed with a definite earlier one.

> Walter Benjamin, "Theses on the Philosophy of History," 1940[2]

Modernity and its discontents

The debates over "modernity" that have reverberated in European cultural theory and history since World War II have not unduly troubled most historians of eighteenth-century Britain. Suspicious of any species of "Whig" (that is, linear) history and confident that Continental theorizing bears little relevance to their inquiries, British historians have been content to fight less epochal battles over the appropriate characterization of their period. Hence whether England was an "aristocratic" or "bourgeois" society, an "ancien régime" or "commercialized" polity, marked predominantly by paternalism and deference or restiveness and resistance are the issues that have traditionally occupied many historians' attention.[3] Although such dichotomous readings have often been geared towards advancing more academic careers than productive debate, the status of eighteenth-century England as a progenitor of modernity has only recently been taken seriously by historians of the Hanoverian period.[4]

Certainly there is cause for skepticism about the historical returns of investigations into the location and meanings of modernity, not least since the term is twisted and turned to serve a variety of scholarly constituencies. Among more positivistic social scientists and historians, for example, modernity has been conceived as the story of "modernization" – that is, of those objective, ineluctably unfolding processes that are believed to have generated the structures and texture of "modern" life: urbanization, industrialization, democratization; bureaucracy, scienticism and technology.[5] But other historians and cultural critics, less interested in structural determinacies than in the meanings, ambiguities and significance of a period's configurations, have engaged more fruitfully with the notion of modernity as an unfolding set of relationships – cognitive, social and intellectual as well as economic and technological – which, however valued or construed, are seen as producing the modern self and its expectations of perfection or progress.[6] The re-theorizing of modernity among the so-called "postmodernists," for example – a disparate group of critics whose perceived unity rests on their intellectual debts to various French post-structuralisms as well as their shared belief in the discontinuity of the late twentieth-century present with the "modern" period that came before it – located in the discursive and institutional matrices of power and resistance shaping late eighteenth-century European societies the genealogies of their own age's discontents and transfigurations.[7] More currently, scholars are examining the relations of power at home and abroad that underwrote and sustained Europeans' perceptions of modernity, demonstrating how the nation-state and imperialism stimulated forms of identification, exclusion and belonging that have refused to fade.[8] In general, the most interesting work continues to focus on modernity as a discursive and cultural construct rather than a set of stereotypic processes or "forces," and some of the most exciting work looks at ways in which emergent ideas about nationality, race, ethnicity and difference became central to the broader social and political transformations of the mid eighteenth to early nineteenth centuries.

Clearly, the analysis of modernity has borne rich scholarly fruit as well as some conceptual vacuities, and it is a rash (not to say naive) historian who would dismiss all efforts to interrogate and theorize modernity as ahistorical, dangerous or irrelevant. For modernity need not be seen as one particular moment, whose "origins" and characteristics can be identified with certainty and mapped onto a specific temporality between the sixteenth and twentieth centuries. Rather, "modernity," the latest point on the continuum of historical change, should be understood as an emphatically historical condition that can be recovered, in Walter Benjamin's resonant phrase, only in "time filled by the presence of the now."[9] Modernity in this sense is not one moment or age, but a set of relations that are constantly being made and unmade, contested and reconfigured, that nonetheless produces among its contemporaneous witnesses the conviction of historical *difference*. Such a conceptualization opens up whole new grounds for theorizing and understanding our histories which do not deny the specificity of a period's configurations or reduce the eighteenth century to the status of the great primordial swamp of a more "modern" world. As an epistemological strategy, the historicization of differential modernities can also disrupt the comforting belief in the dissimilarity of past and present and productively subvert our sense of historical progress.[10]

This chapter will propose that such a reading of modernity can greatly enrich our understanding of English culture and politics in the Georgian decades. In doing so, it is indebted to a number of recent studies that have challenged dominant narratives and periodization of Western history by stressing the complexity, heterogeneity and hybridity of modernity at the moments of its various historical articulations. From this perspective, modernity refers to the cultural practices and representations that produced certain kinds of subjects and objects of knowledge, upheld widely shared notions of space and time or facilitated the formation of cultural identities that resulted in contradictions as well as coherences. The discontinuous and plural nature of the eighteenth-century experience – marked as closely by slavery as liberty, racial, class and gender exclusions as universality, and fractured and "double" as unitary identities – requires nothing less than a modification of the boundaries by which "modernity" and "postmodernity" are demarcated and understood. What follows hopes to contribute to this rethinking of eighteenth-century modernity by focusing on some of the forms of English identity and belonging produced by the British nation-state in the age of its first empire. For not only did the ideological legacies of eighteenth-century war, state and empire building shape the ways in which nationality was understood for two centuries or more to come; they also made possible the naturalization of certain kinds of identities – social, sexual, political, racial and national – whose traces refuse to disappear.[11] In the continual re-inventions of "the nation" – always a constructed, mythic and contested rather than stable or self-evident unit of meaning and coherence – and the ideological significations of its activities at home and abroad may be found a place where, in Paul Gilroy's phrase, a modernity begins in the "constitutive relationships with outsiders that both found and temper a self-conscious sense of western civilization."[12]

Whose Imagined Community?
Citizenship in a National Imaginary

In an immensely influential formulation, Benedict Anderson theorized in 1983 that the "print-capitalism" of the eighteenth century produced one of the founding practices of modernity, namely, the ability and propensity to imagine the "community" of the nation. The commodified production of print in books, novels and especially newspapers, Anderson argued, made possible the dissemination of a national consciousness, not only by stabilizing a vernacular language but also, and most importantly, by organizing distant and proximate events according to a calendrical simultaneity – of "empty, homogeneous time" – that enabled their readers to coordinate social time and space, and thus to think relations to others across countries and continents.[13] Anderson has since been rightly criticized for his unitary notion of the "nation" and its unproblematic transpositioning to the colonial and postcolonial worlds.[14] But his attention to the newspaper press in constructing forms of national belonging is salutary, not least because it reminds historians of the inseparability of any society's historical "reality" from its forms of cultural representation. "The 'lived reality' of national identity," John Tomlinson has noted, "is a reality lived in representations – not in direct communal solidarity." The viability of an imagined community of the nation depends upon the ability of its members to "[project] individual existence into the weft of a collective narrative," as Etienne Balibar has cogently argued, constructed through traditions "lived as the trace of an immemorial past (even when they have been fabricated and inculcated in the recent past)."[15] In this respect, the newspaper press, a strategic part of the print culture of eighteenth-century England that encompassed both the spread of the artifacts of the press and the institutions and forms of sociability that subsidized it, was clearly of great importance in disseminating particularized interpretations of the state, nation and polity. In conjunction with a range of other printed materials that were read in similar ways and social settings in towns throughout the kingdom, the newspaper press was instrumental in structuring national and political consciousness, binding ordinary men and women throughout the localities in particular ways to the processes of state and empire building.

Provincial newspapers, 244 of which sprouted up in fifty-five different towns over the century, offer one intriguing example of the operations of a "national" political imaginary as constructed and supported in the press. The importance of provincial urban life to negotiating the stability of the Hanoverian state at home and abroad has long been underplayed in accounts of the national becoming.[16] Yet catering to provincial urban publics whose interests in the processes of state were galvanized by decades of war and imperial expansion, provincial newspapers coaxed and confirmed their readers' involvement in national and international affairs in ways that gave form to contemporary conceptualizations of power and market relations, at home and abroad. For example, the newspapers of commercial and trading centers such as Newcastle, Norwich, Liverpool, Birmingham and Bristol in the middle decades of the century produced in their structure and content a mercantilist world view in which trade and the accumulation of wealth appeared as the highest national and individual good. The progress of wars in Europe, America, Africa and Asia, the coming and going of merchant and slaving ships and the lists of the contents of their laden bottoms; prices, stocks and bullion values; and advertisements for luxury goods culled from mercantile and military adventures abroad were consistent features of newspapers in the outports.[17]

In addition to an obsession with the moveable products of empire and commerce, newspapers and provincial periodicals also evinced a widespread fascination with the mechanics of colonial acquisition and possession. By the 1740s and 1750s, provincial papers frequently included sections on "American affairs" or "British Plantations" that provided current news on politics and trade, while periodicals crowded their pages with the histories and settlement patterns of individual colonies and beautifully produced maps of British and rival European colonial territories. Such texts did more than literally and figuratively map imperial aspirations and accumulationist desire; they also organized time and space in ways that welded the national and imperial interest, while effacing the crueller aspects of empire, colonialism and "trade" (the horrors of the Middle Passage or the brutalities of plantation slavery, for example) and the subjectivities of the growing numbers of peoples under British rule.[18] Instead, the newspaper and periodical press produced a commercial, sanitized and "patriotic" vision of the British empire and its apparent destiny of spreading profits throughout the nation while disseminating British goods, rights and liberties across the globe.[19] "Leonard Herd's African Coffeehouse" in Liverpool, which boasted of its "genteel accommodation" and current subscriptions to ten London and provincial newspapers and *Votes of the House of Commons* in the *Liverpool General Advertiser*, participated in this conjunction of empire, trade, politics and male sociability at the heart of much of urban print culture.[20]

Other items in the papers integrated the imperial project and Britain's performance and standing abroad with the prosperity, mores and class hierarchies of everyday life at home. Local and national politics, Court gossip, the notable *rites de passage* of the local gentry and bourgeoisie, philanthropic and economic initiatives and the "quaint" customs or "insensible" behaviors of the common people: such content endowed readers with the power of possession (*our* colonies, ships, MPs and gentry) and with the sense of entitlement to be on the right side of the vast social and cultural chasms between those who profited from the processes of imperial expansion and those who did not. In these and other ways, newspapers chronicled the bids of the urban commercial and middling classes to social authority and sketched out the structures of economic, political and discursive power in the society, of market-relations and forms of social, political and sexual commerce, within England, Britain and abroad. Above all, they made manifest the impact of state actions and politics on daily life and regional and national prosperity and standing, and allowed individuals to participate imaginatively as well as materially in the processes of domestic and imperial government.

Newspapers were thus central instruments in the social production of information: representing and verifying local experience and refracting world events into socially meaningful categories and hierarchies of importance, they helped produce, in Anderson's felicitous phrase, an "imagined community" of producers, distributors and consumers on both sides of the Atlantic who shared an avid interest in the fate of the "empire of goods" that linked them together in prosperity and adversity.[21] However, the ascription of "imagined community" to the world of goods and information constructed by newspapers begs a number of questions, not least, whose community? who was imagining it, and what was it imagined to consist of? Clearly newspapers (or other forms of print) did not produce homogeneous cultural identities, but a highly mediated "national" belonging that was constructed through and in tandem with other (local, regional, social) identities. Nevertheless, as the above analysis suggests, we can discern the social, sexual and racial contours of the national community constructed by the newspaper and periodical press. It was imagined to consist of free, flourishing and largely, though not exclusively, white male British subjects within the locality, nation and empire; its boundaries were defined and guarded by gender, race, productivity and profits. Hence despite the participation in the processes of state and imperial expansion by other citizens in the metropolis and provincial towns – women, slave and free Africans, Jews, servants, Catholics, laborers and so on – who worked in urban economies as victuallers, retailers, artisans, carriers and peddlers, supported the state through taxes or otherwise played roles in financing, transporting, distributing, manufacturing or consuming the artifacts of colonial and international commerce, their status as a part of the public appealed to in the newspaper press was usually implicit at best, extrapolated through the claims to status of the male middling sorts or their betters.[22] The accessible, homogenized national identity cultivated by newspapers was in fact a delimiting one that recapitulated the self-representations of the urban upper and middle classes, and especially their male, white and English members. And although such an inscribing of subjectivity was contested by a variety of other practices and genres – from pamphlet writing and novels to dramatic works and women's periodicals – it tended to be bolstered by related sources, such as travel writing.[23]

Further, if we extend the metaphor of "imagined community" to include the *political* imaginary, that is, to partisan representations of the state and its relations with individuals and localities, we can see how the conventional political biases of the provincial press could operate to deepen the identification between citizenship and the male upper and middle classes. G. A. Cranfield pointed out long ago the marked propensity of provincial printers to capitalize on predominant hostility to successive Court Whig ministries by reproducing the parliamentary opposition's point of view.[24] By consistently printing essays and letters from the main opposition tracts, pamphlets and journals, provincial papers such as the *Norwich Gazette, Farley's Bristol Journal, Gloucester Journal, Salisbury Journal, Newcastle Courant* and *York Courant* adopted fairly hostile criteria by which to judge the state and its leaders that played a large role in shaping attitudes to metropolitan hegemony, the activities of the oligarchs and the abuses to which, it was alleged, the constitution was repeatedly subject at their hands. Equally important, through its representations of the state the opposition press in London and the localities also constructed the identity of the citizens positioned outside its confines. For example, in the contexts of Britain's imperial rivalries, wars and ministers who seemed either disinclined to adopt an aggressively expansionist foreign policy or too willing to undertake coercive measures against English citizens wherever they lived, the frequent charges of corruption and "effeminacy" levelled against the state by opposition writers in the middle to late decades of the century inscribed its reader-opponents as activist, virtuous, masculine political subjects. It was only "the people" (a deliberately ambiguous designation in the hands of most opposition journalists), inspired by a "manly, rational love of liberty," who were capable of serving as guardians of the public trust. In this way, the oppositionist reading of politics that was retailed in the newspaper and periodical press produced definitions of patriotism and political subjectivity that were quite at odds with those proffered by ministerial advocates.[25]

"Every subject not only has the right, but is in duty bound, to enquire into the publick measures pursued," one writer asserted, "because by such enquiry he may discover that some of the publick measures tend towards overturning the liberties of his country; and by making such a discovery in time, and acting strenuously . . . he may disappoint their effect."[26] This activist conception of citizenship proclaimed the *duty* of the subject to monitor, ogle and canvass the state to ensure the accountability of those in power. As such it lay at the heart of oppositionist patriotic imperatives, based on "the original Power of the People" to resist illegitimate power, upon which scores of writers from Bolingbroke to John Cartwright insisted. Yet how was such an ideal to be enacted? Over the course of the century supporters offered a variety of answers to this question that differed according to the issues and agendas at hand, ranging from participating in instruction and petitioning movements, voting for Members of Parliament and engaging in political demonstrations or festivals to remonstrating the throne or setting up alternative conventions to speak the sense of the People.[27] Yet one of the perennial and preeminent ways the "manly, rational love of liberty" could be demonstrated was in the public sphere of surveillance and opinion constructed by the press. Against government supporters' claims that "inquiries into the corruptions and mismanagements of those in the administration, properly and solely belong to . . . Parliament," opposition journalists continually asserted the people's right to monitor the state through the mechanisms of spectatorship provided by a free press. As one pamphleteer argued in 1740, since "[t]he People of Britain in general have an indubitable Right to Canvass publick affairs, to express their sentiments freely, and to declare their sense of any grievances under which they labour,"

> treating political subjects freely in print, and thereby submitting them to the view and censure of the Nation in general, is so far from being dangerous that it is really conducive to the Publick Peace. By this means, all Degrees of People, who have leisure and abilities, and a turn to this sort of reading, acquire rational ideas of liberty and submission, of the rights of the church, and of the power of the State, and of their duties as subjects, and of what they may justly claim as *Freemen*.[28]

In this argument, literacy becomes the test of citizenship and the instrument of political subjectivity itself, and through print culture the subject's right to monitor the state and the potential for citizen activism were fulfilled. Clearly, the political press recast politics into spectatorial, critical activities, capable of being exercised privately, but more appropriately enacted within the sphere of public society itself. The alehouse, tavern, newsroom, coffeehouse and club, as well as the counting house, shipyard and shop, made "the people" temporarily visible, but print made it permanent, allowing it to exist through a "steady, solid simultaneity through time" as Anderson has noted.[29] At the same time, through the role of spectator the political subject was delimited in class, gender and racial terms as "independent," sovereign and masculine – a critical, objective, manly and hence white male subject, immune to the emoluments of power, whose contrast to the allegedly corrupt, irrational or effeminate aristocratic state could not be more marked.[30]

Such particularized "national imaginings" encouraged by the newspaper and political press were reinforced elsewhere in the culture of urban life, where a range of pursuits and practices, whether undertaken in the name of politics, science, art, "useful knowledge" or civic improvement, could continually reinscribe the extra legal definition of citizens as independent, male heads of households capable of defining and protecting the national interest. Indeed, the "urban renaissance" itself, that much celebrated and masterfully described phenomenon of provincial urban renewal over the century, provided contexts for social and political action that enabled the middle classes to negotiate the status and authority of established elites in ways that privileged their claims for political recognition and status. Predicated largely on British economic expansion and prosperity, especially the growing importance of England's colonial and foreign trade in the provincial economy, the urban renaissance could also bolster the masculinist patriotism espoused by opposition spokespersons and bellicose merchants alike.[31]

To be sure, the initiatives undertaken to improve public amenities and communications, expand leisure facilities, rebuild churches or found hospitals were dependent upon the willingness and ability of a wide range of residents, men and women, artisans and merchants, shopkeepers and patricians to associate and subscribe money and time in order to refashion and regulate their physical and cultural environments. And arenas of polite culture such as assembly rooms, tea rooms and pleasure gardens promoted the cultivation of heterosociality that afforded upper- and middle-class women a valued status as arbiters of sociability and decorum, or polishers of gruff masculine manners.[32] Yet the institutions of the urban renaissance also advanced definitions of subjectivity that supported the prerogatives of middle- and upper-class men. Voluntary hospitals for the sick poor, for example, those quintessentially mercantilist enterprises dedicated to expanding productivity by remodelling the poor, combined that ubiquitous method of capital mobilization, the subscription, and wide and heterogeneous community support with more delimiting rules of participation and voting that accorded with the gender and financial contribution of the subscriber.[33] Assembly rooms and theaters, built through the contributions of the wealthiest members of their communities, also did less than is usually supposed to disrupt dominant social and gender hierarchies. For example, the use of provincial assembly rooms was strictly regulated, with the formations of minuets and dances as well as the arrival and departures of carriages organized according to social rank and position.[34] Theaters brought together a more volatile cross-section of the public but were nonetheless stridently defended as bulwarks of the national character and fomenters of those manly, civilized and patriotic manners necessary to English success abroad and stability at home. Indeed, in both rationale and performance, theater frequently drew upon and exaggerated the masculinist cultural identities circulating elsewhere in the public sphere in a self-conscious effort to socialize audiences into the mores of gender and national differentiation.[35]

The proliferation of clubs and societies, one of the most celebrated and distinctive aspects of provincial urban culture in the eighteenth century, was perhaps most successful in authorizing particularized definitions of citizenship. Whether devoted to philosophical inquiry, politics or competitive gardening, most provincial clubs provided homosocial enclaves of conviviality, sociability and discipline that, among their many manifest and latent functions, endowed their predominantly male memberships with the identity of decision-making subjects capable of associating for the public good.[36] Certainly associational life per se was not a male preserve. As the politics of trade and empire and the issues raised by state expansion worked to galvanize political consciousness and patriotism in new directions, merchants, traders and shopkeepers, journeymen and servants and men and women were stimulated to initiate political activities on their own or to join national campaigns.[37] But the *signification* of such participatory patriotism was strictly narrowed by the demands and exigencies of politics and international military conflict. Decades of war had tended to bolster a militaristic, masculinist version of the national identity that privileged the claims of the white, trading and commercial classes to political status while excluding a range of "effeminate" others who threatened their supposedly distinctive goals: not only the French or francophilic, but also the aristocratic, the foppish, the irrational, the dependent and the timid.[38] For example, in the virulent national political debates over the nature of the aristocratic leadership and the national character that resounded in the 1740s through 1760s, "effeminacy" denoted a degenerate moral, political and social state that opposed and subverted the vaunted "manly" characteristics – courage, aggression, martial valor, discipline and strength – constituting patriotic virtue. Its denigration intersected with other efforts to eradicate behaviors and practices (sexual and consumer as well as political) that blurred gender lines or otherwise threatened masculinity and resolution in the political and cultural realms. An effeminate Nation was "a Nation which *resembles Women*," John Brown asserted in his influential *Estimate of the Manners and Principles of the Times*, devoid of courage, liberty, principle and endurance, opposed to public spiritedness and martial valor, and destined for international ignominy and derision.[39] As a diagnosis of national political ills, Brown's assessment was to have a recurring, if contested, longevity; as a marker of what was desirable and necessary in the nation's leaders and citizenry, this masculinist version of the national character became common currency in wartime, asserted and circulated in parades, dramatic tableaux, painting, periodicals, sermons and street theater, artifacts and design as well as the press.[40]

Not surprisingly, then, the expanding fiscal-military state forged and defined through war produced in political culture definitions of patriotism and the national character that represented its operations at home and abroad through the axes of class, gender and race, recuperating simultaneously both an anti-conquest, humanitarian version of military acquisition and an aggressive, if compassionate, masculinity, potency and power. The social heterogeneity of subscribers to patriotic societies actually worked to uphold this composite as the primary instrument of the nation's survival and greatness: men and women, aristocrats and servants joining together to promote that "manly, rational patriotism" and martial spirit without which the nation's security, self-sufficiency and destiny would crumble.[41]

The aftermath of war and massive imperial expansion saw these tenets appropriated, renewed and reworked by other means. The political and debating clubs of the Wilkite period, for example, not only articulated an overtly radicalized vision of the polity, but also an ideal of citizenship that recuperated andocentric patriotism for new purposes. Wilkite journalism, street theater, prints and plays retailed to a wide audience the ideology of independence and ideals of resistance and "manly patriotism" that made explicit a hostility to intrusions of the feminine as well as effeminate in the political sphere. Defining as the true patriot one who would resist, at considerable personal cost, the illegitimate powers that threatened to overtake the polity, the model of manly patriotism defined and solicited a particular version of masculinity to be put at the call of the nation that marginalized and opposed non-resisting and hence "effeminate" others. The broadside *Wilkes and Liberty* (Fig. 2)

Figure 2 Wilkes and Liberty (1763). Courtesy of the British Museum, Department of Prints and Drawings.

retails this version of resolute masculine patriotism in visual and textual form, showing Wilkes and his friends, Earl Temple, William Pitt and Charles Churchill, gallantly defending a bare-chested and fainting Britannia from the assaults of Bute and his cronies, above a ballad that celebrates Wilkes's own persecution and heroic resistance to royal and ministerial tyranny. Hence the acerbic attacks of Wilkite journalists on "Scottish" and aristocratic pollutions of the body politic, as well as on "sodomitical" peers and incestuous women behind the scenes exerting "secret influence" at Court, served a number of political purposes that included both privileging the claims of middle-class Englishmen to the prerogatives of political subjectivity and closing down the gender identities available to political subjects.[42]

A constitutive part of this milieu, Wilkite clubs embellished a longstanding belief of Masonic and pseudo-masonic societies that women and "effeminate" men were potential sources of contamination that would undermine the rationality and fraternity of their project.[43] They were also complicit with the rakish, heterosexist libertinism with which Wilkite radicalism was associated. Certainly Wilkite publishers' sustained attack on aristocratic libertinage, royal vice and political corruption allowed their readers to experience the vicarious pleasures of voyeurism and self-righteousness, and so retailed alternative models of masculinity more amenable to the requirements of sensibility.[44] But at the same time, Wilkes's pornographic *Essay on Women*, his flamboyant sexual escapades (including alleged participation in orgies as a member of the notorious Medmenham Monks, a "Hell-Fire Club") combined with his assaults on the royal family and such alleged evidences of aristocratic effeminacy as sodomy, legitimated and mobilized a quite explicit sexual, as well as political, libertarianism among its supporters, from Sylas Neville to political revellers in the provinces.[45] Wilkes was "free from cock to wig," in the words of a humble (male) admirer; while the voting qualification for the Wilkite club members that attended the mock election at Garrat was "having enjoyed a woman in the open air within the district."[46] Although the connection of the libertine version of masculine virility to radical politics did not go unchallenged, and women were participants in Wilkite festival and polemics, at the very least the multiply determined constructions of Wilkite radicalism drove home the point that political subjects and sexual subjects were one and the same.[47]

Hence, Wilkite clubs of the period, such as the Revolution Club in Newport, Isle of Wight, which annually commemorated "the duty and honor of resisting Stuart Tyrants," the Patriotic Society in Leeds, formed to mark the day of Wilkes's enlargement from prison, and the African and American Club in Whitehaven, devoted, with no apparent awareness of contradiction, to promoting the slave trade abroad and the liberties of the subject at home, all equally aimed at a reconstruction capable of shaping notions of the national interest to their advantage and reconfiguring the terms of social exchange and political power. But they were also instrumental in inscribing this broader symbolic valuation of gender identities, upholding a homosocial, heterosexual and predominantly masculine ethos of conviviality and politics that staked out both physically and ideologically a male domain within the socially mixed and potentially transgressive spaces of urban society.[48] Like print culture and other sites where extra legal definitions of citizenship could be enacted or maintained, club life not only imbricated empire, state expansion and local and national prosperity in ways that multiply constituted the national; it also constructed the identity of the citizen, the nature of the state and the contours of the political nation in social, racial and gendered terms.

(Second Class) Citizens and (Non-) Nationals

To restate the argument so far, the politically constructed national imaginings of urban life, and particularly the efforts to enact a "national," rational political public to which the state was held to be accountable, also led to stridently gendered and exclusionary notions of political subjectivity that played central roles in consolidating oppositional categories of the domestic and public spheres. Yet the larger contexts and culture supporting and influenced by the expanding fiscal-military state and its actions at home and abroad also created spaces and sites for a wider range of groups to claim or imagine a status as citizens despite oligarchy and ethnic, class and gender inequalities. To take the most obvious example, in spite of their legal standing as dependants and the masculinist nature of much nation-alistic political discourse, women frequently acted like political subjects within the commercialized world of extra-parliamentary politics. Women made up thirty percent of the patrons at circulating libraries in the country and accounted for between one-third and one-fifth of the membership at various book clubs that have left adequate records; they were avid newspaper readers, and were also patrons of such institutions of politics and print culture as inns and taverns.[49] Further, numbers of women worked in London and provincial towns as writers, printers, engravers, newspaper publishers, newsagents, stationers and booksellers as well as innkeepers and victuallers; as writers they engaged in polemical political debates from the consequences of the Glorious Revolution to the immorality of slavery.[50] Beginning in the 1730s, the development of the market for political artifacts increased the range of things women could buy (and sell) to express their political affiliations. Women in provincial towns wore appropriately colored cockades and silks to assemblies and balls to signal their political affiliations, presided over politically correct tea tables whose cloths commemorated the defeat of the excise bill, or sold ballads, garlands or snuff that honored the opposition hero Admiral Vernon.[51] Women were also participants in riots, demonstrations, chairing and processions; spectators at the ceremonials of state and nation, from anniversary day celebrations to military reviews; avid attenders at the theater and at debating societies; subscribers to philanthropic and patriotic societies; activists in the "home front" during war and invasion scares and occasionally the targets of vigorous propagandizing. Even the government itself interpellated women as political subjects by prosecuting them for seditious or treasonable words.[52]

Clearly, long before the 1790s, the commercialized nature of English politics and culture provided women at virtually all social levels with wider opportunities to act like political subjects and appropriate the mantle of citizenship for

40

themselves; indeed, the injunctions to "manly rationality" could not be bounded by biological sex and emanated from and were a source of identity for women as well as men.[53] As one provincial essayist satirized, "[A]s the times past have seen a nation of Amazons, who drew the bow and wielded the battle-ax, formed encampments and wasted nations, the revolution of years has now produced a race of Amazons of the pen, who, with the spirit of their predecessors, have set masculine tyranny at defiance, and asserted the claim to the regions of science."[54] Nevertheless, the social acceptance and valuation of women's forays into politics was variable, dependent upon class and political context as well as those fluctuating variables that connived at suspending or amplifying the conventional misogyny of English political writers.[55] Aristocratic women's influence at Court, on the canvass or behind the scenes was largely accepted; indeed, elite women in general played a crucial role in establishing, through marriage, sociability and friendships, the social and familial networks upon which high politics depended. Well-positioned women, whether bluestocking or no, clearly felt drawn to the appeals of a sentimental patriotism that encouraged their identification with their country of origin or adoption as "home."[56] Women of less exalted status identified themselves as citizens by their practices and standing in the community, voting in parish and even parliamentary elections, even after the King's Bench decision of 1739 denied any constitutional status to such anomalies. Moreover, some women were recognized as legal individuals in certain poor law cases over the century; and the political aspirations of the more economically fortunate could be nourished through their votes as shareholders in the chartered companies.[57] Yet although an appropriate degree of political interest by elite and bourgeois women was tolerated by most observers, lower-class women's political activism was denounced as evidence of their degraded natures.[58] Above all, national crises or emergencies were liable to make intrusions of the feminine into the political sphere a focus of intense male anxiety, while war both intensified the strident masculinism of patriotic discourse and effaced the extra efforts women made to the "home front" that war simultaneously demanded.[59]

As we have seen, the patriotisms legitimating or authorized by the fiscal-military nation-state depended upon a marginalization or subordination of the feminine in their notions of the national character. Certainly this did not prevent women from identifying with the imperatives of citizenship, nor from developing specific forms of "female patriotism"; but these discourses and practices continued to devalue or relativize women's contributions to national affairs and so naturalized their exclusion from formal politics. Joseph Addison set a pattern in 1716 when he both urged right-minded women to support the Hanoverian Succession and then satirized their propensity to "judge for themselves; look into the State of the Nation with their own Eyes, and be no longer led Blindfold by a Male Legislature."[60] This double bind for women, being simultaneously urged to promote love of country and yet constrained by their lack of legal and political status and injunctions to domesticity, stimulated a great deal of the protofeminist commentary of the day and was ultimately addressed in the ideas of republican motherhood (although many of the more progressive women would come to reject this association). Equally important, however, it also confirmed women's alter status within contemporary political culture, where, as stadial historians and political theorists agreed, their capacities and resources at the service of the fiscal-military state were limited by their supposed "natural" and emotional otherness.

I am *not* suggesting that we should take such eighteenth-century representations at their word: as should be clear by the examples above, women were clearly crucial to political, as to other forms of social and cultural life, and occupied a heterogenous range of positions within it. What I am arguing is that women's participation in politics and public life as a whole had to conform to the roles conventionally assigned to them in an obviously hierarchical gender and social order. Indeed, recent stress on the marvelous capacities of aristocratic women to intervene in political life does not result only in a return to a rather old-fashioned and attenuated view of politics as a realm where kinship and connection were what mattered, and ideology was irrelevant. It also underlines the class-based nature of gender idealizations and identifications, of historians as well as their subjects. Within the self-understanding of this historical society, women's role in public life was secondary and instrumental, geared largely to facilitate and uphold male prerogatives. As Hilda Smith has convincingly argued, the "false universals" permeating political and legal discourse of the early modern period "excluded women without explicitly saying so." Or even by explicitly saying so: as one journalist propounded,

> The central point in the British constitution is common freedom, which makes every Inhabitant of the state a free subject; protects *him* from every controuling will, but the Will of *his* country's laws, which is *his* own will, because *he* hath assented to them by *his* Representatives; and secures to *him* the full enjoyment of *his* property, with as much Right, as *his* Sovereign enjoys his Crown. *His* house is *his* castle, and no man can Enter it without *his* own consent. These are the privileges of every English*man*.[61]

Sir John Strange put the case more baldly in 1739: "in all acts which concern the public, women are put in the same class with infants." In the political and social theory of the day, women's difference and improvement was mapped through culture and education, *not* through property and "independence" (a mental, as much as material, condition) as for men, and without the latter formal political status was unthinkable. Hence women's assertions of subjectivity failed to secure recognition within the larger political culture of the nation, where most commentators agreed that women lacked the "improved understanding" required for political rights.[62] The moral and the material intertwined to keep women in a subordinate, if productive, position in the national polity. Free, rational, tasteful, clean, domestic, sympathetic and decorous, but also fragile, luxurious, sensual and dependent, English women could serve as emblems and demonstrations of national superiority and civilization, or help purify the morally dubious public sphere through their influence. But they could not be independent political subjects, only auxiliary ones, whose ultimate role was to authorize masculine prerogatives and authority. Contemporary representations of the national character and citizenship trenchantly foregrounded these convergences and tensions between the symbolic feminine and the empirical positions of women, stimulating resistance and contestation certainly but also partially structuring women's experience and desire.[63] Hence Elizabeth Robinson Montagu, a highly articulate and integral player in the political gossip networks of the day, fantasized about being the consort of the "conquering hero" (and pathologically violent) Cortés.[64]

Women's contingent and subordinate positioning within the imagined community of the nation was in some ways paralleled by, though in no way homologous to, that of marginalized ethnic and religious groups within the English polity. By the eighteenth century, England had acquired a reputation for providing refuge for groups persecuted elsewhere in Europe (Huguenots, Walloons, Gypsies, Sephardic Jews, for example); it was also a "mother country" for colonial immigrants, both old and new (Irish, Scottish, Americans and West Indians), and a destination for others brought in through the privileges and exigencies of slavery and colonial trade (Africans, East Indians, Chinese).[65] The first European diaspora wrought by colonialism, commerce and exploration, in other words, wrought another, partly involuntary diasporic population living in the English metropole. Some of these immigrants and their children became almost permanent members of poor and disadvantaged communities in the capital and outports; others thrived in partially or wholly assimilated artisan, craft or mercantile occupations. The difficulties of "forging a nation" in the face of such apparently irreducible and inevitable internal difference has been influentially summarized by Linda Colley, who has stressed its considerable successes by the years of the Napoleonic wars.[66] Nevertheless, the crises of the period produced by war, invasion and rebellion could confound the efforts to construct and maintain a unifying national identity. In particular, the presence and resistances of those whose Englishness or Britishness could not be taken as self-evident demonstrated that the continual reinventions of the nation and of the terms of national belonging could not be capacious or elastic enough to accommodate all of "the others" within. Catholics, Jews, foreign Protestants, Irish, Scots and Africans were among the groups targeted for denigration, harassment, physical segregation or forced exile during the various political crises of the century.[67] As such, even if their members could act like citizens in the public sphere of association, opinion and debate and promote their own versions of the public interest, their membership in the nation was tentative, unstable and always revealing of the fictive nature of a "national identity."

To take one example, the "black" population of England, comprised mostly of Africans and West Indians (though including a small contingent of South and East Asians), numbered between ten and fifteen thousand by the 1770s, concentrated in London and those outports having extensive dealings with Africa and the plantation colonies.[68] Although Africans had been present in England since Elizabethan times, Britain's subsequent rise to dominance in the slave trade and changes in the laws meant that from the 1720s until abolition of the slave trade in 1807 they arrived in greater numbers, in all conditions – as slaves, servants, refugees and stowaways, sailors and artisans, students and princes – and from all over the world. Despite endemic prejudices and pervasive economic hardships, their members came to occupy a variety of subject positions within English society. Probably the majority arrived as slaves and lived by custom as servants; if they gained their freedom while in the country, they had to live under the shadow of possible recapture and sale.[69] Free blacks worked as servants and sailors (by the 1790s one-quarter of the British navy was composed of Africans); as shopkeepers, artisans and laborers; as laundry maids, seamstresses and children's nurses; or as peddlers, street musicians, players with travelling fairs, and pugilists; while still others fell into begging or crime. Those with a specific skill or trade usually came in at the bottom of the hierarchy of labor that included the Irish and Jews as well as the mass of "English" laboring poor.[70] English attitudes towards Africans and people of African descent were varied and variable, and among the laboring classes in particular relations between black and white Britons could be cordial and close. Nevertheless, Ukawsaw Gronniosaw, arriving in England as an adult after having been kidnapped into slavery and then held in bondage as a domestic servant in New York, illustrates the struggles that could beset an African immigrant who attempted to gain a livelihood in what he been brought up to believe was a "holy" land. Working as a navvy, carpenter and twisterer in London, Colchester and Norwich, he, his English wife (who was a weaver) and three children fell continually into those economic difficulties common to the insecure life of the laboring poor, but exacerbated in their case by racism. The hostility of the "inferior people" in Norwich, in Gronniosaw's words, was such that resentful laborers resorted to working under price in order to starve the family out of town. "Such is our situation at present," Gronniosaw wrote in 1770 from Kidderminster; "As Pilgrims, and very poor Pilgrims, we are travelling through many difficulties."[71]

Gronniosaw's appropriation of the language of *Pilgrim's Progress*, that most Protestant and English of religious tracts, to make his own claim to subject status in a country hostile to such "outsider's" claims points to another avenue of contestation and survival for former slaves in England, namely, Christianity and especially Anglican Protestantism. Despite several court rulings to the contrary, it was widely believed that baptism would make slaves free, and slaves in England were eager to take advantage of this extralegal loophole; indeed, the majority became Anglican communicants. Although their religious beliefs were probably genuine, and baptism and conversion were far from fail-safe methods of procuring freedom, the use of the privileged religion as a road out of bondage ironically gave Africans a leverage within English society that other persecuted or disadvantaged groups, such as Jews and Catholics, could not access. It "gets the mob on their [i.e., the ex-slaves'] side," Sir John Fielding reported, "and makes it not only difficult, but dangerous, . . . to recover possession of them."[72] The "confessional state," that bulwark of the establishment, and Anglican Protestantism, the cornerstone of the national identity and a marker of the "civilized" in the popular consciousness, thus became avenues through which Africans could make their tormented journeys in the English mind from slave to humanity, or at least live as other English people and claim their rights in the national community. These claims to citizenship were extremely important in promoting the abolitionist cause.[73]

Sociability, politics and propaganda – all activities carried out in the public sphere of eighteenth-century urban life – also provided opportunities for non-white English citizens to promote their own versions of the public interest. The African-English community in London was large and closely knit, and a black variant of English urban culture upheld customs of civility that succored its participants and took the edge off their sense of ethnic isolation. Taverns, assemblies and clubs dominated by black Britons were noted in London in the 1760s; and wealthier individuals attended the theater and pleasure gardens.[74] Further, roused by slave revolts in the colonies and spurring the efforts of abolitionists such as Granville Sharp and Thomas Day, a politicized black community galvanized the antislavery movement beginning in the late 1760s; indeed, African-English writers played a major role in its growing popularity out of doors.[75] Their participation in print culture was multiply significant. As Henry Louis Gates Jr. has argued, blacks were believed to be largely outside of the community of reason in the eighteenth century, and "reason" – rationality, objectivity, logic – was an instrument of delimiting citizenship as well as a commodity to be used in exchange for admission to "humanity." Hence Phyllis Wheatley, domestic slave of a Boston merchant, who visited London in 1772 and charmed aristocratic bluestocking circles with her ardent antislavery poetry and spirit; Ignatius Sancho, butler to the Duke of Montagu, grocer, friend of Garrick and admirer of Sterne, whose posthumously published letters garnered six hundred initial subscribers and a number of editions; Olaudah Equiano, Nigerian, ex-slave, mariner, explorer, writer and radical activist; and Ottabah Cugoano, a Ghanian kidnapped into slavery at age thirteen who in 1787 penned one of the most influential abolitionist tracts of the period, all joined Gronniosaw as Africans who simultaneously "proved" their humanity and indicted European hierarchies of civilization by their writings.[76] Their prose and verse, in fact and content, also pluralized the universal and gave proof of its multiple embodiments, a strategy which aided other groups who were alter to the white, English male bourgeois subjects that political discourse valorized to stake their own claims for recognition.

Nevertheless, the place of Africans and "people of colour" (an eighteenth-century phrase) in the national imaginary was fraught and uncertain. In the newspaper debates that accompanied the Sierra Leone repatriation project in 1786–7 – a moment marked by economic crisis and high anxiety over an influx of black immigrants in the aftermath of the American war – toleration and the longstanding secular racism of the plantocracy and its supporters in England contended, while the contingent nature of black claims to national standing and the ambivalences of "Englishness" itself were made richly apparent. The project to "export" numbers of poor blacks from London to begin their own colony on the

African coast, in an area considered and then rejected as a potential penal colony, was first hatched in May 1786.[77] Yet between October 1786, when the navy commissioned ships to carry the pioneers, and April 1787 when they finally left England, a number of circumstances had intervened to quell the initial enthusiasm for the project among the London African community and its leaders. Five hundred men, women and children had boarded the *Atlantis* and the *Belisarius* (the name of the latter a spectacular if unintended irony)[78] by late October, yet, as the departure was delayed, numbers began to perish with cold and sickness in an unsavory imitation of a slave ship expedition. Other enlisters, unsettled by rumors about the British government's intentions and their own safety once they arrived in Africa, began to leave or refused to join the ships. Cugoano summarized their case sometime later, arguing: "can it be readily conceived that government would establish a free colony for them nearly on the spot, while it supports its forts and garrisons, to ensnare, merchandize, and to carry others into captivity and slavery?" The *Morning Herald*, a liberal, abolitionist newspaper, agreed, asserting that, in opting out, these blacks had shown their English predilections, "prefer[ring] liberty with poverty" to being "transported to a military government, like the white Felons to New Norfolk." "Would it not be dangerous innovation in this land of liberty," an editorial pronounced, "to suffer the exclusion of our fellow creatures from the rights of mankind, on account of difference of complexion?"[79]

Other reactions were less supportive. One writer to the *Public Advertiser* claimed that the Africans' distrust of the government showed how little they comprehended the English constitution and character: "national honour" would prevent any circumvention of Parliament's commitment to protect their liberty. The *Morning Post* ignored the libertarian issues altogether, drawing instead on plantocratic fears of miscegenation and contamination in order to condemn the Africans' refusal to leave. Sarcastically referring to these "dark-colored patriots," it quoted the late Mr. Dunning on the likelihood of London taking on "the appearance of an Ethiopian colony" if the black population was not reduced and immigration stopped.[80] Equally hostile writers drew upon stereotypes that were also used to denigrate other disadvantaged or diasporic populations within: blacks were "naturally indolent" and had to be forced to work (charges also levelled against the Irish); "exporting" them would lower the crime rate (the same argument was used in favor of restraining the "importation" of the Irish and Jews) and reducing their numbers would stave off the inevitable emasculation of English men that Africans' alleged sexual prowess and lasciviousness effected (a recurrent, fetishistic fantasy about racialized others that was also wielded against Irish men, South Sea Islanders and visiting Cherokee Indian warriors).[81] As the *London Chronicle* had put it twenty years before, "there can be no just plea for [black Britons] being put on an equal footing with *natives whose birthright, as members of the community, entitles them to superior dues.*"[82] The satirical print *The Poor Blacks Going to their Settlement* (1786) (Fig. 3) confirms the point that black Britons had no real claim on the nation. Portraying the Prince of Wales (in Indian feathers) and his adherents as displaced black Britons, the print lampoons the opposition's loss of profile since the American

Figure 3 The Poor Blacks Going to their Settlement (1786). Courtesy of the British Museum, Department of Prints and Drawings.

war, conflates the Sierra Leone resettlement project with the plan to found a convict colony at Botany Bay (against which Lord George Gordon, center, petitioned), and so indicts both blacks and their surrogates as no better than paupers and criminals. Blacks and people of color may have been human in this national imaginary, but they certainly were not English, and "English" in these contexts served less as a universally recognized symbol or set of attributes than as a "sign of difference," in Homi Bhabha's words, which could never be naturalized.[83]

As such, Africans living in England clearly experienced the fractured and hybrid identities that in part constituted, and were constituted by, the diasporic experience and the crucibles of nation-state and colonialism. Equiano, whose many occupations included ship's steward under Admiral Boscawen during the Seven Years War, sailor in a merchant ship, participant in Captain Constantine Phipps's expedition to the Arctic, and political organizer in abolitionist and corresponding society politics, adopted in his writings simultaneously the subjectivity of the quintessential English bourgeois (traveller, scientist, trader, explorer, Protestant) and that of an African, a "Son of Africa" (the name of a group of African abolitionists in London), a former slave and a working-class, radical citizen. He was, in his words, "almost an Englishman," and "part of the poor, oppressed, needy and much degraded negroes" – an incompatibility that seemed irreducible. The multiplying "double consciousness" of a diasporic modernity, to use W. E. Du Bois's phrase, permeated his political and autobiographical self-representations.[84] Equally palpable was the dislocation and alienation felt by Ignatius Sancho. Born on a slave ship and brought up in an English household before entering the Duke of Montagu's service, Sancho, with his aristocratic penchants for gambling, womanizing and polite entertainments, was once pointed to by scholars as a case study in successful assimilation. Yet in his private letters Sancho expressed a profound sense of isolation and unbelonging that national crises such as the American war or the Gordon Riots only exaggerated. Reviewing the disasters that accompanied the former in 1779, he wrote that these national tribulations were "nothing to me, as I am only a lodger, and hardly that" – a displaced African, not a black Englishman, as Folarin Shyllon has noted.[85]

In sum, although the sites that enabled or encouraged national imaginings could enact the gulfs between the public and the private, men and women, slaves and freemen or "the people" and the rabble, they also inevitably created spaces for participation, engagement and contestation by those outside of the privileged halves of these oppositions. Such interventions, at the very least, gave embodied proof of the pluralities of the universals of citizenship, humanity and patriotism and contested the unitary deployments of the central tenets of libertarian discourse in the period. On the other hand, the place of England's peoples marked as "other" in the imagined communities of the nation was contingent and incomplete at best, denigrated and despised at worst and always the product of contestation and resistance.

Fractured Desires: Empire, Citizenship and Nation

Finally, empire itself, its imagined forms and seemingly limitless possibilities, brought into sharp relief the fissures and problematic of attempted national imaginings in ways that suggest both the fatal attractions and irreconcilable tensions between empire and nation. Benedict Anderson has argued that the nation was imagined as a "community" because "regardless of the actual inequality and exploitation that may prevail in each, the nation is always conceived as a deep horizontal comradeship."[86] Yet empire and colonies, the knowledge, possession and processes of which were integral in constituting the British nation and English national identity in the eighteenth century, constantly demonstrated the contradictions and strains produced by such attempted "national" imaginings. Certainly England's imperial project at times provided a slate upon which a united national polity could be inscribed that overlaid the social and political tensions within the domestic polity.[87] But if the discourses of nationality sought to construct homogeneities within the territorial boundaries of the nation-state, they also sought to identify and assert *difference*, and those differences, however artificial and tenuous, not only distinguished the nation from other nations but also divided the citizens within its own boundaries. Empire confounded and completed this project in interesting and complex ways.

As we have seen, the English devotion to empire lay as much in its role as a bulwark and emblem of English superiority and benevolence as in its profitability, yet, especially as constituted in oppositionist patriotism, empire was imagined to create a far-reaching and inclusive *British* polity that preserved the most valued components of the national identity. In the 1730s and 1740s, such imaginings, galvanized and focused on the opposition hero Admiral Edward Vernon, who defeated the Spanish at Porto Bello in 1739, supported the spectacular vision of empire as an extensive, homogenous polity bounded only by rights, liberties and duties and guided by manly and virtuous leaders. Clearly this belief was both rose-colored and self-serving, mystifying or obscuring the brutal, exploitative and violent processes of colonization and slavery and glossing over the differences between the various forms of British imperial dominance in the New World (and Old). Nevertheless, it was immensely attractive to domestic publics, who seemed fervently to subscribe to its view of the essentially fair-minded, just and paternalistic nature of British, as opposed to French or Spanish, empire, and the former's ability to "tame the fierce and polish the most savage," civilizing the world through commerce and trade.[88] Through Vernon, empire was refracted back to his supporters as the ultimate patriotic project, diffusing wealth among the domestic population, protecting English freedoms (including the freedom of trade and navigation) from the threats of foreign powers and rapacious ministries, and extending the birthrights of English people throughout the world.

Over the next decade, a Jacobite rebellion and inconclusive war with France did little to satisfy these exalted hopes and much to promote a sense of national malaise and fears about the national character and leadership. By the 1750s, French encroachments on the American colonies and the loss of Minorca in 1756 amplified existing anxieties about the emasculation and degeneracy of the British body politic that seemed to be emanating from above. Empire was now represented as the antidote to aristocratic "cultural treason" and effeteness, the bulwark and proving ground of the true national character and (middle-class) potency and virtue. The ultimately spectacular string of British victories and conquests in 1757–61 – in North America, the East and West Indies, India and Africa – both soothed and reconstituted national masculinity and power, while also enabling the war and the newly extended British empire to be celebrated for saving the world from French tyranny, Spanish cruelty and native barbarity alike.[89] "Britain will never want a Race of Men . . . who choose Dangers in defence of Their Country before an inglorious safety, an honourable Death before the unmanly pleasures of a useless and effeminate life," was how a Newcastle clergyman summed up the situation in late 1759. The Protestant Dissenting Deputies congratulated George III for inaugurating a new era of British imperial ascendancy and expansion, "diffusing freedom and science, political order and Christian Knowledge through those extensive regions which are now sunk in superstitious barbarism . . . and imparting even to the most uncultivated of our species, the happiness of *Britons*."[90]

The homogenizing, "patriotic" vision of empire produced for many citizens by the century's most successful war was soon shattered. The Peace of Paris brought to the fore a long-suppressed unease at the enormity of British possessions, their racial and religious diversity, the domestic divisions they mirrored and reproduced, and the authoritarian techniques used to govern them. Playwrights, political journalists and parliamentarians alike began to condemn the empire's polluting impact, now designated as a conduit of "luxury, effeminacy and profligacy" to those at home. The East India Company and its conquests on the subcontinent were a particular source of concern. "The oppressions of India and even of the English settled there under the rapine and cruelties of the servants of the Company," were a constant topic of conversation in 1772, according to Horace Walpole, as Britons learned of the famine in Bengal that had been exacerbated by the trading practices of Company employees. Lord John Clive emerged as a chief culprit. The parliamentary inquiry leading to the Regulating Act of 1773, precipitated by the Bengal famine and Company financial scandal, publicized Clive's misadventures there and the extent of the huge personal fortune he had amassed. Clive, as Colonel John Burgoyne would charge, used both force and fraud to expand his own and the East India Company's power in the Carnatic, reputedly accepting bribes, issuing threats, procuring monopolies on foodstuffs and otherwise fleecing native nawabs and their subjects. He then used his ill-found wealth to advance his own ambitious political schemes in England. Clive thus seemed to concretize Chatham's famous warning to the House of Lords in 1770, that "The riches of Asia have been poured in upon us, and brought with them not only Asiatic luxury, but, I fear, Asiatic principles of government." He had also become a human barometer of the changes in political climate and imperial thinking since the Seven Years War: once hailed as the sort of intrepid and manly military commander required to extend and maintain distant imperial possessions, Clive found himself reviled in public and private as a mercenary despot and subjected to parliamentary censure and social opprobrium. He took his own life in 1774. But he had clearly been made a scapegoat for the pricking conscience of politicians and public alike.[91]

West Indian debacles also underscored the unsavory aspects of an empire of conquest. British attempts in the late 1760s to expatriate or exterminate the Caribs on the island of St. Vincent in order to appropriate their lands produced a particularly gruesome and bloody war on the island that forced English observers to confront, and decry, the realities of conquest and question the long-vaunted moral superiority of British imperialism over its European competitors. "The honor of the British nation is at stake," Alderman Barlow Trecothick exclaimed in a parliamentary debate on the propriety of the ministry's sending troops to quell the Carib's resistance; "a scene of iniquity and cruelty is transacting . . . on the defenseless natives . . . against [whom] you are exercising the barbarities of the Spaniards against the Mexicans."[92] The Pacific explorations of Captain James Cook and his crews in the same period, widely publicized and celebrated at home, also increased, for the moment, domestic sympathy for indigenous peoples and mobilized sentiments against the use of force and conquest in the "civilizing" process. Not surprisingly, the abolitionist movement had its roots in this period, when colonial examples, African resistance within England and the Somerset case of 1772 forced the English public to acknowledge the brutal ways in which English rights were denied to other Britons throughout the empire, as well as to recognize the growing importance of slavery in the British and American economies.[93]

Significantly, the American war brought these ambivalences about empire to a head, while also underlining the tenuousness of long-held beliefs about the morality, virtue and libertarianism of the imperial project. British commentators had long insisted that Britain's virtue as an imperial nation lay in not seeking conquest, but having conquest thrust upon her: colonial acquisition in the Seven Years War was thus continually justified as a *defense* against French aggression. The policies of the Pelhams and Chatham had done less to undercut these views than those of George III and his ministers, who enacted measures which seriously confounded them. The Quebec Act, the "Coercive Acts" and the entire, massive war effort aimed at coercing or murdering Protestant English people living in America indicated the loss of a virtuous empire, once "as much renowned for the virtues of justice and humanity as for the splendour of its arms," as the Middlesex electors lamented in their address for reconciliation with America in 1775.[94]

Most importantly, the period of the American war forced into the English national consciousness the contradictions, inequities and atrocities perpetuated in the name of the national identity and obscured by the fire and fury of imperial expansion. For it provided irrefutable evidence that the British empire was comprised not just of free British subjects but of large numbers of alien peoples, incorporated into the empire by conquest, not consent, and sustained, in Peter Marshall's words, "by the deployment of British troops across the world in a way that was to last until the 1960s."[95] As such, some English people who lived through the war and its aftermath believed themselves to be at a momentous historical crossroads, when the England that had orchestrated British imperial ascendancy seemed to be in danger of precipitous collapse, and the components of the national identity and the nation's role in the world had been unintentionally reconfigured. At the very least, this forcibly disjunctive moment gave many English people pause, compelling a confrontation between their history and their future, a moment intimated by Edward Gibbon's magisterial jeremiad on Roman decline and reworked by scores of commentators thereafter. "A foolish or effeminate Prince, surrounded by a venal Senate . . . was not born to retain dominions acquired by republican wisdom, and republican valour; nor could a People, which had lost all pretensions to govern itself, long expect to rule over others," was one radical writer's take on Gibbon's history that was meant to explain both the nature and singularity of the current crisis.[96] Imperial dismemberment, military defeat, the penetration of "national" boundaries by the emigration of racialized others whose claims to belonging seemed tenuous at best – all brought into collision, and not for the last time, a present and a past "charged with the time of the now," a self-confrontation that undermined national confidence and underlined both the historical specificity of the present moment in the national becoming and the possibilities for rethinking its future character.[97]

"Are we not compelled to . . . value what we hold most dear, next to our own salvation," one dismayed observer inveighed in the midst of the American crisis, "as we value our rights as Englishmen, our existence as a nation, and the safety and dignity of the BRITISH EMPIRE?"[98] Yet carried out as a right of English men and in the name of English liberties, empire could not secure those rights for Britons, who within the context of a heterogeneous empire were not all created equal. A range of people living within and without the metropole were "others," although not interchangeable ones, to the fair-minded, masculine English subject that the imperial project valorized, and were part of the amalgam which empire's gendered, commercial and aggressive vision of the national identity sought to subordinate, at home and abroad. Within Britain itself, from the perspectives of the metropole, the Welsh and, more gradually, the Scots become naturalized as "British," the Irish, Jews, Africans and Asians perhaps never do; beyond the British isles, the claim of peoples of different races and cultures to British rights and liberties was even more remote and contingent, and "Britishness" was conferred or denied not only in relation to the numbers of white British settlers in residence but also to the degree of acceptance by colonial peoples of English hegemony and the legitimacy of British rule.

Of course, colonized groups could destabilize the identities of Britishness formulated in the days of imperial glory and subvert their hegemonic deployment. The American colonists appropriated the "rights of Englishmen" to reject English-ness and to continue to deny those rights to indigenous and slave populations, an effort that both "heritage" and "race" worked to make relatively successful. The beleaguered Caribs were described by the British planters who desired their land as "idle, ignorant and savage people," exalted by their defenders as exhibiting not only the rights but the temperament of English men – "Fighting for liberty, and every English heart must applaud them"; but they themselves feared they would be made slaves by their new British governors, to the apparent shock and dismay of liberal observers in England.[99] The period of the first British empire thus consolidated a national identity, forged in over two centuries of imperial adventures and national and colonial expansion, that could not be readily naturalized, producing colonial subjects who were "savages" or "almost like Englishmen" but could never be English themselves.[100] The various hierarchical visions of the domestic polity were recognizably if irregularly mapped onto the imperial one, and the incompatibility of the rights of English people and those of Britons laid bare – the first always had to take priority over the second, and national belonging kept within strict territorial, cultural, and increasingly, racial bounds. As a constitutive moment in the "modern" national becoming, the traces still linger, and still confound.

2

THE ISLAND RACE:
CAPTAIN COOK AND ENGLISH
ETHNICITY

BRITANNIA: Mark, votive Islander, thy fate is mine
For mine, the Queen of Isles, the mistress of the Main! . . .
Still shall my sons, by *Cook's* example taught
Thy new found world protect and humanize.
John O'Keeffe, *Omai, or a Trip Around the World* (1785)

The inhabitants of islands . . . have a higher relish for liberty than those
of the continents; and therefore are in general free. Thus the inhabitants of
Great Britain were a free people, according to the first accounts we have
of them.
William Falconer, *Remarks on the Influence of Climate, etc.* (1781)

The philosophical traveller, sailing to the ends of the earth, is in fact travelling in time; he is exploring the past; every step he makes is the passage of
an age. Those unknown islands that he reaches are for him the passage
of human society.
J.-M. Degerando, *The Observation of Savage Peoples* (1800)

The Island Race: the phrase is used by Winston Churchill in his *History of the
English Speaking Peoples* (1956) to describe the inhabitants of Britain from Celtic
society to the Norman Conquest. Reviewing the polyphonic mixtures of tribes and
cultures that made up early British society and acknowledging the role of Roman
imperialism in laying the foundations of modern civilization among the "wild
barbarians" of the island, Churchill nonetheless upheld the primacy of Anglo-
Saxon blood and custom in producing the distinctive "island race" that would
one day stamp its imprint on the globe Three decades later, Margaret Thatcher,
Churchill's ardent admirer, would use the phrase to orchestrate her war against
post-imperial malaise, invoking the fictive affinity of English people with the
beleaguered Falkland Islanders. The Falklanders, like Britons, were "an island race,"
she proclaimed, sharing the historic addiction to freedom that would make them
forever compatriots.[1] Both Churchill's and Thatcher's understanding of the origins
and character of Englishness drew on the various legacies of nineteenth-century

54

imperialism and race science, but their notion of an "island race" also articulated a conception of national identity that eighteenth-century Britons would have recognized. This saw Englishness as defined by a conjuncture of territorial boundaries, topographical features and historical continuities that included language, character and physical attributes. Ideas about nation and race occupied overlapping if not identical cultural and political terrains in this construction. As we have seen, not only did race and nation share etymological origins, but both were also used to distinguish groups by lineage, common descent or origin and to identify political, social and territorial particularity. In the last quarter of the eighteenth century, however, national and imperial events had raised new questions about the relationship between race and nation that were being vigorously debated in political, religious, scientific and literary circles.

This chapter will explore how late eighteenth-century thinking about Englishness and national identity was articulated through representations of Captain Cook and the South Seas. Specifically, I want to argue that, through the figure of Cook and the widely circulated stories of his and his followers' voyages to the South Pacific, an important component of English ethnicity – that of England as a unique "island race" – was authorized and renewed as central to Britain's national identity and imperial mission. Literary critics have argued that the topos of the island in European imaginative literature made possible reflections on origins and dominion, "the site of that contemplation being the uninhabited territory upon which the conditions for return or genesis are made possible."[2] Anthropologists have drawn attention to islands as, variously, sites of geographic and cultural singularity, stages for cross-cultural encounter and conquest, and engines of the geopolitics of empire. For the eighteenth-century English, the topographical and figurative significance of insularity had long served to structure certain crucial beliefs about the "national character" and destiny.[3] But the "discoveries" in the Pacific also turned islands, literally and figuratively, into historical vehicles for the self-realization of humanity and the attainment of a particularly English genius and mission.

The literary and visual representations of Pacific exploration were consolidated and commodified in rhetoric of discovery that combined features of travelogue and empirical description. The resulting observational reportage modeled its techniques of comparative social analysis on the systems of classification initiated in natural sciences, ranking human societies according to material and moral progress, or the "stage" of civilization. Integral to eighteenth-century European imperialism and its larger taxonomic projects of ethnology, natural history and global knowledge, such naturalist reportage also influenced the representation of colonial encounters in a range of forums. It enabled the exotic, unknown and "discovered" to be appropriated, domesticated and rendered plausible.[4] The impact on articulations of English distinctiveness and identity are strikingly illuminated in the apotheosis of Captain Cook. Theatrical extravaganzas, scientific classificatory systems and religious and historical imperatives converged to set the English (and, secondarily, the British) apart as an "island race," a notion that idealized past national and imperial experiences and shaped expectations about the national destiny in ways that would indeed, as Churchill testified, leave its indelible imprint on the globe.

Contexts

In the years surrounding James Cook's three voyages (1768–71, 1772–5, 1776–80) (Map 1), a convergence of political, cultural and imperial crises had raised urgent questions about empire, "race" and their relationship to the national identity. As discussed in Chapter 1, growing disquiet among British publics at the extent and diversity of their nation's colonial possessions and the tyrannical techniques used to govern them galvanized abolitionist and reformist campaigns aimed at re-shaping the domestic and imperial polity. In particular, bloody skirmishes with indigenous peoples on three continents intersected with newly charged anxiety over the dislocations and human devastation wrought by decades of slavery, rebellion and maroon war on the sugar islands. American colonial revolt and the massive war effort to suppress it also did little to quell doubts about the supposed virtue and superiority of the imperial project and the "national character." Britannia's rule of the waves had begun to look like a trial by fire that incinerated justice and liberty in the name of the national interest.[5] If white, Protestant English people living abroad were not able to claim the same liberties as English people at home, what hope was there for the other, proliferating ranks of peoples under British rule?

The arguments of abolitionists and their opponents and the plight of black Britons living within England also raised troubling questions about the nature and accessibility of English rights and liberties for those whose Britishness could not be taken as self-evident. After two centuries of comparative indifference, hostility to the slave trade and to the plantocratic justification for slavery's continuation in the New World were galvanized by British Protestant evangelical outrage and the relentless efforts of black abolitionists such as Olaudah Equiano and Ottabah Cugoano. Horror stories about the brutal treatment of slaves in the colonies and slave-owners' attempts to recapture refugees living in England induced queasiness among even the most phlegmatic portions of the English public. Most infamously, the Zong affair of 1781 saw 133 captive Africans aboard a slave ship bound for Jamaica drowned for the insurance money. At the same time, the apologists for West Indian slavery steadily fanned fears about the dangers of miscegenation that the influx of black immigrants into England during and after the American war did little to allay. The gossip and scandal that accompanied the alleged affairs between African men and aristocratic women, such as Soubize and the Duchess of Queensberry, or Ignatius Sancho and his numerous amours, as well as the animosity ignited by Edward Long's inflammatory allegations about lower-class English women's insatiable taste for black men, influenced the thinking of even antislavery activists such as Granville Sharp. The Sierra Leone resettlement project of 1786–7 was shaped in no small part by the arguments that black Britons would be better off in "their own country."[6] Events of these decades, in other words, had forced a

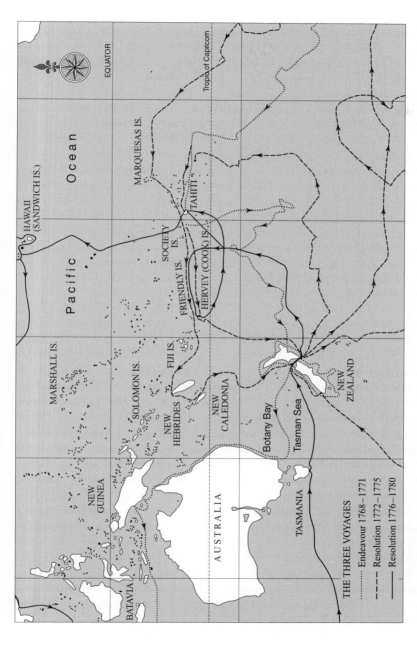

Map 1 The South Pacific voyages of Captain Cook.
From J.C. Beaglehole, *The Life of Captain Cook* (London, A&C Black, 1974).

confrontation between differing claims to national belonging that highlighted not only the miscegenating consequences of empire and the links between territorial and sexual conquest, but also the cultural and physical requirements of "Englishness." By underscoring the role of racialized ideas of difference in legitimating forms of domination to which Britons themselves would not submit, these events demonstrated that the terms of national belonging within an imperial polity could not be rendered capacious or elastic enough to accommodate all of the "others" within.

Finally, the voyages inaugurating what is eurocentrically called the second age of discovery – Byron, Wallis and Carteret to the Pacific, Cartwright to Labrador, Phipps and Pickersgill to the Arctic – provided new information about the diversity of humankind and the extremes of degradation, savagery or refinement in which they could live that renewed old questions about the relative positions of Britons, Europeans and indigenous peoples across the world. If all peoples enjoyed a "natural" equality, as some Enlightenment thinkers had suggested, then why were some so much more advanced than others? If all were alike morally and anatomically, then how could the rights and privileges enjoyed by Europeans in general and English people in particular be justified? The result was an appeal to nature and history that gave philosophers, scientists, clergymen and cultural entrepreneurs alike the task of sorting out the "facts" of human similarity and difference and imbuing them with moral and political significance.

A New Kind of National Hero

The Pacific explorations of Captain James Cook and their widely publicized results gave a much-needed lift to the collective national psyche and imperial self-confidence alike. Indeed, despite the European internationalism, in personnel and goals, of both the exploration projects launched in this period and their popularity, they could still be used for patriotic and narrowly nationalistic purposes. "Maps, names, lists and taxonomies were the plunder of the later eighteenth century," Jonathan Lamb has remarked, and the writing up and translation of accounts of voyages were very real weapons in the wars for empire.[7] Cook's three voyages accordingly generated an industry of highly ethnocentric commentary, praise and critique that commenced with publication of Hawkesworth's *Voyages* in 1773 and continues to the present day. With a distinguished sponsorship that included the Royal Society, George III and the Admiralty, and boasting trained naturalists, astronomers and artists as well as navigators on board, the voyages were celebrated for marking new departures in empirical observation, discovery and collection of data. Their contribution to knowledge was widely hailed as prodigious: perfecting navigation, aiding astronomy, expanding botanical, geographical and cartographic knowledge, preserving seamen's health, and furnishing, through the vast quantities of "first-hand" information acquired on different peoples and customs, the materials for a new "science of Man." Their political importance was more pragmatic if no less profound, for, in the context of the American war and its aftermath, Cook's discoveries pointed out alternatives to the population outposts, raw materials and markets provided by the former colonies and directed imperial energies to the South Seas, New South Wales, India, Madagascar and West Africa, thus stimulating the formation of a more forward-looking, rationalized and authoritarian imperial policy.[8] Equally important, the voyages captured the national imagination with their tales of vast oceans, giant coral reefs, wild cannibals and erotic maidens, and Arcadian tropical islands populated by uncorrupted island races. Cook himself was lionized by the English public in ways that few figures of the era could match, coming to symbolize and embody the combination of intrepidity and humanism that was quickly vaunted as a central feature of Englishness itself.

The interest in and acclaim generated by Cook's P/pacific feats can be quickly demonstrated. The voyages coincided with and stimulated both the professionalization of natural science and an unprecedented expansion in the reach and production of various eighteenth-century media and arenas of polite sociability. Pacific exploration and the diversification of its forms of representation thus became mutually reinforcing. Official and unofficial accounts and images of the voyages proliferated in the 1770s and 1780s across the broadest social terrains, extending from the Court to the tavern and the parlor, and these were endlessly condensed, excerpted and otherwise recirculated in print culture, conversation, letters and diaries.[9] After the English translation of Bougainville's *Voyage autour du monde*, which appeared in 1772, Hawkesworth's three-volume *Voyages* of the following year probably did most to spark the "Pacific craze" in Britain, with its "authentic" account and lavish illustrations of Pacific exploration undertaken successively by Byron, Wallis and Cook. Despite its high price and the controversy sparked by its inaccuracies and scandalously relativistic observations on Providence and Oceanic peoples, Hawkesworth's *Voyages* went into multiple editions in Britain and America, followed by French, German, Italian and Spanish translations from 1774 to 1794, and was excerpted in virtually every London and provincial magazine. The official and unofficial accounts of the second and third voyages were similarly pirated and reproduced, with such distinguished periodicals as the *Annual Register* devoting up to sixty pages per issue to their contents. The vast troves of information on distant lands and peoples garnered on the voyages swelled the seven lines devoted to the South Pacific in the first edition of the *Encyclopaedia Britannica* to forty double-column pages in the third edition of 1788–97.[10]

More importantly for our purposes, Cook's personal fame and nationalist significance swelled with each voyage, overtaking the celebrity that initially attended the naturalists Joseph Banks and Daniel Solander of the *Endeavour* voyage and reaching a crescendo in the years after his death in 1779. His renown reverberated at many social and political levels, but in all he was heralded as a particularly *English* hero who embodied and extended his country's genius for navigation and discovery, aptitude for science, respect for merit, love of liberty and paternalistic regard for humanity. A reviewer in the *Annual Register* in 1785 captured the public mood in his hubristic summary of the national aggrandizement that had resulted from Cook's exploits. Thanks to Cook, he stated,

there is nothing now unknown of this globe, which can intitle any one
to the character of a discoverer . . . our success in exploring unknown
regions, give posterity a convincing proof that we have a more decided
superiority over the other countries of Europe, than could be derived
from the most extensive conquests, and will hold us forth to future ages
as the most powerful people upon this globe.

(149–50)

Cook himself was immortalized in biographies, plays, painting and poetry. All
served as fulsome encomiums to the low-born man who became a great commander
by virtue of his own talents, the supreme English explorer whose amazing forays into
undiscovered countries spread friendship and arts among native peoples while
furthering the national reputation and standing throughout the world. Cook's
superior abilities, judgment and discipline, as well as his humble origins as a
Yorkshire husbandman's son, his auto-didacticism (he taught himself mathematics
and astronomy while master of a warship serving off the coast of America during
the Seven Years War) and his humility (he is endearingly disparaging of his literary
skills in his account of the second voyage[11]) all became inextricable parts of his
heroic character, the Everyman whose hard work and merit, "great qualities and
amiable virtues," paid off for himself, his family and his country. The portrait of
Cook by Nathaniel Dance (Fig. 4) captures this image well: depicting a solitary
figure with a rough-hewn face, exuding common sense and intelligence, whose
intense concentration on the navigational map on the table is momentarily broken,
it is strikingly free of any iconic reference to monarchy or aristocracy. Cook's status
as captain and discoverer, the portrait proclaims, was achieved by perseverance,
discipline and merit, not entitlement.

Cook's humanity was also lauded from all quarters, particularly from among
those who had been repelled by the crass commercialism and aggressive militarism
of earlier maritime adventures. Fanny Burney called him "the most moderate,
humane and gentle circumnavigator that ever went out upon discoveries" and this
verdict was confirmed by Hannah More, Anna Seward, William Cowper, Dr.
Johnson and Mrs. Thrale, to name a few. Cook's reputed respect for the diversity
and commonalty of humankind and his efforts to bring indigenous peoples "within
the pale of the offices of humanity, and to relieve the wants of their imperfect
state of society" while shedding "some rays of light . . . on their infant minds," made
him the exemplar for abolitionists of what could be accomplished once the progress
of all was privileged over the profits of a few. As Hannah More declared in *Slavery,
a Poem*,

> . . . [His] social hands,
> Had link'd disserv'd worlds in brothers' bands,
> Careless, if colour, or if clime divide
> But lov'd, and loving

Figure 4 Nathaniel Dance, *Portrait of Captain Cook* (1776). Courtesy of the National Maritime Museum.

was how Cook lived and died. Even his resistance to the sexual charms of Tahitian women – in marked contrast to the behaviour of most of the rest of his officers and crew – as well as his monogamous marriage and manly offspring were celebrated for confirming his credentials as a man of sensibility and an upholder of non-aristocratic morality.[12] After decades of war and the celebration of leaders whose fame rested on more militaristic and sanguinary acts performed in the service of their country, Cook represented not only an alternative masculinity, but also a new kind of national hero, one who demonstrated both English pluck and humanity, sense and sensibility, to best advantage – the explorer's "man of feeling" who died on the altar of national service with more blood brothers than bloodshed to his credit. As David Samwell, Welsh surgeon's mate aboard the *Discovery*, eulogized, in sentiments expressed in virtually every ode, elegy and verse dedicated to Cook's memory:

> [he was] the animating spirit of the expedition: he was our leading star, which, at its setting, left us involved in darkness and despair . . . There is hardly a corner of the earth, however remote and savage, that will not long remember his benevolence and humanity. The grateful [South Sea] Indian, in time to come, pointing to the herds grazing his fertile plains, will relate to his children how the first stock of them was introduced into the country; and the name of Cook will be remembered . . . as the source of every good, and the fountain of every blessing.[13]

Certainly Cook had his critics. One of the most notable was the Dublin professor, the Rev. Gerald Fitzgerald, whose poem *The Injured Islanders* betrayed a woeful familiarity with its tale of native desecration by avaricious English men. As we shall see, missionaries would also take Cook to task for a number of wayward actions, not least allowing himself to be treated as a deity by incognizant savages. And Cook's quick temper and sudden flashes of violence were all too well known to his crew.[14] Nevertheless, the idealizations described above are important for what they reveal about Cook's instantly mythical stature as a figure capable of reconstituting British imperial authority and English superiority, through what was now seen as the essentially humanitarian and philanthropic enterprise of empire building. These various strands in Cook's apotheosis are amply displayed in a theatrical extravaganza in his honor that is worthy of detailed attention. In the age of the "first empire," English theater did much to consolidate and popularize ideas about English distinctiveness, and to familiarize audiences with the typologies of gender, class and national difference. Lauded as a key element in the emergence of a polished and polite urban culture, the eighteenth-century stage represented and disseminated topical "knowledge" about the world as a central part of its respectability and "civilizing" function. Indeed, in its representations of conquest (sexual and territorial), desire and otherness (both racialized and gendered), Georgian theater supplemented the encyclopedic gaze of print culture in staking out the grounds of identification in the formation of alterity and sameness. It was thus crucial in socializing English people into *recognizing* difference, and especially the historicity and distinctiveness of the English compared to other nations in history.[15] Moreover, the stage played a crucial role in circulating the texts, bodies, ideas and people meant to incarnate the best of an English, and secondarily a British, national identity, all the while demonstrating both the syncreticism of that culture and the performative nature of those essentialized identities that theater was meant to express, invoke and mobilize. The performances of difference on the Georgian stage thus constituted a repository of social knowledge that literally and figuratively embodied the categories through which self and other could be understood, while also revealing, through the skill and artifice of the actors, their fictive nature – making "visible the play of difference and identity within the larger ensemble of [social] relations," as Joseph Roach has noted.[16]

The Cook play *Omai, or a Trip around the World* amplified and reconfigured some of the visual and figurative tropes at work in other literature and drama of the day, enabling English audiences to come to terms with Cook's, and their own, histories and destinies in particular ways. A pantomime written by the Irish playwright John O'Keeffe and the English composer William Shields, and designed by the Alsacean artist and theater designer Philippe Jacques de Loutherbourg, it was produced at Covent Garden in December 1785, one and a half years after the official accounts of Cook's final voyage had been released by the Admiralty.[17] That the canonization of Cook as the most English of heroes was left to the talents of an Irishman and a Frenchman did not seem to trouble contemporaries. All were profoundly invested in the superiority of the English as the premier "mimic men" and in the English stage as the leading site for the enactment of superior national virtue and character: the place where, in and through the bodies of the actors, past met present, and English mastery at becoming the other was made evident, if only for the duration of the show. Pantomime of the late eighteenth century revolved around the story of the frustrated romance of Harlequin and his lover Columbine and their ultimate triumph over their nemeses, Pantaloon and the Clown, but its rapidly changing scenes allowed for both topicality and spectacle. The spectacular, mythic and topical blended in this case to provide, as one contemporary put it, "the stage edition of Captain Cook's voyage."[18]

The title of the pantomime that was to honor Cook was equally significant. It was borrowed from the first Polynesian visitor to England, called by the English Omai, who in 1774 had been brought by Captain Furneaux of the *Adventure* (the consort vessel of the second voyage). Omai came from a mid-ranked Raiatean land-owning family who had been dispossessed of their property in war. He had been on Tahiti when Wallis's ship arrived, and had taken refuge on the island of Huahine by the time the *Adventure* appeared. Once in England, however, Omai performed the role of noble savage for the patrician set, and quickly became the darling of London society for the two years of his stay. Presented to the king, taken to the theater (an established tradition for visiting savages and exotics), and lauded for his "natural" grace, politeness and manners, he was painted in suitably neoclassical

Figure 5 Johann Jacobe, after Sir Joshua Reynolds, *Omai, a Native of the Island of Utietea* [*Ulietea*] (1780). Courtesy of the National Library of Australia.

style by Reynolds (Fig. 5).[19] Omai was ultimately sent back to eastern Polynesia in the specific role of "ambassador" for England, meant to persuade local peoples of the felicities of British civilization and of British proprietary rights to their land, but rather unsuccessful at both. Yet Omai in fact was only the most well known of the series of native informants whose aid, friendship and local knowledge allowed the voyagers not only to "discover" heretofore unknown island societies, but also to survive. Others included the Tahitian priest, advisor and navigator Tupaia, who joined the *Endeavour* when the ship left Tahiti in 1769 (and died in Batavia the next year); Hitihiti or "Mahine" and his servant Poetata from Borabora, who accompanied the *Resolution* on its Antarctic search for the southern continent and mediated the navigators' dealings with Maoris and Easter Islanders; and the aristocratic "queen" Purea or Oberea, gracious friend of Wallis and Cook and the object of much scurrility at the hands of English pundits for her supposed romantic relationship with Joseph Banks.[20] Hitihiti, whose services materially aided the second voyage at several crucial junctures, and Tupaia, who literally gave his life for the mission, do not figure in the play, but Omai and Purea do, in ways that attempted to honor them for important roles in the "discovery" process. Significantly, the stage production bore the same relation to Omai's, Purea's and Cook's "real" circumstances as its representation of Pacific–English encounters did to the empirical politics of exploration, imbricating all present in an "unstable interplay of truth and illusion."[21]

Indeed, the pantomime had a whimsical and romantic plot, which involved Omai, here made heir to the throne of Tahiti, and his betrothed, the beautiful Londina, daughter of Britannia, racing across the world to escape the evil spells of his rival who wants to prevent their union and hence that of the two kingdoms. The lovers' flight provided the theme of the show, bringing them from a Tahitian *marae* to Hyde Park, Plymouth and Margate before whisking them across all the islands and continents Cook had visited or discovered, including Kamchatka, the Ice Islands or Antarctica, New Zealand, the Tongan, or Friendly Islands and the Sandwich Islands. In doing so the pantomime set new standards in scenery and costume for topographic and ethnographic accuracy. Indeed, Loutherbourg's sets were technologically breathtaking. Loutherbourg had made a reputation in the past decade for his naturalistic and spectacular stage designs that used top-lights, silk screens, transparencies and mechanical figures and ships to create the illusion that the stage had become the world, the "imagined place of action."[22] In 1781, he introduced to Londoners the eidophusikon, a miniature theater without actors, described as "Imitations of Natural Phenomena, represented by Moving Pictures" which were made to represent "views" of landscapes and events from all over the globe, from London to Tangiers, Japan and India, in an uncanny predecessor of the newsreel. As Loutherbourg explained the device,

> by adding progressive motion to accurate resemblance, a series of incidents might be reproduced which should display in the liveliest manner those captivating scenes which inexhaustible Nature presents to our view at different periods and in different parts of the globe.[23]

65

This expertise at representing "natural" phenomena and temporal movement proved to be the perfect strategy for this pantomime, where primitive South Sea islanders, English icons and comedic characters confronted each other in a bemused apprehension of historical and cultural difference.

For in *Omai* Loutherbourg proved that the English arts of theatrical representation were equal to the English arts of discovery, merging the naturalistic and mimetic to produce an ethnographic spectacle within a magical setting that showed off English civility and technological superiority to best advantage. Louterbourg had probably familiarized himself with the collections of South Seas artifacts collected by Banks, as well as those displayed at Sir Ashton Lever's private museum in Leicester House; he also paid close attention to the various drawings, sketches and paintings by the voyages' artists, William Hodges and John Webber. Hence his sets for *Omai* brought to stage design the same arts of perspective, light and motion that had helped make navigation such a spectacular science. In conjunction with the ethnographic accuracy of the costumes and weapons, and the use of such sophisticated equipment as the flying balloon, the sets brought home the visuality of exploration to English audiences. Popular actors provided key performances, such as the lovely young Miss Cranfield as Londina, stately Elizabeth Inchbald as Britannia and the ethnic specialist Ralph Wewitzer as a native prophet who paid homage to Cook in extempore chatter that was supposed to be Tahitian and was "translated" in the program (a tactic which mimicked the widespread printed circulation of antipodean vocabularies in voyage accounts and commentaries). All increased the appeal of a show that sparkled with its jumble of exoticism, science, spectacle and "fact." "What can be more delightful than an enchanting fascination that monopolizes the mind to the scene before the eye, and leads the imagination from country to country, from the frigid to the torrid zone, shewing as in a mirror, prospects of different climates, with all the productions of nature in the animal and vegetable worlds, and all the efforts of man to attain nourishment, convenience and luxury, by the world of arts," gushed the critic for *The Times*. The writer in *Rambler's Magazine* put it more succinctly, calling the pantomime "a school for the history of Man."[24]

As an entertainment about encounters in the "contact zone" when English islanders confronted the otherness of Pacific islanders (in a genre appropriated from Italian commedia dell'arte and using all British actors), the pantomime made possible what Walter Benjamin has called the "flash of recognition" between different historical subjects and periods that staked out the grounds of similarity in the construction of historical difference.[25] Capturing Pacific peoples in the ethnographic gaze characteristic of the period's nascent social science, the representation allowed "travel," geographic and temporal, by aid of the latest in visual sciences and technologies, while the Pacific islanders so arrayed provided examples to English audiences of their earlier selves, "mirrors" of a past once deemed lost, but now paraded before them in proof of present-day English ingenuity, civility and cosmopolitanism. At the same time, through the dissemination of apparently neutral topical and "scientific" knowledge, the pantomime demonstrated the role of theater in formulating the notion of a (idealized) history "as it really was" that was also at the heart of burgeoning vogues in painting and fiction (realms where mimesis also transformed the "real" into the ideal, the higher form of knowledge).[26] The music, too, was praised for its realism, Shield's songs described as "beautifully wild" and "capturing the vernacular airs of Otaheite" by including Tahitian words as well as imitations of the sounds of conches and exotic animals. The pantomime thus permitted "science . . . [to] approach barbarity" as the critic for the *London Chronicle* so evocatively remarked.[27]

Not coincidentally, these genres are brought together in the final scene of the pantomime, which takes place in Tahiti. Omai, successfully wed to Londina, is installed as king and a grand marriage procession of all the peoples of the Pacific Islands takes place – Tahitian dancing girls and (male) attendants; New Zealand warriors, with a woman and child; chiefs and men of the Marquesas, Easter Island, Friendly Islands and Sandwich Islands, the latter in feathered and plain helmets; Tannese, Tartars, Russians, Kamtchatkars, Onalaskans, and residents of both Nootka and Prince William Sound of both sexes. British tars and an "English Captain," who presents Omai with a sword, wind up the parade. Two features are remarkable here. First, the British actors cross-dressed as Pacific "natives" solicit through their costuming both identification and its refusal from the audience, the exotic or homely costumes of the women setting off the more graceful, demure and civilized garb of Londina, and the feathers, furs, tattoos, beaded collars and rudimentary weapons of the men distinguishing their degree of civility from the audience's own. Second, and more importantly, this scene of happy miscegenation, dignified by the princely status of Omai, engages in interesting ways with con-temporary English anxieties over "real" interracial sexual union at home, in the colonies and in the act of "discovery." It suspended, for example, the shame over the congress between English tars and Tahitian women that had been a source of venereal contagion on the island, and morally elevated the amorous connections imagined by pundits to have existed between the historical Omai and concupiscent aristocratic English ladies. Omai and Londina's union also, perhaps unwittingly, conformed to colonial legal codes against miscegenation, which attempted to prohibit black/white sexual relations but permitted intermarriage between "Indians" and whites, since Polynesians were consistently referred to as "Indians" in all the voyage accounts and commentaries.[28] Above all, perhaps, the scene enacted that desire for the Other that was an increasingly important feature of Englishness in this period, and also its ultimate goal of possession: as Omai becomes, through marriage, British-identified, bound to the British way of life and to British superiority in arts and arms.[29] "Away my useless spells and magic charms," the enchantress Oberea coos after watching the sexual and material exchange underway: "A British sword is proof against the world in arms."

In the event, these implications are deepened by the entry of the real (non-miscegenating) hero of the piece, for, as soon as the marriage ceremony ends, the English Captain begins to sing a grand lament for Captain Cook. A giant painting of the *Apotheosis of Captain Cook* (the first of what would be a long line of similarly

67

titled paintings) simultaneously descends on the stage, portraying Cook, holding a sextant rather than a sword, resting in clouds over the Hawaiian bay where he had been "sacrificed" as he is crowned by Britannia and Fame (Fig. 6). As the last in the series of "original" island races, Cook represents their final and most advanced form. The tripartite structure of the painting attests to this progression: the space of exploration and discovery, where the exact representation of landscape

Figure 6 Philippe Jacques de Loutherbourg, *The Apotheosis of Captain Cook* (1785). Courtesy of the British Museum, Department of Prints and Drawings.

and British ships evoke an empirical mapping of the "discovered" and exotic terrain where Pacific islanders lived; the intermediate space separating the human and celestial; and the space of the divine, rococo in style, where Cook, in a pose clearly influenced by Benjamin West's *Death of Wolfe* (1773), is deified while looking nobly and sympathetically at the human scene below. The voices of all the various peoples proclaim:

> The hero of Macedon ran o'er the world,
> Yet nothing but death could he give
> 'Twas George's command and the sail was unfurl'd
> And Cook taught mankind how to live.
> He *came* and he *saw*, not to *conquer* but to save.
> The Caesar of Britain was he:
> Who scorn'd the conditions of making a slave
> While Britons themselves are so free.[30]

Reaching back to, and surpassing, both "ancient" and "primitive" time, Cook, Omai and the Pacific islanders thus became figures in the panorama of English progress and achievement, lessons in the "school for the history of man," the "mirror" of past and present. It was, as the playwright himself noted, an immensely gratifying moment for English audiences, who thereby participated in the progress and ultimate canonization of English imperialism itself as the agent of Enlightened civilization. George III, slave trader and soon-to-be staunch opponent of abolition, was nonetheless moved to tears by the pantomime at the performance he attended, and the finale became one of the most popular songs of the late 1780s and 1790s, published in newspapers, demanded by audiences at theaters, concerts and assemblies and sung at tavern societies. As J. Boaden, Kemble's biographer, recalled in 1825, "The success of this elegant entertainment seems to have stampt a character upon the theatre itself, which has since constantly adhered to it."[31]

The significance of *Omai* should be seen in several contexts. Certainly the dramatic presentation of contemporary English heroics in exotic or foreign settings was not new. The *Death of General Wolfe*, first staged in provincial theaters in 1763 (and perhaps influencing West's famous painting), remained a favorite afterpiece into the early 1800s, and contained similarly idealized historical tableaux that aimed at exalting another exemplar of the glorious national character. An episode of less socially elevated but nationalistically useful heroism was represented to Birmingham audiences in the midst of the American war by Richard Brinsley Sheridan's interlude *The Storming of Fort Omoa*, taken from the pantomime of *Harlequin Fortunatus*, which featured (thanks again to Loutherbourg) the astonishing spectacle of a brave British tar scaling the wall of the fort while he furnished an unarmed Spaniard with a cutlass, conquered him and then spared his life.[32] But Loutherbourg both before and after 1785 had transformed scene design, setting new standards of authenticity and "exactness" in stage representation that quickly came to serve as a testimony to British national and imperial expertise.

Spectacles set in India, for example, such as *The Choice of Harlequin, or the Indian Chief* (1782) and *Ramah Droog* (1798) boasted scenery based on the drawings of Indian architecture and topography by Tilly Kettle and Thomas Daniell respectively, artists renowned for their "first-hand knowledge" of the subcontinent. "Exactness" also became crucial to future efforts to turn current affairs and fantasies into heroic history: *The Pirates* (1790) claimed to be an "exact representation" of the *Bounty* mutiny: the capture, rescue and arrival at the Cape of Good Hope of Captain Bligh (played by none other than Ralph Wewitzer), and the celebratory dances of the "Hottentots" at his departure made up some of its central scenes. *The Death of Captain Cook*, a French ballet which in 1789 began a three-year tour of England and Ireland, also used gorgeous, naturalistic scenery to heighten the romantic plot about love and betrayal among Hawaiian islanders, rendering Cook's death all the more tragic and heroic.[33] Hence – and this is a point we will return to – *Omai*, with its blend of fantasy and ethnography, science and spectacle, crystallized the innovations in representation by which theater was able to transform historical idealizations into historical "realities" that helped structure and confirm English beliefs about their own distinctiveness and destiny.

Secondly, the pantomime exhibited a broader shift in contemporary under-standing of historical time and primitivism that moved away from cyclical, classically based models to linear, locally inflected ones, thanks in large part to the proliferation of information about indigenous cultures. In this latter mode, the notion of the ancients as the moderns (or vice versa) gave way to a conception of the primitives as the ancients – gave way, that is, to a progressive notion of histo-rical time that ranked societies according to their "stage" and accomplishments rather than supposed classical origins. The tension between the English mimesis of primitiveness and English men's actual displays of "primitive" behavior in the South Seas (through violence, murder, rapaciousness and so on) was, of course, not addressed. Instead, *Omai* gave English audiences the pleasure of re-imagining themselves as historically alter – as a primitive island race – and of confirming their "real" status as modern – advanced, civilized, tolerant, progressive, the superior Island Race.

The Progress of Nations

To see how and why this was so, we must turn to some of the uses made of Cook's voyages in scientific and missionary literature. Cook's discoveries in the South Pacific initially fostered within Britain a craze for descriptions of the customs and manners of South Sea islanders, feeding the appetite for the exotic, eroticizing the primitive, and bolstering neoclassical or Rousseauian views about the natural equality, universal reason and similarity of human life in the state of nature.[34] Primitivism, or the concept that humanity in the first stages of society was a model of virtue, simplicity and excellence that civilization corrupted, had a long history, going back to Homer and Hesiod. Most commonly invoked when "civilized" protagonists confronted "less advanced" peoples, primitivist thinking placed its objects in an antithetical relation to modernity, remote in either time or place: in Golden Ages in the past, or as Noble Savages at the boundaries of geographic knowledge. In the eighteenth century, primitivist thinking was associated primarily with neoclassical values, especially the view of the ancients as gifted children living at the dawn of civilization, and with the Rousseauian romantic nostalgia for the "noble savage" whose bravery, virtue and spontaneity contrasted starkly with the over-refinement and hypocrisy of the present age.[35] However, although Pacific voyagers and commentators were clearly influenced by both models in their perceptions of native peoples, and neoclassical allusions continued to abound in many of the artistic and literary representations of Cook's discoveries, the dominance of primitivist thinking was short-lived in certain circles. For the publication of the details of the voyages stimulated contending interpretations of the nature of Pacific peoples that revealed the inadequacy of classical or romantic traditions in interpreting so-called primitive cultures. As the "primitive" became subjected to empirical, scientific scrutiny and understanding, it became less a set of aesthetic standards than an ethnological category in the larger effort to assess the progress and development of human society. Indeed, the second and third voyages even had the effect of recasting a longer-held and more ferociously enacted anti-primitivism that had shaped English colonial relations for some time, not least with the Irish, Welsh and Scots.[36]

As we have seen, South Sea exploration occurred at a time when natural and social scientists were under greater pressure to found the study of human society upon as firm an empirical foundation as that of the natural world. As English civil servant and linguist William Marsden put it, in a swipe at the armchair philosophers and natural historians of the day, "the study of their own species is doubtless the most interesting and important that can claim the attention of mankind; and this science, like all others, it is impossible to improve by abstract speculation, merely. *A regular series of authenticated facts is what alone can enable us to rise towards a perfect knowledge in it.*"[37] It was precisely such "authenticated facts" that Cook's later voyages were widely heralded as providing, resulting in a profusion of theories accounting for human difference which despite their real and apparent discrepancies sought to contribute to a new comparative ethnology, the "natural history of man." Thanks to Cook's voyages, one typical enthusiast gushed, natural historians have been able to "eradicate former errors, and to establish permanent truths in the history of Man." As an epistemological project, this new "history" marked the beginnings of modern anthropology, reflecting not only the general-ization and extension of historical time to encompass the whole world, but also its spatialization. As Johannes Fabian has noted, in the travel-as-science literature of the late eighteenth century, "relationships between parts of the world . . . [became] understood as temporal relations. Dispersal in space reflects . . . sequence in Time."[38] The application of nascent anthropology to its objects – "primitive" societies – was important as a prelude to imperial control; in the shorter term, its truths were used to discern in these societies, at best, an early stage in the gradual process of human amelioration, or even less flatteringly, a nastier and less developed version of European society.

First, natural and social scientists, including some of those who had accompanied Cook on his second and third voyages, described the island races encountered in a distinctly unromantic fashion. The Maori "massacre" and dismemberment of an entire boat-crew from the *Adventurer*, the consort vessel of the second voyage, was revealed in the separate accounts of Cook, naturalist J. R. Forster, his son George and Lieutenant James Burney, horrifying the reading public in Britain perhaps more than those who had witnessed it. Although Cook and the young Forster stressed that the Maoris probably had been provoked by the hot-tempered master's mate in charge of the boat, Burney's less measured response was more representative: "Such a shocking scene of Carnage and Barbarity as can never be mentioned or thought of, but with horror," he wrote, recalling the blood and body parts that lay strewn along the beach near the wrecked boat, "For the heads, hearts, and lungs of several of our people, were seen lying on the beach, and at a little distance, the dogs gnawing their intrails."[39] Similar reports of cannibalism and of human sacrifices and infanticide among the Maoris and Tahitians respectively – pronounced by such luminaries as Joseph Banks to be "contrary to the first principles of human nature" – confirmed traditional beliefs about "savages" abroad that had titillated and horrified English and European publics for two centuries, while detailed accounts of the "shivering wretchedness," "treachery" or "stupidity" of other islanders, such as the Aborigines of New Holland, also did much to qualify visions of uncorrupted noble savages.[40] Certainly Cook and many of his men made sustained efforts to assess indigenous peoples against their own rather than European standards, regarding their societies, in good relativist fashion, as having value, or even greater happiness than that obtainable in "civilized" countries.[41] But the information gleaned from the second and third voyages also suggested to many observers that the force of climactic and developmental variations on the human, animal and vegetable kingdoms alike had produced some brutish and irrational people whose absolute difference from Europeans of any rank could not be more arresting.

Accordingly, the tropics, long acknowledged to be geographic spaces of indolence, luxury, sloth and sensuality, also began to be used to promote the idea that humankind had risen stage by stage from a lower to higher form of existence, a progression in which primitive peoples demonstrably lagged behind. This version of social evolution, although overtaken by the unlikely convergence of comparative anatomy, physical anthropology and evangelicalism in the early 1810s and 1820s (until reconfigured in the more absolutist biological and social forms of Darwin and Spencer),[42] nonetheless marked a distinctive initiative in the later eighteenth century's efforts to understand human diversity that impacted theories of natural and human history and political economy. Certainly the four-stage version of human development elaborated by Scottish social scientists, which had held that human society naturally developed over time through stages based on the mode of subsistence, was well established by Cook's time. But the current emphasis on empirical observation had shown that Pacific peoples were prone to exhibit contradictory characteristics that were not subsumable under earlier primitivist or social science models. Proponents of social evolutionism following the Cook voyages tended to envision a more complex configuration of development from savagery to civilization, one that was less mechanistic, unwilling to found explanations for social differences upon a single cause such as climate or subsistence alone and more nuanced in the understanding of history, combining spatialized and progressive notions of time and simultaneity with the perception that economic and cultural growth entailed both progress and corruption. They differed from their nineteenth-century successors in seeing cultural difference as a product of historical development and social convention, rather than inescapable natural laws, and deemed progress among primitive peoples to be possible once "discovery" had planted or nurtured the seeds of improvement or otherwise brought them into the time of History.[43]

The senior Forster, who despite his famously quarrelsome personality brought an impressive background in antiquarian and classical learning, Linnaean and Buffonian method and Scottish moral philosophy to bear on his study of Pacific societies, was both indicative and constitutive of this explanatory trend. His *Observations Made During a Voyage Round the World* (1778) was based, as he stressed, on an intimate and empirical knowledge of the things and peoples described, a "first-hand" knowledge of the local and the particular, so that his analysis of the stages of civilization in which Pacific peoples existed was sustained by his grasp of an equally detailed natural history. Forster rejected an automatic primitivism that saw humanity in its natural state as noble and virtuous in favor of an empirical recounting of differences and similarities in custom, appearance, manners and the attainment of distinct degrees of happiness. Mankind must, he wrote, "be considered in various situations, comparable with the various ages of men from infancy to manhood; with this difference only, that men in their collective capacity ripen but slowly from animality, through the states of savages and barbarians into a civilized society, which has again an infinite variety of situations and degrees of perfection."[44]

Forster's *Observations* adopted within a monogenetic system a comparative approach to classify the various "nations" of the South Pacific into two "races" or "varieties," which he theorized (wrongly, we now know) descended from two distinct migrant populations from northern Asian islands or western islands around New Guinea respectively. The two races were distinguished according to "Colour, Size, Form, Habit and natural Turn of Mind," and ranked according to manners, morals, cultivation and religion (or the "progress towards Civilization," a rubric under which the treatment of women was accorded great significance).[45] The characteristic tension in much Enlightenment thought on human diversity between innate and acquired characteristics appeared here as well: ardently embracing the universalism founded on the belief in essential human nature, Forster's work demonstrated how history, climate and material progress could make that nature so malleable as to confound the question of essence itself. He ascribed, for example, seemingly invariable "natures" to different peoples while emphasizing at other times their mutability from "original" type to improved or degenerated versions. And although physical differences usually initiated Forster's discussions about what was distinctive about each island nation in the Pacific,[46] and climate was taken to exert a strong force on their physical and mental state, it was the intricate interconnection of climate to population size and historical stage of existence that "explained" the variations in culture and physiognomy: "Such are the beginnings of arts and cultivation, such is the rise of civil societies; sooner or later they cause distinctions of rank, and the various degrees of power, influence and wealth . . . Nay, they often produce a material difference in the colour, habits and forms of the human species."[47]

The complexity of Forster's relentlessly comparative perspective lay in its unwillingness to ascribe a single value to any variable in social development. For example, while savage and barbarous societies could be dependent upon climate for their levels of happiness, they could also improve or degenerate in the most auspicious climes, and although civilized societies achieved happiness through laws, education and knowledge, climate and environment could still reshape their moral and mental faculties. Moreover, race and stage of civilization were not identical: New Zealanders, who lived an "unsettled" and peripatetic life, presented a "degraded" version of the first and generally more advanced race of eastern Polynesia, while the Tannese, exemplars of the second race of western Polynesia, had progressed to a dependence upon cultivation and were happier and less violent.[48] On the other hand, it was clear that within this early version of a pre-Benthamite felicitous calculus, it was not physical but *moral* happiness – that is, the "means of improving the intellectual faculties, and preserving the rights and privileges of a free agency in man, without interfering with the happiness of others" – that was the key to progress towards "civil or social felicity." "Men in society advance towards perfection by a strict regard to truth or candour, by *humanity*," Forster stressed; and debasement and degeneracy occur among those societies that "can neither profit by the assistance, nor by the inventions and improvements of others." Hence progress is predicated upon a striving for betterment, which, if not innate, was at best unevenly inculcated.[49] Finally, Forster's narrative sought to inscribe into History peoples who previously had had to depend upon "vague traditional [oral] reports in lieu of historical records" to account for their origins and movement. His work thus held out the hope that the incommensurability of global societies could be overcome through contact, commerce and the example of civilization; but it also tempered the implications of necessary progress by arguing that South Seas peoples showed the importance of the roles of both environment and chronological degeneration in the formation of different character and races.[50]

Forster's son George adopted a similar social evolutionist position in his *Voyage Around the World* (1777), while also being more prone to culturally relativist assessments of primitive peoples' inclinations towards improvement. Significantly, both Forsters used women to assess the levels of savagery and progress towards civilization within Pacific societies. As George explained,

74

> It is the practice of all uncivilized nations to deny their women the common privileges of human beings, and to treat them as creatures inferior to themselves. The ideas of finding happiness and comfort in the bosom of a companion, only arise with a higher degree of culture.[51]

As we have seen, this conflation of eurocentric aesthetic standards and sexual politics with "neutral" empirical observation was a standard trope of late Enlightenment ethnology, where women were frequently used to delineate important features of historical and national difference and to endow those differences with moral significance. And European and particularly English women were believed to have attained the highest levels of physical, mental and moral refinement and good-treatment.[52] In the South Seas, the place of women in local societies was essential to Forster's distinction between the two "races" in the South Pacific and their divergently moving cultures. "The more the women are esteemed in a nation, and enjoy an equality of rights with the men," Johann Forster observed, the more the culture is capable of the social virtues that "naturally lead them toward the blessings of civilization." Yet South Seas discovery encouraged a view of women's historical and cultural differences through the accumulation of local knowledge, even as it proclaimed the potential for progress to overcome them.[53]

Tahitian women, for example, had quickly become legendary in England for their beauty. Joseph Banks typically enthused about their grace and elegance, which, "except in the article of Complexion in which our European Ladies certainly excell," surpassed that of every other nation. He theorized that their superior physical forms were owed to the body being allowed to develop as nature intended, unencumbered by the distorting artifices of European clothing.[54] Even more titillating were their supposed proclivities towards free love: the overtly erotic dances performed by young Tahitian women, accompanied by hip gyrations and other "indecent" movements; the voracious and polygamous sexual antics among the *arioi*, the elite group of performers and religious chiefs associated with the war god, Oro; and the more exogamous sexual trysts of their non-elite sisters with British tars sparked fantasies in English, as well as French, minds about the lack of guilt in the "state of nature." But Tahitian society was set apart by the Forsters for the high esteem and good treatment meted out to its women. Although their greater nonchalance towards matters of the flesh – alternatively explained as a product of class (e.g., of aristocratic luxury or lower-class depravity), simplicity or tropical excess – showed they had some way to go, Tahitian women were still taken quite literally to embody their society's progress.[55] In many of the prints and drawings of the Society Islands, such as in the painting by William Hodges *Tahiti Revisited* (Fig. 7), tattooed Tahitian women are represented in their "natural habitat," and so become part of the island's lush tropical fertility, splendor and exoticism, but also, as in Hodges's *Resolution and Adventure in Matavai Bay* (1776) or John Webber's *Young Woman of Tahiti Dancing* (1784), central to their society's arts and comforts. In Forster's account, too, their bodies were made to bear the signs of both their primitiveness and its transmutation to a higher stage: their

Figure 7 William Hodges, *Tahiti Revisited* (1776). Courtesy of the National Maritime Museum.

tattooed buttocks, well-shaped breasts, and delicate demeanors, along with their "wonderful quickness of parts and sensibility, a sweetness of temper, and a desire to please . . . contribute to captivate the hearts" and soften the manners of their men, and so move their society towards civilization.[56]

Among less advanced peoples, such as the Maoris, where women were not only less attractive (their breasts were "flaccid and pendulous") but also wretchedly treated by their husbands and offspring, their bodily and mental difference could still contribute towards the improvement of their men's intellectual faculties: the "more delicate frame of their bodies" and their "natural" dispositions towards "cooler reflexion," submission and the will to please, "must in time naturally contribute to soften that harshness of manners, which is become habitual in the barbarous races of men."[57] Similarly, women in the New Hebrides and New Caledonia, ground zero of the "second race" of the South Pacific, were not only "generally ill-favoured by Nature," but also were used as the "drudges and pack horses of the Nation; we saw them always loaded with Yams, Bananas etc., weeding their plantations, and working something or other." Yet the effect of this oppression on women's bodies and nerves paradoxically "contributed more towards the improvement and perfection of their intellectual faculties, than those of the males," and thus prepares them to lead their societies towards progress.[58] Women's "nature" and character, although differently situated in time, still provide the grounds against which a complex and diverse masculine civilization can flower, with the European observer serving as representative of the latter's most advanced form.[59]

Other philosophers and social scientists used evolutionary schema to support less optimistic views of Pacific peoples. In his *Origin and Progress of Language* (1773), which drew on accounts of Cook's first voyage, Lord Monboddo had been forthright in proclaiming that humanity's departure from its earliest state was a *progression*, not a corruption, and that the capacity for rational thought and moral improvement was not innate but acquired by toil and struggle. "There cannot be virtue, properly so called, until man is become a rational and political animal; then he shows true courage, very different from the ferocity of the brute or savage . . . the infant of our species." Despite Monboddo's notorious eccentricities, the connection he posited between the historical stage of civilization and the *capacity* for improvement was bolstered or amplified by other stars of the English and Scottish Enlightenment, as well as Continental scientists, and popularized in periodicals, fiction and travel accounts.[60] Polygeneticist Lord Kames shocked his colleagues with his idea about the different species among the human race, but his discussion of how the "capacity" for society and progress varied among nations, which drew upon evidence from Pacific islanders, aroused little comment.[61] John Millar, certainly the most celebrated proponent of stadial theory, whose second edition of his influential *Origin of the Distinction of Ranks* (1779) added a section on Pacific islanders, argued that "the lower its [i.e., savage society's] primitive condition . . . the greater the exertions of labour and activity" that must be exerted for the "seeds of improvement" to take root. And Marsden's acclaimed *History of Sumatra* (1783)

– significantly, not a conventional history at all, but an account of contemporary Sumatra which placed its inhabitants in the "natural history of man" – specified a cultural evolutionary hierarchy of humankind which placed the Europeans and Chinese at the top, Caribs, New Hollanders, Laplanders and Hottentots at the bottom, and the South Seas peoples somewhere in the middle.[62]

On the positive side, theories of social evolution, grounded upon a view of the essentially "progressive" character of humankind and human society, allowed British observers to see in the customs, gender relations or technologies of primitive societies "mirrors" of their earlier selves. "The history . . . of some of the South Sea isles, which the late voyages of discovery have tended to disclose, enables us to glance at society in some of its earlier forms," James Dunbar wrote in his *Essay on the History of Mankind in Rude and Cultivated Ages* (1780).[63] John Marra, the Irish gunner's mate aboard the *Resolution* who scooped the Admiralty by two years with his published account of the voyage, exculpated the Tahitian *arioi* from the charge of excessive sensuality by quoting esteemed antiquarian Sir William Temple on the custom of wife-sharing among the "ancient inhabitants of our own island" – a historical judgment which Gibbon himself entertained in the last volume of his *Decline and Fall* (1788).[64] The custom of tattooing, so elaborately pursued by the New Zealanders (Fig. 8) was, William Falconer noted, a "custom of great antiquity, and very general" among people in a rude or savage state; "Julius Caesar mentions this practice among the ancient Britons . . . and several of the savage nations on Asiatic and African coasts follow the same practice today."[65] And others were encouraged to observe in Pacific cultures, including the Maoris, the signs of the beginnings of progress that was moving them from barbarism into the early stages of civilization. Nevertheless, in the versions of evolutionary progress being canvassed, rationality itself, as well as custom, material culture, sexual politics and physical characteristics, became intractable parts of the progression from a lower to higher humanity. Nature becomes culture, and culture nature, in this mental universe, and mimesis fails the less advanced races as a form of knowledge production. As Cook remarked, when reflecting on Omai's lack of application on returning to his native land in 1776, "this kind of indifference is the true character of his nation. Europeans have visited them at times for these ten years past, yet we find neither new arts nor improvements in the old, nor have they copied after us in any one thing."[66] From the perspective of explorers, social scientists and their interlocutors, Pacific islanders existed in a temporal distance, a different historical stage, than Europeans, whose civilizations were older and hence more advanced, if also in certain respects more degenerated and corrupted.

Cook's own death at the hands of some of these islanders emotionally intensified the transformation from noble to ignoble savages. In the aftermath of his death,[67] Hawaiians and some other more "primitive" peoples of the Pacific began to be compared to the Hottentots and Eskimos – races notorious for their cannibalism, harshness towards their women, hostility to Europeans and disgusting personal habits, repugnantly exhibiting to British people the extreme lower boundary of humanity. Whether immature or degraded, the South Sea peoples lagged

Figure 8 Engraving after Sydney Parkinson, *Head of a New Zealander* (1773). Courtesy of the Henry E. Huntington Library.

behind the Europeans in customs, progress and initiative. They were located in an anterior historical time that, if it allowed Europeans and especially English islanders "to behold, as in a mirror, the features of our own progenitors,"[68] also ensured their place on the lower rungs of the ladder of civilization. In this guise the historical differences among the "races" could serve as guides to understanding the cultural differences among the classes in Europe: in both cases human progress was contingent upon a willingness as well as capacity for self-improvement through the exertion of rationality and the reigning in of baser instinct. Such was the argument, at least, of the Anglican clergyman Thomas Malthus, who placed the South Sea peoples only just above the Tierra del Fuegans and American Indians in the "stages" of human civilization by which men and women learned to exercise the "moral restraint" necessary to control the sexual instinct and avert demographic disaster. Naturally, the European and especially English middle classes were seen to have excelled at liberating reason from the forces of instinct, and as such were taken to be the guarantors of future progress.[69]

Protestant Island

Malthus points to another, harsher source of antiprimitivist thinking that had been gaining ground in religious and political circles in the latter decades of the century, namely evangelical Protestantism. Protestantism itself, of course, was in Britain a great deal more than anti-Catholicism or the last resort of national bonding, as Linda Colley and Liah Greenfeld have recently reminded us. It demonstrated and embodied the Old Testament image of a chosen, godly people who were "an elite and a light to the world because every one of its members was a party to the covenant with God."[70] Protestantism, a rational improving religion – in stark contrast to the superstitious idolatry that dominated across the Channel – thus secured to Britons the certainty of their own excellence and entitlement. In the decades surrounding Cook's voyages, Protestant evangelicals worked to discover, and endow with great urgency, the national mission to save the debased savages from themselves, a project which cultural, imperial and political rivalries with France accelerated.

Evangelicals were among the first to denounce the romanticization of Pacific islanders that followed the publication in English of Bougainville's and then Hawkesworth's *Voyages*. John Wesley, avid and critical purveyor of indigenous peoples in their "natural" states, sat down to read the latter with "huge expectations" but was quickly stunned and appalled: "Men and women coupling together in the face of the sun, and in the sight of scores of people! Men whose skin, cheeks, and lips are as white as milk. Hume or Voltaire might believe this, but I cannot!" Other anonymous and self-styled "Protestants" attacked Hawkesworth's *Voyages* in the newspapers for attempting to "debauch the Morals of our Youth at home," exclaiming that his book gave English women "stronger excitements to vicious Indulgences than the most intriguing French Novel."[71] From this perspective, South Pacific peoples in general and Tahitians in particular exemplified the sloth and sensuality not of the state of nature but of original sin. In the following decades, and in a spirited riposte to Enlightenment niceties, sermons, letters and missionary reports denounced the iniquities of human sacrifice, infanticide, nudity, lasciviousness, transvestism, uncontrolled sexuality and total absence of revealed religion that the accounts of the voyages had shown. The conversion of the South Sea islanders accordingly became a cause célèbre in evangelical circles that sparked the formation of a new spate of missionary societies geared towards saving the debased savages from heathenism and French Enlightenment alike. The Baptist Society, founded in 1792 by William Carey, who led the mission that set out for Bengal the next year; the ecumenical but predominantly Congregationalist London Missionary Society (1795), founded by a handful of Bristol and London clergymen; the Anglican Church Missionary Society (1795); and the Africa Society (1795) all claimed to have been galvanized into action by the accounts of the Pacific peoples provided by the Cook voyages.[72]

Of course, the ultimate goal of evangelicalism was to create universal Christian subjects equal in the eyes of God. But the evangelical belief in good works, benevolence and also the essential sinfulness of humanity legitimated ideas of both savage backwardness and the central role that Protestant England – God's chosen nation – must play as the "Teacher of Nations," showing the way forward to progress and salvation.[73] There was, after all, no apparent contradiction between a potential spiritual equality and a national, social and racial hierarchy, as evangelical efforts to Christianize African slaves in America had long made clear, and current campaigns for reformation of manners and abolition of the slave trade reinforced.[74] The new missionary societies were well connected to the abolitionist cause and to each other in personnel as well as goals, and were equally clear in their insistence that the salvation of heathen souls was the key to the advancement of Britain's imperial and commercial as well as moral ascendancy in the world.[75] As the wars with revolutionary and Napoleonic France intensified, British evangelical missionary work was held up by its proponents as the crucial bulwark for national survival and international order, stamping out simultaneously French and heathen infidelity and idolatry in Europe and the world. As one supporter put it, it was "an honour to England that its inhabitants of all distinctions are so zealous in propagating the knowledge of the Holy Scriptures throughout the world; that true religion and true liberty may be understood and enjoyed by all people."[76]

The London Missionary Society or LMS demonstrated the materiality of these imperatives to convert, subdue and possess the world through the cultural power and superiority of English Protestantism. Conceived in a spirit of competitive zeal with Baptist and Anglican missionary societies on the one hand and Roman Catholic missions on the other, its leaders quickly fixed on the "well-tempered" but culturally degraded South Sea "heathens" as most urgently in need of their ministrations. Thomas Haweis expounded on this theme in an early sermon to the organization, noting the sharp contrast between the lush natural beauty of Tahiti and the spiritual and moral turpitude of its inhabitants: "amidst these enchanting scenes," he warned, "savage nature still feasts on the flesh of its prisoners, appeases its Gods with human sacrifices – whole societies of men and women live promiscuously, and murder every infant born amongst them." From this perspective, it was up to the worthy individuals of the Society and their missionary representatives to correct and complete the tasks the Cook voyages had initiated. The society dispatched the *Duff* to Tahiti in 1796, carrying thirty men, six women and three children, to do God and Britain's work, and their subsequent reports soon began to circulate among the British public in newsletters, travel collections, prints and paintings, joining the accounts of Cook's and Bligh's voyages as authorities on Polynesian culture in the British imperial archive.[77]

The LMS missionary accounts are interesting in a number of ways, not least in their bestowal of implicit cultural and national authority upon the predominantly plebeian and lower-middle-class men and women – mostly skilled artisans and tradesmen – who, along with four clergymen and a surgeon, made up the first mission to the South Seas.[78] Moreover, the accounts demonstrated an intermixture of the rhetoric of travel-as-science and of religious fervor that would be very influential in political judgments about colonization. The resultant missionary ethnography assessed native culture in terms of its peoples' ripeness for conversion, a state inferred from their degree of heathenism (a quality considered particularly "expedient," since it also guaranteed no lasting damage from incidental contact with French superstition) and compliance ("amiable temper"). Missionary publications were accordingly filled with descriptions of native religious and sexual practices, which no doubt contributed to the popularity of these accounts among British publics.[79]

Most importantly for our purposes, however, cultural relativism was eschewed in favor of a more uncompromising view of antipodean savagery that sought to establish simultaneously the redemption, superiority and proprietary rights of the English settlers. These views were dramatically represented in the famous painting, and subsequent engraving, of the missionaries' formal acquisition of the district of Matavai from a Tahitian chieftain: it depicted sober, respectable and heavily dressed English men and women confronting half-naked islanders, "'the untutored offspring of fallen nature' anxiously awaiting the Christian revelation."[80] At the same time, the accounts made clear that the mistakes and indulgences of Cook and his crews would not be tolerated. Spiritual, not sexual, commerce was to be the coin of the realm, and the success of the colonial encounter was to be measured by the degree to which the settlers mastered themselves through fortitude, suffering and faith, and their native charges through example, enlightenment and ultimately conversion.

On landing in Tahiti, the missionaries found their "passion . . . more powerfully excited to find their population greatly diminished, and, through the prevalence of vice, tending to utter extinction" – an assessment which neatly reversed the responsibility for the plague of venereal disease which Cook had lamented as a direct consequence of European contact onto the indigenous islanders themselves. Not that Cook and his crews were held to be blameless: the missionaries attributed the surprise with which the Tongatabu islanders greeted their refusal to sleep with native women to the "practices of our abandoned countrymen making them believe this was a favour we could not well do without."[81] Instead, the missionaries offered a model of man- and womanhood predicated upon (imperialist) evangelical family values, where the imperatives of monogamous marriage, procreative sex and spiritual comradeship went hand-in-hand. The heroes of the missionary accounts thus combined morality, self-restraint and self-denial with spiritual leadership, and if Cook had managed the first three, he never attempted the last.[82]

Such a drastic transformation in the cultural frame of reference as that represented by the missionaries led the locals to suspect that they were "not Englishmen, or like any others they have seen who have ever visited their island." The dangers (in the missionary view) of such mis-recognition led to the adoption, by unanimous vote, of strict rules governing their personal interactions with the natives and with those of their fellowship who may transgress them. Hence in the second year of the mission on Tahiti (1798), Thomas Lewis's decision to take a local woman as his wife caused great distress among the rest of the fellowship, who had no choice but to excommunicate him from their Church, although he continued to attend the public religious services, and "to bring this native with him." John Jefferson, Secretary to the society, justified this particular rejection of English–Tahitian miscegenation as absolutely central to the maintenance of those cultural boundaries upon which the success of the mission depended:

> It must be borne in mind in this and in all similar circumstances that the woman remained *heathen*, not only ignorant of Christianity, but also addicted to all the abominable practices of a savage life. It was not a case of a missionary marrying a native convert but of a Christian man uniting himself to a heathen woman, and that on an island where the testimony of the missionaries, after a residence of eighteen months, was that in all probability not one single female on the island over ten or twelve years of age had escaped pollution.[83]

Lewis's wife, in other words, was not only willfully incognizant of the spiritual authority of English Protestantism as the representative of Christendom, but also tainted by possibility that she had contracted venereal disease through earlier sexual encounters. As *Omai* had earlier implied, acceptable intermarriage depended upon cultural, spiritual and bodily submission to "English" values on the part of the colonized, without which carnal knowledge could not be sanctified.

Through its representations, the LMS, like other missionary efforts of the day, provided the moral counterpart and corrective to the changing ethnographic representations of so-called primitive races. "The missionaries have done a great deal for us in clearing up our notions of savage nations," Coleridge reportedly asserted, for they have shown that "[t]here scarcely ever existed such a set of blood-thirsty barbarians."[84] Only through the interventions of the Holy Spirit and British civility in *Protestant*-Christian conversion could such peoples be transformed into obedient Christian subjects, thus confirming the pedagogical relationship set up between them. As "God's elect among the islanders," as the LMS missionaries were wont to remind themselves in times of hardship, their duty was to endure intense provocation, temptation and tribulation in order to effect the salvation of the corrupted and debased whose conversion would constitute the ultimate homage to English superiority and resolve. Interestingly, in the evangelical publications of the next two decades, the original naturalist repertoire of images – plants, animals, landscapes, native peoples – that dominated the earlier accounts of the voyages were supplanted by appropriately evocative scenes of native brutality, superstition and backwardness. Hence Webber's *Human Sacrifice at Tahiti* was retrieved from Cook and King's *Voyage to the Pacific Ocean* of 1784 to become one of the best-known illustrations of the nineteenth century; while the new editions of Cook's voyages were both purged of their "indecent" contents and extended with new illustrations of brutish-looking savages whose skin and intentions grew ever darker.[85] As with the antislavery movement, missionary work combined humanitarianism with anti-French invective and hierarchical notions of British superiority and English difference in ways that bolstered conceptions of the gulfs between and distinctiveness of "nations." Significantly, after a number of disastrous setbacks, the great victory of conversion the missionaries proclaimed to have achieved among the Tahitians by 1820 did little to dislodge this perception of the hierarchical and pedagogical relationship that existed between them. The English success in "transforming . . . [the] barbarous, indolent and idolatrous inhabitants" of the Tahitian and Society islands "into a *comparatively* civilized, industrious and Christian people," the celebrated LMS missionary John Williams argued, had inaugurated for the Polynesians a "new era . . . not only in their moral history, but also in their intellectual." This bringing of savage peoples into History, and the gratitude and filial piety it inspired, was acknowledged by the former heathens themselves, according to Williams, who recalled a Raiatean chief telling him "although we have ten thousand instructors in Christ, we have not many fathers, for, in Christ Jesus, *you* have begotten us through the Gospel."[86]

Island of History

Drama, science and religion, then, worked in tandem to classify the English and British as a superior and distinctive people. But the ethnicity reconstituted through Cook and the South Seas was experienced not just oppositionally, that is, through contrasts between England and its Others, but also self-referentially, through the heightened interest in recounting the historical origins of British ethnicities themselves. Concomitant with the notion of "universal history" and continuous time, the period witnessed a proliferation of writing on particularist national history that shared a topical and epistemological propinquity to the ethnology of the day. Organized according to notions of qualitative progress in the material, scientific and intellectual realms (themselves influenced by the comparative study of ancient, Oriental and indigenous societies) and predicated upon the firm foundation of demonstrable "facts", this history sought to emphasize the rationality, modernity and distinctiveness of the present through the objective presentation of specificities, antecedents, origins. "The only certain means by which nations can indulge their curiosity in researches concerning their remote origin, is to consider the language, manners and customs of their ancestors, and to compare them with those of neighbouring nations," David Hume asserted. "The fables which are commonly employed to supply the place of true history ought entirely to be disregarded."[87] Not surprisingly, the history of England loomed large in this enterprise. Hume's disclaimer notwithstanding, a selective use of "fables" about ancient Britons and Saxons, their relationship to Britain's current ethnic groupings and England's future place in world affairs became peculiarly charged features of cultural production in the last quarter of the century, marking the boundaries between the civilized and non-civilized while also inscribing national and ethnic particularity. As Johann Forster (member of the Society of Antiquaries and essayist on King Alfred and Saxon geography) put it, History must be taken to be one of the "blessings of a more exalted civilization and education, which give us in every respect so great a superiority over these [primitive] nations, and assign us so high a rank in the scale of rational beings."[88] At the same time, the Pacific craze and fascination with South Sea "primitives" inspired some new perspectives on ancient Britain and its inhabitants, combining contemporary respect for empirically based scholarship with the impulse to reinvent the ancient Angles, Jutes and Saxons as Britain's noblest savages. The central myths of Anglo-Saxonism were thus lent a factual coloration by association with current social science, which aided their widespread acceptance.[89]

For example, the production and popularization of multivolume national histories of England (some of which were written, with no apparent sense of irony, by Scots) abbreviated or ignored the Celtic or pre-Saxon past. Hume's *History of England*, unquestionably the most popular and influential history of the century, and convincingly characterized as "cosmopolitan" in intention, was nonetheless arguably Anglo-Saxonist, in that it painted, in Samuel Klinger's words, "a vision of world renewal through the mass migration of the Germanic tribesmen." In the first volume, Hume notes that the conquered Romanized Britons were too "abject," "effeminate" and weak to resist the Saxons, who carried to their highest pitch the manly "virtue of valour and love of liberty"; while the Irish, never conquered by the Romans, remained buried in the "most profound ignorance and barbarism" until the English took up Rome's mantle some centuries later – judgments that were later confirmed by Gibbon in his *Decline and Fall*.[90] Antiquarian Thomas Percy's *Northern Antiquities* (1770), a translation of Paul-Henri Mallet's history of ancient Danes, stressed the different ethnic origins of "Gothic" northern and Celtic nations, and argued that it was the love of liberty that particularly distinguished the former. Expanding on these themes were the "nationalist" historians of the same decades, such as Catherine Macaulay, Obadiah Hulme and John Pinkerton, who despite their political differences were explicitly, even rabidly, interested in questions about racial and national origins, the virtues of the "native stock," and the connections of both to Anglo-Saxon liberties. All agreed not only that the Saxons had provided the most perfect constitution the world had ever seen, but also that they set the standards of political liberty and civilization which other peoples, including the Celts, could only emulate. Pinkerton went the furthest, asserting that the Celts "are savages, have been savages since the world began, and will be for ever savages while a separate people."[91] A less virulent and xenophobic acknowledgment of the blessings of the Anglo-Saxon inheritance, stimulated by neoclassicism's revival of interest in the antique, was commercialized in popular literature, prints and tourism: sections on "Antiquities" in periodicals abounded with Saxon examples, while the affluent urban classes were seized with a passion for both touring "Gothic ruins" and owning prints of Gothic architecture in testimony to their collective, if barbarous, ethnic heritage.[92] And Anglo-Saxon history and political traditions were held up as a viable counter to pernicious French or foreign influences by patriotic and cultural commentators from the Anti-Gallican Society to John Cartwright and Granville Sharp; the latter proposed the establishment of Anglo-Saxon communities in England in order to encourage an appreciation for the pre-conquest, Teutonic "original principles" of liberty and freedom that could then serve as a model for less fortunate peoples.[93]

The coincidence of historical (racialist) theories of the "Norman yoke" and democratic political ideas during the period 1760–90 has been ably examined elsewhere.[94] What needs to be emphasized for our purposes is that there emerged in the last quarter of the century a renewed interest in the links between ethnic and national identity that it was up to history to document. The English were not the only Britons intent on recovering their ethnic roots. The Irish, Scots and Welsh were similarly occupied in this period, producing a rush to document the ethnic origins of the tribes that made up ancient Britain before and after contact with Rome in order to restore the Celts to their rightful place in their own and in Britain's past and future.[95] Within these competing histories, the techniques and orientations of the ethnologists of the Pacific were drawn on to corroborate rival views. For example, the faith that philological study could discern the origins of different "races," subscribed to by ethnologists such as Monboddo, J. R. Forster and William Marsden, was also taken up by antiquarians, prompting investigations into the origins of English in order to prove the racial as well as linguistic distinctiveness of the national character. "[T]he investigation and analysis of Language conduces to point out the genius of a people," wrote Burgess in An Essay on the Study of Antiquities (1782). The study of Old English, Cornish and other Gaelic languages could thus demonstrate the "original" and presumably enduring differences between their speakers; as one analyst wrote, "the British, to speak plainly, has little or no resemblance to the English . . . their idioms and genius are as radically and essentially different as any two languages can possibly be."[96]

The influence of South Sea islanders on views of Britain's own ancient primitives was even more directly demonstrated in the rise of an antiquarian ethnography devoted to interpreting the material remains of antiquity. English naturalist George Pearson used remnants of ancient Roman and Saxon weapons found in Lincolnshire to make extensive comparisons between the state of British society at the time of the Roman conquest, and "that in which our late discovers found the natives of the South Sea islands." Rev. Frederick Clark, a professor of mineralogy at Cambridge, reported to Joseph Banks in 1812 that diggers had found an ancient weapon "exactingly resembling the Stone Hatchets of the South

Seas." Falconer's frequent parallels between the manners and customs of ancient Anglo-Saxon and present-day Pacific islanders were a standard feature of his work, although he made it clear that it was in Britain alone that the association between insularity and freedom, quoted at the beginning of this chapter, held true over the ages. Other commentators noted the similarities between native and Oceanic arts, music and poetry. The Oxford Prize Poem of 1791, *The Aboriginal Britons* by George Richards, opened with an address to Cook and his South Sea navigators that exhorted them to remember, as they viewed the "wondering Savage" on those distant shores, that "a form like this, illustrious souls, of yore / Your own Britannia's sea-girt island wore."[97] The romanticization of Celtic traditions by Scots, Irish and Welsh writers such as James Macpherson and Sylvester O'Halloran who decried the excessive Englishness of British culture was also indebted to the interest in ethnology prompted by the South Seas "discoveries," not least since they allowed comparisons between ancient Celtic and Pacific island customs, such as the Druidical and Tahitian *arioi* practices of human sacrifice, that redeemed the former from being just embarrassing. Even the evangelicals tried to exploit the identification of ancient Britons with Oceanic primitives: the Rev. Melville Horne, in his "Letters on Missions," exhorted potential supporters to remember that "Britain, Christian Britain, was once an island of idolatrous barbarians; and such it had yet remained, unless some of God's dear people in distant countries . . . had formed the benevolent plan of sending missionaries hither."[98] Through such comparisons, the Pacific present and British past mirrored each other, and Pacific peoples became imaginatively associated with the customs of English people's own ancestors. Here, if ever, we have a "past filled with the time of the now" in Benjamin's mellifluous phrase, but even further, a present filled with temporally disjunctive pasts, rendered homologous through the radical simultaneity of primitive and modern space-time.

Not surprisingly, this antiquarian ethnography could also focus on more contemporary subjects. Perhaps in a riposte to those who held out for the inventiveness and superiority of the ancient Celts, English writers turned their ethnographic analysis on contemporary Celts as holdouts of the "primitives within." The Highlanders, for example, became the objects of much discussion in popular periodicals, travel literature and scientific journals in these decades as atavistic survivors of an earlier age, whom the march of modernity could only extinguish. Equally indicative of the pernicious imperialist distancing involved in such views, touring enthusiast Gilbert White advocated the adoption of a plan of "exploration" of Ireland identical to that undertaken by Banks and Cook in the Pacific, in order to illumine not only the varieties of flora and fauna, but also "the manners of the wild natives, their superstitions, their prejudices, their sordid way of life."[99] Here, as above, factual "discovery" in history and science converged in the service of establishing ethnic authenticity. The anachronism of the Highlanders, Macpherson's Ossian cult, the London Welsh literary societies, and Sharp's proposals for re-establishment of the witenagemot or Saxon parliaments all depended upon both to produce their versions of cultural distinctiveness and ethnic particularity.[100] Hence as the origins of Englishness as well as other

British ethnicities come to seem more historically specific and authentically ascertained, they also become less naturalizable, established in and inherited from, as Edmund Burke made clear in his *Reflections on the Revolution in France* (1790), a common, venerable and *induplicable* past. Hence History emerged, like Science, as an "art of (self) discovery" that underwrote English distinctiveness and modernity. In this context, the representation of Cook as the standard-bearer of a peculiarly national genius, and of South Seas peoples as a "mirror" of divergent British "national" pasts demonstrated how the tangled circuitry of colonial identification, alterity, exchange and transformation could produce both an inter-locution of similarity and difference, and an ineradicable otherness.

The argument will end where it began, for theater conjoined these different strands of cultural production into a syncretic vision that transmuted the past and the present into the mythical, and the mythical into History. In the work of Loutherbourg in particular, the techniques of naturalist visual technologies made the fictive and illusory into the "exact" representation of "history as it really was." *Omai* was his last, best effort, but his earlier productions had also made evident the interplay of difference and identity in the construction of a visual regime of historical authenticity, some of which we have seen. Others drew upon and amplified the upsurge of interest in the sublime and picturesque within Great Britain. Loutherbourg's *The Wonders of Derbyshire* (1779) was a harlequinade that represented, with the "exactness" for which he was known, the wildness and sublimity of the northern English locality (a topography that was also believed to reflect the "savage" nature of the local Peak people).[101] *Robinson Crusoe*, widely understood in the eighteenth century and after to be based on the "real" experiences of shipwrecked mariner Alexander Selkirk, had profoundly influenced voyagers' tales and travel writing as well as fiction over the century. Produced for the stage for the first time in 1781, with scenery by Loutherbourg, it proved to be one of the most successful afterpieces of the decade. The pantomime's most crucial scene was that which re-enacted the island setting of English imperial genesis, when Crusoe secures Friday's loyalty by saving him from invading savages. As in other famous English island fictions, such as *The Tempest*, mastery over both sea and land and their various inhabitants is deemed crucial for sea-girted civilizations, and this scene was accordingly both critiqued and celebrated by critics and audiences alike for its "authenticity" and likeness to the "original."[102] But this analysis will be best concluded by turning in more detail to a pantomime from Loutherbourg's earlier years that meshed most interestingly with *Omai* and the trends discussed above.

Loutherbourg had begun his theatrical career in London by working closely with David Garrick on a number of Garrick's present-minded historical projects. Garrick had done more than perhaps any other playwright to bring the past into the present in order to bear witness to current progress, and his dramaturgical influence was felt in British theater long after his naturalistic acting style had grown passé.[103] In 1773, one year after Cook's second voyage to the South Seas had begun, Garrick revived at Drury Lane a revision of Thomson and Mallet's *Alfred, a Masque*. This story of the tribulations and ultimate triumph of Alfred the Great, Saxon king (871–901), at the time of the Danish invasion, was first produced in 1740 as part of the Patriot opposition's anti-Walpolean assault. Its refurbishment reflected the newly charged interest in Saxon history as a source of a distinctive national inheritance and character, and particularly in Alfred himself as a native symbol of Englishness that mirrored past, present and future greatness. Yet it was Loutherbourg's elaborate new scenes that most struck spectators with reflection and wonder. In the prologue, Alfred is referred to as "the Godlike figure, in arms renown'd, for arts of peace ador'd . . . the nation's father, more than lord," who ousted "Danish fury" and restored peace and freedom to his "sacred isle." In the final scene, Alfred, contemplating his victory and the future of his country, is enjoined by a hermit to "backward cast your eyes / on this unfolding scene; where pictur'd true / *As in a mirror*, rises fair to sight / Our England's genius, strength and future fame!" With a wave of his wand, the scene changes from the "naturalistic" scenery of ancient Britain into a grand representation of the late naval review at Portsmouth, replete with an ocean in prospect, merchant ships and men-of-war. Sailors jump ashore and begin to sing Arne's *Rule Britannia*:

> The nations, not so blest as thee,
> Must in their turns to tyrants fall,
> While thou shalt flourish great and free
> The dread and envy of them all.
> . . .
> The Muses still, with freedom found
> Shall to thy happy coasts repair,
> Blest isle, with matchless beauty crown'd
> And manly hearts to guard the fair![104]

Liberty, the arts and (feminine) beauty are destined to flourish, then, on the "blest isle," secured under the dual protections of topography and a paternalistic, yet ultimately coercive, masculinity. These themes would be embellished in John Home's romantic version of *Alfred* in 1778 and in the dramatic version of Alexander Bicknell's *The Life of Alfred the Great, King of the Anglo-Saxons* (1777) a decade later. Just as *Omai* projected backwards in contemporary time English origins as an island race, so *Alfred* bequeathed to posterity from the past modern English time, concretized through British men of war. These panoramas provided a "mirror" of English history and futurity that reflected current English manliness, ingenuity and achievement. *Omai*, then, must be read as part of a larger reconfiguration in thinking about time and the "primitive" that reverberated in scientific, missionary and literary circles, and as an emergent theatrical style. This melded topical events, scientific reportage and knowledge and mythic histories into fable and visual spectacle in order to impart to English audiences the origins of the *difference* and *modernity* of the national character. The Island Race, it seems, even in its infancy, would never ever be slaves.

An Island Race Supreme

Captain Cook, "famous civiliser and secret terroriser," in Marshall Sahlins's words,[105] reached a heroic stature in the English national consciousness that few figures before or since have matched. His continued importance in academic and popular historical mythology is demonstrated in the quantities of biographies, monographs and journals that continue to be devoted to assessing his impact and legacy. In the later eighteenth century, in the aftermath of war and imperial dismemberment, the representations of Cook's achievements helped recuperate British political and imperial authority, rescue the national reputation for liberty and restore faith in the superiority of the *English* national character. Deployed alternately as a figure for the English genius for "discovery," observation and monogamous, non-miscegenating heterosexuality, Cook was also in contemporary eyes "a spirit precise, scientific, severe," as J. C. Beaglehole put it, a matter of fact individual whose "competence changed the face of the world." In this light, he could be seen as a prototype for the ideal British colonial administrator. James Joyce once described Defoe's most famous character, Robinson Crusoe, as incarnating "the whole Anglo-Saxon spirit . . . : the manly independence; the unconscious cruelty; the persistence; the slow yet efficient intelligence; the sexual apathy; the practical, well-balanced religiousness; the calculating taciturnity." Cook provided a longed-for, real-life embodiment of many of these same myths and mystifications of Englishness, charting for the nation a new imperial theater for the demonstration of English finesse, expertise and greatness.[106] For by inaugurating a period of fervid British imperialism and settlement in the South Seas – one that their present-day aboriginal descendants still lament – Cook and the South Seas gave the English both a history and a future.

Cook's voyages also had the effect in his own day of embroiling an array of religious, cultural and scientific spokespersons in controversies over the meaning and consequences of human diversity. By the early nineteenth century, the new "science of man" engendered by the voyages became a movement to classify humanity by "racial" types, defined through a conjuncture of physical and cultural characteristics. (In perhaps the ultimate, if telling, confusion of artistic genre, "fact", history and fable that such science configured, Reynolds's neoclassical rendering of the historical Omai (Fig. 5) was used by Johann Blumenbach to illustrate the "Malay race" in his five-race classification of mankind of 1810.[107]) More immediately, in the progress that the history of humanity narrated, diversity signaled temporal disjunctiveness and necessitated hierarchy. Indeed, as *Omai* demonstrated, South Sea islanders could be celebrated as noble savages, "mirrors of our earlier selves," while also providing the ethnographic evidence of a less advanced stage of society than that which the English enjoyed. In this context, the historical, cultural and physical difference of South Sea islanders became evidence of a *lack* that left them lower on the ladder of civilization. Obviously, these temporal and cultural mappings were as unstable as they were fictitious, requiring multiple layers of cultural production in history, technology, theater arts, natural science and literature to give them the appearance of grounding in empirical knowledge and the arts of discovery. And they also envisaged the possibility that such differences among peoples could be eradicated through contact, commerce and will. But in the conceptualization of national belonging articulated through South Seas "discovery," old and new languages of "nation" and "race" converged, and reinforced the belief that "national character," if not innate, was mutable only through the glacial processes of historical time.

Significantly, the proliferation of representations of Cook's human and inanimate discoveries, the endless and repetitive attempts in elite and popular literature to sort out their significance and meanings, served to distance the British in their own eyes even from their European compatriots – a process which the French Revolution intensified. Edmund Burke was not alone in comparing the French Revolutionaries to "savages," for the trope circulated in high and low culture. Job Nott, Birmingham buckle-maker, could think of no greater insult to hurl against French Jacobins than to compare them unfavorably to Hawaiian "savages": "bloody minded barbarians . . . worse than the Antipoads that kill'd and chop'd our brave sailor Captain Cook to pieces . . . they [Jacobins] cut out Gentlemen's hearts, and squeezed the blood into wine and drank it."[108] As such, the French Revolutionaries joined South Sea islanders and other "cannibals" in marking the lower boundaries of humanity and bolstering Britons' sense of difference, superiority and resolve.

Captain James Cook, "mirror" of an English past and present, served (and perhaps continues to serve) as a figure through which these various strands of cultural interpretation could be brought into some coherence. Through the intertwining of the religious, scientific and nationalistic myths described above, this low-born English islander who charted brave new worlds would emerge as the emblem of the Island Race, forged through history, ingenuity, Protestantism, and liberty, whose character marked it out to become the "Teacher of Nations" and so impose a Pax Britannica on the world.

3

BRITANNIA INTO BATTLE: WOMEN, WAR AND IDENTITIES IN ENGLAND AND AMERICA

> I cannot help thinking the Belle Marine [La Malinche, Cortés's Mexican mistress] the happiest woman that ever existed; she seems to have matched herself with a superior species; and I figure to myself how her heart must exult, when she saw her consort (for I supposed she looked on her connection with Cortés as a marriage) leading captive that monarch [Montezuma], whom none of her fellow subjects dared look in the face.
>
> Elizabeth Robinson Montagu to Lord Lyttelton, 1758

So wrote the famous bluestocking, after reading Antonio de Solís's *History of the Conquest of Mexico*, which had just been translated into French.[1] Solís is notorious among historians of the Spanish empire for his whitewash of Cortés's bloody exploits in the New World. Montagu's ardent admiration, articulated to a male correspondent in the midst of Britain's own attempt to conquer an empire in North America, nevertheless raises a number of questions that historians of eighteenth-century Britain have yet to pose, much less answer. In particular, how can we account for Montagu's obvious identification with conquest and empire, those quintessential masculine pursuits, in the eighteenth century? What was at stake for her, and others, in embracing or rejecting the fiscal-military state, and its bloody and extensive wars for dominion? How did such engagement authorize particular national, racial and sexual identities? And how did "the nation" work to organize female desire?

Such questions take on a special urgency in light of recent studies of eighteenth-century British women. Proliferating accounts of their roles in public and political life, in the culture of clubs, sociability and politeness, in artistic, scientific and literary production, in consumption and philanthropy and in the law have wreaked havoc on long-established categories of British women's history. Scholars are now focused on formulating new analytics that go beyond "separate spheres" and gendered oppositions of "public and private" to better capture Georgian women's complex social roles and status.[2] Far from being expelled from the new public culture of the period, women, it seems, were pivotal creators and participants in it; and if their status remained circumscribed by custom and law, they nonetheless maintained vital engagement with the initiatives, problems and pleasures of their society.

However, the new world of eighteenth-century women veers at times towards a rather excessive idealization. Some accounts mistakenly conflate women's presence with women's influence and authority; others, as suggested in an earlier chapter, return us to a Namierite world of kinship and connection in which ideology vanishes.[3] Most importantly, however, the triumphal "exposure" of the empirical falsity of ideological constructions between public and private still begs the question as to why male and female Georgians, from moralists to mothers, stressed the importance of such distinctions in social life. As one critic has argued with regard to "race," criticizing ideas, dogmas or ideologies because they are not empirically verifiable "is without meaning, because it is not the function of an idea to describe social reality but to assist in its constitution. An idea is always 'wrong' in the epistemological sense, but this relation to reality is its very principle."[4] Within the citational practices that established and helped change gender roles, the ideological oppositions between public and domestic life could pack quite a punch when wielded by the guardians of order or reform to fix or refashion the expectations and values of men and women alike. How then should we account for the often asymmetrical relationship between representations of gender and women's own "experience"?[5] If, as several historians have argued, gender and women's history is best conceptualized through a "problematic of continuity" rather than change, it still behooves scholars to strive to understand the ways in which discursive and social power produced historically specific forms of consciousness. In other words, if we are to explore *how* certain gender ideals and roles become hegemonic or contested, across decades or even centuries, and avoid the twin traps of empiricism and idealism, we must place the irreducible relationships between the imaginative and the material at the center of our historical projects. A politics of location that recognizes the links between social ontology and epistemology – between everyday life and the structures of knowledge and authority that shape it – reveals that difference is less a verifiable descriptive category than a highly mobile signifier for power relations and "a cultural and political form of domination" in historical settings.[6]

Such considerations are especially pertinent to Georgian women's relationship to the nation, where the clash between dominant ideologies of patriotism and gender and individual identities seemed especially fraught. For within the matrices of discursive and social power mapped by an emerging nation-state, where the contradictions bedevilling their location as subjects and as individuals were mediated and rendered meaningful by expressive forms, women require attention as both represented and representers.[7] Women's bodies and minds functioned symbolically and literally as the bearers of national values and ideals, just as their alleged "characters" were taken to encapsulate the best and worst features of national manners, yet in both cases, the abstract and symbolic could serve very particularized purposes. To take the most crucial example, the figure of Britannia has loomed large in recent accounts of patriotism of both the loyalist and radical variety. Yet the practice of embodying eighteenth-century English patriotism as a white woman has attracted surprisingly little commentary from historians and critics. Women's bodies were conventionally used to display geopolitical images of power as well as civic and national ideals, of course, but by the mid eighteenth century, a time of war, imperial expansion and loss, new social theories were gaining currency whereby the language of climates and environment linked certain kinds of bodies to specific places. Even the most "abstract" iconographic prints attempted to differentiate the physical as well as mental and moral features of the "national character," as the allegories of the continents, from the 1740s through the 1790s, clearly demonstrate (Fig. 9). At the same time, visual representations of English encounters with new worlds were crucial in gendering and racializing those worlds, often creating the "fantasy of colonial relations, intersecting . . . with traditional gender roles" to create a hierarchy between the imperial and colonized lands and peoples.[8] Britannia, when she first came to prominence as the symbol of the English/ British nation, was personalized, sexualized, abused and otherwise made to stand for a living woman, albeit one who was mother of the race. As such, she could concretize politicized views of national and personal life and mobilize identifications and resistances among diverse audiences. Visual as well as textual representations, material and symbolic conditions and the contexts and practices of everyday life form the semiotic circuits through which meaning was created, contested and ascribed, by eighteenth-century women, their contemporaries and their historians.[9]

In this chapter I want to contribute to the re-thinking of the theoretical grounds and historical enactments of women's status in national life by considering their empirical and imaginative participation in war. Certainly eighteenth-century warfare placed women in ambiguous relationships to state and nation. On the one hand, war made extraordinary demands upon women's financial, physical and emotional resources, forcing them to endure shortage, deprivations, and invasion scares, bear up under trade and agricultural depressions and suffer the loss of fathers, husbands and sons. On the other hand, war also afforded, indeed demanded, greater female activism in the "home front." War stimulated women to take on direct roles in battle as soldiers, sailors, spies, nurses and messengers, to rally anti- or pro-war sentiments among those left behind, to conspire to prevent the impressment of their menfolk, and even to fantasize, as does Montagu, about becoming lovers of the "conquering heroes" at the front. Yet while historians' knowledge of the parameters of eighteenth-century (and especially lower-class) women's participation in war has been expanding, the impact of war on women's own identities remains under-researched and under-theorized. Warfare clearly depended upon the fiscal-military state's ability to co-opt female labor and succor in a variety of acknowledged and unacknowledged forms, and stimulated a consciousness and activism that enabled women to shape and perform their national and gender identities in innovative and imaginative ways. Yet war also, as I shall suggest here, underlined the subordinate place of women in social life and the national imaginary, and the double consciousness that eighteenth-century women had to take on, as "women" and as national subjects.

Figure 9 Peace Introducing America and Britannia (1775). Courtesy of the Henry E. Huntington Library.

If eighteenth-century war was the crucible of the "modern nation," then it was equally an experience that made painfully visible the hierarchies and privileges ordering the various members of the "imagined community." As a result, the romance of nation emplotted by war and conquest – that of "self-sacrificing love," as Benedict Anderson would have it – produced multiple readings of nationality and gender that fit uneasily with dominant constructions.[10] Indeed, war was as likely to produce a sense of dispossession and lawlessness as of community and solidarity for many living within its purview. At the same time, women's struggles to place themselves in its narratives demonstrate how the acquisition of "national identity" was an episodic and necessarily incomplete process, for, as with all identity, its promise of a unity, a full and final recognition, could not be achieved. Identification, that "structuring presence of alterity in the very formulation of the 'I'," as Judith Butler has written, "must be constantly marshaled, consolidated, retrenched, contested, and, on occasion, forced to give way"; it is not an event but a "phantasmatic staging of the event," an event that takes place in the imaginary.[11] While certainly there is no easy relationship that exists between the psycho-dynamics of the individual and that of political life, their intricate mediations are played out within specific historical conditions.[12] And it is their inbetween-ness, rather than similarity or difference, that makes women a problem in the production of national identity.[13] War in the eighteenth century galvanized contests over the right of the nation-state to compel individuals to do its bidding, to serve as the voice of the people, or to express the national will. War produced national subjects, certainly, but it placed them in a range of class, gender and racialized positions within the nation that were discrepantly valued, and that contested the symbolic representations of war as a defense of home and hearth, of Englishness and civilization – a nexus of signification that allows us to take neither identity nor experience for granted.[14] The experience of being a "woman," in other words, in the everyday life of eighteenth-century British society thus shaped, and was shaped by, the experience of being a Briton at war.

This chapter will suggest some ways to approach the analysis of the grounds of female identification and contestation with the imperial, fiscal-military state of eighteenth-century Britain, looking at examples from the period between the defeat of the Jacobite rebellion of 1745 and the end of the American war in 1783. We will turn, first, to women's empirical and imaginative participation in war in England and America, drawing upon diaries, letters, memoirs, newspaper reports, magazines and army regimental lists. Then we will examine the representations by and of three particular women: Elizabeth Robinson Montagu, avid commentator on the Seven Years War (which she admired for its similarities, in her mind, to Cortés's conquest of Mexico); Elizabeth Brown Wheeler of Bedfordshire, Quaker and uneasy critic of the American war; and Lady Harriet Acland of Hampshire, wife and companion to Major John Acland, whom she accompanied on his regimental march in America, joining him in captivity after he was captured by enemy troops at the Battle of Saratoga (1777). Their divergent adventures suggest how eighteenth-century British women's engagement with the romance of war and empire generated possibilities for both complicity with and resistance to the nation-state's injunction to militarism. Equally important, their involvement created conditions that construed the terms and iconography of national belonging, circulating competing notions of nation, liberty and political identity.

Warrior Women

Although the nature of the relationship between the army and civil society was changing over the course of the eighteenth century, one thing is clear: women accompanied the British army in substantial numbers during the Seven Years and American wars. Linda Colley's compelling argument that the French and Napoleonic wars forced women to come to terms, for the first time, "with the demands and meanings of Britishness" ignores English women's long historical involvement with war organization and relief activities and activism on the front.[15] For example, women "on the strength," or officially allowed by the army, were determined by the commanding officers, who strove to limit their number to between three and six women per company; but these proportions were greatly exceeded by the greater numbers of women accompanying the army "off the strength" – in unpaid but still critically important and extensively exploited capacities. During the former war, the numbers of women exceeded one-quarter of total personnel in several places, while in the latter five thousand women and twelve thousand children accompanied an army of 47,640 combatants.[16] The sheer number of women in the army was a constant source of aggravation for army authorities (and ridicule by French and American opponents), and aggressive steps were taken to limit their number during the American war, although apparently to little effect.[17] General Burgoyne's defeat was widely attributed to the great numbers of women – allegedly numbering two thousand – attached to his 4,700 soldiers, whom General Gates then had to provision after the surrender at Saratoga. At the parliamentary inquiry into the expedition in London two years later, Burgoyne did not bother denying the charge outright; rather he dryly noted that although he could not attest to "their beauty or their numbers," he would have been "very sorry to have had two thousand women" experiencing army victuals. Burgoyne's libertinism, well known back in England, was far from amusing to his officers and their wives, who decried his nightly cavorting with his mistress, the wife of a commissary, throughout the north country battles. Burgoyne placed the blame for defeat squarely on General William Howe, whose promised detachment never arrived. Significantly, Howe also had a reputation as a ladies' man, who persisted in putting gallantry and the pursuit of pleasure above military duty on the front. As one of his lieutenants recalled, "Nothing seemed to engross his attention but the faro table, the play house, the dancing assembly, and Mrs. Loring" – wife of the commissary of prisoners and Howe's mistress – who "like Cleopatra, lost Mark Anthony the world."[18] As Hogarth's *March to Finchley* (1746) and Rowlandson's *The English Review* (1786) suggest, amorous women were believed to undermine military discipline, and their disruptive influence was especially resented during the American conflict.

Yet, as in civilian life, women's paid and unpaid labor was crucial to the political economy of early modern armies, supplying the necessary services that kept the troops fed, clothed, nursed and in residence.[19] Soldiers' wives and servants made up the majority of the numbers who were denigrated as "camp followers" by authorities, but who nevertheless labored as nurses, tailors, laundresses, cooks and couriers in return for their rations. In addition women performed unpaid services as sexual partners to the men, bore and looked after children, and moved the camps from one location to another. Trudging along, laden with bushel baskets and children, and bent double with the weight of the loads of pots, kettle and furniture on their backs, they made an arresting sight (Fig. 10). Women also joined the military operation at the front as professional sutlers, medics and clerks, as well as wagoners, laborers and prostitutes. But the majority were soldiers' wives, some acquired in the course of military service, who performed what can only be described as heroic levels of spousal duty for their country's good. The comparatively low number of such female caregivers on the American side in the Revolutionary war was evinced in the tattered and unkempt appearance of the troops, since the men refused to undertake "housekeeping" chores for themselves.

Women also experienced the dubious pleasures of military conveyance by sea, on board royal navy and merchant marine ships. Despite the long standing superstition among seamen that women were bad luck on a voyage, their presence was connived at and unofficially sanctioned. They were thus able to experience the disease, overcrowding, limited fresh water (which precluded the possibilities of bathing or washing clothes), rotten food, drunken crews, rough seas and recurrent threat of capture by hostile vessels that were standard features of shipboard life.[20] The voyage east may have been especially fraught with peril, as Eliza Fay's experience suggested. On her first passage to India, where her new husband was to take up a post as advocate at the Supreme Court of Calcutta, dangerous surfs, marauding pirates and shipboard fevers were but a prelude to the fifteen-week imprisonment of her party by the Haidar Ali at Calicut.[21] Despite such travails, India continued to be an important outpost in the transnational English marriage market. East India merchantmen carried increasing numbers of married, betrothed or marriageable women to the male servants of the company on the subcontinent, much to the alarm and disgust of observers back home.[22] A print that lampooned this practice, James Gilray's A Sale of English Beauties in the East Indies (1786) (Fig. 11), depicts such "exported" women as commodities, to be weighed, poked and assessed by mercenary English East India officers and lascivious Indian nabobs alike. As a foppish auctioneer attempts to procure the highest price for his "goods," a warehouse in the background, "For Unsaleable Goods from Europe, to be returned by the Next Ship," shows the unhappy fate of the ladies who failed to meet expectations. But the voyages west to the American colonies and West Indies could also be harrowing, with pirates and privateers lying in wait to surprise English vessels. On the warships, in addition to bearing up under the twin threats of shipwreck and capture, sailors' wives worked in the same variety of unglamorous employments as those on the march and were liable to similar hazards and sicknesses. Meanwhile,

Figure 10 Thomas Rowlandson, *Soldiers on the March* (1808). Courtesy of the British Museum, Department of Prints and Drawings.

Figure 11 James Gilray, *A Sale of English Beauties in the East Indies* (1786). Courtesy of the British Museum, Department of Prints and Drawings.

those women who stayed on shore, in the maritime communities, victualled, sewed, kept lodgers, lent money and ran the pawnshops essential to the daily lives and provisioning of sailors. It was not for nothing that the "Women and Children of Sea Officers" considered themselves to be, as their petition to the House of Commons put it, "always ready and willing to hazard their lives in the Service of their King and Country," or that they demanded reciprocal rights and rewards from the state.[23]

No matter their provenance, women, like soldiers and sailors, were bound by the harsh conditions and discipline of military life. The diary of Charlotte Browne provides a vivid picture. This formidable lady, a widow, came to America as a matron of the British army hospital organized for General Edward Braddock's campaign against the French and Indians on the frontier of the British colonies, the Ohio River Valley, immediately preceding the formal outbreak of the Seven Years War in 1754–6. By the time Braddock left for America, virtually all British army nurses were female, and the practice of assembling nursing staffs in England, and sailing with them to the fronts was well established.[24] Many had relatives in the service. Browne's husband had probably been a soldier or army medic, as was her brother, who accompanied her, along with their two servants, on the first part of her journey. Browne's maid soon married a soldier in the regiment and left service to tend to him at the camp near Fort Cumberland. Browne nevertheless stalwartly continued on the march, where she endured insect-infested beds, drenched camps, treacherous roads, her brother's death and the news of her daughter's passing in England, while also attempting to minister to wounded British and colonial American soldiers and their bereft partners. "My Lodgings not being very clean I had so many close Companions call'd Ticks that depriv'd me on my Nights Rest . . . we halted this Day, all the Nurses Baking Bread and Boiling Beef for the March to Morrow," she wrote in June, 1755 (180). Following the news of Braddock's defeat later that year, Browne recorded that "it is not possible to describe the Distraction of the poor Women for their Husbands" (184). She also had to fend off the unwanted advances of a senior officer, for it was crucially important for respectable women to keep up not only the fact but the appearance of propriety. "Went to the Fort [at Albany] to deliver a Letter from Dr. Bard at New York to Col'n Marshall [commander of the fort] and was receiv'd with great politeness but the Dutch had a very bad opinion of me saying I could not be good to come so far without a Husband," she recalled (194). In fact, Browne's ready acceptance by the ladies of the towns of Philadelphia and Frederickstown owed a great deal to her sterling reputation for good sense and strict chastity.

Browne's journal records her observations on the ethnic and religious diversity of the frontier, testifying to the considerable efforts of will and imagination required to make sense of an exotic colonial world. "An Express is arriv'd from Lancaster with an Account that the Indians are scalping all before them" (190), she wrote; some days previously, she had noted that she had "Rec'd the Comp't of all the English Ladies in [Frederickstown, Maryland] . . . I had an Invitation to go to a Ball which was compos'd of Romans, Jews, and Hereticks who in this Town flock together. The Ladys danced without Stays or Hoops and it ended with a Jig from each Lady" (187). Her entries clearly conveyed her own feelings of exile amid the harshness of day-to-day life for an army matron; for example, her observance while on the march of the anniversary of her husband's death two years before reminded her that ever since his passing, "my Life has been once continual Scene of Anxiety and Care" (176). Yet although her experience in America produced a profound sense of unbelonging, she felt equally uneasy back in civilian life.[25]

Clearly for many women, army service became as much a duty for them as it was for their husbands: the camp wife, as much as the "female warrior," was a ubiquitous fixture of the British army in fact and fiction. As Martha May put it in a petition to Colonel Bousquest in June 1758, "I have been a Wife 22 Years and have Traveld with my Husband ever Place or Country the Company Marcht to."[26] During the Seven Years War, the majority of women who accompanied their husbands to America were, like them, drawn from the lower orders, coming primarily from agricultural and craft occupations in England, Scotland, Ireland and the German states, and had to adapt to both the direct class control of the British elite and the transculturated "wilderness" of the British frontier.[27] Yet some still chose to demonstrate their patriotism by joining the ranks in combatant roles on land and sea, occasionally cross-dressed as men. Whether one accepts or not the claims that "tens of thousands" of women served as combatants in the American Revolutionary War, it became clear in that conflict, as in the French and Indian war that preceded it, that women could fight. Hannah Snell is only the most famous of the woman warriors who fought Britain's enemies in India, Africa and America. Others, who did not leave literary testaments behind, turn up in army regimental lists and order books, usually to the considerable surprise of their commanding officers. A typical example was Christian Walsh, "who notwithstanding her being a Woman serv'd many years very faithfully in the late Wars in Flanders in the habit of a Man and received sevl Dangerous wounds" received an outpension from Chelsea Hospital in 1720.[28] Most "warrior women" played their roles in battle openly, as women and adjuncts to the fighting force. Jenny Cameron of Glendessary, Scotland, raised three hundred men for the Young Pretender and led them to the raising of the standard at Glenfinnanon on 19 August 1745. Mary Ludwig Hays, or "Molly Pitcher," as she became known, carried buckets of water to the soldiers and manned an artillery piece for the Americans in the Battle of Monmouth (1778). Molly Stark organized hospitals, cared for the sick and carted ammunition for her husband John, commander of the First New Hampshire Regiment of 1775. The intrepid Mrs. Stone, wife of a British sergeant in a marching regiment sent to America during the Seven Years War, refused to leave her husband's side through nine engagements, occupying herself with carrying the wounded off the battlefield, fetching powder cartridges and rallying the courage of the men around her.[29] Other women served as spies, scouts and couriers. The British were adept at using women provisioners for espionage: one of their most effective agents was a sutler who followed the Americans during the Revolutionary war and relayed valuable information about the location, movement and condition of the infantry troops of

General Gates, Colonel Morgan, and Lafayette.[30] And of course there were also the "ladies" – wives of senior and sometimes junior officers, who joined their husbands in camp in order to distribute domestic cheer, anchor social life, and give aid and comfort to the men. In contrast to their social inferiors, elite women were privy to official strategy, plans and gossip, had passes and protections issued them and their servants for traveling, and were generally well treated, with officers on each side courteously returning each other's captured wives. The eighteenth-century military, which modeled its hierarchy on an idealized vision of patrician–plebeian society, did not always see itself as necessarily antithetical to domestic concerns, and indeed signified its entitlements and justified its extraordinary demands on individuals of both sexes and all classes and races through images of idealized family life, through which the fiscal-military state could be made to stand for the nation. In the American war in particular, this imagery was used to contrast "natural" political and class hierarchies with debased colonial ones through the images of "unnatural mothers," patricidal daughters and rebellious sons (Fig. 12).[31]

Although noncombatants usually waited in camp during battle, thousands of women were nonetheless taken captive or killed over the course of these two wars. Significantly, these women seldom appeared on casualty lists, and must be tracked through incidental reports in newspapers and diaries.[32] Such official inattention to the loss and death of female noncombatants speaks volumes about their status and place in army policy and vision. For example, law provided medical care to every soldier, but soldiers' families were not so protected, and regimental surgeons treated them only at their own pleasure. As a consequence, many were left to suffer or die on their own.[33] Indeed, despite their sacrifices, British officials rarely acknowledged their debt to these women, preferring instead to regard them as unnecessary drains on the Crown's finances. Predictably, in a period in England when excessive feminine influences in the polity were perceived to be damaging the nation's martial resolve, women's presence in the camp and on the march was attacked for disrupting the cut and thrust of homosocial bonding and male solidarity necessary for a strong fighting force. Those off the strength were widely regarded by officers as being little more than tramps and prostitutes, lazy, defiant and totally undermining of good discipline. The belief that they debauched the troops and spread disease led some commanding officers, some hundred years before the Contagious Diseases Acts, to order the army surgeons to examine vaginally all soldiers' wives to make sure they were "clean."[34] The women who followed the army were thus treated as conduits of infection and disorder. It is not surprising that officers described them as "odd and disgusting." As one officer put it, the women following the troops "were the ugliest in the world to be collected," exhibiting "deformity of Aspect and Shape" and "low and Scandalous examples" of life: "furies who inhabit the infernal Regions can never be painted half so hideous as these women," he asserted, contrasting them with "those of the Sex who possess the delicacy that is naturally great in them."[35]

Certainly, ordinary soldiers came in for their share of class-conscious abuse from their commanding officers, who derided their underlings' lack of skill, education

and discipline. The troops' alleged tendency to "degenerate" from European cultural standards in the comparatively uncivilized society of the American frontier meant officers had to be especially vigilant against their men's attempts to desert or "go native."[36] Nevertheless, warfare had the potential, at least, to transform ordinary soldiers into patriots and heroes, and to allow them to be lauded as defenders of the nation: men who "sacrific[ed] their domestick and social Enjoyments, their very Lives, in her [their country's] Defense," as one propagandist put it. Warfare turned the same class of women, conversely, into low, immoral and vicious creatures, vulgar examples of female degeneracy in its most extreme state, as contemporary satires and satiric prints also confirmed. In this way as in others, war heightened gender and class difference even as its labors simultaneously blurred their boundaries.[37]

The contradictions that bedeviled women's position within the military, then, where their presence was both necessary and derided, also highlights the double standard that resulted from eighteenth-century constructions of the role of gender difference in political and national life. While giving one's life for one's country was held to be the ultimate political obligation that legitimized men's political and legal prerogatives, women who equally fulfilled this duty were marginalized as "out of place," needless and heedless casualties of the sanctified goal of militarism in the service of national aggrandizement.

Military Madness

On the home front, women took equally significant roles in supporting or contesting the fiscal-military state and its war efforts abroad. War extended women's usual roles in social, familial and economic life, but also generated additional pressures on food supplies, labor and political liberties that impinged upon military mobilization. "Militarization" may well "automatically entail a resurgence of the authority of the father," as Frantz Fanon asserted, but it also forced other members of the family to perform an unwelcome paternal role as head of household, which made them in turn both dangerous and vulnerable.[38] Women alone were seen as easy targets by libertines and government officials alike. Recruiting officers, for example, mythically set their sights on the seduction of women whose husbands were away in the service; but probably more frequently attempted to press women into the cause of enlisting their men. On both counts, their efforts had uneven results. Sometimes, indeed, a disgruntled woman would turn over a lover who had scorned her, but more often women would engage in elaborate subterfuges to get the recruiters off their men's trails, or even stage rescue efforts to retrieve their men from the gangs and the tender.[39] Women who lost their spouse by design or

Figure 12 (facing) *The Battle of Bunker's Hill, or the Blessed Effects of Family Quarrels* (1775). Courtesy of the British Museum, Department of Prints and Drawings.

impressment to the military service had to take on men's work in the effort to keep their families afloat; not surprisingly, they can be found taking part in many of the riots that attended mobilization during the Seven Years and American wars.[40] Their experience of violence at the hands of the press and crimping gangs and the local militia calls into serious question recent arguments about the remoteness of eighteenth-century wars to the majority of the population.[41] Women were prominently involved in the impressment riots of 1757–8, 1761 and 1776–8, sometimes with fatal results. In the Hexham anti-militia riots a heavily pregnant women who was shot and killed by Yorkshire militiamen – "the ball found in the child's belly" as Captain John Dawson of the Northumberland militia soberly noted – could be said to have given two lives for choosing her family over her empire.[42] Lower-class women faced brutal choices in times of war, and like their men were victims as well as instruments of state violence, which they wrestled with as valiantly as their counterparts in the service.

Middle- and upper-class women had rather different experiences of war. Many devoted themselves to domestic chores in service of the national effort, making clothes for the troops and contributing to patriotic societies; many also took up their pens to spread news and opinions about military actions through extensive national and regional correspondence networks. "A pacquet which arrived yesterday from Calais brings an account that thirty transports were there, and several pieces of cannon and mortars just arrived, which looks no very friendly circumstance to this neighborhood," Elizabeth Carter reported to Catherine Talbot from Deal, Kent, in March 1756. She confirmed in July that the soldiers' decampment from Barham Downs produced "great disappointment . . . to several parties formed for visiting the camp, and great wailing among ladies whose hearts are gone beyond the sea."[43] Most middle-class women probably had less direct experience with the war than those either above or below them – unless they were officers' wives – but their imaginative engagement with the trials and tribulations of the military seemed to be no less intense for all that. In the localities, the war effort was felt in the rhythms of everyday life. Mary Hardy, wife of a prosperous farmer in Holt, Norfolk, kept abreast of developments in the American war not only through newspaper-reading, coffee house and tavern gossip and the observance of fast days and victory celebrations, but also through the spectacles of local food and impressment riots, balloting for the militia and the reviews of regimental and volunteer troops which the whole family attended.[44] Most sobering for her seemed to be the report of the sinking of the *Royal George* as the ship lay anchored at Spithead on August 29, 1782, which she copied out in her diary from the *Norfolk Chronicle*. The vessel's frames were so rotten that the bottom simply dropped out – killing most of the 821 crew and the three hundred women and children on board.[45]

Elite women had both direct and indirect interactions with the military during wartime. The social lives of port towns such as Plymouth, Portsmouth, Bristol, Yarmouth and Liverpool as well as London were much enlivened by embarking and disembarking vessels whose officers and men lent glamour and excitement to conventional gatherings at assemblies, theaters and balls. The prettiest and most eligible young ladies, suitably chaperoned, could be invited to dining parties aboard ship.[46] The camp-culture mania that seized upper-class women during the American war, recently described by Gillian Russell, brought these opportunities inland. Coxheath and Warley camps provided extravagant spectacles of a glamorous and benign fiscal-military complex, where silken tents, sparkling uniforms, mock battles and parades kept the nobility, gentry and the ton cavorting. Such fabulous female "volunteers" as Georgiana, Duchess of Devonshire, who organized the officers' wives into donning regimentals and forming "battalions," matched the macaroni officers in élan and esprit. She also patriotically instituted a ladies' mess, "to which no officer was admitted unless he was distinguished by good conduct and strict attention to his duty."[47] The general public's ardor for all things military and especially the spectacle of camp life was solicited, if not sated, by several dramatic productions of 1778, such as A Trip to Coxheath performed at Sadler's Wells, Colman Sr.'s adaptation of Bonduca and his The Female Chevalier (which also played on current fascination with the French transvestite diplomat and swordsman the Chevalier D'Eon) at the Haymarket, and Sheridan's The Camp at Drury Lane. Sheridan's production had a thin but agreeable comic plot involving a foppish officer, a blundering Irishman and a cross-dressed heroine who disguised herself as a recruit in order to remain with her lover, in traditional female warrior fashion. But the most celebrated part of the show was provided by the maestro of the mise-en-scène and the mechanical device, Philippe de Loutherbourg, who had painted a "beautiful perspective view of the Coxheath Camp" before which "by a kind of magic peculiar to himself, he makes the different battalions, composed of small figures, march out in excellent order, into the front of their lines to the astonishment of every spectator." Not surprisingly, Loutherbourg's history-painting of The Troops at Warley Common reviewed by his Majesty, 1778, was exhibited at the Royal Academy in 1780 to much acclaim.[48]

Recruiting, spectacle, painting and theater drew an array of domestic publics into the glamour and heroics of war. However, more typical of the war time experience of middle- and upper-class women was that of Frances Boscawen, wife of Admiral Edward Boscawen. Despite being the spouse, mother and ultimately the widow of navy officers, Boscawen shared many of the same experiences of war as Mary Hardy. Raising their five children largely on her own while also maintaining a busy social life, Boscawen's knowledge of the progress of the war was still acquired through representations of the English media, which she shared with her husband at sea, and the occasional express from abroad, which she shared with the politicians.[49] Edward, made Admiral of the Blue in 1758, led the successful attack on Louisbourg in June 1758, the first British victory of the war, which was greeted with frenzied joy at home. She described the celebrations to her husband in her letters, along with other domestic political developments that she gleaned from friends and newspapers. But she seemed to feel some sense of kindred with the less privileged women who accompanied their husbands to the front: when a company of Hessians passed her estate in Hatchlands in December 1756, their women in tow in a wagon, she sent them bottles of rum and brandy. "They all seemed much pleased, and very thankful, and indeed it was peculiarly proper, for it snowed all the time they passed."[50]

Middle- and upper-class women's intended roles as domestic auxiliaries to the military were carefully laid out in contemporary literature. They were exhorted to become proper "Female Patriots" by giving up imported French luxury goods and novels, and so "become *Nursing Mothers* of the Manufactures of their native Island"; or, as Hannah More would later urge, to "come forward with a patriotism at once firm and feminine for the general good."[51] In addition to refusing effeminizing luxuries themselves, patriotic women had to promote the stoicism and love of country within the home that produced a manly and intrepid fighting service at the front. A broadside of 1746 entitled *The Female Volunteer* (Fig. 13) depicted the actress Peg Woffington (famous for her breeches roles) in the garb of a volunteer, admonishing the "Patriot-Fair" to "exert the sacred Influence of [their] Eyes" and "vindicate the glory of our Isle" by refusing their favors to cowards and deserters; in this way they shall "fire each Hero to his Duty / And *British* Rights be sav'd by *British* beauty." Women, as the bearers of national values, had to provide the examples of domestic virtue that complemented and invoked masculine patriotism. Eliza Haywood's *Female Spectator* also spoke directly to this imbrication of the

Figure 13 *The Female Volunteer* (1746). Courtesy of the Theater Collection, Houghton Library, Harvard University.

military in domestic life by outlining women's role in turning Britain's effeminate soldiers into an intrepid fighting force that would in turn be more worthy of their women's love. Why do women love soldiers? Haywood asks.

> surely not because they wear red Coats? – *that* many others do, who sometimes sit behind a Counter . . . but it is because a Soldier is supposed . . . to have the Courage to defend, in any Exigence, all who are under his Protection; and also because the Character of a brave Man is, of all other, the most esteem'd in the World, as that of a Coward is the most contemn'd.

Haywood's piece, like the broadside above, was written in the aftermath of the infamous battle of Falkirk (1746), when panicked British troops fled from Jacobite Highlanders without firing a single shot.[52] Nevertheless, the point was clear: it was women's duty to bring forth male bravery by putting aside their private feelings, and convincing their lovers that nothing was so much desired as their success in battle. Even Hannah Snell asserted that her call to arms rested largely on the need to rouse her country's men from the "Effeminacy and Debauchery [that] have taken Place of the Love of Glory, and that noble Ardor after warlike Exploits."[53] Women, their bodies and minds, must serve as the visible markers of national homogeneity, and selfless femininity had to be put to work in the service of masculine vigilance. Female agency here is a *designated* agency, in Anne McClintock's phrase, one that finds legitimation in relationship to men; women's status as auxiliary national subjects depended upon their skills in promoting masculine patriotism. As Lord Kames explained in his survey of female progress, "The master of a family is immediately connected with his country: his wife, his children, his servants, are immediately connected with him and with their country only through him. Women accordingly have less patriotism than men; and less bitterness against the enemies of their country."[54] Even so hallowed a feminine icon as Boadicea could be used to stress this point. During a particularly dangerous juncture of the American war, when France joined forces with the American rebels and the Earl of Chatham's death crystallized fears of an imperiled martial spirit, Colman Senior staged his adaptation of *Bonduca* (1778). It portrayed the Icenian queen to be as stern a bulwark of bellicose patriotism for her troops as her daughters were its solvent, when they allowed their romantic feelings to undermine the resolve and stoic virtue at the heart of love of country. Fortunately, Garrick's prologue neatly routed Boadicea's ancient British fire to the present through manly historical figures such as Edward I, Henry V, Marlborough and Chatham.[55] If male virtue lay in the willingness to sacrifice all in the service of the country, then female virtue rested on the willingness to sacrifice everything in the service of their men. Just as the impact of Britain's wars on the domestic English, Scottish and Irish populations was highly variable, so gender worked at various levels to legitimate the division of risks, benefits, duties and privileges among those who left and those left behind. At the very least, such directives indicate the degree to which "*all* members of the national collectivity are incorporated, at least symbolically, into the military," though the benefits that resulted were unevenly distributed.[56]

Desire and the History of Nations

Elizabeth Montagu provides a good example of a woman who was conflicted by the dual injunctions to feminine virtue and patriotism. Indeed, her desire to be both conqueror and conquered, expressed in the quotation with which the chapter began, has to be read in the context of the uneasy match made between the dominant discourses of patriotism and liberty and her own experience and sensibility. As is well known, Montagu was at the center of a literary and social circle that would later be called the "bluestockings," in constant contact with the leading intellectual and political figures of the day. Her female correspondents included such luminaries as her sister, novelist Sarah Scott, Elizabeth Carter, Catherine Talbot and Frances Boscawen. Eighteenth-century letter-writing has recently received a great deal of attention from scholars. Letters were a form of performance that "staged" the self and its relation to the world; evincing the reach of female networks, they also allowed women to engage in discussion and debate on the entire gamut of domestic, political and worldly topics.[57] Some of the blue-stockings' letters were clearly meant to be read by a wide audience; others were obviously more personal, but all served a social purpose that both mimicked and supplemented the reportage of print culture. During the Seven Years War, Montagu and her correspondents circulated news and intelligence sometimes even in advance of the "prints," and exchanged views on the political affairs publicized in newspapers and pamphlets. Writing to Frances Boscawen on the occasion of Byng's court martial, Montagu interrupted her narrative to report "Mr Montagu has just come from the Coffee house" and then relayed the latest developments. She also urged Boscawen to have the "courage of an Englishwoman" in coping with her husband's prolonged "quest of glorious danger."[58] But if affairs of war and state loomed large in Montagu's letters of the 1750s, so too did remarks on the inequities and indignities that bedeviled women's place in the nation. Hence Montagu's ardent identification with issues of war and conquest must be located in the complex nexus of personal experience, intellectual orientation and frustrated desire.

Montagu had acquired early on a sense of the constrictions placed on her gender, compared to that of her brothers, and openly envied their greater educational opportunities and freedom of movement.[59] This was especially so as she grew up, and her small dowry made marriage seem unlikely. "Is it not a Sad thing to be brought up in the Patriot din of Liberty and property and to be allow'd neither?" she remarked to her father in 1740. Although she satirized the venality of courtship and marriage, Montagu found little humor in the experience of her own "bargain and sale" to the aging bachelor Edward Montagu, a grandson of the Earl of Sandwich. Their only child's tragic death a year after their marriage brought an end to the couple's physical relations and an increasing distance in their emotional ones. Montagu particularly chafed at the "lordly power" assumed by men over their wives. After her husband attempted first to block and then shorten a planned visit to Frances Boscawen at Hatchlands, Montagu denounced his attempted exertion of "prerogative" in a letter to her sister, Sarah Scott: "Do not you admire these lovers of liberty! What do the generality of men mean by a love of liberty, but the liberty to be saucy to their superiors, and arrogant to their inferiors, to resist the power of others over them, and to exert their power over others. I am not sure that Cato did not kick his wife."[60]

Montagu's reference to Cato, classical paragon of patriotism, was also important, for it points to her and her friends' predilection for studying the history of nations. By the mid eighteenth century, history had emerged as a primary vehicle of national self-understanding and identity as well as philosophical reflection, meant to promote both a cosmopolitan interpretive perspective and a deeply grounded sense of national specificity. As Karen O'Brien has recently argued, historical *writing* was meant to serve as "an arena in which both historian and reader exercise political, emotional and aesthetic choices," and which made evident "the interplay of likeness and difference within the family of Christian churches and nations."[61] A mode of inquiry believed to display and contribute to the advanced condition of the age, history was meant to be both didactic and rhetorical, engaging the reader's imagination and reason in the spectacle of the past and its lessons while also bestowing narrative unity on dissimilar phenomena. By allowing the mind to associate contiguous events and ideas, History thus facilitated "the Passage of the Thought or Imagination from one to another, facilitat[ing] also the transfusion of the Passions, and preserv[ing] the Affection still in the same Channel and Direction," as Hume remarked.[62] Interestingly, *reading* history had become by mid-century not only a favorite pastime of educated women, but also the prescribed corrective to frivolous ones, who could thereby improve their understanding and reform their hearts.[63] Hume himself urged that there was nothing he "would recommend more earnestly to his female readers than the study of *History*." If his directive had a satirical edge, women nonetheless heeded the call in spirit if not always in substance, becoming avid attenders of historical drama, rapt students of anthropological treatises and travelogues (the "natural histories of man"), eager purchasers of prints with historical subject matter, and critics of the androcentric bias of conventional history. Hume's *History of England* itself had a wide female audience, who seemed to appreciate his somewhat severe if fair-handed assessments of the female historical actors. George Ballard's *Memoirs of Several Ladies of Great Britain* (1752), which celebrated the cerebral accomplishments of the bluestockings' female forebears, Valentine Green's *Queens of England* (1779), which identified many examples of feminine heroism in the national past, and William Alexander's *History of Women, from the Earliest Antiquity to the Present Time* (1778), which assured the fair sex of the superior treatment always afforded British women compared to others in history, were thus clearly responding to, as well as extending, a substantial female audience.[64] Their narratives, and others like them, displayed the extraordinary circumstances faced by heroic women of the ages, who, as Green put it, "in the hour of impending ruin, in scenes of personal danger and calamity, and in the most awful moment, . . . have been seen rising superior to misfortune, and encountering even death itself without dismay."[65] Hence William Woollett's engraving of Benjamin West's painting of *The Battle of La Hogue* (1781), which commemorated England's defeat of Louis XIV's plans to invade England with a depiction of English sailors saving women from a sinking French warship, proved to be very popular with the ladies for its female as well as male patriotic élan (Fig. 14).

Montagu confirmed history's role for her in sharpening both her reason and her imagination. In her words, reading history familiarized her with people "whom superior parts and noble ambition led from the silent path of life, to its busiest & most turbulent scenes; if I can get some of their experience without any of their dangers, and a little of their knowledge without any of their passions, I may keep my tranquillity without falling into that stupidity and insensibility which I think still more unworthy of the human mind than vain sollicitude, and idle perturbation."[66] She accordingly used ancient and modern history as a way to acquire "experience" with the world, providing her the opportunity to engage in speculative statecraft, to discern the causes behind the rise and fall of nations, to examine the duties and rights of citizenship, and to work out the appropriate place for women in the polity. In the letters exchanged between her and her friends, the war takes on a prismatic historical character, refracting episodes, events and personalities of the present onto competing distant times and places, and bringing contingent and dissimilar events into the same narrative frame. Time and agency are dispersed and non-linear in these readings, rendering disjunctive pasts homologous and contiguous. Montagu's sister-in-law, Lady Jemima Montagu Meadows, offered these reflections on the coming conflict in a letter to her of November 1755: "What passes in north America at this time puts one in mind of the first part of our history when the Romans came here, a great number of petty Kings, barbarity to enemys, Idolatry, a people untamed, and in a great many respects uncorrupted, and enjoying the health, and vigour of a natural way of living . . . I have a particular respect for Monacachuta the Indian general, and am out of patience with Braddock."[67]

Montagu and her friends, then, inserted themselves into their reading of history, comparing their own lot with those who had preceded them, imagining themselves as great rulers and their mistresses, and emplotting themselves in the tragedies and comedies of the past. By positioning them within national narratives while allowing full scope for agency and judgment, if only on an imaginary level, history became a place where the much-vaunted "liberty" of an English woman was less constrained by the notions of gender difference that structured the fiscal-military state and its ideas of political subjectivity. At the same time, history was used to ruminate on the fate of empires and their relation to the luxury, degeneracy or civility of a nation. Was empire a beneficial system of exchange and emulation, as William Robertson suggested, a place of exploitation and rapaciousness, as James Burgh, John Brown and Elizabeth Carter contended, or a conduit of effeminacy and corruption, as theologists and civic humanists warned?

112

Figure 14 William Woollett after Benjamin West, *Battle of La Hogue* (1781). Courtesy of the British Museum, Department of Prints and Drawings.

These considerations illuminate the significance of Montagu's reflections on Cortés and the Seven Years War. In Solís's work, Montagu found a more recent historical model through which to interpret Britain's conflict. Indeed, in a war in which the feasibility and defense of Britain's empire, the nature of the national character and the fungibility of the national identity were believed to be at stake, Montagu was anxious about its violence and its possible outcomes. "Wars abroad, faction at home, so much ambition among the great, such discontents among the people! ah! poor England," she wrote to Frances Boscawen in late 1756. She became particularly concerned about the furore surrounding the loss of Minorca, which sparked demonstrations across the country and was painted in the national press as a humiliating defeat that underscored the emasculation and degeneracy of the British body politic. Hence despite her friends' and her own growing anti-war sentiments, Montagu found herself being seduced by the romance of war and conquest that the Cortés epic presented. In her imaginings, we can see the ways in which desire became positioned "at the heart of the rationalist discourse of history," as Gyan Prakash has pointed out in another context, underlining the fissures of identity and alterity produced by colonial projects themselves.[68]

Writing to George Lyttelton, a historian and poet as well as a politician, who had recommended Solís's history to her and acted as both mentor and intellectual suitor (and perhaps more),[69] Montagu was eager to impress him with her intellectual acumen. Solís, she averred, "by the simplicity of his narrations, the dignity of his speeches, and the good sense of his reflections," put himself "in the rank of Thucydides and Tacitus." Although she thought him blind to "the great concerns of religion" – by which she means the Spaniards' wholesale extirpation of indigenous religious life – she also agreed with Solís that "there was some supernatural assistance given to the Spaniards in this enterprise." The British view of North American indigenes as culturally static and temporally backward if occasionally noble is fancifully reflected in her musing to Lyttelton that Admiral Boscawen's message "from the Indian savages, . . . expressed in hieroglyphics . . . will give him an idea of the expresses sent by the Mexicans and Montezuma."[70] But her remarks then draw attention to her own status as a woman with romantic impulses and sexual desires that were not unrelated to domination and submission. "The character of Cortés is not among the ordinary productions of nature, but composed of those various and contrary qualities, that are requisite to bring about great events," she wrote; "I cannot help thinking the Belle Marine the happiest woman that ever existed; she seems to have matched herself with a superior species; and I figure to myself how her heart must exult, when she saw her consort (for I suppose she looked on her connection with Cortés as a marriage) leading captive that monarch [Montezuma],whom none of her fellow subjects dared look in the face."[71]

Even if we acknowledge the correspondents' propensity for hyperbole, the intellectual and personal identifications expressed in this statement are remarkable and complicated, functioning simultaneously as both personal and political allegory. First, Cortés, "my Spanish hero," as Montagu called him, was considered to be so removed from ordinary mortals that he seemed a higher "species" of human;

his sexual difference (from women) was exceeded by his racialized difference (from men), where his courage, resolution and apparently supernatural backing rivaled History's other great conquerors, such as Alexander the Great (perhaps as Montagu's own difference from other women, which Lyttelton always stressed, put her in the pantheon of History's female worthies).[72] At the same time, Montezuma, the vanquished prince, may stand in for both her husband, Edward Montagu, as well as for Britain's indigenous foes in the New World; in both cases the defeated are forced to become spectators to the victor's conquest of land and women. Moreover, just as Montagu's enjoyment of the spectacle of conquest reflects current pressures on Britain to conquer anew the New World, it also allows her to place herself in the role of conqueror, a role which only History, as imagination, can allow her. By the 1750s, triumphal military and naval figures had seized the British imagination in ways that rivaled and may have exceeded kings and queens.[73] Yet the national celebration of aggressive, conquering masculinity – in a decade when the manliness and resolve of the national character was believed to be in question – was not without its darker and overcompensatory side. Indeed, conquests of both the territorial and sexual varieties were believed to be ambiguous in their results, the first allowing luxury, effeminacy and dishonor to contaminate the body politic, as civic humanists warned, and the second blurring the boundaries between domination and submission (as when the male climax becomes the female triumph, leaving him "spent" and her invigorated), as early modern models of heterosexuality suggested. These ambiguities play themselves out in Montagu's letter, where the conquest of the New World becomes conflated with the conquest of the native woman, an act which displaces the anxiety generated by conquest by making it part of the "natural" gender order. Hence the conflation of sexual and political conquest is made useful at a time when British aggression had to masquerade as defense.[74]

Montagu's envy of Malinche expresses similarly intricate identifications and refusals. Malinche was the mediator between colonizers and colonized in this epic of European conquest, an Aztec embodiment of that transculture of the New World achieved at the cost of considerable violence and bloodshed. Further, Malinche was made to stand in for the young virgin land, poised to be invaded and vanquished, that prints of the New World expressed since Jan van deer Staat's *Vespucci Discovering America* (c. 1600), and that more recently were realized in some of the anti-French, pro-expansionist prints of the 1750s.[75] Political and sexual conquest are again twinned, as Montagu imagines that it is the conquest and domination of the indigenous prince that most sparks the Belle Marine's ardor. Yet Malinche is restricted neither by the European sanctities of marriage, nor by love of country, but can align herself with freedom, so Montagu imagines, to the man she most desires. Hence, as befitting her uneasy place in the gender and class hierarchies of her own society, Montagu identifies with both subjects – the (masculine) colonizer to whom history ascribes agency, and the (feminine) colonized who possesses the agency of alterity, both sexually and politically an auxiliary to her lover, but a radical rearticulation of woman's liberty to Montagu. The "Spanish hero" and his lover become the screens on which she projects her own fantasies of alterity and subjectivity, of becoming a different sort of national subject and woman. Through the fantasy that cannot be fulfilled, Montagu fuels the economy of desire created by the structures of national identity and its failures.[76]

Quaker Nation

If we turn to the diary of the Bedfordshire Quaker Elizabeth Brown Wheeler (1754–93), we see a very different, though not unrelated, set of issues arising around the question of national identity, and an equally reconstitutive notion of "nation" at work that shaped her own consciousness. Wheeler begins her diary in December 1778, when she was single and living with her brother's family, and ends it in July 1791, ten years after her marriage to woolstapler Joshua Wheeler and the beginning of the unexpected illness that would hasten her death. The diary shares many features with other Quaker journals of the period, its primary purpose being to monitor the writer's interior and spiritual life, make sure one's outer deportment is brought into line with one's spiritual values, and so offer a testament to the progress of the Inner Light that could serve as a model for other seekers. Equally important for our purposes, Wheeler's diary also provides a strikingly original account of the great national affair of the day, the American war.[77] Her lively engagement with the world around her was aided by her propensity to insert herself into the weft of more than one collective narrative.

Wheeler, the daughter of William Brown, a prosperous draper in the market town of Ampthill, was a descendant of one of the earliest Quaker families in Bedfordshire, long an important center for Friends in England.[78] Wheeler's life before marriage was filled with a variety of industrious and philanthropic activities that were typical for many female Friends: keeping shop for her brother, who owned a dry goods store,[79] preparing cotton and linen for sale, and visiting the sick and the poor. "Nothing can induce so much to a desire of administering to the necessities of the poor as to visit them in their Cottages, and to behold their many wants . . . which will beget a desire to assist those who in the course of divine providence are placed out of the reach of many of the comforts if not the necessaries of Life," she wrote on July 9, 1779. Wheeler also attended weekly and quarterly women's Meetings and numerous social gatherings of Friends, while pursuing her nightly study of ancient and sacred history, spiritual issues and current events. Time was "profitably" spent when it furthered her reflections on the meaning of life, or gave her new insight into the providential plan: as she put it, "unremitting industry [w]as the only means of preservation from the many entanglements that tend to retard our progress heavenward" (March 23, 1779). Indeed, bound by the Inner Law and leavened by the Inner Light, English Quakers in the last quarter of the eighteenth century continued to maintain a way of life that marked them off from their neighbors.[80]

Wheeler's diary reveals a sturdy independence of thought and judgment. She made up her own mind on the theological and political disputes of the day and was skeptical of the different sources of national authority, from the monarch and the military to the Church. She scorned the artifice of "politeness" as a "vain custom," disapproved of "superfluity" in fashion and consumption and spurned such "licentious" activities as magazine-reading and theater, which she felt "tend so much to corrupt the morals of the people" (December 31, 1778; February 27, 1779; April 16, 1779). She clearly felt more connected to her religious kindred in distant parts of the country than to nonbelievers close by. When she traveled she attended meetings in Huntingdonshire, Oxfordshire, Cambridgeshire, Buckinghamshire and Northamptonshire; when sea air was prescribed for her illness in 1783, Wheeler journeyed to the Kentish coast, staying at Friends' houses and inns and attending Meetings. Not surprisingly, perhaps, given Friends' assiduously maintained national and international networks, Wheeler felt the sufferings of the American Quakers with a special intensity, even receiving some Friends from New Jersey and Massachusetts at her home.[81] Hence, while she is against war in general for religious reasons, Wheeler is particularly critical of the American colonists for their persecution of Quakers who refused to contribute to the war effort. Competing notions of "nation" are in clear evidence here: to whose nation does she belong? The "national" identity was bound to fail or succeed for Wheeler only in part, because her self-identification as a Quaker was primary.

Wheeler read widely in secular as well as religious literature, from the *Northampton Mercury* to Purver's *Bible*.[82] These interests melded for her in ancient history. She scoured "old histories" as she called them in part for proof of the "ideas of an hereafter" held by such "great warriours" as the king Darius and his son, Alexander the Great, concluding that their spiritual notions, if any, were "very dark" (December 29, 1778). But the rise and fall of empires and the role of family rivalries in their demise also resonated with England's current crisis, which was substantiated for the English public through images of familial bonds and betrayals. In the triumphs and demise of nations and empires, Wheeler felt, where luxury and sin played overwhelming roles, "sacrificing every thing to . . . ungovern'd passions" (January 20, 1779), men and women played comparable parts. Reviewing the bloody plotting of Darius's mother and daughters, for example, she asserted that Persian history provided "an account of diverse cruelties practised by those of the weaker sex one destroying another lest she should have the higher place," while among Roman women, "valour and constancy" vied with destructive cruelty (January 26, 27, 1779). Such was "the precarious standing of those in high stations," she concluded at the end of her reading one evening, "where truth is not suffer'd to overballance . . . aspiring pride." (January 26, 27, 29, 1779). Greek history she found to be a model of a "barbarous age" where the few "that acted from a principle of virtue" were hardly treated (February 12, 1779). And just as Alexander died, in her view, from too much luxury and freedom, by which she meant lack of self-restraint, and his empire reduced through "Civil wars and bloodshed," so England could expect little succor from heaven until the tide of luxury and corruption had turned. The travelogue *The Beauties of England* (1778), which Wheeler read to learn about "some particular parts of this Nation" instead provided her with a catalogue of follies that contributed to England's depraved state. The luxurious palaces of King George were "not capable giving any solid satisfaction," Wheeler asserted, but, like the fast days he proclaimed to try to stave off defeat at the hands of national enemies, were distractions from the real issues: "regulating those things, that are so destructive to the Nation, and bringing down the luxury which abounds to a very high degree to the bringing in of almost every vice and exterpation of Righteousness which is the thing necessary to exalt a Nation" (February 10, 1779). As these remarks suggest, Wheeler saw history not as a progress but as a series of great questions presenting stark and timeless contests between good and evil, truth and sin. If "righteousness exalteth a nation" then those governments that were depraved or corrupted would be destroyed. Hence her understanding of such crucial political signifiers as "nation," "liberty" and "truth" provided counter-points to dominant definitions that undermined, for her, the latter's prescriptive authority.

Wheeler's views on the American conflict were shaped by her spiritual concerns. Certainly the war with the colonists confused accepted categories of national belonging, for her as for others, underlining the Americans' cultural and national "in-betweeness," their peculiar state of being both similar to and different from their English cousins.[83] Within southern Bedfordshire, as elsewhere, opinion on the war was divided, but there was considerable anti-war and reformist sentiment among property-owners at all levels: local elites had led the movement for the Bedfordshire petition for economical reform, and two Foxites were returned for the county in the critical 1780 parliamentary election.[84] The common metaphors used to capture the dilemma of "loyalty" in the crisis attempted to convey the uniqueness of the "civil war" or "rebellion" as rival sides named it. Indeed, news-paper columnists, graphic satirists and pamphlet writers competed with each other in parading the images of familial dysfunction (blood brothers, unnatural mothers, patricidal daughters and over-indulgent parents) before the public. One writer who questioned the familial metaphor still demonstrated how ties of consanguinity and history muddied claims to national belonging:

> The present Body of the People of America were born there of American Parents, and consequently can no more be our Children than we can be theirs. If there be Englishmen among them, are there not Americans in England? . . . Surely when Children grow to Maturity, and do for themselves, they are from under the Controul of their Parents. Does not all Nature follow this Rule? . . . It is true the Americans are originally descended from Britons, but are not Britons originally from the Continent, and Europeans originally from Asia? What Connexion have Englishmen now with Jutland, the Seat of their Forefathers? Or what Connexion have such as are of Norman Blood amongst us with Normandy?[85]

The war, in other words, raised questions about origins and the automatic link between nativity, descent and nation. But for Wheeler such questions were always at play. Surrounded by the day-to-day evidence of war – mobilization efforts, processions of dignitaries, men-of-war at dock on the coast – Wheeler consistently saw the conflict as the latest in the series of abominations carried out by secular nations for worldly ends. "War still continues, with the natural consequences," she wrote on January 4, 1779, "perhaps for a scourge to the nation" – a view which others in her meeting shared. "The nation was arrived to a great pitch of wickedness as should not wonder if it should please providence to permit our enemies the French to oppress us to a great degree," she later reflected (February 17, 1779). Yet on the other hand, much as she disapproved of the war – "who can rejoice at the loss of lives on either side!" (March 1, 1779) – the "revolted Colonists" were in her view the basest hypocrites for their persecution of Friends on a matter of conscience.[86] The "arbitrary proceedings of the Americans, those that pretend to be such advocates for liberty," was a recurrent topic at teatime. They made "our fellow professors" suffer greatly: "many are reduced to the want of necessaries and some deprived of life . . . men of unblemish'd character, one of whom left a Wife and ten children: such arbitrary proceedings by those who pretend to fight for liberty!" (January 1, 1779). Liberty, in her view, was a civil and spiritual state, which bestowed not only freedom from persecution for religious beliefs, but also freedom from the "vain desires" and competitions of the world – a "liberty spiritual" which was "contrary to that of the Flesh" (March 23, 1779).

However, Wheeler also dwelled on persecution because persecution was never far from her mind. She remarked, "what a wonderful privilege [it is] thus peaceably to be favor'd to keep our Meetings compared with the many difficulties our worthy ancestors had to encounter" (January 1, 1779). Yet the tolerance of English society, which still prevented the full participation of dissenters in civic life, was given substance mainly by the bloodier intolerance of the previous century. Memories were kept alive in such publications as Joseph Besse's A Collection of the Sufferings of the People called Quakers (London, 1753), which counted 12,465 separate persecutions in England and Wales in the seventeenth century. Wheeler found Besse's enumeration to be a great comfort, for it reminded her and her contemporaries of "the sufferings of our worthy ancestors who stood boldly for the testimony of Jesus amidst such great persecutions" (January 28, 1779).[87] Contemporary newpaper writers also dwelled on whether Quakers' refusal to observe fast days by closing their shops constituted disloyalty to the king and country.[88] Wheeler's gratitude thus competed with an equally pervasive sense of insecurity that this freedom could come to an end at any point, intensifying her bonds of community with those across the Atlantic. As she put it, "we hear much of the sufferings of those that are well-affected in America from which at present we are protected, but know not how soon the same may overtake us" (February 16, 1779). Despairing of the excesses committed by the mob on the acquittal of Admiral Keppel in 1779, Wheeler described the riot that precipitated an attack on her household, when several of their unilluminated windows were broken.

> In the evening had such a riot on account of the acquittal of Admiral Keppel as is seldom remembered: the effigy of Hugh Palliser, his accuser, was carried about, then hanged on a gibbet and burned. Friends were threatened with having their windows broke if they did not conform to the practice of setting up candles.

Although their broken windows constituted "the first instance I remember of that sort," she and her family imagined that such actions could inaugurate "a portion of those sufferings . . . undergone by our Friends in America" (February 16, 1779). The nation in Wheeler's narrative emerges as a contested and ambiguous community, one as liable to betray as protect one's family and livelihood. While her status as a member of the nation of Quakers was secured for her by her devotion to her Inner Light, her status within the English nation was tentative and contingent. The presence and resistances of those whose Englishness could not be performed (as, for example, at victory celebrations or fast days) could confound the larger effort to construct and maintain a unifying national identity in wartime. It was some comfort to Wheeler, perhaps, that for her the English nation, like other nations in history, was but a temporary and passing vanity, but the nation of the well-affected would eternally endure.

Britannia into Battle

Lady Christian Henrietta Caroline Acland, or Lady Harriet, as she was generally called, provides our final example of the complex interrelations of women, war and identity. Acland accompanied her husband to Canada in 1776 to become part of Burgoyne's campaign against the Americans, and left a journal which, penned in part by her and in part by an unknown male attendant, probably her husband's valet or the military chaplain Edward Brudenell, gives some account of life aboard the transport ship that took them to America, living conditions on the northern frontier of empire and the chaos of the battlefield.[89] Acland's diary contains few observations on policy or proclamations of public-spirited motives, and no direct personal accounts of the most exciting moments of her adventure. This is in striking contrast, of course, to the celebrated journal of one of her contemporaries and part-time companion on the march, the Baroness von Riedesel. Daughter of a Prussian general and wife to the Hessian commander, Frederich von Riedesel, who led the German troops sent to aid Burgoyne, Riedesel penned astute remarks on everything from military strategy to rebel marksmanship. But, I would argue, Acland's journal is no less important for not containing what we would like to find there. For if Acland speaks little for herself, she is made to speak for others, and in doing so brings into sharp relief the shifting registers of cultural and national community in the American Revolution. What emerges from the journal and supplementary diaries and memoirs is a portrait of "female patriotism" that salvages an otherwise disastrous military campaign. As the *Dictionary of National Biography* proclaimed over a century after her adventures, "the narrative of her sufferings during the campaign, which has been often printed in both England and America, forms one of the brightest episodes in the war with the American people."[90] Acland's frontier experience and the uses made of it by others thus crystallize the ways in which women and war became inextricably bound in the forging of both individual and collective narratives of nation.

She was born Lady Christian Henrietta Caroline Fox-Strangeways in 1749; her father was the first Earl of Ilchester and part of the Whig aristocratic coterie at Holland House; her second cousin was Charles James Fox. Her immediate family also maintained links with prominent Tory families such as the Chathams, so her marriage in 1770 to John Dyke Acland, a strong Tory landowner with Devonshire and Somerset estates, was not, perhaps, too surprising. Colonel of the Devon militia, and pronounced opponent of American independence, Acland's rough West-Country manners and habits, which included a fondness for strong drink, did not detract from his attractiveness, amiability and courage. His name appears prominently on the loyal address to the King of October 1775 from the officers of the first regiment of the Devonshire Militia, which denounced "the unnatural Behaviour of your American subjects" and the "Enemies of your Majesty's Government and this Constitution." After his offer to Lord North to raise a regiment for the King's service at the outbreak of the American war was declined, Acland rose by purchase in the regular army to the rank of major in the 20th Regiment of Foot, which was mobilized on January 9, 1776. When in America he commanded the company of Grenadiers chosen to form the advance with Burgoyne down from Canada to Albany.[91] Lady Acland attended her husband throughout the eighteen-month campaign that ended in the surrender at Saratoga (October 14, 1777). This was an arduous trek: save for brief stays in Montreal, there was little of the social life that accompanied camp life in the campaigns around colonial cities like Boston, Philadelphia or New York. The handful of officers' wives, children and servants accompanying the troops, which included, besides Lady Harriet, the indomitable Madame Riedesel and her three small children, and Mrs. Harnage and Mrs. Reynell, wives of an English major and lieutenant respectively, were usually kept at a safe distance from the battles. Here they listened to the cannonades and gunfire with their hearts in their mouths ("more dead than alive" as Madame Riedesel was wont to remark), had their dinners disrupted by the intrusion of dismembered bodies, and turned their huts into hospitals for the wounded and dying. The women joined the action when unavoidable or necessary, to nurse the sick or for safety's sake. Occasionally the officers' wives and children would even ride in their caleshes in the midst of the soldiers' march, literalizing the symbolic role of domesticity and its defense in warfare. The alarms and trauma they all had to endure is suggested, in part, by the fact that Riedesel was the only woman among the officer's wives whose husband was not killed or wounded on the campaign.[92]

The convoy of three transport ships which embarked in April 1776 from Cork landed at Nova Scotia in late May, and quickly began the descent south, moving along the Great Lakes to Quebec and the St. Lawrence in order to take advantage of the last campaigning months before November. During the winter, the British troops were quartered at Vergère, Canada, before beginning the descent again down Lake Champlain on April 5, 1777. Lady Acland accompanied the artillery and baggage train with the rest of the women for the most part. However, as Burgoyne later recalled, in the course of the march Lady Acland "traversed a vast space of country, in different extremities of season, and with difficulties that an European traveler will not easily conceive."[93] For example, when Major Acland fell sick at Fort St. John near Montreal in the summer of 1776, Lady Acland hurried "to attend him upon his sickbed in a miserable hut at Chamblée" (Fort Chambly). When Acland was wounded in the leg shortly thereafter at the Battle of Valcour Bay in October, 1776, Lady Acland traveled the length of Lake Champlain to nurse him. Her other travails included a life-threatening fire in her and her husband's tent at Dovecote (Coveville), from which both narrowly escaped alive, an outbreak of measles and a pregnancy that began in May of 1777. The biggest adventure of Lady Acland's American journey, however, was yet to come.

In the journal entries that can be straightforwardly attributed to her, we can see a lively interest in military maneuvers of the British and the "rebels," as she unvaryingly called the Americans, and in the conduct and recruitment of the "Savages," as she and the other journal writer called the native Americans who fought on the loyalist side. Indeed, the adjustment of the categories of national belonging necessitated by this war for empire clearly confirmed for Lady Acland her own position as civilized English woman, one who understood the nature of political obligation more clearly than those engaged in the current "unnatural rebellion." Yet she and her companions also found it more difficult than expected to categorize, differentiate and maintain the boundaries between the denizens of a culturally hybrid North America. The American colonies had long been seen as a potential source of degeneration for English people. In 1759, a Highland officer castigated the "inhumanity" of American rangers and their Native American allies in war. Such "cowardice and barbarity," he remarked, "seems so natural to a native of America, whether of Indian or European extraction." During the Revolution, the Americans continued to be depicted by hostile British observers as "savages," prone to deploy such barbaric tactics as scalping their enemies in their inevitable descent into godlessness and rebellion.[94] Recalling an American prisoner who declared his pleasure of "dying in a good cause, that of gaining independence to the American Colonies," Thomas Anburey remarked "how cheerfully some of them will sacrifice their lives in pursuit of this favourite idol." Conversely, American settlers and indigenes alike had also long sparked European fantasies about the nobility of humanity in its "original state," the virtues of hardiness and self-reliance, and the possibilities for social regeneration. Both tropes appear in the Acland journal to make sense of the extraordinary encounters and casualties of war. The pro-American colonists appear as rebels, certainly, but colonial loyalists were more often pointed to as rather imperfect illustrations of the stages through which civilizations develop. The valet or Brudenell described a Canadian family living near Coudres on the Labrador coast. Greeting him with "a natural ease and frankness," from "a small but exquisitely clean house," this family presented to my imagination the outlines of original society, excepting that being descended from ancestors who had lived in a polished country they had left behind them the barbarity which generally attends the first stages of infant manners. Happy people may the speculator say amongst whom simplicity can exist without barbarism & civility, & a softened not weaken'd mind, without affectation, without luxury.

(May 25, 1776, p. 18)

Nevertheless, the writer was forced to admit that the attempts of this family to exploit the company for profit – "they knew how much we wanted refreshment, and they asked 3 times the value of every thing we wanted" – demonstrated "that the nature of man is everywhere the same, tho' the incitements to action and the application to his passions may be different in different places" (19). French in origin, English by conquest and affiliation, the Canadians displayed non-synchronous cultural attributes, and so unwittingly illustrated the tensions in late eighteenth-century British ideas about human nature and the capacity for improvement. The Riedesels, in contrast, ever conscious of their own status as Germans, and alternately admiring of the Americans' independence and disdainful of their apparent republicanism, referred to the colonists indiscriminately as "the English."[95]

Part of the mission as the British-led troops descended the northern frontier was to persuade the notoriously fickle Canadian Indian nations met with en route to support the loyalist cause.[96] When the Aclands and their entourage went in a calesh to a small village called Indian Lorette outside Quebec to negotiate for aid, they witnessed the Ottawa ceremony for declaring war, which ended with a dance in which the women as well as the men participated, all "very much ornamented" and "painted in a very curious manner." Watching the dancers shouting and setting up "the War Hoop," the writer found the ceremony to be "a curious but a very horrible and disagreeable sight" (May 31, 1776, p. 21). The Ottawa proved to be brave and able on the British side, but when, in an incident described by Lady Acland in the journal, one of their nation was killed, they demanded a prisoner to make up for the man they had lost: "General Fraser consented to their having a black man who was taken deliver'd over to them – which was done – but immediately after the General bought him of them for 50 dollars – to the great joy of the poor wrech who had been in the utmost distress at knowing his fate" (July 26, 1776, p. 25). The literal surrogation of a black British servant for a Native American – and back again – was seen by Lady Acland as a testament to British beneficence and humanitarianism in war, which complements the views of the officers and ladies on the campaign.[97] Her observations served to confirm English difference, just as her presence in the imperial conflict thus brought into stark relief the boundaries of national belonging and dis-possession.

The high drama of Acland's American adventure occurred during and after the Battle of Bemis Heights (which immediately preceded Burgoyne's surrender at

Saratoga), when Major Acland was wounded and captured by American forces. "Towards the close of evening Major Acland was wounded in both legs and notwithstanding every effort that was made to carry him off it was found impossible and he of course fell into Enemie's hands", the journal laconically reported. The American Colonel James Wilkinson remembered that incident more vividly:

> With the troops I pursued the hard-pressed, flying enemy, passing over killed and wounded until I heard one exclaim: "Protect me, Sir, against this boy." Turning my eyes, it was my fortune to arrest the purpose of a lad, thirteen or fourteen years old, in the act of taking aim at a wounded officer . . . Inquiring his rank, he answered, "I had the honour to command the Grenadiers." Of course I knew him to be Major Ackland, who had been brought from the field to this place on the back of a Captain Shrimpton of his own corps, under heavy fire, and was here deposited, to save the lives of both. I dismounted, took him by the hand, and expressed hopes that he was not badly wounded. "Not badly," replied this gallant officer and accomplished gentleman, "but very inconveniently, I am shot through both legs. Will you, Sir, have the goodness to have me conveyed to your camp?"

Wilkinson complied, and Acland was taken to American headquarters.[98] Meanwhile, his valet took a bullet in his shoulder searching for him on the battlefield.

Major Acland had directed his wife to follow the route of the artillery and baggage before the battle. Once the action began, it quickly became bloody and fierce, and the surgeons appropriated the women's hut as a hospital. Here she was joined by Madame Riedesel, Mrs. Harnage and Mrs. Reynell. Harnage was soon brought to the surgeons badly wounded, and Reynell dead. "Imagination will want no help to figure the state of the whole groupe," Burgyone recalled. The six-month-pregnant Lady Acland, hearing her husband had been shot and taken prisoner, according to most accounts, determinedly approached Burgoyne about getting a pass to request General Gates's permission to attend her husband across the Hudson. He consented,[99] and she, her maid, Brudenell and the major's valet got into a boat and rowed down the river to the American camp, in a scene that would be immortalized in painting, engravings and bronze bas-relief.[100] The American sentinel would not let the boat pass or the company come on shore until morning, and the passengers were forced to wait eight hours in the dark and cold. In daylight, however, she was received warmly by General Gates, "with all the humanity and respect her rank, her merits and her fortunes deserved." As Burgoyne put it,

> Let such as are affected by these circumstances of alarm, hardship and danger, recollect, that the subject of them was a woman; of the most tender and delicate frame; of the gentlest manners; habituated to all the soft elegancies, and refined enjoyments, that attend high birth and fortune; and far advanced in a state in which the tender cares, always

due to the sex, become indispensibly necessary. Her mind alone was formed for such trials.

In this scenario, her body alone betrayed the "sex" that her mind eschewed; but both her mind and (reproductive) body worked to underline the importance of a comparative masculine resolve, wielded in the service of the mother country. In a riposte to the domestic representations of a "macaroni war" allegedly fought by "fribbles," Lady Acland affirmed gender difference even as she transgressed its boundaries, providing an assurance of both the honor and virtue of the war effort in America while also rousing every man to his proper duty. The bearer of national and imperial values, Lady Acland showed the "courage of an Englishwoman" in the face of threats to her family and country's honor. Her husband's courage and fortitude, and her selfless devotion were thus *mutually* reinforcing, and showed the synergy of gender difference in *mutually* constituting national self-definition and resolve.

Lady Acland also confirmed the British representations of the American war as, indeed, a gentlemen's war, where the gallant and respectful treatment of elite women – and men – by the British demonstrated the civility and humaneness of the civilized and wronged mother country. This is significant, given that American soldiers within the vicinity of Burgyone's march reported a rather different treatment of colonial women by the "British Tyrants." "The common appellation is to Women Damn'd Rebel Bitches and whores . . . and often kicked when met in the street," wrote the Nova Scotia patriot John Allen in June 1777. Allen's wife, imprisoned by the British at Halifax, and separated from her husband and children, allegedly suffered much mistreatment, and other documents of the war indicate a similar disregard for civility on all sides in the conduct towards prisoners, whether men, women or children.[101] In the case of Lady Acland, however, gender and rank trumped nationality in the widespread admiration for her accomplishments. Officers on both sides expressed their regard for her beauty and courage, her loyalty to her husband, and her kindness to the grenadiers under her husband's command, to each of whom she gave a Cheshire cheese. This "was not such small present as you may imagine," Thomas Anburey recalled, "English cheese then being a dollar per pound: . . . there is no present you can send to a European abroad so great as a good Cheshire cheese." His memoirs, to which she later subscribed, celebrate her appearance and character.[102] Another British officer was more lyrical: "There is scarcely an instance," he asserted,

> either in ancient or modern history, that more finely depicts the resolution, affection and fortitude of woman toward the husband of her heart and vows than this. If war sometimes in bad men, calls forth all the viler passions of our nature, in woman it is otherwise; it rouzes into action a heroism otherwise unknown, an intrepidity almost incompatible with the sex, and awakens all the dormant susceptibilities of their mind.

The crisis, in other words, calls into action resources and capabilities in women otherwise "dormant" – provided they are of good enough stock to begin with. The Americans were equally enthralled by her aristocratic charm and the grace she lent the otherwise gritty proceedings. "The feminine figure, the benign aspect, the polished manners of this woman were alone sufficient to attract the sympathy of the most obdurate," wrote Colonel Wilkinson; and General Gates himself recorded, in a letter to his wife on the day of the British surrender, "I hope Lady Harriet Ackland will be here when you arrive. She is the most amiable, delicate little piece of quality you ever beheld."[103] Significantly, Madame Riedesel, not one to suffer fools gladly, asserted that she had had to persuade Lady Acland to go to her wounded husband behind the lines – although no independent confirmation for this version of the story can be found. Rumours did fly across the transatlantic gossip networks about Lady Acland's relationship with Brudenell, however, some of which, concerning an alleged bout of insanity and a remarriage to the chaplain, were repeated by Victorian historians, only to be firmly rejected by their twentieth-century successors.[104]

But for the moment, Lady Acland's wartime adventures provided an empirical example of the eighteenth century's idealized portrait of female patriotism, in which gender, rank and danger conjoin to produce the heroine. Indeed, her story, spread by Burgoyne, Anburey and the periodical press, helped write a history of the American war for the British that organized and shaped a narrative of loss into one of triumph. An oil painting commemorating this achievement was exhibited at the Royal Academy in the early 1780s (Fig. 15), and subsequently engraved by Pollard above. It depicts Lady Acland, ambiguously pregnant, disheveled and a bit tattered but still stylishly dressed in a gown and regiment frock coat and flowered straw hat, offering the *laissez-passer* to an unseen sentinel, as Brudenell holds the flag of truce, the maid looks on apprehensively and the valet watches a ship exploding up river in the distance. Interestingly, Pollard's print truncates the expansive vista depicted by the painting, which opposes Acland's feminine figure in the boat with armed sentries on the riverbank, rifles at the ready. But this omission may aid the image's attempt to popularize Lady Acland's adventure as History, providing a more labile and evocative representation onto which women and men of all ranks – those who had been in war or had lost loved ones to its brutalities – could project their own identifications and desires. In both cases, as the stand-in for Britannia, Lady Acland turns the national icon into a pregnant wife, and demonstrates how the figure of the woman can mobilize the ultimate nationalist fantasy about war as both death and reproduction. The iconography of nation and women's experience come together in the painting and engraving, as Acland's body becomes the *national* body, symbolically defining and upholding the boundaries of national difference and power between men. A metaphorical and literal bearer of the nation – the aristocratic woman who temporarily gave up luxuries and entitlements, and, still more risked her life and that of her unborn child, to help make her husband, and hence the nation, strong – she vindicated the hierarchies of gender, class and race in the construction of the national character.

126

Figure 15 Lady Harriet Acland during the American Revolution (c. 1784). Courtesy of the National Trust Picture Library.

This chapter has sketched in some of the ways that the shifting registers of women's "experience" and its representation – by themselves, and by others – form the semiotic circuitry through which meaning was constructed: there can be no "return to the archives," or even to the telling of good stories, without an appreciation for the ways in which ideology, representation, social practice and material conditions intertwine in symbiotic relation, to shape both "experience" and our access to it. By exploring the heterogeneous identifications and refusals of women with the nation, these examples suggest how the histories and myths of national becoming, the ideologies of patriotism and the boundary experience of war could shape British women's perceptions of self, community and other and organize mental space, time and consciousness in unexpected ways. They also demonstrate, across a variety of generic forms, how *representation* of and by women became central to collective narratives of national struggle, triumph or loss. The relationships between eighteenth-century imaginaries of gender and national identity were not fixed or straightforward, but were continually formed and re-formed by women's involvement with the romance of war and empire, generating unauthorized as well as conventional notions of liberty, belonging and identity.

Burgoyne and Gates negotiated the release of Acland in return for the colorful patriot Ethan Allen, who was taken prisoner at Bemis Heights, and the Aclands were able to return to England for the baptism, if not the birth, of their son in March 1778. Major Acland never recovered fully from the experience, and died later that year,[105] while Lady Acland lived until 1815. But her story provides the fitting end to this exploration of women, war and identities in eighteenth-century Britain. For her status as a rather lonely heroine in the national trauma of the American war marked the ways that class, gender and reproductive resourcefulness could be made to bear the evidence, on the field of death, that the nation would go on.

4

THE BLACK WIDOW: GENDER, RACE AND PERFORMANCE IN ENGLAND AND JAMAICA

After having buffeted the Billows of the *Law* upwards of Twenty Years in Search of *Justice*, and only to arrive at this desart *Island of Poverty* at last, may furnish an instructive Caution to others how they embark in so romantic an Expedition.

Teresia Phillips, *An Apology for the Conduct of Mrs. T. C. Phillips* (1748)

There are several [creole] Gentlemen who are well acquainted with Learning . . . but these are few and the Generality seem to have a greater Affection for the Modish Vice of Gambling than the Belles Lettres, and love a Pack of Cards better than the Bible . . . A Boy, till the age of Seven or Eight, diverts himself with the Negroes, acquires their broken way of talking, their Manner of Behaviour, and all the Vices these unthinking Creatures can teach; . . . Some of the Ladies read, they all dance a great deal, coquette much, dress for Admirers; and at last, for the most part, run away with the most insignificant of their humble Servants.

[Charles Leslie], *A New and Exact Account of Jamaica* (1740)

Many causes of national character are so mixed as to be almost inscrutable. It may, perhaps, be partly ascribed to the sensibility that a warm climate excites, that Creoles are said to be impatient of subordination and addicted to juridical controversy . . . ostentatious, and extravagant.

R. C. Dallas, *History of the Maroons* (1803)

Black widow n. a spider of the New World, the female of which is highly venomous, and commonly eats its mate.

British Book of Spiders (1958)

The British West Indies served a Janus-faced function in eighteenth-century English imagination and policy. Irresistibly attractive to travelers, playwrights, philosophers and naturalists as well as merchants and planters as outposts of New World exoticism and its mastery, the islands presented a theater of savagery and conquest, adventure and economic enterprise that also reflected changing imperial strategies towards a cultural frontier at the heart of English prestige, wealth and authority. By the eighteenth century, when the lethal but fabulously profitable combination of sugar and slaves had become entrenched in plantation mono-culture, the islands attracted the younger sons, older daughters and otherwise disadvantaged offspring of the British isles who sought to acquire status or fortunes, usually with the hopes of returning "home" remade.[1] However, the complexities and complicities of British Caribbean culture prevented the islands from serving as a "city on the hill" or a progenitive version of modern England, as the New England colonies had and the South Seas islands soon would. For the West Indies retained in experience, imagination and representation an ineffable otherness. Literally and figuratively islands of slavery, exploitation and physical and social death, they seemed to promise obliteration for the enslaved, the penurious and the prosperous alike. As economic boon and cultural miasma, they hinted at the strangeness and hybridity of colonial power and the danger it posed to the honor of the English nation and the virtue and integrity of its imperial project. The fabulously wealthy Caribbean planter that emerged in fact and fiction came to represent the West Indian uncouthness, backwardness and degeneracy that inverted the acclaimed standards of English civility and culture. Incarnating the acquisitive possessiveness of empire and its licensed rapacity, the Caribbean was that "secret, underground Self" of English society, and the projected screen of an imagined West Indian "national character" was constantly disrupted with recognition as well as disavowal.[2]

For some time the Caribbean retained something of this ambiguity in British historical studies as either a shadowy presence in the success story of the eighteenth-century British/English nation, or a place "out there" in the empire best dealt with by "regional" specialists. Fortunately Caribbean and Anglo-American poets, novelists, critics and historians have worked successfully to repair the links between British and Caribbean history that early modern writers first labored to forge.[3] The most recent work has recast the Caribbean as a crucial entrepot of an "oceanic interculture" that, propelled by the dark economic tides of slavery, did not begin and end at national borders.[4] For scholars who wish to explore the mobility and instability of "national" identities in an imperial age, the eighteenth-century Caribbean promises to yield rich case studies in the disruption of the polarities of metropole–colony. Through the circulation of ideas, people, artifacts and cultural forms, the islands energized a circuitry of identity, alterity, exchange and trans-formation in which racial, national, sexual and gender identities transected colonizers and colonized. This is not to suggest that colonial and metropolitan culture were somehow "the same." Rather, it is to emphasize the importance to the larger imperial network of those local translations of "Englishness" that adapted and reconfigured cultural categories and customs, endowing them with new political meanings.[5] Site of the most advanced form of eighteenth-century European capitalism, and of a "transculture" achieved at the cost of considerable bloodshed and violence, the antinomies of West Indian everyday life supported and propelled the century's modernities and the terms of national belonging.[6] English recognition of, and profound ambivalence towards, the elements of their own culture in the "creolisation," "métissage," or "hybridity"[7] of the Caribbean should not blind us to the fact that the values and goals of acquisition, display, maximization of assets, profit and dominion underwrote the British civilization of both places.

This chapter will explore some of the intersections of British Atlantic culture through the focal point of an English woman colonist. The notorious Teresia Constantia Phillips (1709–65) lived in Jamaica in 1738 to 1741 and again from 1751 until her death in 1765, a period bounded by slave insurrection and global war. Phillips was well known to contemporaries as a courtesan and memoirist, parading her marriages and love affairs with highborn and well-connected men before the English public in a three-volume autobiography. Living at both the center and the margins of fashionable high life in Paris, London, Boston, Kingston and Spanish Town, Phillips represented herself as a model of victimized woman-hood, a metropolitan subject whose heritage as an Englishwoman was denied her by sexist prejudice, but whose resourceful English character nonetheless sustained her in the face of ostracizing condemnation and colonial exile. Yet through her reputation as a bigamist, her later husbands' mysterious deaths and her remarkable success in positioning herself close to the centers of privilege, this "spider" or "female Bluebeard" became a source of scandal and myth in the colony and metropole, serving as a warning against the twinned dangers of female sexuality and colonial power.

Not surprisingly, Phillips has been intensively studied by late twentieth-century scholars, serving variously as an example of the "scandalous memoirist," victim of the double standard, or "serial bigamist."[8] But the colonial contexts of Phillips's rebellious subjectivity and her experiences as a transnational subject of the British Atlantic have yet to be examined. Partly this is because the details of her later life in Jamaica are clouded in obscurity and rumor. But Phillips left a colorful account of her first extended stay in Jamaica and a permanent imprint on Jamaican cultural life during her second when she became Mistress of the Revels under Lieutenant-Governor Henry Moore, and thus responsible for licensing all theatrical presentations and public entertainments in Spanish Town and Kingston. Through the fragments this notorious woman left behind, and in light of current academic and popular obsessions with Atlantic crossings, Phillips's life as an Anglo-Caribbean subject allow us to ruminate upon a number of significant historical issues: the convergence of the identities of foreign and colonial others, and particularly West Indian Creoles, in English imagination and practice; the role of performance in establishing and contesting hierarchies of gender, race and nationality in England and Jamaica; and the status of white English women in reproducing the ideological and social contours of Creole colonial life. Equally important, Phillips's adventures bear witness to both the vitality and the predatory nature of the Atlantic interculture that articulated the everyday lives of people of all colors, slave and free, in England and Jamaica, commodifying gossip, retailing reputation and fomenting resistance across an imperial cultural marketplace. Phillips's relationship to English national and colonial culture was contested, alternately embracing and redefining "English" values of display, exchange, "conquest," resourcefulness and self-invention; but if those values were at odds with conventional notions of English womanhood, they were perfectly complicit with imperial power.

Penitent performance and the savage within

Phillips, one of the most beautiful women of her day (Fig. 16), was known among fashionable London circles of the 1720s, 1730s and 1740s for her series of sexual liaisons with prominent men and for her marriage woes. Her proclivities for extravagance in dress and conspicuous consumption also contributed to her fame, as she became a familiar figure on the London scene, parading from theater to assembly room, pleasure garden and Court bejewelled and bedecked with finery and accompanied by clouds of servants. Her writings added notoriety to an already complicated reputation. An Apology for the Conduct of Mrs. T. C. Phillips was produced at a particularly impecunious juncture in her life, in part to blackmail the Earl of Chesterfield, a former amour, into paying her an annuity. First published serially, and then in volumes in 1748–9, and running to three more editions, the last appearing in 1761, the Apology narrated the story of her tribulations from her "ruin" as an adolescent through her subsequent sexual dalliances and series of matrimonial lawsuits that stretched over twenty-six years. It won her sympathizers as well as critics, for it exposed the abuses suffered by dependent women and the chicanery that underwrote English legal culture and matrimonial law. Her memoir so greatly influenced law reformer Jeremy Bentham that he claimed it as "the first, and not the least effective, in the train of causes in which the works by which my name is known had their origin." Less positively impressed, Henry Fielding and Horace Walpole saw fit to list her as among the great female sexual predators of all time, Grub Street vilified her as an insatiable and polymorphously perverse man-eater and Creole Jamaicans, apocryphally, referred to her more respectfully as the "The Black Widow," a natural history metaphor that hinted at the dangers West Indian topography posed to civilized English people. Two years after the first volume of her autobiography appeared, she published A Letter Humbly Address'd to the Right Honourable the Earl of Chesterfield.[9] These texts, together with their published responses and some incidental writings and verses Phillips produced in Jamaica in the mid-1750s, provide the starting point for the following discussion. They provided a vivid account of her trials and tribulations as a mistress, wife and public figure, a virulent indictment of the sexual double standard that allowed women to be treated so shabbily at law and by custom, and an intimate view of the alliances and identities at the heart of colonial society in Kingston and Spanish Town.

A brief outline of the main events in her life will facilitate our examination of Phillips's overdetermined status as a scandalous woman within the British Atlantic world.[10] She was born into an ancient and well-connected Welsh family in January, 1709; her father, a Lieutenant-Colonel in the Grenadier Guards, was discharged from the army sometime between the end of the War of the Spanish Succession

Figure 16 J. Highmore, *Teresia Constantia Phillips* (1748). Courtesy of the British Museum, Department of Prints and Drawings.

and the suppression of the Jacobite rebellion of 1715; his possible collusion in Jacobite intrigue must remain a subject of speculation, but Phillips does record that a "Catastrophe" occurring in her family when she was "not above five" (I: 46) resulted in the loss of all of her father's commission and employments. Lawrence Stone has surmised that Phillips was raised a Catholic by a French Catholic mother, a guess supported by Phillips's bilingualism, Catholic lovers and propensity to escape from her troubles to a nunnery at Ghent. Somewhat incongruously, Phillips's paternal family connections were firmly Whig, as shown by the fact that the illegitimate daughter of the Duke of Monmouth, the Duchess of Bolton, was her godmother, and the wife of Horace Walpole, to whom her father claimed a relation by marriage, was her sister's protector. Phillips herself seemed little troubled by sectarian feelings – although she would insist despite her mistakes upon her own morality and goodness until the end of her life – but by the time she wrote her vindication she had become, in her social circles at least, opposition identified. Her *Apology* was introduced and edited by Paul Whitehead, a journalistic scourge of the successive Whig administrations and a valued member of Prince Frederick's circle at Leicester-House. According to the *Dictionary of National Biography*, Whitehead also reveled in a scandalous sexual life as secretary and steward to Sir Francis Dashwood's libertine group, the "Medmenham Monks," of which Wilkes was later a member.[11] On various levels he made a sympathetic person to edit her memoirs.

After Phillips and her family came to London in 1717, her sister and brother were dispatched to the care of Mrs. Walpole and an uncle in Barbados respectively; like Phillips, their fortunes would rest on the exigencies of empire-wide patronage networks. Phillips herself enjoyed for a time the protection of the Duchess of Bolton, who educated her at an elite Westminster girls' boarding school. However, a series of family disasters – including the death of her mother and her father's marriage to a servant who harbored murderous sentiments towards his children – left Phillips on her own and in charge of her younger sister at the age of thirteen. She attempted to make a living for them in London with her needlework, lodging at a respectable widow's house, but soon she was drawn into a disreputable life, initially by the young Philip Stanhope (nephew and heir to the Earl of Chesterfield) whose taste for young girls led him to court, then rape and afterwards briefly maintain Phillips as his mistress. Her father's abdication of responsibility for her, and Stanhope's desertion, set the pattern for the patriarchal and aristocratic betrayal that Phillips maintains characterized her entire life. "[W]hat shall we say of a Man, who, through mere Wantonness, debauches a Child of that Age, in the base, ungenerous Manner just related," Phillips asks, and then "abandons her to all the Miseries a young Creature in these Circumstances must be necessarily exposed?" (I: 65). Phillips was equally adamant that her chastity – that most precious jewel of womanhood which, according to the conventions of the day, was negotiated away to future husbands in conventional marriage arrangements – had a price, and that she was the one to whom it should be paid.[12]

Hopelessly in debt, Phillips was convinced by her confidants that the only way out of her troubles was to effect a Fleet marriage, since a married woman's debts were by law the responsibility of her husband. This she did, to a professional bigamist named Delafield, which had the desired effect of putting off her creditors. In 1723, at the age of fifteen, she became the mistress and then the wife of Henry Muilman, a wealthy Dutch merchant and son of a very rich Amsterdam commercial family. When his parents discovered the truth of Phillips's penury and dubious sexual past, they were appalled, and insisted that Muilman get the marriage annulled. The threat of disinheritance was too much for Muilman, who secretly began a nullity suit in the Consistory Court on the grounds of Phillips's previous marriage. This he supplemented with a range of cruel and brutal treatment designed to obtain Phillips's promise not to contest the suit by bringing up Delafield's previous marriage (which would have made her marriage to him void and her marriage to Muilman legal). Muilman set "ruffians" and bailiffs upon her to retrieve her clothes and jewels, abused her verbally and physically, once even branding her with a red-hot poker on the breast when she refused to sleep with him, and lodged her in a bawdy house in the effort to persuade her to become again his mistress.[13] Phillips's lawyers finally negotiated a deal with Muilman whereby she got a bond to secure an annuity, cash and the return of her valuables, and Phillips agreed not to defend the nullity suit, and left the country for France. As a result, Muilman's marriage suit went through, although it "made a great deal of noise," as Phillips's proctor reported to her (I: 194). After returning from Paris, Phillips foolishly borrowed money from Muilman, giving him the bond for her annuity as collateral – and then spent much of the next twenty years suing him for its return.

Muilman was soon remarried to an heiress, leading to Phillips's life long claim that he, not she, was the bigamist. As Stone has summarized the resulting legal thicket: "The legal status of four marriages: Delafield to Miss Yeomans [his wife], Delafield to Con Phillips, Muilman to Con Phillips, and Muilman to Miss Darnell [his second wife] – now depended on whether it was possible to find hard evidence to prove the first of them. If so, the second and fourth became bigamous, and the third valid."[14] Phillips's protracted effort to prove the validity of their marriage formed the basis for her second set of suits against Muilman that she pursued fervently in King's Bench and the ecclesiastical courts. The chicanery of Muilman and his father-in-law, the lawyer Sargent Darnell, included slandering Phillips in the press, as well as allegedly murdering a penitent Delafield to keep him from testifying on her behalf. These actions foiled her legal maneuvers, but make for breathtaking reading over hundreds of pages of the Apology.[15] Her case seemed to justify Whitehead's bitter observation that "in a country where the best laws that ever were made subsist, they are so corruptly executed that they are become our greatest oppression, while we are overcome with a swarm of the vermin ministers of it, who loll in their coaches and wallow in the spoils of a ruined people" (I: 196).

Throughout these troubles, Phillips maintained a gay and extravagant life in London and Paris, going to Court, attending the theater, opera and fashionable assemblies and masquerades, and passing her time in France among Gallican and expatriate English nobility, such as the Duke of Beaufort. After her return to England, she embarked on a series of liaisons with dashing and rich men, escaping when necessary to the convent in Ghent. Her lovers included a Mr. B—, handsome heir to a general, with whom she lived with a great deal of style and vivacity in London and Paris on and off for seven years. Her next amour, the Worcestershire baronet and suspected Jacobite Sir Herbert Pakington, reduced himself to a "skeleton" and twice attempted suicide in his effort to keep Phillips under lock and key. Lord F—proved to be a more amiable and caring partner, and she lived quite happily with him as mistress of his household in Hertfordshire in 1732–3, until he married an heiress worth £80,000 per year. A more problematic lover was one "Tartuffe" or "S—te," the son of Sir John Southcote, a prominent Catholic and heir to great estates. Foppish, lascivious and sexually inexhaustible (he had a reputation for being able to impregnate barren women), Southcote caused Phillips by her own account to fall madly in love with him. She gave him money and jewels, sustaining his extravagance with her own as she played the devoted partner to a hopeless rake. In 1732 he left Phillips for the Grand Tour, and, when she saw him again in the difficult year of 1746, he joined the ranks of her previous lovers in rejecting her pleas for aid.[16] Her hatred and bitterness over this affair increased, if possible, her loathing for the "great men" who so casually used and discarded young women like pocket-handkerchiefs. To Phillips men were the "perfidious Sex": "all they purpose is to make Women instrumental to their Vanities, and subject to the Gratification of their grosser Appetites" (I: 260).

Phillips's next, and, for our purposes, most important, lover was "Mr. Worthy" or Henry Needham, a handsome, Oxford-educated son of a wealthy Jamaican planter. Their "violet passion of love" (III: 112) led Phillips to follow him to Jamaica in 1738–41 and then to Boston in 1741, before an unhappy end to the affair brought her back to England. Taking to sea to follow her man in time-tested "female warrior" tradition, Phillips braved numerous natural and human catastrophes in her journeys across the Atlantic. Her adventures are related with the verve and excitement of other voyage accounts, with Phillips surviving not only a near-shipwreck, a lascivious captain and French and Spanish privateers with her virtue intact, but also displaying such "masculine spirit and composure" (III: 119) as to win her universal regard. On one occasion, she reports that she performed deckside surgery upon wounded British seamen who had bravely defended their vessel from a Spanish privateer, for which she was later thanked publicly in the papers by the grateful captain. In Jamaica, she and Needham lived in his country-house at Sixteen-Mile Walk, ten miles from Spanish Town, in a haze of happiness that outlasted earthquakes and the dreaded fever. The gallant Needham was at one point roused to fight a secret duel over Phillips's honor following a verbal slight made by neighboring planter Ballard Beckford, but not before he made provision for Phillips in his will. In the event, Needham emerged wounded but alive, and Phillips nursed him back to health before she contracted the yellow fever, which ultimately forced her to leave the island. She returned to England briefly before sailing intrepidly again in man-of-war-infested waters, accompanied by her four Jamaican servants, to meet her beloved Needham in Boston in late 1741. Her experience in New England was not a happy one, for unfortunately, in Phillips's view, the "quality" of Boston seemed to share the same "caballing spirit" (III: 157) as those elsewhere in the New World: Needham's distant cousin, the new governor of Massachusetts, William Shirley, refused to meet her socially and frustrated her attempts to pass as Needham's wife. Meanwhile the rumors "industriously propagated" (III: 162) about her by Shirley's friends and family and Boston society's

Jamaican connections succeeded in breaking up the lovers.[17] Phillips nevertheless retained a lasting fondness for Needham that was openly expressed in a poem she wrote after she had moved to Jamaica permanently.

Once back in England, Phillips began to spend the fortune she had acquired on the litigation with Muilman. But bouts of pleurisy, aggressive creditors and ultimately the unending lawsuits made the 1740s an anxious and miserable time. She had no spectacular suitors or lovers, but supported her sister (whose husband, an East India merchant,[18] lived abroad in total disregard for her and their offspring) and her children with the help of a number of male friends. Improvident as always, spending freely and accompanied everywhere by her Jamaican servants, Phillips found herself twice arrested for debt and taken to the Liberties of King's Bench Prison, and was once confined there for nearly two years. While in the Rules, she began two more lawsuits, one against a crooked ex-solicitor, and one against the Marshal of the Prison for his fees. But her series of confrontations with the "great Men" of England and America, as she collectively called them, from Chesterfield and Shirley to Lord Chancellor Hardwicke and the gaolkeeper, were coming to a close. On her release she began threatening former lovers with exposure unless they gave her financial help, resulting in the serial publication of her *Apology*, which she was forced to sell from the window of her apartments. Its revelations, particularly about Chesterfield, provoked a war of words between her and those who chose to defend her alleged persecutors, until around 1751 Muilman finally succeeded in bribing her to go into exile in Jamaica. "What a literally good Husband was this Mortal?" she asks sarcastically in her *Apology*; "he was for *letting nothing lie waste*, you see, and plainly shews the true mercantile Spirit, to make the most of everything. What a laudable Instance of conjugal Oeconomy!" (III: 222). Her memoir ends here; but Phillips's marital adventures would begin anew after her emigration to Jamaica, as we shall see.

As even this cursory synopsis of her early affairs may suggest, Phillips's status as a scandalous woman in England rested upon the particular features of her self-presentation, the salacious details of her life, and the transatlantic reach of her reputation. First, her autobiography was a performance in the theatrical sense, portraying the victimized woman who chose to use her hard-won knowledge of the world to instruct and warn off the naive. "This performance," she declares in the *Apology*, is meant to be didactic, to "deter others, to whom Nature has given more Beauty than is needful for a wise Woman to build her Happiness upon, from following her Examples" (III: 245). But it was also performative in the philosophical sense, "constituting as an effect the very subject it purport[ed] to express."[19] That is, in portraying a character who exceeded the categories and confounded the stereotypes of gender and genre, and revealing the serial impersonations that the role of scandalous woman required, Phillips's memoir intervened in contemporary debates about relations between the sexes and revealed the constructed and performative nature of social identities in eighteenth-century England.

Secondly, Phillips's movements across the circum-Atlantic world and her pursuit of pleasure and profit within it illustrate the importance of gossip and reputation in the imperial cultural marketplace (Map 2). In the traffic of goods, people, patronage, kinship and ideas that flowed back and forth across the sea, hearsay and reputed "character" were important commodities that facilitated a range of social and economic transactions from the regulation of business dealings, extension of credit and negotiation of lucrative marriages to the escape from slavery.[20] Just as a merchant's credit and success were dependent upon a reputation that preceded him in his various ports of call, so a woman's reputation circulated from one country to the other as an ineffable representation of her character and worth, preceding her arrival and leaving ghostly traces long after she had departed. However, whereas a man's reputation depends upon his behavior in a number of contexts, a woman's reputation depended largely upon her sexual conduct, an activity that was in turn the especial purview of gossip.[21] Hence Phillips's reputation as bigamist, courtesan and troublemaker was transmitted via verbal and written accounts through the trade and postal routes, family connections and printed materials that comprised the variegated communication channels of the Atlantic world.[22] Her reputation accompanied or even preceded her arrivals in the entrepots of Amsterdam, London, Paris, Spanish Town and Boston, making her the object of voyeuristic pleasure as well as opprobrium. Moreover, her *Apology*, which among other things purveyed unflattering and salacious details about elite men, was not surprisingly read by some critics as a form of gossip: an example of unreliable female chatter, displaying women's propensities to use words as weapons and to exercise power behind the scenes in a dual display of self-aggrandizement and aggression. In all of these ways, as we shall see, gossip, as a "medium through which third parties circulate first persons," and reputation, which turned "male agency into female responsibility," were commodities that lubricated the channels of material exchange and anchored the social hierarchies of the Atlantic interculture.[23]

Phillips's narrative drew on several genres of the day – picaresque and epistolary novels, travel accounts and legal tracts, for example – and there are some striking parallels between the life presented in the *Apology* and those of such colorful characters as Moll Flanders, Roxana and Pamela, a point to which we shall return.[24] Yet significantly, Phillips deliberately identified herself and her plight with the higher-born heroines of sentimental English *drama*, and especially the domestic or "she-tragedies" of the late Augustan period that continued to be immensely popular after the Licensing Act had banished overly political plays. An avid theater goer, she was familiar with the poetic justice that imposed death sentences or banishment on seduced ladies, and took evident delight in the ironic twist to these cautionary tales provided by her own survival. Her *Apology* begins with a quotation from Nicholas Rowe's *Fair Penitent* (1708), the first of his "she-tragedies," whose protagonist Calista, daughter of a nobleman, was secretly loved and abandoned by Lothario, amoral ravisher of women:

> Were ye, ye Fair, but cautious whom ye trust,
> Did ye but know how seldom Fools are just,
> So many of your Sex wou'd not, in vain,

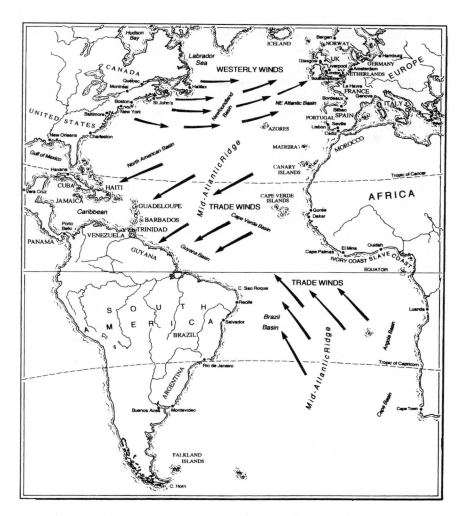

Map 2 Atlantic worlds, *c.* 1750. Courtesy of Paul Butel and Routledge.

> Of broken Vows and faithless Men complain:
> Of all the various Wretches Love has made,
> How few have been by *Men of Sense* betray'd?

Like Calista, Phillips sees herself as a victim of male lust and betrayal, whose "drama," as she calls her life, becomes one long punishment for an initial fall from grace. Like the theatrical penitent, she too was both ashamed of her lack of control over her sexual passions, but also deeply resentful of the double standard of sexual behavior that made "the condition of our sex / Through ev'ry state of life the slaves of man!" (Rowe, III: 39–40). As Phillips put it, "I think, in Honour and Justice, there should be some lesser Punishment, than that of eternal Infamy, affix'd to a Crime in which [men] are the principal Aiders and Abetters, or else that the Crime should be equally odious in both: *for at present the Thief is exempted from Punishment, and it is only the Party despoiled who suffers Death*" (*Letter*, 18–19).[25] Yet unlike Calista, or indeed Calista's literary heirs such as Clarissa, Phillips brazenly survived her "disgrace" to demand vindication of her own innocence, her subsequent conduct and her essential human worth. Indeed, in persistently fighting back, Phillips exceeded the conventions of the female character.

For Phillips was, as she and her editor repeatedly insist, more than a woman – her character exceeded her gender. Against the foppish, cruel and weak men who betray her, she appears in the *Apology* to have the sterling "manly" virtues – steadiness, loyalty, resolution, compassion and courage – so evidently lacking in them, enabling her to transcend "the Instability and Weakness of the Sex" (II: 57). "Never was Oppression equal to that attempted to be put upon me," declares Phillips in her preface, and yet she proved herself repeatedly to be "formed with a Disposition very opposite to this *Female Supineness*. Her Misfortunes have shewn her the Necessity of becoming superior to them, and every new Oppression she meets with, adds fresh Vigour to her Fortitude, for she has a Soul too masculine, to become an Opponent fit to answer . . . in the *Bilingsgate Stile*" (III: 28). Unfairly calumniated by wicked conspirators while she shouldered the responsibilities abdicated by mothers, husbands and fathers, "I am no Woman," Phillips pronounced, in these and other matters (II: 93). Secondly, in a legal and political culture that relegated women to the status of subordinates to men, Phillips claimed the rights of citizenship in the public spheres of print culture and the law. In her preface she lays claim to "that Liberty of the Press . . . as our only Bulwark" against attempted tyranny, and upholds the role of public as judge and jury, for she is sure that "when the Public have perused her Story they will unanimously become her Protectors" (I: v, ix). Litigious and combative, she also took up with absolute sincerity the shibboleth that the "rule of law" was every English person's birthright and was what distinguished Britannic freedom from Continental slavery. Phillips appeared personally before hallowed judges to offer a spirited defense of her rights and character. She thus constructed herself as both a legal and political subject, a freeborn English woman who used her "liberties and properties" in these realms, as in others, to support and defend herself against oppression.

Moreover, as a commoner who dares take on a lord, Phillips singlehandedly proffers a blistering assault on class and sexual politics that stressed her right to fight back against both male vice and aristocratic arrogance. "Titles may give . . . Place and Precedence, but unless their high Rank be dignified by Virtues . . . they are only to be pitied, and conspicuous to be despised" (II: 112), Phillips asserts in the midst of a fine anti-aristocratic diatribe that would not have been out of place in a tract by Burgh or Shebbeare. "Once in a *thousand Years*, a Woman should be found who has the Courage to take up Arms against her Oppressors, and prove that even an *Lord* may be – *a Villain*" (III: 38). The male characters in her drama, all of whom were recognizable types in contemporary theater – the "*high-born* DEBAUCHEE," the "bigamous Merchant" and the "Beau Adventurer" (III: 246–7) – incarnated the male and aristocratic prerogatives that exploited women. In many ways, then, Phillips's theatrical rendering of her life gave her dramatic license for the public and textual performance of herself as a victimized woman while simultaneously demonstrating that the stereotype of the fallen woman was insufficient to capture the complexities of her character,[26] mobilizing sympathy, indignity, outrage and pleasure among her audience.

Phillips's contested self-fashioning focused and propelled a number of existing anxieties about female sexuality and consumption, male degeneracy and the fungibility of the national identity that circulated in cultural and political circles in the 1740s and 1750s. In the wake of the Richardsonian revolution, an outpouring of novels and conduct literature attempted to convey female interiority and to regulate female conduct.[27] This literature expanded a growing anxiety about the relationship between women's agency, sexuality and their control. Providing evidence of women's sexual desire, and absolving them of responsibility for it, memoirs like Phillips's "both confirm and deny that every woman is at heart a rake," as Felicity Nussbaum has wittily noted.[28] This inner state of femininity was authenticated in such popular works as the French *chroniques scandaleuses*, or, still more, John Cleland's overtly sexualized narrative *Fanny Hill, or Memoirs of a Woman of Pleasure*. Further, although Phillips vowed that "every Syllable [of the Apology] was true" (I: ix), the narrative's generic hybridity also allowed it to be consumed not only as gossip, but also like a novel, so that as with the sparring "pamelists vs. anti-pamelists" of the period the walls between fiction and non-fiction collapsed as the public struggled to decide whether Phillips was saint or sinner. In this context, the performativity of Phillips's text, and her own public performances as fine lady and tragic heroine, struck both chords and nerves.[29]

At the same time, Phillips's status as a courtesan and bigamist played on a long-standing fascination with fallen women, adultery and polygamy that runs through eighteenth-century writing, but which in this period is sharpened and extended in the realms of the dramatic, the religious and the anthropological. In novels, plays and periodical essays, for example, these sexual suspects appear variously as evil temptresses (and thus allied with Frenchness, foreignness and depravity), or more sympathetically as ladies whose "triple accidents" of beauty, frailty and poverty forced them to become wantons.[30] Such imaginative interpellations intersected with empirical developments, as social commentators and moralists began to "discover" the problem of fallen women. The blight of prostitution was seen to plague the metropolis morally and physically in an unproductive waste of female corporeality, a crisis crystallized by the Penlez brothel riots of 1749.[31] The Rev. James Fordyce's perfervid sermon, *The Folly, Infamy and Misery of UNLAWFUL PLEASURE* (1761) made Fordyce famous as it exhibited the anxiety about morally compromised women and their enervating, inflammatory sexual energy that had been building to a cacophony since the early 1750s. The formation of Lock and Magdalene hospitals to reclaim and reform these lost souls seemed to

141

offer one solution to the "swarms" of their sort polluting the streets of the capital.[32] Another was to ship off redundant women to the colonies in order to provide a much needed boost to the white populations, or even, as the chaplain of the Lock Hospital suggested, to marry them off polygamously – a recommendation that echoed those of a handful of explorers, travel writers and philosophers about the efficacy of polygamy in keeping women under control in Africa and other "savage" lands. Not coincidentally, it was also in this period that social scientists had identified sexual mores and marriage customs as markers in the "stages" through which societies progressed from savagery to (British) civilization: here polygamy and the promiscuity of woman were both held to be infallible signs of a lower stage of culture.[33] Phillips's Apology, then, appeared at a time when female agency, sexual desire, purity and pollution were subjects of considerable attention and debate, and the particular "character" of English women under sustained investigation, rendering her revelations of autonomous female sexuality dangerous indeed.

Political developments had done nothing to allay these fears. Between 1745 and 1757, rebellion, military defeat and the insidious impact of French and Catholic influence on English culture and consumption had stirred up fears about a slide into national "effeminacy." As we have seen, effeminacy referred to a complex of values and practices that augured a failure of masculinity in the public and private realms. The charges of "effeminacy" in this period targeted the supposed collapse of English martial spirit, self-sufficiency and strength in the face of French assaults, and required men and women to return to their proper roles and duties. All were matters of urgent concern to English political observers. James Burgh denounced the "restless and indefatigable spirit of the papists to overthrow our constitution, and extirpate the protestant religion in these kingdoms, and to bring upon us their damnable idolatry" at the same time as he condemned the materialist practices and French imports that increased the desire and aggrandized the vanity, luxury and corruption of national manners and spirit. Other writers pointed to the return of Cape Breton to the French by the terms of the treaty of Aix-la-Chapelle as a particularly heinous instance of ministerial supineness that threatened to seep down and corrode the martial spirit of the polity.[34] These themes reached a heightened pitch in the 1750s, when charges of aristocratic malfeasance intersected with the condemnation of behaviors and practices – sexual, consumer, political – that blurred gender lines, threatened masculinity and austerity in the political and cultural realms, and exacerbated England's decline into "a Province of France."[35]

In these contexts, Phillips appeared to be a particularly dangerous and rebellious woman. "An artful prostitute, in falshood practis'd / To make advantage of her coxcomb's follies," said one pamphleteer, quoting Otway's Orphan; while others maligned her as a "French Whore," idolatrous Catholic, and polygamous aberrant. "How vilely can a smooth tongue polish over the ugly countenance of vice!" Catherine Talbot remarked, and her correspondent, Elizabeth Carter, agreed that Phillips was "a very bad woman." Conflating Christian sin and civic vice, Phillips epitomized the excessive feminine influences that were causing a degenerate slide of the national character into effeminacy. As the reviewer in the *Gentleman's Magazine* put it, when surveying the spate of pamphlets which sought to diminish the impact of her memoirs by painting Phillips as a "vain, insolent and Whorish" creature, "some persons are not pleased with her making the best of her cause."[36] As courtesan, she exemplified the perpetual spirals of allure and pleasure which Foucault has argued are constitutive of sexual power, but which in eighteenth-century sexual ideology threatened young men with corruption and respectable womanhood with contagion. A living, breathing "woman of pleasure" she was simultaneously fantasy, menace and commodity.

Indeed, in pursuit of her lifestyle Phillips not only contravened accepted conventions of respectable womanhood, but also exhibited qualities considered in other contexts to be highly commendable: resourcefulness, persistence, resilience, self-respect, an eye for profit and the bottom line, and an appreciation of assets – "for letting nothing lie waste . . . a true mercantile Spirit" as she said in another context. Circulating through the circum-Atlantic world like other goods and peoples, and using her bodily assets to gain favours and wealth and acquire prestige – "My Beauty, while it lasted, amply supplied the Deficiencies of my Fortune . . . No Woman, let her Fortune be what it will (out of *England*) made a genteeler [figure] than my Self" – she also was able to turn her life itself into a commodity, and "reap considerable Benefit" (*Letter*, 20–1) from its sale. At the same time, her extravagant lifestyle, proclivity for vulgar display, recurrent overwhelming debts and lavish attention to her own natural resources made it clear that she had taken the laws of imperial mercantile capitalism to heart, underlining their contradictions in the process. As one pseudonymous pamphleteer put it, "these admirable Adventures, will afford indisputable Proofs that Pleasure was the reigning Taste; that Profusion passed for Magnificence; that Show and Equipage gained Admittance every where; that Money was the one thing necessary, and that all ways of coming at it were esteemed lawful amongst those who lived in a continual State of Dissipation."[37] One could offer the correction that Phillips demonstrated that money was not always necessary, for she seldom had any and lived for long periods of time entirely off credit to supply her very considerable needs and desires.

Phillips, then, was an excessively consuming female whose taste for the sensual, the sensational and the luxurious promised to enervate the nation and make it a colony of France. This aspect of feminine excess was further supported by her frank sexual desires on the one hand and by her singleminded dedication to living off men on the other, exploiting her bodily assets to attain the lifestyle she felt she had been born to. Leaving her victims suicidal, consumptive (spent) or otherwise robbed of their masculinity and virility, she refused to be contained within the legal bounds of the state-sanctioned heterosexual coupling that was soon to be codified in Hardwicke's Marriage Act. A model of voracious womanhood, she was resolutely nonproductive in a material and corporeal sense (she never had children of her own, or, it appears, became pregnant), so that she could be neither made to fit into socially sanctioned models of maternity nor forced to bear the damning stain of illegitimate offspring.

The foreign as well as sexual menace presented by Phillips is expounded on in a number of pamphlets, most interestingly in *The Happy Courtezan: An Epistle from Teresia Constantia Phillips to Signor Farinelli* (1735). Farinelli, the famous Italian castrato, was the object of much fascination, lust and loathing during his London performances of 1731. To many he was the perfect example of the depths of "degeneracy" to which modern Italians had plunged, and encapsulated the dangers of foreign influence and corruption in a too-permeable England. As one writer queried, after reviewing his performance at the Royal Opera House, is it any wonder that England has become "so debauch'd with Effeminacy and *Italian* airs . . . [that] we daily see our Male Children . . . dwindle almost into Women?" Farinelli's fictional liaison with the courtesan signified both as specimens of the unnatural. In this epistle, Phillips appears as a voracious man-eater of the most non-discriminating kind, having "Dukes, Earls, Colonels Captains . . . The courtier gay, prim cit and purse-proud clown; Jew Merchants too, the richest in the City" as her conquests. But she needs the castrato to satisfy her lusts, for "Eunuchs can give uninterrupted joys, / Without the shameful curse of girls or boys."[38] Foreign and "unnatural," effeminate and unwomanly, virtual spectacles of degeneracy, Farinelli and Phillips broke the links between sexuality and reproduction, inverted or perverted the natural order, and appropriated sexual and political prerogatives that rightly belonged to manly men.

The relations between Phillips's denigration as a courtesan and bigamist and the pejorative construction of foreign others can be seen even more particularly in the colonial context. Certainly the "fallen woman" turned colonial adventurer had become a stock figure in English accounts of the Caribbean and North America, given swashbuckling credibility by real-life Jamaican pirates Anne Bonney and Mary Reed, and mimetic form by Defoe's eponymous heroines. The low moral character of English women in Jamaica was also a concern of travel writers. Edward Ward reported that "they are such who have been Scandalous in England to the utmost Degree, either transported by the State or led by their vicious inclinations; where they may be Wicked without shame, and Whore without punishment." John Oldmixon soberly confirmed forty years later that "of late years, it has been customary for young Women, who are fallen into Disgrace in England, or are ill-used by their Parents, to transport themselves thither, and, as they say, Try their fortunes." But Phillips was also taken to embody a range of those attributes of West Indian Creole life that English observers were wont to decry. Indeed, at a moment when expanded concepts of civility – taste, refinement, discernment, generosity of spirit – were heralded as the essence of a superior English culture, the transculturated West Indian Creole seemed to exhibit exuberantly antithetical values.[39] Sensuality, indolence and love of luxury and display were said to be endemic features of white (and black) society in Jamaica by virtually every English observer from Sir Hans Sloane to Monk Lewis. "The Ladies . . . coquette much, dress for Admirers" and are prone "to run away with . . . their . . . [black] servants," was how Charles Leslie delicately put it in 1739, conveying their irreducibly corrupted sensibilities. Edward Long made the charge more explicit: "the Creoles

. . . are possessed with a degree of supiness and indolence in their affairs, which renders them bad oeconomists . . . With a strong natural propensity to the other sex, they are not always the most chaste and faithful . . . They are liable to sudden transports of anger . . . are not apt to forget or forgive injuries . . . they are fickle and desultory in their pursuits . . . [and] too much addicted to expensive living, costly entertainments, dress and equipage." In contrast to the North American colonies, there were few antimiscegenation laws in the West Indies. The ubiquity of black concubinage among European men of all ranks, married and unmarried was widely accepted and tolerated. Such liaisons, however, were believed by the English to impede conventional marriages and dissipate legitimate male fortunes, while white Creole women were deliberately dalliant in the duty of reproduction, preferring "unnatural" remedies to pregnancy and the rearing of "an unadulterated race of children."[40] Although these characteristics could be attributed by English observers to climate or felonious social origins, they were more often blamed on spending too much time around their black slaves and concubines, whose gross mannerisms, savage temperament and promiscuous appetites irreversibly infected their masters and mistresses (a point to which we shall return). Nevertheless, that white Creole women were parasitical consumers (a view recently given empirical support by Hilary McD. Beckles[41]), prone to vulgar displays of wealth and debased in their morality and sexual tastes became as common an English prejudice in this period as that African women were depraved, sexually promiscuous (as their men were polygamous) and especially fond of Europeans. Oversexed, excessively sensual and consuming, fiery-tempered and litigious, Creoles' love of "gaudy exhibition" was the outward performance of an inner excess produced by the hybrid, mis- cegenated culture of the Caribbean. Clearly, Phillips both reflected and shaped these associations of unconventional sexuality and miscegenation with West Indian colonial life. Her multiple lovers, French connections and mulatto servants cemented her identification with the foreign, the dark, and the uncivilized, demonstrating to her critics how her colonial adventures had further tainted an already corrupted sensibility. Phillips, "like a spider, wrought a Webb so fine" that the "Artifice hid under the specious Appearance of Truth." Hence some critics suggested she would be more comfortable in Jamaica, a country where "slavery, piracy and thievery," polygamy and miscegenation were entrenched parts of the social landscape.[42] Significantly, John Highmore's famous portrait of Phillips sets her against a tropical background, replete with palm trees, ships and a plantation house in the distance (Fig. 16 above).

In sum, as both a fine lady and a wanton, and as a legal, political and sexual subject, Phillips appropriated prerogatives and independence that, however precarious and compromised, could not be tolerated by most observers. She was, in short, a domestic "fierce savage," a woman who refused to be tamed.[43] Not surprisingly, Phillips never was "at home" in England, which for her had become a "desart *Island of Poverty*" where she experienced a kind of social death. Her frequent retreats to France, where she was celebrated as "La Belle Angloise," and her peripatetic wanderings in Jamaica and New England, all provided greater succor for her than did her experiences in the country of her nativity. "I wandered in foreign Countries, because Strangers paid me those Honours I was denied in my own," she remarks, "till tir'd with seeing and being seen, I return'd to my native Home, always pined after, tho' the only one in which I have been treated ill" (*Letter*, 20). Turning the colonialist gaze back on the metropole, Phillips proclaimed England to be the "barbaric land" (*Letter*, 20–1), an unchristian, despotic and cannibalistic country where wealth, position and gender allowed men to exert tyrannical power over their dependants, and an oppressive double standard degraded women to such an extent that abortion and infanticide (both held to be features of "savage" societies) were regular practices.[44] English men took "the Savage example," she remarks, for "the chief Use the Majority of them make of superior Fortune, is to oppress, if possible, their Equals, and devour their Inferiors: Supported by this Maxim, the Great are never in the Wrong" (I: 172). Yet as we shall see, once in Jamaica, the outsider mobilized her nationality to ensure her superior position in local power structures, revealing how intimately colonialist sensibilities became intertwined with the performance of national identity, race and character. Hence if in a period of protracted imperial wars punctuated by intense anxieties about the firmness and manliness of the national character, Phillips took on within England the negative attributes of the inhabitants of British tropical colonies, once in those colonies she brilliantly performed her *English* difference, not least by mimicking the English imperative "to rule."

Performances of Difference

The Jamaica that Phillips visited from 1739 to 1741 and ultimately settled in from 1752 until her death in 1765 stood out as exemplar of the best and the worst of British civilization in the Caribbean. Renowned for its mountainous beauty, picturesque Spanish ruins, luxuriousness and abundance of tropical "civilities and delicacies," the island by mid-century had become the richest British colony. Its social, economic and political life was dominated by a sugar-planting elite whose combined land-owning, banking and mercantile functions had made them some of the wealthiest subjects of the king, and Jamaica a linchpin in Britain's world-wide commercial and maritime network. Local prosperity was also aided by the vigorous illicit trade with the Spanish, French and North American colonies and the energetic privateering engaged in by British vessels that continued the buccaneering traditions of the Caribbean by lawful means. That the Spanish had great cause to complain of British depredations in the decades before the War of Jenkins's Ear seems indisputable: indeed, Captain Jenkins himself, a Jamaican land-owner, was well known locally as a great plunderer of Spanish vessels in the Caribbean.[45]

Yet amidst the apparent ease, natural beauty and plenty, the shadows of slavery, internecine rivalries and death fell heavily. The rigorous slave labor regimes instituted by the planter class were notorious for their brutality and for the resistance, desertions and rebellions they fomented.[46] The various other ethnic, class, caste, racial and political divisions on the island – between English, Scots, Irish and Jews; white traders and indentured servants, mulattos or "coloureds," free blacks and Maroons; highly mobile populations of soldiers and sailors; merchants and planters; small and large land-owners; and local and metropolitan officials – produced great squabbling and factions among the colonists, endless lawsuits and explosive quarrels between planter-mercantile elites and the imperial government. As if in divine reprisal for these shortcomings, hurricanes and earthquakes regularly devastated settlements on the island while yellow fever, malaria and dysentery stalked the inhabitants in ruthlessly leveling fashion. Overall then, the island seemed to embody the combination of tropical plentitude, economic and mortal precariousness and cultural motley that was believed to produce political irascibility and sexual and moral lassitude in its inhabitants. The contrast with England was felt with a "pang of remorse" by one visitor to the island, who longingly compared "Britannia . . . with native Freedom blest, the Seat of Arts, the Nurse of Learning, and the Friend of Every Virtue" to lush and verdant Jamaica, "A Place not half inhabited, cursed with intestine Broils, where Slavery was established, and the poor toiling Wretches worked in the sultry Heat, and never knew the Sweets of Liberty, or reap'd the Advantage of their painful Industry."[47]

Politically, Jamaica shared in the battles between the contending rights and powers of metropolitan and colonial government that forced itself into American life as the Board of Trade and secretaries of state for the southern department became more vigilant over the century. If in the eyes of the governors of Jamaica there was "too great power . . . lodged in the Assemblies," the Assemblymen and even the Councilors considered the governors, patent officers and other royal appointees to be alien placemen, "unjust and tyrannical" officials whose actions and policies tended to risk the lives, liberties and properties of the honest British subjects placed under their authority.[48] The tendency of sinecurists like the patent officers to exploit the colony for profit was particularly despised, while the limited abilities and knowledge of all royal appointees from the governors down were constantly ridiculed.[49] Moreover, the recurrent threats of invasion, piracy and privateering during Britain's long wars and the ever-present fear of slave insurrection made the island's meagre military defenses a festering grievance, one that the parish-based island militia did little to ameliorate. Edward Long summed up established local feeling when he remarked that "a faithful description of our Provincial governors and men in power, would be little better than a portrait of artifice, duplicity, haughtiness, violence, rapine, avarice, meanness, rancor and dishonesty, ranged in succession." From this perspective, it was the local planters who were able to appear as the true patriots of the island, alone exemplifying "the native spirit of freedom, which distinguishes British subjects beyond most others . . . in the remotest part of her empire."[50]

Yet the Britishness of the island's political culture notwithstanding, Jamaica appeared, even to some of its residents, to be a colonial marchland, a hybridized outpost of empire. English travelers and visitors to the island remarked on the transculturated customs of the white inhabitants: drinking "Spanish" chocolate and sangria; using African "chewsticks" to clean their teeth; eating quantities of turtle, which was believed to contribute to white Creoles' "yellowish" complexions; and sleeping in hammocks, a custom borrowed from the Indians. The flora and fauna of the tropical island seemed as dangerous as they were exotic, replete with scorpions, venomous spiders and poisonous plants.[51] The lethal climate, its proclivity for natural disasters and the social and ethnic diversity of the population combined to create waves of anxiety, resentment and siege-mentality among land-owners and shopkeepers alike.[52] A recurrent worry was the way in which people perceived to be "foreigners" – in a colony where, by the early 1700s, all of the inhabitants, as well as most of the crops, were not autochthonous, the indigenes having been wiped out – infringed upon the British population's "rights and liberties." Along with the more generalized angst about maintaining Englishness in a colonial setting, these sensibilities shaped Jamaican law, which aimed to enshrine distinctions between the inhabitants on the basis of a racialized nationality, defined by origin, descent and religion. Hence a 1733 law provided that "no one shall be deemed a Mulatto after the Third Generation . . . but . . . shall have all the Privileges and Immunities of His Majesty's white Subjects of this Island, provided they are brought up in the Christian Religion." This act, giving "legislative countenance to the social ascent of mulattoes," as Winthrop Jordan pointed out some time ago, was singular among the British colonies in America. But it also made clear the racial basis of claims to national belonging: English rights and liberties belonged to English, or British, subjects, "born of British parents" or sufficiently removed from miscegenated roots to be seen as white and Christian; to be "called English" meant to be "free from all taint of the Negroe race." Later in the century, after it had restricted the amount of property a planter could leave to his mulatto children, the Assembly felt emboldened to declare, in a nice inversion of English shibboleths, that Jamaican law's essential task was "to preserve a marked distinction between the white inhabitants and the people of colour and free blacks."[53]

The law, in other words, stepped in to shore up distinctions that social practice frequently abridged, and that family, blood and business connections transected. Jamaican law created a bifurcated system that divided the numerous castes into four classes: whites, who alone had access to English common law and its most sacred plank, trial by jury; free people of color having special privileges granted by private acts; free people of color not possessing such privileges; and slaves. Among whites, under the planters, rich merchants, colonial officials and military officers were ranked the professionals, mid-sized farmers, overseers, bookkeepers, and retailers; *petit blancs* who comprised the estate staffs; small landowners, traders, white indentured servants and most soldiers and sailors and their families. Class distinctions among these groupings may not have been as rigid as in Europe, as the majority population of Africans and their descendants, who outnumbered whites by a ratio of about 11 to 1 in 1748, worked to keep white society more cohesive, mobile and paranoid.[54] Nevertheless, ethnicity and class formed important axes of European social hierarchy. Men of English descent maintained predominance on the island until after the American war. They dominated white immigration to an island with a small native-born population, owned the biggest plantations (perhaps one-sixth as absentees) and largest mercantile houses, and dominated the Council, Assembly and militia leadership.[55] Underneath them were arrayed, in ascending numerical order, the Jews, Irish and Scots. Jews, hailing mostly from Portugal and its colonies, carried on lively businesses as traders with the Spanish colonies and retailers in Spanish Town and Kingston, despite being plagued by a range of civil disabilities and restrictions that included the Assembly's frequent attempts to impose special taxes on them. In the 1750s Jamaican Jews waged an early, if unsuccessful, campaign for civil rights by agitating for the right to vote. Although probably considered "white," their non-Christian status made them ambiguous, and liable to accusations of collusion with rebellious blacks.[56] The Irish were considered to be the "poor whites" of the island, arriving originally as indentured servants and Roman Catholics, and their loyalties were suspect. In 1729, according to Governor Robert Hunter, most of the militia were of this stock. "Our Militia consists cheefly of hir'd or indented servants," Hunter wrote to the Board of Trade, "and these for much the greatest part of the native Irish [who] by their backwardnesse, mutinys and desertion damp'd or rather destroyed the hopes I had of their assistance in the defence of the country." In fact, a number of Irish men occupied high-profile legal and professional offices in the colony over the century. The resident English generally regarded Scots, arriving in increasing numbers after 1707 as lawyers, doctors, managers and merchants, as ambitious and successful interlopers. By the 1760s, Scots made up between one-fifth and one-third of the white population, owned about one-fifth of the island's plantations, and contributed a distinctive ethos to local social life.[57] Within this society forged by diasporic flows and complex notions of "home," plantocratic culture of the island maintained, self-consciously, an "English" identification and orientation, modeling its rituals and customs on an exaggerated gentry paternalism while sending its children "home" to England to be educated[58] – an identification of some importance in assessing local life, as we shall see.

Underneath the whites in power and status although not in numbers were the people of African descent, most of whom were enslaved.[59] Working on plantations and in towns in a great variety of occupations and capacities, the enslaved were chattels by law and custom, cut off from the antislavery bias of English Common Law, and deprived of almost all personal liberties and properties. Significantly, Jamaican practice implicitly acknowledged the contradictions inherent in the concept of human property by allowing the enslaved limited distributive and munerary rights, such as rights to food, clothing, religious instruction; to raise and sell provisions; and to avoid "bloody, inhuman and wanton killing." As the Rev. Robert Robertson observed of slaves in Antigua, slaves were well aware of their rights, "of which they are as tenacious as any Freeman upon Earth . . . and which no Master of common Sense will once attempt to violate." In Jamaica, slaves pursued, when circumstances permitted, their right to market gardening and craft work, the products of which were sold at the markets in Kingston and Spanish

Town, effectively provisioning the entire urban population.[60] Ethnic and linguistic divisions among the enslaved Africans (brought in at a rate of about 7,500 to 10,000 per year, with a quarter destined for "re-export") could undermine social cohesion: at mid-century, well over half the slave population was West African, 40 percent of the latter group comprising Akan-speaking Koromanti (from present-day Ghana), thus hailing from a highly developed militaristic culture. Transculturation ultimately forged racialized notions of connectedness with Creole slaves, but African slaves or their children were the instigators of almost every one of the seventy-five slave rebellions recorded over the century.[61] Ironically, within the contemporary paradigms of colonization, enslaved West Africans became the surrogates for the extirpated Arawak Indians as the "natives" whose "savagery," "treachery," "perversity," "laziness" and "rebel nature" necessitated and vindicated British stewardship and culture in an outpost of empire.[62]

In addition to the enslaved, in 1738 there were estimated to be 3,408 free blacks and colored or mulattos, and an additional thousand Maroons, or rebel ex-slaves. Of the first group, many were artisans, craftspeople and hucksters in Spanish Town and Kingston; indeed, their success in trade not only belied white assertions about blacks' inherent laziness but also led to recurrent protests by white traders and artisans and to a recommendation by the lieutenant-governor in 1736 to "suppress" them. Many free persons of color were descendants of planters, some having risen through the ranks to become slave owners themselves. Freed and mulatto women, for example, particularly in the relative hinterland of the western parishes, could become property-owners through their attachments to white planters and managers. Other free persons of color worked as servants, while the poorer ones may have been made on occasion to wear a cross as a badge of freedom. All were denied most basic civil and political rights, except those who had acquired them by private acts of assembly.[63] The Maroons, descended from an early seventeenth-century intermix of Arawaks and escaped African slaves brought to the island by the Spanish, had their stock continually replenished by runaways into the next century, and were differentiated on the basis of ethnicity and region. The western or Leeward Maroons, comprised largely of the warlike Akan and Ga-Adangme-speaking Koromanti from the Gold Coast, lived in an autocratic, kinship-based polity in Ashanti style, with the women doing most of the farming, cooking and housekeeping and the men playing the role of hunters and warriors; the leaders usually had several wives. The eastern or Windward Maroons followed a more Amerindian pattern of less rigidly structured leadership and greater political and ritual roles for women. By the 1720s the struggle for survival in the mountainous interior had eliminated many of these differences, and the Windward Maroons, inspired by the priestess Nanny, practitioner of *obi* or "obeah" magic rituals and namesake of Nannytown, joined the Leeward Maroons and their leader Cudjoe in waging a series of raids and war against the planters. In response, the plantocracy attempted to seize the initiative during the long Walpolean peace to separate the Maroon bands and extinguish each in turn, even hiring Muskito Indians from the Isthmus as trackers. Despite some English successes, the artful guerrilla war waged by Colonel Cudjoe, Captain Accompong and their men forced the English to make peace in the treaties of 1738–9. These treaties recognized the Maroons' freedom in return for their help in capturing runaway slaves, and so allowed them to establish more permanent communities in the eastern and western interior.[64] Thereafter, Maroons became picaresque characters in the local ethnic topography, elaborately dressed in ruffled shirts and buttoned coats to sell their game in Kingston markets or roam across plantations with hunting parties. They were essential to plantation security and the preservation of the slave system itself.[65]

The social contours of Jamaican society were worth examining in some detail. For within this cultural mélange, performance became particularly important in rendering visible the privileges and alleged superiority of white "civilization." As in Georgian Britain, colonial Jamaican society was a world where performance, display and spectatorship were essential aspects of the social mechanism, but where the stakes in the "theater of class relations" had been raised by the transecting caste and class divisions and the minority status of the white population in general and the English in particular.[66] The politics of location at work in such a setting meant that racial difference was a feature of everyday life on the island, but the meaning and significance of that difference was labile, constantly marshaled, contested, and even forced to give way. "Race" was constructed and codified on Jamaica through a nexus of variables – origin, religion, language, legal status, property and political rights, and skin color figuring most prominently. But within this technology of power, skin color alone was not enough to maintain and render credible racial hierarchies, but had to be seen to express an *internal* difference of character which physical appearance alone was insufficient to secure. At the same time, "English-ness" could become a performance of non-English or even non-British peoples, a trope of white "civilization" on the island that set its denizens off from slaves. The performance of difference was thus both theatrical in the mimetic sense and "performative" in the deconstructive sense described earlier – that is, its non-referentiality constituting the imagined internal difference of character it was supposedly expressing, that separated white from black, English from Irish, and so on.

The conspicuous consumption, extravagant hospitality and notorious brutality of the plantocracy must be seen in this context. Oldmixon observed,

> The Master of Families in *Jamaica*, Planters and Merchants, live with as much Pomp and Pleasure as any Gentlemen in the World; they keep their Coaches and six Horses, have their Train of Servants in Liveries running before and behind them, and for Magnificence and Luxury they have always got the start of the other Colonies.

(II, 412)

Such display was integral to the performance of social power that enacted and maintained the distinctions of rank, caste, class and race on the island. The custom of the "visitation," for example, which involved a planter's entire household, family, slaves, pets and all, coming to stay at a neighbor or kin's plantation for weeks or even months at a time, institutionalized the grandiosity of local sociability as it emphasized the essentially feudal mentality of the planters.[67] Signifying their sense of impermanence, the planters' love of grandiosity did not necessarily translate into architecture: until the 1770s, the houses on Jamaican estates tended to be "mean" and undistinguished, as numerous contemporaries complained, built in a single level to better survive the tempests and earthquakes that periodically stormed the island, although some of the gardens were beautiful, painstakingly laid out to maximize the tropical or mountain views.[68] But the planters made up for their makeshift houses in their indefatigable pursuit of more immediate gratification. Their manic revelry, ardent gambling, intemperate drinking, love of lavish dress and devotion to litigation all bespoke an opulence and security that those who beheld them were meant to view with awe and emulation. The Church of England clergy were reputed to follow the planters in their indulgence in the "Vices and Immoralities of this Island"; while lower-class whites mimicked their betters in dress and style, so that a cooper's wife "goes forth in the best flowered silk and the richest silver and gold lace . . . with a couple of Negroes at her tail."[69] That much of this display was financed by credit, given both the chronic shortage of specie on the island and the practice of mortgaging each crop to the coming year, is also important in underlining the insistently visual nature of this regime. Hence the dedicated dissipation of the planter may have been due in part to the knowledge that "a slight shift of fortune's wheel might mean bankruptcy or even debtor's prison"[70] but it was equally part of the enactment of difference, the performance or rank, nationality and entitlement upon which the plantation system depended.

The brutality of slave punishments was of course the other side of the coin of display. "No Country exceeds them in the barbarous Treatment of Slaves, or in the cruel Methods by which they put them to Death," Leslie reported of the Jamaican planters. For relatively menial offenses slaves could be hanged and starved to death, staked to the ground and burnt with a fire that began slowly at the feet and slowly consumed the body or have salt and sealing wax rubbed into wounds caused by flogging.[71] These punishments were justified as necessary given both the weakness of the local colonial state apparatus (which allowed slave owners to claim considerable regulatory powers) and the allegedly "savage" nature of the slaves. But as with Damiens the regicide, the main point of such excessive torture was to enact, through the ceremonial of gruesome death, the absolute power of the planter over his slave and so engage the spectator in the *visual* and *corporeal* regime that enacted the power of the law. Such a violent "performance of waste," as Roach has called it, demonstrated the plantocracy's willingness to expend any asset, including the lives of slaves, in defense of their own privileges,[72] while effacing their dependence on slaves for the necessities of everyday life. Indeed, given that penal remedy for the enslaved was transmitted through performance and custom rather than statute, slave punishments did not enact a prior law, but *were* the law performed.[73] The "paternalism" of the masters performed through hospitality and conspicuous consumption was thus reinforced by the retaliatory terror of the whip, the stake and the gallows.

The audiences for these performances of white privilege were various, but the largest, of course, was the enslaved. Their opportunities for "counter-theatre" may have been circumscribed, but were no less cogent for all that. Within the theatre of terror described above, for example, West Africans' and especially Koromantis' widely reported shows of stoicism and defiance – exhibiting "resolution and firmness . . . smiling with an air of disdain at their executioners," or even a preference for death – never failed to strike onlookers with fear and awe while also confirming slaves' supposedly "ungovernable" nature.[74] Indeed, on many different levels, the alternative culture created by the enslaved provided a counterpoint to the dominant structures of colonial society that could influence the forms and meaning of the socioeconomic and cultural exchanges under way, allowing the enslaved to exploit their status as both capital assets and exotic spectacles. For example, forms of slave resistance to the imposed labor regime, from lethargy, complaining and gossip to "petit marronage" and suicide could seem almost as dangerous to the masters as armed insurrection.[75] At the same time, syncretic forms of West African cosmology and culture, from obeah, a complex set of rituals and beliefs which attempted to manipulate the natural and social worlds, to dances or "plays" and funeral rituals, which sought to connect supernatural and everyday life, remained mysterious to white observers. As Thomas Thistlewood complained, "There is no way of knowing what they say on these occasions." Such performances provided powerful expressions of self-ownership and dis-possession to the enslaved, while also extending contacts and cohesion among slaves of diverse backgrounds within and across the pickets of the plantation. On these occasions, too, gossip, considered to be an art form in West African culture, a verbal performance that was judged on the basis of acuity and choice of words, could also function as a form of aggression to enact harm, spread information or coordinate action: indeed, Maroons used gossip and taunts to try to lure Indians and blacks away from white hunting parties.[76] That social performance could focus slave discontent was demonstrated decisively in the insurrection on St. Thomas in 1733, planned at a customary dance, which gave Africans control of the island for six months. Similarly, on Antigua slaves conspired at a funeral to blow up the local elites at George II's birthday celebration in 1736.[77] As we shall see, black Jamaicans were crucial players in the spectacles of difference and transculturation on the island, and the attempts to define white English "culture" against black "nature" were liable to collapse under the weight of social practice.

Two more points must be made about the complex relationships between performativity, mimesis and difference in Jamaica and England. Despite white avowals of the deep, abiding internal disparities and abilities between the "races," the mimesis of racial difference was seen to threaten the gulfs between plantocratic and slave classes. The frequent complaints about the influence of African social customs on whites, especially on children and women, demonstrate this point eloquently. Charles Leslie decried the ways that children learned to talk and imitate all the "behaviour, . . . and . . . the Vices these unthinking Creatures can teach" (36–7). Other behaviors borrowed from African slaves spawned similar anxieties, such as white women's carrying of baskets on heads and children on hips in the African manner, or, more seriously in contemporaries' views, the ways that planters' daughters and wives, from the "constant intercourse" with black servants, "insensibly adopted" their speech, movements, dress and attitudes:

> We may see in some of these places, a very fine young woman awkwardly dangling her arms, with the air of a Negro servant lolling almost the whole day upon beds or settees, her head muffed up with two or three handkerchiefs, her dress loose, and without stays. At noon, we find her employed in gobbling pepper-pot, seated on the floor, with her sable hand-maids around her.
>
> (II: 412–13)[78]

Clearly, Long paints a picture of cultural miscegenation and degeneration where uncontrolled mimesis subverts domestic life and threatens to turn white Creole girls into an inferior species. Their drawling language and mannerisms also reflected their too-close association with their slaves.[79] The unfolding and visible consequences of this miscegenating process were what led English observers to speak of Creoles as exemplifying a "national character" of their own, one that was litigious, extravagant, generous, sensual, promiscuous and so on. The slippage between "race" and an equally essentialized "national character" is displayed in the way that Long, and other English observers, tracked the progress of cultural difference through the *physical* changes that allegedly occurred as Creoles adapted to their environment. Long describes white Creole men in the following way: "their cheeks are remarkably high-boned, and the sockets of their eyes deeper than is commonly observed among the natives of England; by this conformation, they are guarded from those ill effects which an almost continued strong glare of sunshine might otherwise produce." He also describes their more supple joints and "keen and penetrating sight": "Although descended from British ancestors, they are stamped with these characteristic deviations" (II: 261–2). Here climate intersects with culture to produce a "national character" that gets presented and understood as a racial phenotype. Forty years before Long's observation, Charles Leslie had also noted that English people in Jamaica were not only too *white* – looking "sickly and wan", with "scarce a face that resembles the gay bloom of a *Briton*" (2) – but also seemed shorter: performers in the spectacle of degeneracy produced by tropical torpor and the mimetic effects of cultural hybridity and difference.[80]

The contradictions surrounding the role of white women in the frontier of Jamaican Creole culture also participated in these performative systems. By the mid eighteenth century, to put it crudely, white women were at a premium, and (despite their varied social and economic positions) law and custom worked to put them on a pedestal that emphasized the cultural distinctions of "race" as it endowed planter society with respectability.[81] Against the black woman's alleged voracious sexuality, physicality, and cultural and moral primitiveness, white women on the island were idealized as fragile, maternal, pristine and inviolable to attempted improprieties. Indeed, as noted above, the plantation system deliberately linked white women to the reproduction of freedom by legislating that black women's children, even if fathered by a white man, were slaves, while all white women's children were free.[82] Yet though white women's social and symbolic position was secure,[83] Creole women's "inner nature" placed them somewhere outside of European standards of femininity and beauty. Unfavorably compared to the stylish mulatto beauties of the island, white Creole women were considered by male and female observers to be gauche, simpering, indolent, sluttish, vain, not only prone to display the "vulgar manners" of their black servants but also singularly lacking in the wit and grace of their European counterparts. The openness and ubiquity of black and colored concubinage was blamed in part on the physical and cultural insufficiencies of white Creole women, whose own extravagance and primitive excess was also displayed in their predilections to "run off with the most insignificant of their [black] servants" as Leslie had noted.[84] Hence when in 1739 Edward Manning brought his divorce case to the Assembly, he charged his wife Elizabeth not only with her recent love affair with planter Ballard Beckford, but also with the allegations that she had been sleeping with a number of black men on the estate.[85] Creole women were not quite/not white Englishwomen in contemporaries' eyes, and their idealization only thinly masked their otherwise suspect essential nature. Even the young ladies wanted "that indispensable requisite of complete beauty, the glow of youthful vermilion," Bryan Edwards opined, "which heightens the graces of the English fair."[86] The different kinds of whiteness in Jamaica called into being through such characterizations underlined the colony's dangerous status as a site of transition and degeneration.

At the same time, the material realities of existence on the island – where, despite the high mortality rates among the men, they still outnumbered women by a substantial proportion – meant not only that women from fairly petty backgrounds could aspire to good marriages, but also that widows, as women of property, were highly desirable prizes. As elsewhere in the New World, marriage was a critical social act in a colonial society where the public authority of Church and state were weak. Governor Sir Nicholas Lawes was alleged to have remarked that "the female art of getting rich" quickly in Jamaica was summed up in the words "Marry and Bury." But the same was also quite clearly true for men, the most fit and ambitious of whom were particularly eager to acquire well-connected and propertied women. To this end, Lawes himself married five widows, by which he related himself to five distinguished families and so rose steadily in the ranks of colonial administration.[87] The shortage of marriageable women also made Jamaica an attractive destination for young English ladies and their ambitious mothers, ever-hopeful of catching the eyes of wealthy planters, although this did not always turn out as planned. Frances Storer, successful singer at the Covent Garden Theatre, brought her four daughters with her on a visit to Jamaica in 1762, only to see three of them serially mated and married by the actor John Henry.[88] Still, such an environment could be a fertile one for a socially ambitious, witty and beautiful woman determined to acquire the recognition, status and financial security that she felt had been unfairly denied her in her native land.

We can now place Teresia Phillips into our Jamaican social-scape. From her first visit in May 1739 to January 1741, a period marked by peace with the Maroons and war with Spain, she inserted herself into local political, social and racial narratives of the island with a vengeance. The flip side of the coin of her anti-aristocratic sentiments was that she was supremely aristocratic-identified, convinced she was a great lady who had more intellect, polish and refinement than all the grandees who had shunned her. She quickly appreciated her cachet as an émigré who could perform the role of the poised and witty English lady with considerable aplomb, and used her status to position her within the upper echelons of Creole culture. Despite the exciting voyage across the Atlantic and her own apprehensions about the unhealthful climate, she landed in Port Royal harbor in good spirits. The first "Spectacle" she beheld "was seven great tall Negro Men in a Boat that brought two white men on Board, and in no other than the very Dress in which Nature first presented them to the Light" (III: 104). Phillips's shock, which she represents as stemming from "the natural Modesty of a Woman," marked her as English, since the nakedness of Africans was apparently a common enough sight in this period that white Creole women could be seen inspecting the genitals of newly arrived slaves in the marketplace.[89] She soon was taken to Spanish Town, where her arrival "made the usual Noise: These Islands are like Country Towns," Phillips remarked, "where every Person knows his Neighbour; and to fill up their vacant Hours, are generally obliged to employ them in other Peoples Affairs" (III, 106). More to the point, her reputation as Needham's mistress had preceded her, in a testament to the speed and efficacy of transatlantic gossip networks.

Phillips spent her first three years in Jamaica immersed in the social life that swirled around Henry Needham at his country house at Sixteen-Mile Walk, ten miles outside Spanish Town, a pleasant and healthy part of the island which sported a number of "gentlemen's seats," fresh air, a spring and a river with an abundance of fish. Indeed, Needham's immediate and extended family owned sizeable plantations on the island and his uncle, William Needham, was currently speaker of the Assembly, so that Phillips's social circle was made up of the elite of colonial society.[90] Among the local celebrities she came to know were Ballard Beckford, a neighbor whose estate bordered Needham's and who had just been expelled from the Assembly for his affair with merchant Edward Manning's wife; Hampson Needham, cousin of her lover, whom she thought to be brash and insensitive; and Governor Edward Trelawney, a "genteel, behaved Gentleman," planters' advocate and factionalizing political influence on the island whom Phillips greatly admired. She may also at this time have met Henry Moore, her future patron, owner of a neighboring estate and political ally of Trelawney.[91] And while some of her contemporaries who visited the island, such as Mary Ricketts, found it to be "a Dull, illiterate Part of the World," Phillips exulted in the charm and liveliness of Creole society. She proclaimed the "native Creolians" to be "the most hospitable, friendly, faithful People upon Earth" (III: 129), while the local style of conspicuous consumption and display and her lover's money allowed her to indulge herself in her favorite pursuits. Significantly, however, her view of white Creole women endorsed that of some of her male English contemporaries: devoid "of beauty, wit and soft good nature" and harboring tongues tinged "with the meanest satire," Phillips found them to be immodest, dull and crass. In contrast to other English women visiting the island, who were frightened or disgusted by ubiquitous house slaves, Phillips preferred the company of her numerous colored servants, whom she found to be particularly "tender" and "generous" (III: 130–1).[92]

Phillips staunchly embraced the viewpoints and attitudes of the planter class with whom she lived and associated. She decided, for example, that the high mortality rate amongst European men arose from their "free Living, Irregularity, and Want of Management of themselves" and that there was nothing about the climate that would prevent Jamaica from "being made one of the most delightful Spots in the World" except bad imperial management. Her examples of the latter included many of the standard grievances listed in Assembly records, pamphlets and memorials to the metropolitan government: the monopolization of land into relatively few hands, "by which Means there are no small Settlements, not one fourth of it being opened;" the level of "faction" within the Assembly and Council, which Phillips blamed on the "Scots and Irish," who as merchants "with inde-fatigable Pains endeavor each to keep the upper Hand, and wrest the whole Power from the [English] landed Gentlemen"; and the corruption of colonial office holders, whose methods of tax-gathering and legal administration allowed them to expropriate properties from struggling planters.[93] On more immediate political issues, such as the war with Spain, local opinion was divided: many merchants believed the "haughty Spaniards" deserved some retaliation for their frequent "depredations" and that a British victory would open the door to further colo-nization in the Caribbean basin; planters thought the war would be bad for the sugar trade (which in fact it was). Phillips predictably agreed with the planters, while also offering some sharp comments on the conduct of Vernon and Ogle who, despite having "the largest and finest fleet" ever assembled, were unable to prevent the demoralizing spectacle of French privateers capturing Spanish treasure at Cartagena (III: 139–40).[94] Finally, Phillips complained of the "Evil" arising from the ominous disproportion between the plantocracy, the lower classes and still more the vast slave population, which she estimated at twenty to one, an exaggeration indicative of the siege mentality of whites on the island. In Phillips's view, and one that was more widely shared, deficiencies of the African "character" meant that the late treaties with the Maroons could prove to be "very destructive," for they provided a beacon and example for disaffected slaves (III: 140–1).[95]

Phillips, then, clearly enacted her Englishness as a sign of difference that upheld the systems of political, racial and gender subordination in Jamaica. Her nationality and race ensured her a superior position in local power structures, where her propensity for extravagance and display were recognized signs of that entitlement. At the same time however, her role again exceeded the one conventionally assigned to white women as decorative consumers, for she interested herself in the social and political affairs of the island, and made those opinions known to others. She was, in this way, as Hilary McD. Beckles has suggested of Caribbean white women in general, a "conduit in the process of socio-ideological transmission" that ensured the reproduction of the plantation system.[96] Phillips's and her four servants' departure early in 1741 was precipitated by the malaria epidemic that had sickened her lover and then herself; it would later claim the lives of some ten thousand soldiers and sailors under Vernon and Ogle's command.[97] But this passage to Jamaica, which Phillips would call "the most pleasing Remembrance of her Life" (III: 131), embodied for her the kind of civil and gracious life she had been born to lead. Significantly, several years later, when Phillips was about to be taken to the rules of King's Bench for debt, she reported that her mulatto and black servants offered to sell themselves to procure her liberty, and had a number of prospective buyers, but Phillips adamantly refused to let them make such a sacrifice. "Is there any *European* Proof of fidelity and affection in a Servant that Equals this?" (II: 227), Phillips exclaimed. In the Atlantic interculture, nationality, loyalty, and "character," like human beings themselves, were commodities that both bolstered and dissolved the categories of difference upholding European order, retailing reputation, servitude and freedom across an imperial cultural marketplace.

Theater of transatlanticism

Phillips's immigration to Jamaica in 1752 inaugurated a new phase in her life, one that is somewhat less accessible to historians because it is based on gossip and rumors, with some thin first-hand accounts written by Phillips herself.[98] Nevertheless, the basic outlines of her life as a resident of the colony are easy to reconstruct: a heady, successful and extravagant period as a wealthy widow and colonial official followed by a predictable period of debt and decline leading to her death. For after a brief stint of running a "boarding school for young ladies,"[99] Phillips embarked on a new "career," that of marrying and burying a string of rich husbands that enabled her to amass a fortune and live in considerable style.

Her continuing English identifications notwithstanding, Phillips's first two husbands were wealthy Celts from the professional and merchant classes. Hugh Montgomery, whom she married in 1754, was a well-to-do Irish land surveyor who lived in Kingston. As in England at the time, road building was a politically divisive but commercially profitable business, and Montgomery had made a fortune in surveying estate boundaries and rights-of-way for planters and the colonial government. Their marriage went well for a time, but within two years Montgomery came down with an undetermined illness, allegedly provoked by his wife's extravagances, that "reduced him almost to a skeleton." He decided to go live in the country, and to leave Phillips nothing in his will, but Phillips got wind of his plan and forced him to leave her everything by deed of gift. Some days later he was dead, and she inherited his considerable estate, even pursuing the Council for the back-fees for

Montgomery's services.[100] Her next husband, whom she married a year later, was Samuel Callender, a Scottish commissary for the French prisoners of war and "a young gentleman of good interest in *Britain*, and well respected in *Jamaica* by all who knew him," as one observer attested. Despite blooming premarital health, Callender soon became a recluse who was "not seen more than three times out of his house" before his death two years later, while Phillips handled his affairs. Inheriting all his possessions and estate, including a cargo consigned to him, she soon amassed a ready fortune of some £2,000, and acquired a new coach and horses to live in great style. Before his illness, Callender had conveniently brought to Jamaica as prisoner one Adhamar de Lantagnac, nephew to Vaudreille, a handsome young French officer, who became Phillips's third husband on the island. They married in the Kingston parish church in 1762, when she was fifty-three. Loving dissipation as much as she, he disappeared after a year without a trace, said by Phillips to have "decamped" to Martinique or Hispaniola. What actually happened to him, however, was never clear. In each case Phillips was able to profit from her partner's demise and carry on her proclivity for the high life, so availing herself of the time-tested strategy for social advance in Jamaica. Sometime during this period, too, Phillips's niece may have come from England to live with her; the evidence for this visit however is tantalizingly small.[101]

During her first marriage, Phillips intervened in local politics in a way that confirmed her reputation as a woman to be reckoned with. The ill-fated Admiral Knowles, who served as governor from 1752 to 1756, was a once-popular figure who had distinguished himself at Chagres and who was celebrated locally for his successful capture of two Spanish privateers carrying 120,000 pieces of eight. Yet as governor he became embroiled in the battles between the planters and merchants that were waged with singleminded dedication within the institutions of colonial government. In 1756 these divisions provoked the most serious political crisis of the century. Partly to please his merchant allies on Assembly and Council, partly because of the unhealthy and defenseless location of Spanish Town, and partly out of fears for his own safety at the hands of the planters, Knowles attempted to transfer the capital of Jamaica from Spanish Town to Kingston. The resulting volleys of petitions and addresses to the metropolitan government procured Knowles's recall later that year.[102] His successor, Lieutenant-Governor Henry Moore, quickly disallowed the act authorizing the transfer. The planters and residents of Spanish Town celebrated their victory by retrieving the colony's archives from the Kingston town hall and carrying them under strong military guard back to Spanish Town. Illuminations, fireworks and "a great general rejoicing" followed that included the burning in effigy of Knowles, and his ship, the HMS *Cornwall*, "which they sacrificed to the flames, with infinite rage and contempt, after the first striking and burning the flag," as a writer in the *Kingston Journal* reported. This letter quickly became the focus of a new political furore. The burning of Knowles was regrettable enough, the writer noted, but burning his ship was an insult to King and Country, and an act that, in light of "the benefits so lately received from the throne, . . . is a most atrocious mark of their ingratitude to his majesty, as well as a very impudent insult upon the gentlemen of the Navy." At the very least, such "ignominious treatment" provided scant evidence of "that healing balsam that was intended to reconcile all parties."[103] The planters in the Assembly took great offense at this piece, calling it "a false, scandalous, infamous and seditious libel, tending to inflame the minds of the people of this island, and to keep up the unhappy divisions that have too long subsisted amongst them" and ordered the printer, Thomas Woolhead, into custody. Woolhead gallantly fingered one Teresia Constantia Phillips Montgomery as the writer. She was taken into custody in turn, but was discharged upon making an apology, and the affair brought to an end. Nevertheless, Phillips's published remarks on local politics indicate her continuing, if self-appointed, role as political subject and critic: in this case, as the recent English émigré and loyalist who needed to teach untutored Creoles the meaning of patriotism. Taking on the role of the King's protector in his absence, Phillips's performance of Englishness was meant to remind others of their over-riding loyalties to the mother country, which had to trump those of locality within the transatlantic empire. Clearly, her sense of entitlement was as strong as ever, impacting her tenure as a colonial official in interesting ways.

The next year (1757), Phillips was appointed Mistress of the Revels by Moore, Lieutenant-Governor from 1755 to 1759, and again in 1759 to 1762, with whom she had struck up a warm friendship. Son of a prominent Jamaican planter, Moore had been educated at Eton and Leiden, where he became a close friend with another well-known sugar heir and future Lord Mayor of London, William Beckford. A handsome gallant, Moore was eventually married to Catherine Long, daughter of prominent planter Samuel Long and eldest sister of Edward Long, whom Moore appointed as his private secretary during his tenure as Lieutenant-Governor of the island. Moore was well liked for his generosity, fairness and attention to the military needs of the island – he became especially admired for his role in putting down the slave insurrection known as "Tacky's Rebellion" in 1760 – but he was also criticized for his extravagance and frivolity. "There were united in him the opposite qualities of great vivacity and love of pleasure, with intense thinking and profound application," his brother-in-law diplomatically remarked. Moore's devotion to music and theater did indeed seem to exceed his political judgment: on his father's death, Moore brought to Jamaica a band of musicians and players, among whom was the estranged husband of Charlotte Cibber Charke; as Lieutenant-Governor of Jamaica he appointed Phillips to office; and while Governor of New York (1765–9) he aroused considerable Presbyterian ire by attempting to establish a playhouse.[104] Phillips had thus found a sympathetic spirit in Moore, and her popularity with him, as well as her continuing friendship with former lover Henry Needham, now Speaker of the Assembly and married to an American heiress, allowed her to navigate local political disputes and achieve considerable acclaim. Through these alliances, Phillips's reputation came full circle, as she became known in England, Jamaica and New England as a "black widow," a woman who consumed and killed her mates for pleasure and survival. Hence the 1750s brought Phillips to the pinnacle of social success and authority, while also ultimately cementing her association with the chicanery and alterity of colonial life.

Phillips's appointment as Mistress of the Revels put her at the apex of social life in Spanish Town and Kingston in the late 1750s, a time of both anxiety and catharsis on the island. The outbreak of war with France in 1756, when Jamaica was in its usual state of military weakness, suppressed local feuds as residents braced for possible invasion and attacks by French fleets. Commodore Townshend, in charge of Jamaica station, put a press for seamen into effect, and Moore declared martial law. By early 1758, however, the arrival of a British fleet with military reinforcements secured the island and made Jamaica the seat of a major West-Indian offensive, while also restoring trade to near-normal levels. Ultimately the Seven Years War would accelerate Jamaica's economic development, as the British capture of the French sugar islands of Martinique and Guadaloupe, which made French sugar expensive and Jamaican sugar cheap, allowed Jamaica to become the most important sugar producer in the imperial system.[105] In the shorter term, the middle years of the war brought widespread relief and renewed attention to the pursuit of pleasure in the two lowland towns. Spanish Town was the seat of the government and, as noted above, considered to be the planters' special outpost. Choked with carriages that waited for their occupants amongst the ramshackle public buildings and picturesque Spanish ruins, Spanish Town incarnated the spirit of private opulence, love of pleasure and lack of civic spirit that was the hall-mark of Jamaican society as a whole. The town particularly came to life from October to Christmas, when the Assembly was sitting. Occasions as grand as the Governor's annual speeches and as mundane as the anniversary days of the Free and Accepted Masons brought local notables together for processions from the Governor's House or Brown's tavern to St. Catherine's Church. Balls and assemblies on state anniversaries, such as the fourth of November and the monarch's birthday, races on the savanna and medicinal baths near the local hot springs provided opportunities for residents and visitors to display themselves in (and out of) their silk finery and silver and gold-trimmed cloaks. Indeed, on these occasions, planter and merchant, local and international "quality" mingled: English visitors and expatriates alike were always surprised and pleased to meet friends, or friends of friends, "from home," and gossip was a favorite pastime, although the three main topics of conversation were said to be "Debt, disease and death."[106] A theatre boasting an "excellent" company of players and numerous gambling houses provided residents with two other favorite entertainments. Meanwhile, the rickety bridge over the Rio Cobre stood in disrepair, and there was no printing press in the town until 1755, when two printers opened shops, each producing a weekly newspaper.[107]

The capital's rival was Kingston, built up river from Port Royal following the series of hurricanes that had devastated that settlement at the turn of the eigh-teenth century. The merchants' center, entrepot of the sugar and slave trades, and site of the customs and excise offices, Kingston also had a church, two synagogues, a Quaker meeting house, a school and a gaol. The naval officer of the island lived

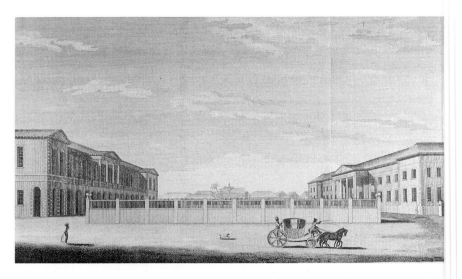

Figure 17 Parade at Kingston (1774). Courtesy of Steve Larese.

here, as did the regiments stationed on the island, in barracks situated on the outskirts. Kingston boasted in addition a handsome square (Fig. 17), an impressive market and attractive buildings, which included abundant taverns, the principal two of which were called Ranelagh and Vauxhall, each having long rooms for concerts, balls and assemblies. Merchant coffeehouses took in all the "prints," while gambling houses and after 1756 a "very pretty theatre" provided important alternative diversions. In the 1750s there were at least two printing shops, one run by Mary Baldwin, who had inherited her husband's business, and at least two engravers, one of whom, Michael Hay, provided maps and plans of North American and Caribbean colonies settled or taken by the British. The two weekly newspapers produced in Kingston in this decade, as those published in Spanish Town, retailed news about British and local politics, declarations of war, gossip about London and Court society, and snippets from Irish, Scottish and American newspapers. They also circulated information about prices, arrival and departure of ships and cargoes, runaway slaves and indentured servants; and inventoried goods and properties for sale, especially by those who were returning "home." The newspapers thus mapped the loyalties, interests and connections that linked Jamaicans of all colors with Britain and the Atlantic colonies, concretized the transatlantic flow of goods, peoples and ideas and gave form to growing local pride in Jamaica's importance as a conduit of British capital and culture in the region – an imperial center, not merely an outpost, of Englishness in the West Indies.[108]

As Mistress of the Revels, Phillips promoted the Anglophilia of white culture on the island while also contributing to its distinctive local translations. First, she oversaw all the events given by and for the governor. For example, in addition to the balls and assemblies in his or the king's honor, a new governor traditionally spent three days being fêted in Spanish Town before making a public entrance into Kingston, where the richest inhabitants subscribed a purse to cover the costs of the lavish entertainments. More centrally, she gave official approval to the theatrical productions in the two towns, had a place on the stage at every performance, and a benefit every season, by which she would earn at least 200 guineas. She thus licensed and profited on the parade of English expatriates, suspected Jacobites and other transatlantic subjects who made up the Jamaican theater companies, and who like herself had chosen to wander the empire in search of fortune or fame.

The importance of colonial Jamaican theater lay in its links to the maintenance of the theatre of power itself. For the playhouses in Kingston and Spanish Town brought together a wide cross-section of local society in the thrice-weekly performance of English cultural difference, an enterprise that both encoded the hierarchies of class, caste, "nationality" and race and displayed the possibilities for their transgression.[109] Meant to serve as a site of didactic experience that also embodied British people's rights to free expression, theatre also provided the arenas for the display of emotion, for spectacle and the spectacular, allowing the public to confront itself in distinctive ways. As in Georgian England, the transgressive power of the theater lay in its status as a forum where power was visualized and political meanings intensified.[110] At the same time, colonial as well as English theaters functioned as sites for the definition, performance and dissemination of Englishness, "carry[ing] abroad a Taste of Politeness and Generosity, and giving the World a Better Idea of *English* Manners," as one theatrical proponent asserted. The theater buildings, the plays acted in them and the style of performance were all part of the effort to transplant English culture to Britain's colonial possessions, and the players performed primarily, though by no means exclusively, for a European clientele.[111]

But this privileging was bound to be a particularly charged effort within the culturally hybrid spaces of the Caribbean, where English theater was necessarily a minority effort, and the majority of the population were neither European nor American. Indeed, English theater in Jamaica was challenged by the competing traditions from the majority population, the real meanings of which baffled whites. For example, Jonkonnu, or "John Connu," which is today the Jamaican national festival, was in the eighteenth century a slave masquerade with dancing and masks that was performed on Boxing Day and harvest festivals. It grew in importance over the century. Sloane described the performers as dancing with

> Rattles ty'd to their Legs and Wrists and in their hands, keeping time with one who makes a sound answering it on the mouth of an empty Gourd or Jar with his hand. Their Dances consist in great activity and strength of Body and keeping time . . . They very often tie Cows Tails to their Rumps and add such other things to their bodies in several places, as gives them a very extraordinary appearance.

Soon thereafter, players also began to add masks based on ethic origin and male and female Connus; by the 1760s the masks were described as having "a horrid sort of vizor, which about the mouth is rendered very terrific with large boar tusks" which they would use to menace the spectators who watched or danced in response (Fig. 18). A circum-Atlantic invention rooted in a syncretic combination of West African and West Indian customs, Jonkonnu seemed a quaint or fascinating expression of Africans' primitive nature to white onlookers. Yet for the enslaved the dances served, in addition to their obvious social functions, more subversive ends: a chance to communicate with each other while providing demonstrable proof of the illegible nature of African culture to Europeans – a performance, in other words, that reveled in its opaqueness to the white gaze.[112] Indeed, British observers fretted over the similarities between the masquerade and music of Jonkonnu with those of the "witchcraft" of obeah, employed to revenge injuries or protect against theft, which also used masks and charms. In the event, they had cause to worry, for African horns and drums had been used by warring maroons to incite slaves to join them, and obeah played an organizing role in a number of slave rebellions. In the serious uprising of 1760, planned in great secrecy among the Koromanti slaves throughout the island, an obeah-man took a leading part in orchestrating the offensive of the over one thousand men and women involved, administering oaths of secrecy and the fetishes meant to protect them. The rebels' strategy was *marronage*, but, when that seemed likely to fail, the masked obeah-man hanged himself as a warning. In Kingston, "Cubah" or "Abera," a female slave owned by a Jewess, was crowned "Queen of Kingston" and fêted in rituals reminiscent of Jonkonnu; a sword with a red feather stuck into the handle (a Koromanti symbol of war) found near her "court" left no doubt in white Creoles' minds that she was another leader of the conspiracy. From the perspective of planter society, African performances at opposite ends of the ritual spectrum blurred imperceptibly; secrecy and gossip were equally threatening; and the counter-theater of the enslaved seemed likely to slip from festival to menace without warning.[113]

Given these stakes, the Kingston and Spanish Town theaters presented indeed a microcosm of the plantocracy's vision of society. Crowded with colorfully dressed black slaves, some in livery, who held the places for their masters and mistresses, most though not all of whom would trickle out as the latter arrived; the officers, government officials, planters, merchants and their expensively dressed wives in the boxes, prosperous Jewish merchants, retailers, shopkeepers, clerks, overseers, and bookkeepers in the pit, and a mix of mulattos, household servants, prostitutes, fruit sellers and "young squires." The castes and classes were on display and confronted themselves in the mutual spectatorship of cultural difference. The theater of the town square, as much as slave masquerade and the broader theater of social relations, was an intensely *visual* and *corporeal* space, where the body was the praxis invested with the performance of history and ideology, thus rendering what they mapped on the body seem natural and inescapable. Alternatively, theater could also work to defamiliarize the natural (as in the ubiquitous cross-dressing of the eighteenth-century stage) by exposing it as mimesis or performance.[114] Finally,

Figure 18 Isaac Belisario, *Jonkonnu* (*c.* 1836), National Library of Jamaica. This Belisario drawing probably presents a more formalized version of the performance than those enacted in Phillips's day.

colonial Jamaican theater had the additional task of attesting to English cultural superiority while also asserting the inviolability of colonists' cultural link with the "mother country" in a counter to the charges of the Creole culture as alien, exotic, foreign or otherwise un-English.

It is thus of interest that the role of cultural emissary was taken up by those held in lowest repute by metropolitan culture – the disreputable and sexually suspect "strolling players" whose professional and personal respectability was always questioned. These men, women and children, hailing from England, Ireland and the American colonies, criss-crossed the Atlantic in their indefatigable devotion to the performance of Englishness, a craft and a performance that revealed both the strengths and instabilities of national culture in a transatlantic world. The "vagrants of the Thespian race," as one American prologue described them, were nonetheless crucial to the success of English colonization and its "civilizing" process, exceeding metropolitan culture in their "capacity to perform the values of the center." By showing the mimesis involved in the performance of Englishness, they undermined the essentialism claimed for the "national character" – the performance, in other words, damaged the performative by breaking its context.[115]

Such considerations significantly illumine Phillips's own love for theater and her pleasure in her role as Mistress of the Revels in Jamaica. The company of comedians she licensed was an amalgamated crew comprised of players from England, Ireland and America, some of whom had been performing on the island for years, and some who had arrived only recently.[116] Prior to Phillips's tenure the local stage had been dominated by the company of Irish actor John Moody who had come to Jamaica to avoid conscription during the '45 Jacobite rebellion. Moody grew up in Cork, where Shakespearean productions were particularly strong, and so may be credited with inaugurating local enthusiasm for the Bard with his dazzling portrayals of Lear, Hamlet, Macbeth and Romeo. By 1746 he had raised a subscription to erect a regular theater in Harbour Street in Kingston and had recruited more English actors, including David Douglass, before returning permanently in 1749 to England (where Moody would become famous for his roles as ethnic figures, from black servants to the blundering Irish officer, Major O'Flaherty, in Richard Cumberland's *West Indian*).[117] Shortly after Moody's departure, and encouraged by the news of his success, a bankrupt London theater manager, William Hallam, gathered together a small group of actors, including his brother Lewis, and, taking along wives and children, props, costumes and scripts from the failed venture at Goodman's Fields, left for the American colonies. After playing along the eastern seaboard from Newport to Charleston, the company came in 1755 to Jamaica and joined forces with Douglass's group, staying on the island for three years. It was this amalgamated group that performed at Phillips's pleasure.[118]

Despite a paucity of local records, it is clear that theater flourished in Jamaica during the middle years of the Seven Years War, when prize money circulated through the town, soldiers and sailors were thick on the ground and people were in the mood to be entertained. Fortunately, the Hallam company left accounts of the twenty-four plays they had in repertoire. These include *The Merchant of Venice, Othello, King Lear* and *Romeo and Juliet* (although *Richard III, Hamlet* and *Macbeth* were probably contributed by the remnants of the Moody company). "Contemporary" plays ranged from Addison's *Cato* and Farquhar's *Beaux' Stratagem* to Lillo's *London Merchant* and Garrick's farces; and among the tragedies performed were Otway's *Orphan* and of course Rowe's *Fair Penitent*, which continued to castigate women's perilous lot in love and life in ways familiar at least to some Jamaican women. The repertoire thus set the pattern for the Jamaican stage of the next half century in combining new and established favorites of the metropolitan stage that were meant to display the best of the English character. As Hallam's prologue put it, "To this New World, from famed Britannia's shore, / . . . The Muse, who Britons charm'd for many an age, / Now Sends her servants forth to tread your stage; / Britain's own race, though far removed, to shew / Patterns of every virtue they should know."[119] For Phillips, seated on the stage in full public view, her earlier self-representations must have seem vindicated: the scandalous woman who was now a colonial authority, who had read her life through the tragedy of *The Fair Penitent*, took considerable pleasure in officiating over the premier tradition in English culture, a privileged spectator who continued to be part of the spectacle, thereby authorizing her own English superiority.

Still, the cultural capital of the Jamaican stage flowed outwards as well as inwards.[120] As noted above, the slaves' theatrical traditions, such as Jonkonnu, evolved out of a mix of customs and traditions, Akan, Ibo and European, on the island.[121] But some of the songs that accompanied them were Scottish airs, and in a number of other street performances the slaves would recite English verse. Most noteworthy in our period were the "actor boys" – that is, slave children who for a tip would enact a scene from an English play. Learned either by rote or by sneaking into the playhouse, these performances delighted and confused white spectators on the streets of Kingston and Spanish Town. *Richard III* was one of the favorites performed by the actor boys, but so too was the fourth act of *The Fair Penitent*, where a duel between the two main characters ends in death, and everyone joined in the victory dance. Clearly, the performance here could call the performative – of race, identity, "national character" – into question, breaking with context in a way that Phillips herself would have understood. The theatre of transatlanticism was a dangerous place, where mimesis and citation could exalt and transgress as well as debase – a volatile social space indeed.

Conclusion: the Black Widow

Phillips spent the last several years of her life much in a familiar pattern, dodging creditors whilst attempting to maintain her gay and frivolous life. Her chariot and horses were seized several times for debt, but she always found friends to get them returned. Yet by the time of her death in February 1765, these appeared to be much thinner on the ground, for she went to her grave unattended by a single mourner, an insult in a country where death, in part because it came so swiftly, was marked at all levels with elaborate ceremony and great crowds. She was said to have had a mirror placed over her bed, so she could view her face during her last moments, remarking, "alas! what is beauty! I who was once the pride of *England*, am become an ugly object!" Her final victory was that, because she died on a Saturday night, the apothecary could not seize her corpse as it went to the grave the next day. The "Letter from a Gentleman in Jamaica" that appeared in *Gentleman's Magazine* in 1766 described this incident and summarized her life in Jamaica: the frequent marriages, the husbands' mysterious illnesses and suspicious deaths, her amassing of fortunes which she just as quickly spent, her stint as Mistress of the Revels, all of which became incorporated into her legend. Jamaicans – perhaps black Jamaicans? – were said to call her the "black widow", an epitaph that allied her with the malignity, menace and sudden death associated with the Caribbean, but also expressed an admiration for resourcefulness and survival.

The scandalous woman, rebel and outcast, had nevertheless achieved success, by eighteenth-century standards, within the territorial and imaginative space of the British West Indies. Her mobility and survival depended upon the ebbs and flows of the Atlantic interculture, where reputation was a commodity, opportunism a virtue and self-fashioning a necessity, a transculture whose inventions, practices and identities did not begin and end at national borders. Phillips figured and circulated alternative views of gossip, of English womanhood and of colonial authority, defied and upheld hierarchies of class, race and gender and performed the English imperative "to rule." She thus mirrored back to the English their "national" characteristics in a way that repelled yet fascinated. Significantly, her last husband, Lantagnac, was said to have been raised from infancy among the Five Nations of Canada, and was thus covered all over his body with their "savage marks" – a final comment, perhaps, on Phillips' own "savage" affinities and those of colonial life.

At the same time, Phillips's historical experience not only highlights the dangers of unconventional female subjectivity and sexuality within England, but also the ways that English and other white women were located within the theaters of power and debasement in the West Indies, and their own roles in the performances of difference. Phillips may have been the only woman to hold colonial office in that century, but she nevertheless demonstrated some, although certainly not all, of the survival strategies available to women "within the unstable and socially hostile colonial culture fashioned by competitive market forces."[122] Phillips's experience suggests how and why the attitudes and activities of white women mainly served the establishment, making their solidarity with white men and slavery in many cases inevitable.

Finally, Jamaican slaves and Phillips may have had the last word. For the black widow is a spider, and Anancy, the spider-man of the Akan peoples, was the folk hero of black Jamaicans. A "trickster hero," a fiddler, magician and cheat, he imposes on people by use of his superior cunning. Sexually voracious, cannibalistic, selfish and indolent, his hearty charm makes even his victims quite ready to forgive his offenses. It may not be too fanciful to see in Phillips, the courtesan turned colonial official, the trickster black widow who demonstrates the performativity of nation, gender, race and class, turning the establishment on its head and surveying her dominion with a smile.

5

BREASTS, SODOMY AND THE LASH: MASCULINITY AND ENLIGHTENMENT ABOARD THE COOK VOYAGES

Punish'd John Marra with one dozen lashes for behaving Insolent to his Superior Officer.

Resolution Log, July 2, 1772

The breasts of the women of O-Taheitee, the Society Isles, Marquesas and Friendly-Isles, are not so flaccid and pendulous as is commonly observed in Negro-women, and as we likewise noticed them in all the Western islands, in New Zeeland, and some of the females of the lower sort at the Society Isles.

Johann Forster, *Observations on a Voyage Round the World* (1778)

From the shelter of the Roman empire, it extends over the length and breadth of the earth; at the destruction of the empire, it takes refuge near the papacy, it follows the arts into Italy, it reaches us when we civilize ourselves. If we discover a hemisphere, we find sodomy there. Cook drops anchor in a new world: there it reigns ... It is to be a villain, a monster, to want to play the role of a sex that is not one's own!

Marquis de Sade, *La Philosophie dans le boudoir*, 1795[1]

Breasts, sodomy and the lash are not the triad usually invoked to talk about the justly celebrated and preeminently civilizing voyages of discovery undertaken by Captain James Cook and his crews between 1768 and 1780. While gender and sexuality have always been central to academic and popular representations of the South Pacific, the sex is usually straight and the possibilities for transgression represented as a function of abundance rather than object choice.[2] Yet breasts, sodomy and the lash became crucial signs in the cultural system through which particular versions of masculinity, national identity and racial difference were constituted, transmitted and destabilized on the voyages. In this final chapter, their examination as objects and subjects of British explorers' discourse about the South Pacific will allow us to appreciate the intriguing roles of gender misrecognition and

169

the entanglements of desire in the production of Enlightenment typologies of difference. Recent scholarship has variously, if not entirely incompatibly, characterized the Cook voyages as being a "diagnostic" of modern geography and Enlightenment *mentalité*, and an incarnation of the local, fragmented and dispersed character of Enlightenment cultural production.[3] We shall begin by embracing both assertions, and add a third: the Cook voyages were groundbreaking, even revolutionary, in their aims (the substitution of the benevolent goals of "discovery" for the bloody annihilations of conquest) and discursive results (the inauguration of "modern" anthropology). Rejecting the notion of a unitary Enlightenment which it is the job here to "unmask," and accepting the importance of the voyages as one of many sites of enlightened processes and ideas, this chapter will nevertheless be concerned with indeterminacies rather than radical departures. In particular, we will take seriously the mutual confusions that abounded as Cook and his men attempted to use gender and sexual practice as guides to Pacific social systems, and Pacific islanders in turn tried to map their cosmogonies onto European bodies. Far from exhibiting some simple or unilateral process of "othering" at work in the art of discovery, our exploration of breasts, sodomy and the lash suggests how much the categories of Enlightenment social science depended upon the familiarity of bodies, and highlights the multiple (mis) recognitions and ambiguous identifications at play in the crucible of first contact – even, or perhaps especially, in the eyes of their beholders.

Enlightened Explorers

The mapping and colonizing of the South Seas, with all their potential promise and glory, had become a competitive and nationalist obsession with European statesmen and intellectuals by the middle of the eighteenth century. In the wake of the Seven Years War, the Scottish hydrographer Alexander Dalrymple and projector John Callander issued urgent treatises on the centrality of British control of the region to the maintenance and extension of national power. Callander, in particular, simply stole French *parlementaire* Charles de Brosse's plan and rhetoric when he claimed the project to be part of a uniquely British mission. "United among ourselves, respected by foreigners, with our marine force entire, and (humanly speaking) invincible, aided by a set of Naval officers superior in every respect to those of the nations around us," Callander hubristically asserted in his *Terra Australis Cognita* (1766), "[and] with a sovereign on the throne who is filled with the most ardent and laudable desire of seeing his native country great and flourishing," the settlement of the South Pacific seemed to be the gold ring within Britain's grasp.[4] Once in the sights of the Royal Society, the Admiralty and George III, the southern Pacific voyages became the most ambitious and well-funded mission of scientific and imperial discovery ever undertaken by Europeans. According to the British social theory of the day, the vessels for navigation displayed the genius of a country: "by the formation of them the ingenuity of a people may be estimated."[5] Accordingly, no effort was spared in making these vessels exhibit the superiority of British technology and invention. Cook's ships were outfitted with the most advanced instruments of navigation and astronomy and boasted naturalists, artists and astronomers on board, whose specially designed rooms could house their accumulating collections of plant, animal and mineral specimens. Each specialist aimed at setting new standards of data collection and empirical observation that promised to demonstrate once and for all British superiority in the arts of discovery, and to vindicate the nation, as one journalist put it, "to future ages, as the most powerful people upon this globe."[6] The official directive for the voyagers to boldly go where no man had gone before and claim all new and old discoveries for Britain also required that they adopt the new techniques of record keeping, recommended by the Royal Society, that were best suited to organize and transmit the fruits of discovery. As James Hevia has argued, these required that

> Global phenomena . . . be collected and placed into a meaningful set of hierarchized units, which could then be comparatively evaluated through exact description. Charting the world in this form had a corollary in writing, a writing which assumed a subject and author who captured the objective world in disinterested prose.

The resulting naturalist reportage, as we have seen in Chapter 2, modeled its methodology on the systems of classification initiated in the natural sciences in order to describe and rank human societies according to stage of subsistence, morality and culture.[7]

Cook's voyages, occurring in the midst of an escalating colonial and national crisis, were crucial to reconstituting the imperial project as an essentially scientific and philanthropic enterprise, designed to benefit all of humankind.[8] Within this context, the enlightened explorer emerged as a new kind of national hero, combining expertise with the taste for adventure, manly action with the sensibility and restraint capable of fostering the "brotherhood among men" that would facilitate British possession. The secret instructions of Cook and his crew sketched in this ideal character: he would "observe the Genius, Temper, Disposition and number of the Natives or Inhabitants" of each land, treat them with "every kind of Civility and Regard" and thereby procure "the consent of the Natives to take possession of convenient Situations in the Country in the Name of the King of Great Britain." The enlightened man of exploration would use civility, tolerance and political arts rather than force to persuade indigenous peoples at once of British benevolence and British proprietary rights to their lands. Simultaneously, he would collect data to formulate general laws discerning the "truth" behind human differences, their causes and consequences. Hence his keen skill for dispassionate, empirical observation and fact-gathering would provide the foundations for "a new Science of Man." Cook himself of course was the primary exemplar of this alternative masculinity, exhibiting the requisite curiosity dissociated from sexual interest, and a self-control crystallized by decisive action. "No man could be better

171

calculated to gain the confidence of Savages than Cap. Cook, " one of his officers recalled. "He was brave, uncommonly Cool, Humane and Patient. He would land alone unarmed, or lay aside his Arms, and sit down when they threatened with theirs, throwing them Beads, Knives, and other little presents, then by degrees advancing nearer, till by patience and forbearance, he gained their friendship."[9] But this mantle of expectation also fell on the shoulders of his officers and crew, all of whom were intensely conscious of the imperative to embrace the goals of masculine, unbiased but compassionate observation and reporting that would vindicate British superiority in the arts of discovery.

The ideal of the enlightened explorer did present certain epistemological and material problems for eighteenth-century theorists and practitioners alike. Royal Society intellectuals had come to question the reliability of sense experience alone in the accumulation of empirical data, yet they nonetheless found themselves forced to depend upon the eyewitness observation of men positioned far from the structures of civil society (and thus liable to degeneration themselves). Such problems could be allayed, if not vitiated, by the adoption of the "naturalist's gaze" by officer and seaman alike, a gentlemanly ideal that would allow the explorer to observe, not with an eye to commerce or conquest, but "vacant to every object of curiosity, and at leisure for the most minute remarks."[10] That the journals and logs of the senior and petty officers would be collected by Cook and later used as the basis for the Admiralty accounts of the voyages gave credibility to crew members' rather inflated sense of their own roles in turning the voyages into History.

Secondly, and perhaps more irreducibly, class disrupted the masculinity and perspicacity attributed to the enlightened explorer. The gentleman naturalist of the first voyage, Joseph Banks, returned to England with eight thousand new botanical specimen only to be lampooned in prints and squibs as a "butterfly catcher" and sensualist whose excessively refined tastes exemplified aristocratic effeminacy. Cook himself resented Banks's preciousness and pretensions, and frustrated his efforts to smuggle women aboard ship at various ports.[11] Conversely, the officers and gentlemen on board also worried that the common seamen and marines lacked the sensibility and restraint to do the work of humanizing imperialism. George Forster, son and assistant to the senior naturalist on board the *Resolution*, complained constantly about the crew's excesses: their swearing, drinking, violence and apparently unquenchable sexual lusts; their cruelty; their "inhuman propensity to destroy the poor harmless people of the South Seas." Although he attributed such behavior to the hardships of a seafaring life, which, in the fashion of eighteenth-century environmentalism, he believed made "their muscles rigid and their nerves obtuse, . . . [and] communicated insensibility to the mind," Forster ultimately hazarded this judgment: "Subjected to a very strict command, they also exercise a tyrannical sway over those whom fortune places in their power . . . Though they are members of a civilized society, they are in some measure to be looked upon as a body of uncivilized men, rough, passionate, revengeful, but likewise brave, sincere and true to one another."[12] Yet despite such doubts, the common seamen were ostentatious in their embrace of the empirical values of the voyage, even as they combined with it the sailor's historically sharp eye for commercial gain. Indeed, the merging of curiosity, science and profit was a distinctive aspect of the voyages as a whole, which marked a turning point in the emphasis on empirical accuracy and collecting.[13] The crew's mania for acquiring "curiosities" – from Tahitian feathers and cloths to severed Maori heads – was important in helping to turn the ship into a kind of floating museum or curiosity cabinet. Their enthusiasm also lubricated the wheels of exchange across the Pacific, as local people became increasingly interested in the artifacts of their near or distant neighbors. The seamen's interest in observation (and its potential profitability) was also, perhaps, revealed in the energy devoted to ethnographic inquiry. Hence the *Resolution*'s gunner's mate, irascible Irishman James Marra, who had first come aboard on the *Endeavour* at Batavia, used his unauthorized account of the second voyage to justify his two attempts to desert the ship at Tahiti as part of a secret mission to do detailed anthropological research. A "pity it was that he happened to be discovered," Marra recalled, "as from him a more copious and accurate account of the religion and civil government of these people might have been expected."[14]

The investigative mission of the voyages intersected with, and reinforced, another normative masculinity legislated aboard ship, namely that of the British explorers' vessel itself. A number of writers have stressed the symbolic, tropic and political significance of the ship in the age of revolution. For Michel Foucault, the ship was the "heterotopia *par excellence*," a chronotope that moved through space, compressing, inventing and inverting terrestrial social relations and re-shaping the human imaginary. For Paul Gilroy, the linguistic and political hybridity of the ship constituted a "counter-culture of modernity" that enabled men and women to cross and transgress social, geographical and national boundaries. For Marcus Rediker and Peter Linebaugh, the ship, with its dangers, monotonies and tyrannies, its paradoxical imperatives of cooperation and coercion, was the engine of radical proletarian consciousness. And for Greg Dening, the ship was both a floating island and a "beach" where cultures were made to reveal themselves to each other.[15] But none of these striking characterizations alone captures the distinctiveness of the explorer's sloop. Its imperative to chart and claim "undiscovered" regions of the globe required, first, that the commanders and crews had the toughness to face down the terrors of terra incognita in the human, climactic and ecological realms. The arts of discovery also necessitated weathering the psychological tedium of seemingly endless months at sea (most other navy vessels spent as much as half their time in port), and accommodating the contending goals and disparate abilities of the peculiar mix of mostly *volunteer* seamen, marines, warrant and Commissioned officers, and supernumerary gentlemen, naturalists and artists on board. The clash of personalities, purposes and pretensions that ensued exacerbated the more customary divisions of social class, ethnicity and nationality with which most navy vessels were familiar.[16]

Indeed, the diversity of Cook's seamen matched and may have exceeded that of other naval vessels, underlining both the difficulties of attributing some undifferentiated "Englishness" or "European-ness" to men sharply divided by national and class background and interest, and incorporating all equally into a coherent mission. On the first voyage, Cook's crew and supernumeraries included twenty-nine provincial Englishmen, nine Londoners, seven Scots, three Irishmen, three Americans, two Welshmen, two Brazilians, two Swedes, two black Britons and a Eurasian, as well as five Tahitians taken on the strength temporarily to help navigate the South Pacific waters. On the second voyage, the crew hailed from England, Scotland, Ireland, Wales, America, India, the Dutch East Indies, Holland, Germany, Sweden and the Azores as well as Polynesia. The company of the third voyage was only slightly less colorful, coming from America, Guernsey, Germany and India as well as the British Isles. Of the black Britons among the ships' companies on the voyages, at least three gave their lives in the cause of national glory: Joseph Banks's servants Thomas Richmond and George Dorlton of the *Endeavour* froze to death during an unlucky inland expedition to Tierra del Fuego in January of 1769, and able-bodied seaman James Swiley of the *Adventure* was killed by Maoris at Grass Cove in 1773.[17] But whatever the provenance of the individual men, and despite their often blustery shows of bravado, all present felt, and were, vulnerable, at sea in exotic locales that offered them so little, and so much, that was familiar.

In this context, authority was maintained by everyone knowing their place, and that survival was possible only if everyone did their duty. Discipline was legislated through the prohibitory system enacted though the Articles of War – the British "rule of law" at sea, passed by Parliament – and the navy's own, and more frequently adjusted, Regulations and Instructions. Both were used to order and legitimate what since the early eighteenth century had become the primary instrument of corporeal navy punishment, the lash or, more precisely, the cat o' nine tails.[18] The lash served as the remedy for an array of behavioral offenses – drunkenness, insubordination, incivility, neglect of duty, waste of food, uncleanness, theft, and threats or implementation of assault on others, including indigenous peoples – and, although the number of lashes was limited to twelve by the Articles of War (any more requiring the order of a court martial), this rule was frequently transgressed by captains, including Cook himself. Indeed, violence, or the threat of violence, was at the heart of the system of maritime authority, and Cook's sloops in this respect were no exception.[19] Given seamen's notorious love of liberty and intolerance of arbitrary power, officers had to run a tight ship capable of making visible the absolute authority and sole right to corporal remedy that they wielded over their crew. The cat was central to the system. Cook flogged 20, 26 and 37 percent of his sailors on his three voyages respectively, and also used irons as a way to placate habitually bad tempers.[20] Admittedly, this may have been a fairly low percentage by military standards (although estimates of this statistic differ), and the number of lashes fairly light, especially compared to that inflicted on West Indian and American plantation slaves (who could be flogged with six hundred lashes or more for behavioral offences).[21] And certainly background and training played a role in the likelihood of corporal punishment: marines were more likely, it seems, to get in trouble than seamen; Irishmen and Welshmen were twice as likely to get flogged as Englishmen and Scots.[22] Flogging was always intended to disgrace, and, given the goals of the voyages to set new standards in virtually all areas, from discovery to seamen's health, it seems likely that the lash took on an even greater symbolic authority as drastic remedy. As Lieutenant Charles Clerke noted in his journal of the second voyage with regard to a typical troublemaker, Charles Logge, the command felt "Ye Common Safety of the Ship['s] Company render'd it necessary to disgrace him with Corporal punishment."[23]

The way a man responded to the lash spoke, in his crewmembers' eyes, to his masculine toughness and resolve. Just as the flogging, done coolly and deliberately, "directed the gaze from the man in power to the power itself and its necessity," as Greg Dening has remarked,[24] so the response of the victim determined the respect shown him by his fellows. Executed with the arms and legs tied to the grating, back bared and legs spread, the crews arrayed on one side of the mainmast and the officers on the other, the spectacle of the flogging was intended to impress through the power of example (Fig. 19). This it did, though not always in the ways intended. Witnesses spoke of the way the first flogging "made the man," transforming the lad into the seaman.[25] As such, the lash was also a badge and guarantee of manly spirit and hierarchy necessary to the ship. Further, it bonded the men in a common fellowship in opposition to that of the officers: however the individual reacted during the punishment, in the eyes of the lower deck he was turned into a man's man and welcome shipmate. Significantly, the lash was also a terrorist weapon in the "civilizing process," used not only to tame recalcitrant seamen but also to educate native peoples in the sanctities of private property and British authority. In these cases there were no Admiralty-set limits on the number of lashes inflicted, and severe punishments of six dozen lashes were imposed on indigenous peoples – chiefs included – who had the temerity to steal equipment or even glasses and eating utensils from the ships. "The [Tahitian] Natives cannot withstand thieving," Clerke reported on the second voyage; "great numbers of them constantly coming on board & going about the Ship & rig[g]ing they frequently steal things, & whenever catched . . . we immediately seize them up to the Shrouds & give them a dozen or two according to the nature of the Theft, without any respect to rank or distinction." Others could be shot and killed – an outcome statistically more likely on the first and third voyages, but occurring in all three. As Cook recorded with reference to his first encounter with the Maori (labeled by the British press in the aftermath of the first voyage as "cannibals," despite the fact that only Maori had been killed),

They are a brave, war-like people, with sentiments void of treachery . . . We had frequent skirmishes with them, always where we were not known, but firearms gave us the superiority. At first some of them were killed, but we at last learned how to manage them without taking away their lives; and once peace was settled, they ever after were our very good friends.

Figure 19 The Point of Honor. From G. Cruikshank, Greenwich Hospital (London: 1826). Courtesy of the British Library.

Maori cannibalism was later theorized by Forster senior as the result of the excess militarism of Maori society; but it was the less severe Hawaiians who would prove to be most in need of the lesson of British superiority secured by physical force.[26]

Needless to say, not only women but all things "effeminate" were considered to be antithetical to the homosociality of the ship, and sexuality was particularly disruptive: there were no European women passengers allowed on these voyages (although some Oceanic women were given passage on the sloops to neighboring islands),[27] and women were *officially* prohibited from coming on board. Obviously when in port this rule was more honored in the breach than in the practice, but the first sign of the commanders' intention to re-impose normative shipboard discipline was to order all the women off the ships.[28] More seriously, in the homo-social space of the ship sodomy was one of the eight crimes for which the death sentence was mandatory – indeed, it was allegedly considered by seamen to be a worse offense than murder – although in practice the less draconian remedies of "running the gauntlet" or the lash were also used to punish or discourage this otherwise lethal vice.[29] There is no unambiguous evidence that any member of Cook's crews was flogged for sodomy, but two were flogged for "uncleanliness", and the Articles of War, which ostentatiously listed "the unnatural and detestable sin of buggery and sodomy with man or beast" as a capital offense, were read aboard ship and on shore on a number of occasions in the course of the voyages.[30] As we shall see, the homophobia as well as the violence of the ship also extended to encompass the semiotics of colonial encounter. At the same time, however, where sexual customs seemed part of a larger social alterity, the intimation or implication of same-sex desire could serve as an entrée into exotic culture and so itself become an instrument of colonization.

In sum, the discipline, power and masculinity aboard the explorer's sloop were visual and corporeal; once engaged in the arts of discovery, the visual and corporeal equally became "evidence" in the effort to classify human difference in evolutionary stages from the primitive to the civilized. The masculinities of the ship thus were bound to a "national identity continuous with that of the universal connoisseur" as Harriet Guest has remarked.[31] These values and expectations profoundly influenced the voyagers' assessments of and interactions with the indigenous peoples of the South Pacific, when British officers and seamen alike confronted political, gender and religious systems beyond European knowledge and experience. In this mélange of Pacific otherness, the shape of women's breasts, and rumors of sodomitical practices among men, were used as metonyms of aesthetic, moral and cultural difference, revealing in the process the unstable and fictive nature of the essentialized identities they were mobilized to express.

The Traffic in Women

"The breasts of the women of O-Taheitee, the Society Isles, Marquesas and Friendly-Isles, are not so flaccid and pendulous as is commonly observed in Negro-women," Johann Reinhold Forster, naturalist aboard the *Resolution* scientifically recorded, "and as we likewise noticed them in all the Western islands [Mallicollo, Tanna, New Caledonia], in New Zeeland, and some of the females of the lower sort at the Society Isles."[32] This observation on the size and shape of indigenous women's breasts was offered in a chapter of Forster's *Observations on a Voyage Round the World* (1778), a work widely renowned to provide the most complete eighteenth-century record of South Pacific natural and human history. Part of a chapter entitled "On the Causes of the Difference in the Races of Men in the South Seas, their Origin and Migrations," Forster's mammary assessment contributed to a larger theory that made women the central signifiers and engines of Pacific societies' potential progress. Forster classified the various "nations" of the South Pacific into two "races," distinguished according to "Custom, Colour, Size, Form, Habit and natural Turn of Mind" and ranked according to manners, morals, cultivation and the "progress towards Civilization", a rubric under which treatment of women loomed large. How did breasts work as signs within this classificatory scheme?

Metonyms of female beauty and sexuality in European culture, women's breasts were something that voyagers of all ranks felt qualified to judge. Joseph Banks thought that Tahitian women's beautiful breasts were the result of being allowed to develop "undistorted by bandages": "Nature has full liberty [of] the growing form in whatever direction she pleases and amply does she repay this indulgence." John Marra and William Wales, both of the *Resolution*, also ventured considered opinions on the subject in remarks that suggest shared aesthetic tastes and perhaps a frequent topic of conversation. "The breasts of the women of Tahiti are round and beautifully shaped," Marra exulted, while the more sober Wales added that although "the Breasts of the young ones are very round and beautiful . . . those of the old ones hang down to their navals."[33] In England, of course, breasts had recently become politicized objects in the debates, inspired by Rousseau, over women's proper role in the polity. The breast-feeding tirelessly promoted by male moralists and adopted with alacrity by some elite and bourgeois women reflected a new emphasis on maternity that, although contested, was swiftly becoming hegemonic. Women's breasts had long served to signify female defenselessness or threat; the pendulous breasts of the witch or the savage both conveyed in early modern visual images a deformed or stunted femininity. In the later eighteenth century, however, as maternity became eroticized, the size and shape of European women's breasts took on additional aesthetic and practical importance: both were believed to determine the quality of the milk, the best coming from round and moderately sized breasts with well-formed nipples.[34] In these and other ways, breasts became integral to the debate on women's place and their role in public life. As moralists emphasized, albeit ineffectually, the need for women to disengage from "public" affairs, the maternal bosom becomes prominently displayed in the portraits and fashions of the period.[35]

In the South Seas, in the equally politicized project of human ethnology, women's position and treatment, their sexual traits and their breasts also became the objects of scrutiny. Linnaeus's "fixation on the female mammae" has been colorfully and convincingly described by Londa Schiebinger as a basis for his classificatory schemes. Other feminine characteristics – skin color, lip pigment, fertility, hair texture, and pelvic and clitoris shape – also provided grounds for scientists' comparisons across cultures and, increasingly, across classes.[36] Johann and George Forster were clearly influenced by Linnaeus, seeing, like him, breast shape as a sign of a broader debasement or inversion of European prototypes among primitive peoples. The remarks quoted above on breast shape thus accorded well with the theories of social progress they advanced about South Pacific peoples. "It is the practice of all uncivilized nations to deny their women the common privileges of human beings, and to treat them as creatures inferior to themselves," George Forster asserted, and his father concurred that "the more women are esteemed in a nation, and enjoy an equality of rights with the men," the more likely the society is to advance towards civilization.[37] Indeed, in the senior Forster's work, this long-established trope of Enlightenment thought is given new resonance by what Nicholas Thomas has called an "aesthetic evolutionism" that ranked the various islanders from the most beautiful (Tahitian and Society Islanders) to the least (Australian Aborigines and Melanesians). In this semiotic system, physiognomy could signify national character: climate and the material bases of subsistence are linked to physical beauty, cultural progress and the prospects or actuality of degeneration, and breasts became a sign of the levels of "savagery" of island societies and their degree of movement towards civilization. Hence, those societies where the women's breasts were "round and beautiful" were among those where women were esteemed and well treated, and held to be advancing out of savagery; conversely, in the cultures where women's breasts were "flaccid and pendulous," women were wretchedly used as beasts of burden or punching bags by their own offspring.

These attitudes found expression in graphic representations of the voyage. As noted above, Europeans from Pliny the Elder to Edward Long, had used women's breasts, to signal the monstrosity or sexual excess of marginalized groups and indigenous peoples. Saartje Baartman or the "Hottentot Venus," who was brought from Cape Colony to London and exhibited to show Khoikhoi women's allegedly protruding buttocks and overdeveloped clitoris, would soon loom large as an example of the ways in which colonized women's bodies were used to mark a deviant sexuality.[38] But on the South Pacific voyages the effort is to show indigenous people in their "native habitats," closely and "objectively" observed – a "naturalist" visual idiom that nonetheless conveyed its own cultural politics, and that sometimes confirmed, sometimes contrasted strangely with the descriptions in the voyagers' journals.[39] In the official art of the voyages, although laden with neoclassical allusion, native women were associated with the relative fecundity or barrenness of the landscape, and their bodies made to bear the signs of their societies' primitiveness or transmutation to a higher stage. Tahitian women, with their "beautifully proportioned shape, . . . irresistible smile, and eyes full of sweetness and sparkling with fire" as Forster senior rhapsodized, of course, were appropriately depicted in sensual, luminous images (which, importantly, were as avidly consumed by women as by men within Britain). And given that physical adornments, including tattoos, were also used to rank and characterize local women, Tahitian women also earned high marks from the explorers for tattooing only their buttocks and hands rather than their upper bodies or lips, as New Zealand and Hawaiian women did. Hence Hodges's *Tahiti Revisited* (1776) (Fig. 7 above) memorializes all of these commendable features of Tahitian culture by representing the women's tattooed buttocks as part of the island's lush tropical fertility and exoticism. His painting, indeed, offered the perfect visual illustration of George Forster's remark that "[t]he View of several of these nymphs swimming nimbly all around the sloop, such as nature had formed them was perhaps more than sufficient entirely to subvert the little reason which a mariner might have left to govern his passions."[40] At the same time, the painting's attention to the buttocks, like the "idol" or *tii* and draped corpse in the distance, hints at the alterity and danger of South Sea social and sexual systems that were elaborated upon in the journals.[41] Yet Hodges also produced attractive depictions of ni-Vanuatu and New Caledonian women, whose large sparkling eyes, round cheeks and high breasts contrast strikingly with Cook's and the Forsters' verbal description of them as "disagreeable" and "ill-favoured" in beauty, customs and hospitality. Malekulan women were apparently too "ugly and ill-proportioned" – having "Monkey faces and Woolly hair" – to warrant visual representation, despite their high intelligence and facility with sign language, which far exceeded that of the Tahitians.[42] More conventionally, John Webber's painting of Poedooa, (*Poedua* [Poetua], *Daughter of Oree, Chief of Ulietea, One of the Society Islands* (1777) (Fig. 20), displays the high and well-rounded breasts of an advancing society, albeit one with an uncanny resemblance to classical statuary.[43]

Conversely, the visual and literary depictions of the Aboriginals of New Holland – held by all the voyagers to be among the lowest on the scale of civilization – were much less allusive, if equally embedded in a landscape described by Joseph Banks as "in every respect the most barren" in the Pacific. To be sure, the Quaker Sydney Parkinson, artist on the *Endeavour*, drew portraits of Aboriginal men as noble savages, and Cook offered one of his more famous reflections when he mused that they were probably "far more happier than we Europeans" because of their austere and simple life.[44] But it is the more deprecatory assessments of New Holland's native inhabitants, first offered by Dampier, confirmed by later commentators, and alluded to in Forster senior's description, which inaugurate a tradition that becomes instantiated in visual representations.[45] Hence John Webber's *A Woman of New Holland* (1777) (Fig. 21) set the tone for subsequent depictions, such as those by Scots convict Thomas Watling's *Group on the North Shore of Port Jackson, New South Wales* (1794) and Frenchman Nicolas Martin-Petit's *A Young Australian Aboriginal Woman* (c. 1800), which also use the pendulous breasts and stark

---

Figure 20 John Webber, *Poedua* [Poetua] (1777). Courtesy of the National Maritime Museum.

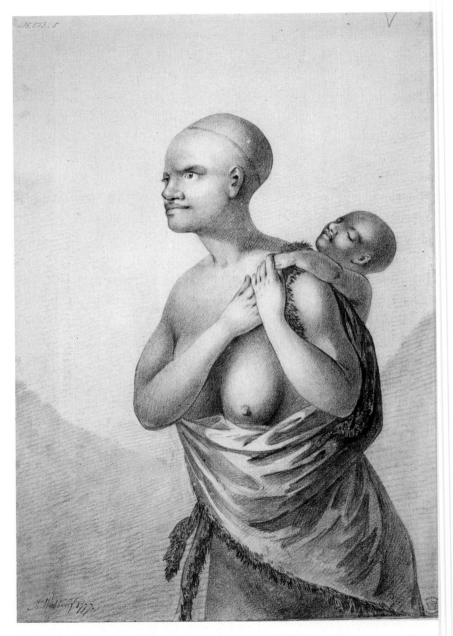

Figure 21 John Webber, *A Woman of New Holland* (1777). Courtesy of the British Library, Department of Manuscripts.

topographical setting described in voyagers' accounts to convey the allegedly more technologically and aesthetically "primitive" nature of Aboriginal culture. Even William Blake, whose sympathetic drawings of African and Amerindian women depicted them with high, firm breasts, portrayed the Iora with pendulous breasts in an otherwise admiring engraving, *A Family of New South Wales* (1792) (Fig. 22). Through "naturalism" in visual and textual accounts, the conflation of the cultural and the physical gets presented as a social fact, and pendulous breasts come to signify, and legitimate, the ethnological notion of the savage.

Figure 22 William Blake, *A Family of New South Wales* (1792). Courtesy of the Henry E. Huntington Library.

The use of breast as metonym of cultural progress or degeneration seems to suggest a successful incorporation of Pacific women by the enlightened explorers into the "history of Man." But these representations simultaneously attempt to mask the chaos attendant on the sexual commerce under way in the South Pacific. Indeed, the journals of the Forsters and other officers and crew reveal patterns of misrecognition and confusion that was not amenable to the imposition of European order. These local representatives of the Royal Society proved unable to cope effectively with the desires and identifications provoked by the radically different sexual and gender systems of the Pacific that neither mirrored nor inverted European models, to the point that the confrontation could interfere with the successful provisioning of the ship, preservation of the crew and survival of the mission. The genital symbolism of temples and monuments, the overt erotic content of dances, poetry and songs, and the polygamy, polyandry and even occasional incest in eastern Polynesia all convinced British seamen that these were sex-mad peoples. "No people in the world . . . indulge their sexual appetites as much as these," the surgeon William Ellis reflected of the Hawaiians. But what the British crews were empirically observing was not the "free love" of Polynesian culture but its sanctification of sexuality. This is not to treat our eighteenth-century explorers with condescension: the complexity of Polynesian social systems has continued to elude well-intentioned Western observers.[46] Although the cultural diversity of Polynesian, as other Pacific island, culture makes it difficult to generalize, in the pre-Christian period gender seemed to function as a complex realm of social relations vested with maintaining the separation and balance of the sacred (tapu) and the everyday, in each of which men and women played indispensable roles.[47] Certainly British tars were delighted that nails, bits of mirror and red feathers, could win the favors of the local beauties and they eagerly projected their own desires onto the women. According to David Samwell, Welshman, poet and surgeon on the *Discovery*, Tahitian women had complained of the "unmanly behavior" of the Spanish crews who had recently visited the Society Islands and had refused their embraces: "This appeared very strange to these blooming Girls, who had always been so eagerly courted by us, and who could have no Idea of any defect that would render young Women undesirable Objects except the Want of Personal Charms . . . We gave them every consolation in our power," Samwell concluded.[48] The sailors, however, refined the gift into an exchange, by rewarding the women with goods in return for sex.[49] What to the British were sexual encounters exchanging sex for goods – a traffic in women that vindicated British Protestant masculinity and marked the women in British eyes as lower-class, akin to English prostitutes in the port towns – was to Polynesians a traffic in European men: first for supernatural access; second, as that illusion faded, to get highly desirable manufactured goods that allowed locals to raise their own status or wage war on their rivals.

For it seems likely that Polynesian cosmogony linked sexual intercourse with access to divine power and social advancement, explicating "the creation of the world from a primordial act of sexual intercourse or from the separation of merged conjugal bodies."[50] Women's offering themselves to British sailors may have been influenced by their beliefs that as foreigners they had close links to this sacred power and the offspring sired by them would give the women access to supernatural benefits in the form of ancestral *mana* (supernatural power). As Marshall Sahlins has famously argued, for Polynesians "sex was everything: rank, power, wealth, land and the security of all these." Sexual acts engaged men and women in a common opposition to the divine: "For men, the Promethean task of wresting the substance of humanity from its divine overseers in the form of food. For the women to attract and transform the divine generative forces in the form of children."[51] These beliefs underlay, for example, the proscription against intersexual dining and certain foods for women: men ate in the company of ancestral gods, and women's spiritual potency was believed to be so strong (the Tahitian word for vagina was "pathway to the gods") that it could interfere with the divinity of the men. Their cosmology also contributed to pagan Polynesian disregard of premarital sex, a moderate amount of which was held to bring on the much-anticipated onset of adulthood at all social levels, and the lack of any Christian notion of a "wife."[52] Because women were active in political and religious realms in much the same way as men, at high and low levels – for example, as chiefs and goddesses as well as in making of sacred barkcloth – differences in rank affected the political and economic power they wielded and the impact of tapu regulations on their lives.[53]

These social features of eastern Polynesia were of course not static, and were reshaped by local regional and political conflicts and further complicated by cross-cultural encounter. In the Society Islands, for example, as in Hawaii subsequently, local dynastic rivalries were intensified by the waves of European visitors. Wallis's bloody encounter with the Maohi on Tahiti 1767 was followed by Frenchman Comte Louis-Antoine de Bougainville's more peaceful visitation in 1768 and Cook's eventful stay a year after that; in between Cook's second and third sojourns on Tahiti, Spanish ships had come and gone, after unsuccessfully attempting to set up a mission. This backdrop of European rivalry and intervention exacerbated local tensions still fermenting over the relatively recent spread of the cult of Oro, god of war, through the Society Islands, the conquest of Raiaitea and Tahaa by Hau Fa'naui of Borabora in the early 1760s and the continuing dynastic ambitions among and wars between the *ari'i*, or ruling class, of the various islands in the archipelago. Members of the *manahune*, or land-owning class, who had lost land and power in these battles also attempted to use the European presence and arms to their advantage. Hence Cook was inveigled by chiefs and commoners alike to wage war on their behalf.[54]

In these and other ways, then, the Maohi or Society Islanders clearly sought to engage with the British through their own cosmological traditions, political requirements and complex perceptions and motives. In the context of the unsettled social hierarchies described above, it seems clear that the appearance of foreigners provided unparalleled avenues for self-promotion. Hence the women as well as the men were determined to seize the opportunity offered them by the arrival of shiploads of strangers. This was often executed against the will of their objects, the

British tars. "[We] found all the Women of these Island but little influenced by interested motives in their intercourse with us, as they would almost use violence to force you into their Embrace regardless whether we gave them any thing or not," Samwell complained at one point. (He seems to have got used to it: some months later he boasted that he and his mates lived on Hawaii "in the greatest Luxury, and as to the Choice and number of fine women there is hardly one among us that may not vie with the grand Turk himself" – an allusion that had some theoretical standing in the work of Lord Kames, among others, who linked sexual aggressiveness in women with the torrid climates and degenerate cultures of Turkey and Asia.)[55]

As Polynesian women mapped their culture onto the European male body, they made that body the object in the process of their own spiritual and social aggrandizement. The apparently boundless appetite of lower-rank women for sex with British tars also mirrored the performative nature of Polynesian culture, "continuously making relationships out of practice" – that is, inventing social relationships out of performances, rather than using performances to guarantee the relationships: which is to say that European contact did remold indigenous sexuality.[56] This cultural traffic flowed both ways. After the seamen had been demoted, in Polynesian eyes, from strangers to locals, women would then offer themselves in return for "curiosities" – thereby displaying an admirable regard for ethnographic investigation themselves.[57] Maohi women quickly worked out the semiotics of European rank, and made their most energetic addresses to officers in uniform, which led inventive ABs in search of amorous encounters to don full dress.[58] The sailors in turn attempted to map their own notions of domesticity as well as sexuality onto the women, inviting them to dinner aboard ship (and thus de-sacralizing themselves as foreigners through intersexual dining), or taking them as "wives." At the very least, through these encounters Oceanic and European History become inextricably entangled. Significantly, a large part of Cook's authority as commander rested upon his resolve to stand outside this history by refusing to participate in the traffic as object or subject. His crews admired him immensely for his self-restraint with native women as well as the men: "Great was the indifference with which he submitted to every kind of self-denial," Lieutenant King would later recall. "The qualities of his mind were of the same hardy, vigorous kind with those of his body."[59] His romantic aloofness and sexual self-control, however, elicited contempt from the women themselves. Hence at Tonga in June 1774 when Cook declined a beautiful young girl offered by her mother for his "personal use," he was roundly abused: "I understood very little of what she said, but her actions were expressive enough and shew'd that her words were to this effect, Sneering in my face and saying, what sort of a man are you thus to refuse the embraces of so fine a young Woman."[60]

Two other consequences of the confusion attendant upon heterosexual commerce in the Pacific stand out. First, although the importance of sex in Polynesian culture could never be reconciled with Christian or European mores, the enlightened voyagers nonetheless struggled valiantly to turn the exchanges under way into facts that could be used in social theories of progress and degeneration. Both Cook and the Forsters suggested that it was European contact that had corrupted Oceanic morals and led to the "promiscuous trade." Reflecting on the Maoris' apparently learned propensity, by the second voyage, to prostitute their wives and daughters for European goods, Cook reflected that "we debauch their Morals already too prone to vice and we interduce among them wants and perhaps diseases which they never before knew and which serves only to disturb the happy tranquility they and their fore Fathers had injoy'd."[61] That in some cases island men were clearly forcing women into sexual commerce was also decried by the gentlemen as evidence of the corruption enjoined by contact with British culture. In Queen Charlotte's Sound, some Maori men came on board the *Resolution* and "went through the whole vessell, offering their daughters and sisters promiscuously to every person's embraces," as Forster junior wrote in his account, "in exchange for our iron tools, which they knew could not be purchased at an easier rate."[62] Here British crews' sexual lusts made them an easy mark for the locals, while also increasing the exploitation of the women. These remarks draw attention to the way in which European contact not only exacerbated divisions within Polynesian island societies, but also altered local sexual customs, spread venereal disease and begat children, with long-lasting consequences for Pacific peoples and European colonization. But they also laid bare the performative nature of Enlightenment social science, which also invented social relationships out of performances, and codified them through stadial theory.[63] Hence Cook himself ventured a universal law on female chastity when, on the third voyage, the women of Van Diemen's Land (Tasmania) refused the tars' advances: "I believe it has generally been found amongst uncivilized people that where the Women are easy of access, the Men are the first who offer them to strangers, and where this is not the case they are not easily come at, neither large presents nor privacy will induce them to violate the laws of chastity or custom."[64]

Secondly, just as the complex transactions under way would set commoners at odds with rulers on the islands, so it exacerbated the divisions among the British crews. From the officers' point of view, the sexual commerce between islanders and seamen was inevitable but regrettable, for it undermined good discipline and encouraged the degenerative tendency among the common men far from civilized society to "go native." Indeed, miscegenation with Pacific islanders played a large role in fomenting desertions, and so "rendered visible a collusion between uncivilized natives and subaltern seamen that could have dangerous results for British authority," as Bridget Orr has argued.[65] Moreover, the apparently uncontrollable sexual "instincts" of the crews were on a par, in the eyes of the gentlemen and officers, with those of the barbarous nations. When Mahine, the native of Borabora who accompanied the *Resolution* to Antarctica, "did not hesitate to gratify his appetites in New Zeeland, though he was too clear-sighted at the same time not to perceive the vast falling off from his own country-women," his behavior was explained as "the force of instinct triumphing over his delicacy, – and can we wonder at it, when our civilized Europeans set the example?"[66] Here Forster articulates a notion of sexual desire as a "natural urge" that civil society needed to regulate, but that civil society was striated by class as well as national divisions.[67] The failure of such regulation was most dramatically and poignantly marked by the encounters that crossed the line into outright rape. Forster senior wrote in his journal of two Maori women who "I believe served with reluctancy to the pleasures of the young Men, and cried bitterly, who were hardhearted enough to use them in the Spite of their tears." Such "brutal lust," which "breaks through all social ties, extinguishes all principles of true honor, virtue and humanity in every being . . . only eyes sensuality and lewdness, as the only things which ought to be satisfied," Forster concluded.[68] But although the gentleman naturalist recorded his disgust, significantly he did not intervene. At the very least, such assaults should have thwarted any attempt to ascribe universal proclivities for amorous activity to Pacific women as a whole, but they had that effect only in part.

The relations between territorial and sexual exploration were harder to read than the British had been led to believe. The frustration of expectation could lead to resentment. When the anticipation of sex for goods was confounded, the British became indignant. On the second voyage, a young Maori woman who came aboard the *Resolution* with an old man was besieged with gifts from the sailors, for she was the first woman they had seen in several months. Yet Clerke remarked with some annoyance "the Young Gypsey did not seem at all inclin'd to repay them in the Kind Indian Women in general trade in, and indeed the Kind that's most esteem'd I believe by all men after so long an absence from the Sex."[69] Polynesian women's supposedly wanton behavior made Johann Forster compare them in his journal unfavorably to British women, whose white and pink complexions, "innocence and chastity" and "improved minds" were so far superior to the superficial physical attractions of Pacific women. Here a corrupted femininity becomes a sign of racial otherness, as Forster upbraids the Polynesians not only for their lack of chastity, but also for their refusal to engage straightforwardly in sexual commerce: "The women coquet in the most impudent manner, and shew uncommon fondness for Foreigners, but are all Jilts and coax the Foreigners out of anything they can get: and will not comply to sleep with them, unless they be common prostitutes, or the bribe very great and tempting."[70] As with the native men's alleged propensity for "theft," which was probably undertaken as a form of compensation for an unwelcome visit, and for which, as already noted, they could be lashed or even shot and killed, local women's refusal to conform to the British rules of "fair trade," and even more, to insist upon their own rights to be subjects in sexual exchange, was read as a sign of their "deceitful" natures, one that frustrated Forster's scientific aim to know and understand them, to possess their cultures' "curiosities."[71]

Clearly, the female gaze that made the women into connoisseurs and the men into objects was very destabilizing. In this context, the classification of female bodies could allay the anxieties arising from the arts of discovery, while also displacing the immense shame felt by Cook and his officers for British tars' "brutishness" towards and venereal infection of unsuspecting islanders. Breasts, a site of sexual commerce that did not betray that commerce's potentially lethal effects, were thus a sign that could impose order on chaos and anchor the process of classifying humanity into discrete categories or stages. Breasts also helped recuperate British masculinity threatened by the perceived excesses and irrationality of Oceanic sexualities and confirm the British officer, gentlemen and crews' status alike as insightful enlightened explorers and connoisseurs of female beauty. In these, and in other ways, white English masculinity was actively produced through the observation and ordering of the indigenous woman's body.

The Traffic in Men

Male sexuality was another area where misrecognition confounded the voyagers' encounters with Pacific islanders. Let us listen to William Wales, astronomer aboard the *Resolution*, talk about his attempts to put to rest among his own men the fear that the "natives" were "sodomites." Recording the details of his exploration of the island of Tana in the New Hebrides (Vanuatu) – one of the islands of the western Pacific that was universally regarded by Cook and his crew to be lagging far behind the Tahitians in civilization and physical beauty – Wales reported that some of his men had been followed into the bushes by ni-Vanuatu males "for a purpose I need not mention." He then remarked,

> there are People who . . . are not capable of defending the Whims they Adopt otherwise than by *It is so – I know it* . . . and some of this Cast have asserted, and I make no doubt *written down* . . . that most of the People we have lately been among are Sodomites, or Canibals, or both . . . [yet] no person had been attempted who had not either a softness in his features, or whose employment it was to Carry bundles of one kind or other which is the Office of their own Women.

Here Wales, like Cook a bluff and self-made Yorkshireman, tries to use his well-trained powers of observation to combat the prejudices of his crew and resolve the crisis brought on by the perception of sexual difference by chalking up the miscues of the Tannese to gender confusion.[72] The visual and corporeal cues upon which European order depended were insufficient, it seems, in antipodean encounters, where British tars projected their own fears of sodomitical desire onto the ni-Vanuatu, and the ni-Vanuatu mapped their own culture on the European male body. From the latter perspective, in a culture where women did most (though certainly not all) the carrying, and were in George Forster's view obliged "to perform all sorts of laborious, and humiliating operations," European men who did women's work looked like, or could be used as, women, in a telling demonstration of the performativity of gender in ni-Vanuatu society. Equally possible is that the ni-Vanuatu could not conceive that shiploads of men could appear without women in tow to do their carrying for them. Wales himself put the burden of proof of masculinity back on the British tars themselves, admitting that the "softness" of features of some contributed to their misrecognition by the natives. In doing so

189

he reflects a widely held view in Britain that "the prevalency of this passion [for sodomy] has for its object effeminate delicate beings only."[73]

Perhaps, as Gannath Obeyesekere has argued about Pacific cannibalism, the British sailors' suspicions about sodomy, arising after several months' incarceration in the cramped and homosocial holds of two sloops, revealed more about the practices aboard ship than they would like to think. Alternatively, to follow this line of inquiry may be to treat these texts to what Lee Edelman has called, following Foucault, a "hermeneutics of suspicion," through which any sexual practice and all forms of homosociality become doubled, permeable and suspect, and homosexuality is called into being through the forensic investigation for "subtexts."[74] Yet I would contend, contrary to both positions, that a (non-homophobic) hermeneutics of suspicion may be precisely what is needed in order to illuminate what is at issue in these accounts: the dense sites of signification that nationalized bodies were made to bear, the failure (from the enlightened explorers' perspective) of native bodies to speak for themselves, and the murkiness created when cultures of identity circulate between nations at the point of contact. From this perspective, Wales's entry speaks to an array of issues surrounding sodomy and masculinity, both in English culture and in the art of discovery, when for a variety of historical reasons the homophobic hermeneutics of suspicion that entangled the ship was projected onto indigenous societies.[75]

For British seamen's prejudices were consistent with the growing antipathy to "effeminates" that was a marked feature of the social and political landscape of England in the 1770s. Within England, sodomy was increasingly identified with aristocratic debauchery and excess or, still worse, with the perception of a depraved and degenerate character. Randolph Trumbach's recent argument that sodomy was becoming the touchstone of a gender revolution that legislated heterosexuality as the norm receives solid empirical support by the evidence of a rise in the expression of English hostility to sodomy in the last quarter of the eighteenth century, a hostility that exceeded perhaps anywhere else in Europe. In this period, bi- or homosexual men were banished to the Continent by their families, and the numbers of pardons for the capital crime of sodomy steadily diminished.[76] There was also an upsurge in formal charges of sodomy that began in the 1770s and reached a peak in the early 1800s, reflecting a backlash in England over non-procreative forms of sex in general. However, on the Continent, too, sodomy carried with it a host of associations that underlined its social status as an "unnatural" act. Its French euphemisms, "le péché anti-naturel," or "le péché philosophique," signaled that sodomy, as a sexual practice that did not bother to hide its status as a purely non-reproductive pleasure, was both an act and a trope that signaled a crossing over into disorder. The Marquis de Sade, whose quotation at the beginning of the chapter may also testify to the rapidity and breadth of the gossip networks that sustained the celebrity of the Cook voyages, was well aware of the social trangressiveness of sodomitical desire. Sade was fond of documenting the naturalness, or ubiquity, of supposed "unnatural" practices, and made no secret of his own pleasure at being penetrated; but it is still clear that sodomy functioned in his writing, as well as in eighteenth-century European civil and martial law, theology and social jeremiad, as the sign of a social, cultural and sexual alterity that could otherwise not be named. Hence a sex manual of the period that trumpeted its usefulness in providing the "forty positions of fucking" added on sodomy as number forty-one, the dangerous supplement, in all senses of the term, that threatened to engulf conventional pleasures.[77]

Characteristically, in Britain such "effeminacy" was coming under scientific scrutiny as a symptom of a moral weakness that "pervert[ed] those appetites which nature has bestowed for the most beneficial purposes." Social theorists such as Lord Kames, William Robertson and John Millar were at pains to explain same-sex desire as a feature of the degeneracy that is produced by luxury and excess in advanced societies, when the "free indulgence of appetites" is unrestrained, and the passions debased; yet they also hinted at its existence among "primitive" cultures, where emotional languor and lack of sensibility could fail to spark "that passion which was destined to perpetuate life, to be the bond of social union, and the source of tenderness and joy."[78] The problematics of "effeminacy" and its complex relations to the "man of feeling" in this period rested, as discussed in the Introduction, on the status of gender difference as innate or acquired and on the dynamic relations existing between sexual practice and gender in late eighteenth-century British culture. For now it is important to note that the apprehension of and anxiety about "effeminacy" – which I would describe in this context as the attribution of a damaged or failed gender to certain kinds of men, which may or may not be evinced in sodomitical desire – influenced our explorers' views of South Pacific peoples.[79] Marra's assessment of Society Islanders was clearly colored by these concerns of Enlightenment social and political theory. "The women, in particular, are without modesty," he recorded, "and the men without courage; they have neither the manly boldness of the Ohoteroans, nor the savage fierceness of the New-Zealanders; but are in general an effeminate race, intoxicated with pleasure, and enfeebled by indulgence."[80] The sensual overindulgence and promiscuity of the Tahitians, and especially the *arioi*, who combined their sexual omnivorousness with abortion and infanticide, were also interpreted by the British as a sign of effeminacy and corruption attendant upon tropical plenty.[81] In this context, the perception of sodomitical desires or practices among indigenous peoples of the Pacific mobilized the fears of difference and social exile involved with the signification of sodomy in England. British tars' concerns certainly seemed to express a terror over losing proper gender through the intimation of inappropriate desire in the antipodes of the world.[82]

Such anxieties were clearly exacerbated in the art of discovery, when the exploration of foreign territories and bodies invoked the concomitant fear of being explored.[83] On the first voyage, Joseph Banks noted that one of the "gentlemen" of the *Endeavour* had come back to the ship after a land excursion on the New Zealand coast, "abusing the natives most heartily whom he said he had found to be given to the detestable Vice of Sodomy." Apparently he had made his addresses to a Maori family for the favors of "any one young woman" they chose for him, and was dismayed to find they had attempted to foist a boy off on him – not once, but twice. Banks recorded his own skepticism of the accuracy of the charge, but others among the ship's company subscribed to it nonetheless.[84] Contact in the brave, and strange, new world of the South Pacific, where the regulatory apparatus of civilization (which seemed here to be read, by Banks's companion, as hetero-sexuality) was suspended, the homophobic hermeneutics of the ship had to be made to stand in the breach. When the gender misrecognition worked the other way, as it did at different points on all three voyages, the psychic trauma produced by erotic entanglement seemed less pronounced. Again in New Zealand, where the problem was caused, in Wales's eyes, by the fact that men and women dressed alike, a young Maori woman who was, like many of her nation according to the explorers, "rather masculine" in personal appearance, mistook a young seaman for a member of her own sex, offering him gifts and rubbing his hair with oil. But she was apprised of her error when, according to one account, the boy tried to seduce her, or, according to another, she saw him urinating.[85] The imperative to close observation – coupled with British guilt and anxiety over the spread of venereal disease in the South Pacific – could lead to some uncomfortable identi-fications for the British. Cook's own identificatory projections, for example, are suggested through his squeamish fascination with Malekulan men's use of the penis sheath: "This Apish Nation," he recorded not once but twice in a single journal entry, barely "cover their Natural parts, the testicles are quite exposed, but they wrap a piece of cloth or leafe round the yard which they tye up to the belly to a cord, and so tight that it is a wonder to us how they could endure it."[86] In these scenarios, gender, sexual practice and "national" difference seemed easily confused, under-lining the degree to which the *familiarity* of bodies was the foundation for more complex and elaborate forms of classification and distinction; at the same time, bodies both exceeded and failed normative European and Oceanic categories of gender. Certainly, as a number of scholars have observed, the projection of the desires and fears of the explorer onto the explored results in an image of the othered as licentious and unrepressed.[87] But what is much less remarked upon is the circu-lation of subjectivity in such scenarios: as in these examples, who is the explorer and who the explored?

The Polynesians certainly had their own doubts about the virility of their visitors. Given their deep investment in the sexual and procreative avenues to spiritual and material advance, it was clear that Polynesians regarded the homosociality of European culture, as manifested in the British explorers' sloop, as suspect, even derisive. Lieutenant King reported that the Hawaiian chiefs were very curious about the provenance and intentions of their guests, but one circumstance "puzzled them exceedingly, our having no women with us; together with our quiet conduct, and unwarlike appearance" – the act of war being one of the few events neces-sitating travel without women in Polynesia.[88] In several islands, as we have seen, the manhood of sailors and officers alike who refused the embraces of island women became the object of taunts by the locals; and following Cook's prohibition of intercourse with Hawaiian women for fear of introducing the "venereals," the women in question were said to have ridiculed the Europeans for their lack of virility. In some other cases, investigations were undertaken to determine whether the Europeans were "whole men."[89] These Oceanic men and women, mutually interdependent in their everyday and sacred relationships, seemed not to conceive of sexual segregation, except for specific sacred or bellicose purposes, as a viable social arrangement. Even after conversion to Christianity, Polynesians remained intensely suspicious of men who remained unmarried into their mature years.[90] Hence the explorers' sloops seemed to raise questions in the eyes of their hosts as to the explorers' inclinations and civility that the British themselves could never quite satisfactorily answer.

Wales's journal entry invites us further into this tangled circuitry of colonial identification, alterity, exchange and transformation. He goes on to elaborate his theory about the gender confusion that gave rise to the unfortunate misapprehension that the ni-Vanuatu were sodomites, while also making clear that the purpose he "need not mention" was universally recognized, and *could* be signed without difficulty in the gestural economy of encounter:

> The Man who carried Mr. Forster's Plant Bag had, I was told, been two or three times attemp[t]ed, and he happening to go into the Bushes on some occastion or other whilst we were set down drinking our Cocoa-nuts etc. I pointed it out to the Natives who sat round us, with a sort of sly look and *significant action* at the same time, on which two of them Jump'd up and were following him with great glee; but some of our Party bursting out into a laugh, those who were by . . . called out *Erramange! Erramange!* (it's a Man! It's a Man!) on which the others returned, very much abashed on the Occasion.

The "sly look and *significant action*" were both conveyed through gestural signs common in encounters in which neither party spoke the other's language; yet the acceptance of gestural language as a reliable indicator of sexual intention is, and was, clearly problematical. The Forsters would also hypothesize, entirely on the basis of such gestural signs, that the ni-Vanuatu were also eaters of human flesh. Wales, however, had initially refused to believe that Maori were "cannibals" despite mounting "evidence" (the pantomime of cannibalism put on by the Maori) and the conviction to the contrary of all the rest of the company. He protested "how far we are liable to be misled by Signs, report and prejudice."[91] In the passage above, however, Wales indicates both that gestural sign (of sodomy? or heterosexual intercourse? It is unclear which sign was being made, or indeed if they were different) could convey the truth both to and of the ni-Vanuatu, and that the suspicious traffic flowed both ways. What should we make of this exchange?

European prejudices were both inverted and confirmed in this social performance. As previously noted, while sodomy and same-sex desire were by no means seen as unitary in the last quarter of the eighteenth century, both were, to varying degrees, coming to be attached to the same object of suspicion: the "effeminate" man.[92] In Britain, this (usually elite-identified) individual was the product of spending too much time around women, or, as Millar theorized, of societies where women had too much civil or political power; in either case, he was beginning to be thought to be the most likely to harbor same-sex desires.[93] There was an increasing, although not invariable, convergence, in other words, between gender and sexual practice, and a demand for men that the outward performance of gender be matched by inner desire. Hence the great surprise and alarm among the British public at the sodomy prosecution and subsequent exile of the manly Isaac Bickerstaffe, playwright and collaborator of Garrick.[94] In the encounter above, however, same-sex or sodomitical desire is feared as a function of primitive, rather than advanced and corrupted, sensibilities, which would require, according to late eighteenth-century stadial models of social development, that it had been there all along, a part of humanity in its "original" as in its "advanced" state (a view which anticipated missionaries' condemnation of sodomy as a "heathenish" practice at all levels).[95] That the ni-Vanuatu were in a "primitive" state was not in doubt, although the Forsters theorized that their nation might have degenerated from the happiness of the Tahitians owing to their less advantageous climate. And certainly gestural sign was associated by some with cultural primitiveness. The case had been made very eloquently by Rousseau, who argued that "if the only needs we ever experience were physical, we should most likely never have been able to speak; we would fully express our meanings by the language of gestures alone." Conversely, on the basis of evidence culled from the voyages of Bougainville and Cook, as well as European communities of the deaf, some Enlightenment thinkers had elevated gestural sign to the level of a philosophical artifact, as a "natural" and possibly even universal language. From that perspective, sign language provided a theatrical, if provisional, "mode of exchange, a physical and symbolic space inscribed with meaning," as Paul Carter has argued of contact performances in general.[96] Yet what that meaning was to the different parties remains elusive. In other words, the indeterminacy of both sign and sodomy is glossed in Wales's account of encounter: in the state of nature being enacted for the British in western Polynesia through a gestural economy, even the most stalwart empiricist was led to believe the "unnatural crime" was not only recognized but could be made intelligible through a sort of kinesthetic lingua franca, the wink and the nod. Communication is achieved as meaning is deferred, and sodomy becomes the place where civilized and savage meet – a predilection of those with too much luxury and too much contact with women (as the British had long believed of Islamic nations), as well as, apparently, those who neither spent time with nor appreciated women.[97] Clearly, the enlightened explorers identified themselves with neither camp.

Of course, just as there was some ritual cannibalism practiced in certain South Pacific societies, so there were people who engaged in sodomy. The expectations of sexual exchange that the British fostered did not necessarily translate into the "natural" sex roles ordained by European culture. But what is most striking here is that Pacific social codes continued to elude European categories of identity. Among the ni-Vanuatu, male-to-male sexual contact may have been part of the complex rituals involved in the invocation and transmission of male and especially chiefly power, although the British had no way of knowing this.[98] Probably more transgressive from the European point of view (and perhaps more accessible to our voyagers) were the *mahu* of Tahiti and the Marquesas, young boys who were deliberately brought up to dress and behave as women and as grown men openly practiced transvestism, fellatio and – perhaps – sodomy. Within the gender complementarity of eastern Polynesian culture, the *mahu* were seen possibly as a third gender, or as women; men having sexual relations with them did not think of themselves as "sodomites," nor did *mahu* have sex with each other.[99] The *mahu* may have been "discovered" by the British on the second voyage as they prepared for final departure in 1774: Wales described some men "who are forbid the use of Women" and Forster senior may have been alluding to them when he decried that "appetite for sensual pleasure" accompanying opulence in a society, which, "if no restraint is laid on its gratification, it grows stronger and stronger, so as at last to extinguish all the notions of propriety and decency."[100] Transvestism was certainly not unknown in England, as the public campaigns to stamp out molly houses attested, and some of the more sensational trials for sodomy confirmed.[101] But what is noteworthy is that the explorers, if they noticed the *mahu*, did not condemn them. Ten years later, Captain Bligh (himself suspected of being "a bit peculiar" by his own men) was less restrained by Enlightenment relativism in his denunciation of the *mahu*. Bligh's close and manual examination of a *mahu* led him to express his revulsion at this example of Tahitian "effeminacy" privately, but in lurid tones: "it is strange that in so prolific a country as this, men should be led to such sensual and beastly acts of gratification," he wrote in his journal. Significantly, he goes on to note "those connected with [the *mahu*] have their beastly pleasures gratified between his thighs, but are no farther sodomites as they all positively deny the crime." The LMS missionaries who arrived in *The Duff* ten years later were more public in their condemnations, recording in their writings the similarity between "these heathens" and "the heathens of old," both groups being "given up to vile affections; the men leaving the natural use of woman, burn in their lusts towards one another." British audiences thus learned of the

> unnatural crimes which we dare not name, committed daily without the idea of shame or guilt. In various districts of the island there are men who dress as women; work with them at the cloth; are confined to the same provisions and rule of eating and dressing; may not eat with the men, or of their food, but have separate plantations for their peculiar use.

Worse yet, the chiefs had their favorites among them.[102] By the 1790s, then, when the enlightened ethnography of Tahitian culture was giving way to the evangelical, both explorers and missionaries interpellated the *mahu* as "unnatural" (whether as fellaters or sodomites), and so confirm the threat that such transvestite practices posed to normative social morality in the counter-revolutionary fervor of the day.

As such, these descriptions and valuations of Polynesian culture fed back into metropolitan categories not only of civilized and savage but also of respectability and depravity.

Nevertheless, despite the irony of explorer and evangelical alike castigating the practice of men living as women as degradation (given their simultaneous British belief that high esteem for women was a measure of progress in a society), both rather missed the point.[103] The social acceptance of the *mahu* in eastern Polynesian societies may have actually expressed the associations of women's reproductive functions with the divine – and hence the association of the feminine with positive, rather than negative, hierarchies and characteristics.[104] Indeed, the *mahu* had their female counterpart in the "female headmen" who took on a role usually fulfilled by male members of chiefly families. Aggressive, masculine in appearance, and large in size, female headmen were known for their skill in warfare, sometimes took youths as husbands or surrounded themselves with *mahu* for their court.[105] Only slightly less transgressive, from the British perspective, was the *pekio* of the Marquesas: men who became secondary husbands to women of high status and provided them with both sexual and domestic service – a role which had its opposite number in Hawaii *āikane*.[106]

The Hawaiian *āikane* was indeed less hidden from the History made on the Cook voyages than the *mahu*, and so they will complete this reading of the circuitry of colonial encounter, misrecognition and transformation. In Hawaii the *āikane* were a distinctive social and cultural presence: young male warriors who served as inter-mediaries, agents and male sexual companions to the chiefs of the islands. Unlike the *mahu*, they otherwise fulfilled typical male roles, including having wives and children.[107] The British were openly fascinated by them, as both Robert Morris and Lee Wallace have recently discussed. The journals of the voyage record several instances in which Hawaiian chiefs or *āikane* expressed interest in British officers and crew, offering hogs in exchange for the younger and better-looking men. Samwell typically records their interest, and British investigation, in lively fashion:

> Another Sett of Servants [of the chief, Kalani'opu'u] . . . are called Ikany and are of superior Rank . . . their business is to commit the Sin of Onan upon the old King. This . . . we learnt from frequent Enquiries about this curious Custom, and it is an office that is esteemed honourable among them and they have frequently asked us on seeing a handsome young fellow if he was not an Ikany to some of us.[108]

Samwell's description of the *āikane*, moving from wonder to knowing and coy detachment, suggests the explorers' propensity to view same-sex desire *not* as a "sin," but as a cultural practice that needed to be analyzed. At the same time, his remarks speak volumes in their silences about his own predilections as the straight man in the comic scene he constructs. A few days later he reported, "we have great reason to think that that Unnatural Crime which ought never to be mentioned is not unknown amongst them" (1184). "[S]uch is the strange depravity of these

Indians," he concluded, after Captain Clerke had been offered several large Hogs to let one of his crew stand as *āikane* to a close relative of the King of Kaua'i.[109] Samwell's gallantry and archness about the sexual proclivities of South Sea islanders thus extended from the women to the men; yet he still managed to suggest, in the latter case, that if he was intrigued intellectually he was not personally attracted by such proposals.

The interest in the *āikane* among some of the other crewmembers was tempered more by anxiety and ambivalence. Given the increasing importance of the belief, later codified through historical examples by Millar, Robertson and Malthus, that civil society's restraints were necessary to inflame the passion and refine the desires for, and good treatment of, the opposite sex, the Hawaiians' base appetites signaled an obstacle to social and spiritual progress.[110] This play between same-sex practices as both an object of ethnographic analysis and a religious abomination was evident in New Englander John Ledyard's assessment. Ledyard used Biblical language to condemn a practice he nonetheless felt it his duty to describe, through the "historian's" obligation to tell the truth:

> It is however very manifest among the chiefs, that not only marriage, but a commerce with the women in any other respect is in very indifferent estimation, and it is a disagreeable circumstance to the historian that truth obliges him to inform the world of a custom among them contrary to nature . . . it would be to omit the most material and useful part of historical narration to omit it; the custom alluded to is that of sodomy, which is very prevalent if not universal among the chiefs. As this was the first instance we had ever seen of it in our travels, we were cautious how we credited the first indications of it, and waited until the opportunity gave full proof of the circumstance. The cohabitation is between the chiefs and the most beautiful males they can procure about 17 years old, these they call Kikuana, which in their language signifies a relation. These youths follow them wherever they go, and are as narrowly looked after as the women in those countries where jealousy is so predominant a passion; they are extremely fond of them, and by a shocking inversion of the laws of nature, they bestow all those affections upon them that were intended for the other sex . . . though we had no right to attack or ever to disapprove of customs in general that differed from our own, yet this one so apparently infringed and insulted the first and strongest dictate of nature, and we had from education and a diffusive observation of the world, so strong a prejudice against it, that the first instance we saw of it we condemned a man fully reprobated. Our officers indeed did not insult the chiefs by any means, but our soldiers and tars to vindicate their own wonderful modesty, and at the same time oblige the insulted women . . . became severe arbitrators, and the most valourous defenders and supporters of their own tenets.[111]

197

The enlightened explorer had to record the facts, and verify the accuracy of the record, but in doing so was roused to condemn a custom "contrary to nature," and to condone the British tars' manly and seemingly compulsory heterosexual response. Indeed, heterosexuality itself is produced and asserted by this reading of the *āikane* as sodomites. There are also many assumptions in this passage – about male beauty, sexual jealousy and romantic love, for example – that also suggest the complicated and ambiguous nature of Ledyard's response to the alter sexual customs and same-sex desire expressed by the Hawaiians.

The journal entries and accounts by Lieutenant James King, handsome and respected young officer aboard the *Resolution*, allow us to track these ambivalences with some care. On leaving the island of Hawaii, following Cook's death, King recorded his overall impressions of the Hawaiian people, and determined that they "will fall very short of the Society and Friendly Isles in that very good test of Civilization, the rank and consequence of Women" for not only were the women forced to eat separately and but were also "depriv'd of the natural affections of their Husbands . . . [since] the foulest polutions disgrace the Men."[112] King perhaps had reason to be worried: Hawaiians mistook him repeatedly not only as Cook's son but also as his *āikane*. Yet his later rather phlegmatic report that one Hawaiian chief had negotiated with Cook "to leave me behind; I had proposals by our friends to elope, and they promised to hide me in the hills till the Ships were gone, and to make me a great man"[113] attempted to make light of the concern, expressed elsewhere by himself and some of the other men, at the effort to make him an object in an "unnatural" and "foul" sexual exchange. King's more fulsome published account of this encounter is even more striking in its apparent indifference to the desire being openly expressed by a Hawaiian chief and one of his warriors. "It was ridiculous enough to see them [the Hawaiians] stroking the sides, and patting the bellies of the sailors (who were certainly much improved in the sleekness of their looks), during our short stay in the island," he wrote.

> On my part, I spared no endeavours to conciliate their affections, and gain their esteem; and I had the good fortune to succeed so far, that, when the time of our departure was made known, I was strongly solicited to remain behind, not without offers of the most flattering kind. When I excused myself, by saying, that Captain Cook would not give his consent, they proposed, that I should retire into the mountains; where, they said, they would conceal me, till after the departure of the ships; and on my farther assuring them, that the Captain would not leave the bay without me, Terreeoboo and Koa [Kalani'opu'u, the chief and Koa, his *āikane*] waited upon Captain Cook, whose son they supposed I was, with a formal request, that I might be left behind. The Captain, to avoid giving a positive refusal, to an offer so kindly intended, told them, that he could not part with me, at that time, but that he should return to the island next year, and would then endeavour to settle the matter to their satisfaction.[114]

As Wallace has suggested, perhaps "despite themselves . . . the Europeans kept signaling this particular sexual availability to [Hawaiian] men."[115]

Wallace's insight also points us to another intriguing aspect of these encounters: the allure of the homoeroticism of Polynesian culture to British explorers. Certainly we have no way of knowing whether same-sex desire between British and Polynesian islanders of the different nations was common or ignored. But it is clear in a number of ways – not least through the abundant descriptions of the genital symbolism of eastern Polynesia (which the British compared to "the Priapus of the Romans"), the "frequent Enquiries" made about the *āikane*, the bond-friendships made between the officers and chiefs (which involved "kissing" or nose-rubbing), and the apparent ease with which King recorded the effort to traffic in male bodies – that the homoerotic aspects of native culture were not rejected by some of the explorers, and could even provide a kind of entree into local life.[116] King himself may have used his own physical attractiveness (described by Beaglehole as "too small-bodied, too well-bred, too genteel, for a young man who . . . may have considered himself a tar") to "conciliate" the islanders and "gain their esteem."[117] The politics of identity within Britain may also help illuminate those at work in these encounters. As Bickerstaffe's case eloquently proved, even by the last quarter of the century sexual identity was not solely determined by object choice, nor was gender an automatic outcome of sexual practice, and the efforts to make them meld (through reformation of manners campaigns, executions for sodomy, and other aspects of the "gender revolution") were not invariably successful. For the seaman, oceans away from the soothing commonplaces and coercive social pressures of "home," homoeroticism or the expression of same-sex desire may have offered a "liminal" space, as Victor Turner has defined it, "a realm of pure possibility whence novel configurations of ideas and relations may arise," that allowed him to cross over to a multiply determined "other side." Tattooing constituted another such act and symbol of transgressiveness, through which the sailor expressed his identification with Oceanic mores and gained the islanders' acceptance. Significantly, tattoos were also associated in British accounts with Oceanic sexual excess.[118] As Peter Heywood, mutineer of the infamous *Bounty*, explained: "I was tattooed, not to gratify my own desire, but theirs; for it was my constant endeavour to acquiesce in any little custom which I thought agreeable to them . . . provided I gained by it their friendship and esteem."[119] The intimation of same-sex desire may have similarly eased some of the anxiety generated through the arts of discovery by allowing the stranger to cross over into the native culture – and perhaps even to become a different kind of national and sexual subject. At the very least, given that, within the terms of eighteenth-century social science, desire was not extinguished but inflamed by restraint, the homophobia of the ship could produce its own rebellion.[120] Ideologies of identity, then, sexual and national, circulated between the two cultures at their points of meeting, and their nature or outcomes were neither predictable nor codifiable.

Hence, the traffic in men transformed the enlightened explorers into the objects of Polynesian knowledge, who thereby read their own culture on the European male body. But this exchange is of much broader historical significance. The tensions between notions of gender and national difference as innate or learned, the shifting dynamics of relations between sexual practice and gender, and the "crime that can never be mentioned" but was everywhere suspected all point to the circuitry of identity, alterity, exchange and transformation that was both charged and recuperated by the systems of observation and empirical recording. Who is the object and who the subject of these exchanges? Who is ethnographer and who the "primitive"? The rape, flogging and killing of natives on the voyages as part of the "civilizing" process established one kind of masculinity and power but did little to impress upon indigenous peoples that the British were representatives of a superior, masculine and civilized race. Indeed, the attempted imposition of British "order" could only temporarily divert attention from what Michael Taussig has called in another context the "unstable interplay of truth and illusion."[121] The differential and contested accounts of Pacific peoples laid bare in the journals and published voyage accounts revealed the insufficiencies of the social typologies that Britain's enlightened explorers were so keen to formulate and apply. These misrecognitions, articulated through the axes of sexuality and gender, produced ideas about racial difference that staked out the grounds of similarity as well as alterity, and possibilities for identification on both sides that were not fixed or predetermined. Significantly, they also suggest that it was religious, rather than secular, valuations of difference that produced the more absolutist definitions that begin to take hold in the late Georgian period.

Cook and his men aimed to discover and record empirical facts about an unknown world, and their cultural as well as topographical mappings changed the world in the process. The psychic impact of these processes on the colonizers and their forms of knowledge has received, perhaps, too little direct attention. The empirical "facts" of territorial and sexual conquest clearly summoned up the fantasy of being taken, as well as taking; and as desire, identification and dis-identification worked to naturalize conquest and allay its anxieties, the "unnatural" nature of the act of conquest comes back to haunt in the figure of the sodomite – the absent presence (or present absence) on all the voyages. Perhaps these examples suggest that through the arts of discovery the emergence of the "modern" sexual regime was indeed being felt and fabricated across the world. But it is also clear that suspect practices could not produce and certainly could not prove the essentialized identities that such a regime required. The multiple images of Oceanic and British bodies reveal the fictive nature and irresolvable tensions within those categories of difference invented in the crucible of first contact. The same accounts that inaugurate the labor of colonial discourse in the South Pacific thus raise the central question, who was looking at whom? What was seen in the act of looking and who was the discoverer? Looking at natives looking back at them, could the enlightened explorers of Cook's voyages be so sure they were not looking at themselves? From this perspective, breasts, sodomy and lash become markers of the instabilities of nationality, race and gender and the indeterminacies of sexual practices – in the time of the great Captain Cook, as well as in our own.

EPILOGUE: "SAVE THE STONES!" KING ALFRED AND THE PERFORMANCE OF ORIGINS

ALFRED, go forth! lead on the radiant years,
To thee reveal'd in vision . . .
. . .
See, where, beyond the vast *Atlantic* surge,
By boldest keels untouch'd, a dreadful space!
Shores, yet unfound, arise! in youthful prime,
With towering forests, mighty rivers crown'd!
These stoop to *Britain's* thunder. This new world,
Shook to its center, trembles at her name:
And there, her sons, with aim exalted, sow
The seeds of rising empire, arts and arms.
>   David Garrick and David Mallet, *Alfred, a Masque* (1773)

If you have any great reverence for the memory of our Saxon kings, as I have, you will wander about the environs of Merton in search of the spot where Ethelred and Alfred, with such noble though unsuccessful valour, defended their country against its brutal invaders; the only instance in which I am willing to allow that fighting makes a hero.
>   Elizabeth Carter to Mrs. Vesey, July 15, 1776

Nation is a moral essence, not a geographical arrangement, or a denomination of the nomenclator.
>   Edmund Burke, "First Letter on a Regicide Peace," 1796

In the spring of 2000, a battle began over a rather unprepossessing artifact of English national history in the village of Kingston Deverill, Wiltshire. The inhabitants, led by the parish council and village hall committee, engaged in a vigorous campaign to prevent the removal of one of two Sarsen stones from a paddock of the local rectory, Kingston House. The stones, claimed to have been in the parish for over 3,500 years, had been moved in the late eighteenth century from a hillside above the valley and used for a variety of mundane purposes before ending up in the rectory garden. But on their original site, antiquarians believe, King Egbert and his Witan, or band of advisors, held court, and, even more momentously, Egbert's grandson, King Alfred, gathered his armies the day before his victorious battle over the Danes at Ethandun in 878. The present owner of the rectory, the Ralph family, wanted to accept a proposal of the Ethandun Memorial Committee to move one of the stones from the paddock for incorporation into a "national monument" to King Alfred's victory at Bratton Camp near Westbury, several miles away, as a centerpiece of local millennium celebrations. The Upper Deverill Parish Council and Village Hall Committee were alarmed: "one of the stones could leave its historic village," they warned, "perhaps for ever," and they called a series of public meetings to rally opposition to such an outcome. The Ralph family countered with its own campaign of photocopies and speeches, including a painstakingly researched and rather interesting history of the Kingston Deverill Sarsen Stones. This pamphlet combined antiquarian lore and oral history (for example, an interview with the son of a local resident who had helped move the stones to the rectory garden) with traditional historical evidence drawn from such august sources as Asser, the *Anglo-Saxon Chronicles*, Georgian maps and parish registers, to convince the Kingston Deverill parishioners that their sacrifice for the memorial to "King Alfred, Father of the English nation," was for a greater national good. However, the self-proclaimed "Alfredists" lost, at least for the moment, and the stone has yet to be moved, its meaning caught between competing claims on the "national" heritage.

This story, laden as it is with allusions to rootedness, insularity, invented traditions and a venerable past, seems to be in many ways a typically English one. But, charming as it is, it is also emblematic of many of the questions raised in the preceding chapters: whose memory? Whose history? And whose heritage was at stake? To Chris Ralph (himself considered to be something of an upstart and foreigner by local residents), the issues were clear. The village's guardianship of the stones had been marked by neglect, he averred – at one point, the paddock was used as a caravan site, and the stones deployed as drying racks for the washing of otherwise unwashed travelers – and subsequent owners repeatedly refused to take appropriate measures to protect the stones. But even more urgent was the current historical emergency, in which, Ralph contended, local schoolchildren learned more about "the American Wild West, Nelson Mandela and Adolf Hitler" than about "the difference between Edward IV and George IV, or how the English nation came into being." Hence the pressing imperative to reach beyond narrow parochial concerns and modern cynicism to ask "How have we all benefited from the efforts and sacrifices of our ancestors? How can we pass this precious knowledge and sense of identity on to succeeding generations? And how can we rekindle the feeling of unity and purpose which has always characterised this English nation in its most challenging times?" Ralph's concluding "call to arms" was for locals to recognize that "[t]he present day enemies, those of spiritual and social rootlessness, are equally destructive, and just as real, but . . . far subtler invaders than those Alfred encountered and defeated."[1]

Ralph's effort to perform the ancient spirit that allowed the English to "fight, and win, and survive" against unseen but real invaders of the national spirit is not an unfamiliar feature of heritage politics in contemporary Britain. Most extreme, of course, is the rhetoric of the British National Party, which also urges (white) English people to "fight for their heritage," preserve "their racial and cultural identity" and combat "multiracialism" in all its forms. Significantly, their party icon is none other than King Alfred the Great.[2] This is not to suggest any collusion, real or potential, between the Ethandun Memorial Committee and neo-fascist politicking. Rather, it is to underline the many purposes and divergent agendas that the clarion call to recognize and preserve a "nation's heritage" can serve. "[T]he relentless search for the purity of origins is a voyage not of discovery but of erasure," Joseph Roach has asserted, and this observation can be used to pinpoint the sources of past, as present, discontents.[3] In the eighteenth century, the main concern of this study, the denizens of what appeared to be a relentlessly progressing England and empire engaged in their own efforts to preserve, re-shape and participate in the definition of a national identity partly through the inventions and re-fashionings of an immemorial past. Alfred himself became a potent symbol of ancestry and origins for partisans across the political spectrum: the hero of English constitutional purity, bicameral parliaments and trial by jury to radicals and reformers, an anti-democratic emblem of hierarchical loyalism and "familial patriotism" to conservatives.[4] Similarly, the "Gothic" past that Alfred embodied became an obsession in cultural inquiry and production, appealing to diverse audiences, from antiquarians to tourists, and stimulating a range of competing and not always compatible constructions. Henry Hoare's plan for the Alfred Tower at Stourhead included an inscription crediting the Saxon King with the whole host of English political and familial virtues, from paternal leadership to the establishment of the navy and the growth of "our Trade to the remote parts of the The Globe."[5] In Garrick and Mallet's masque, quoted above, Alfred becomes the genius of modern English imperial dominion and its extension into the Pacific as well as the conduit of ancient Saxon spirit and liberties.[6] Even such cosmopolitan and anti-war intellectuals as Elizabeth Carter and Johann Forster were caught up in the mania for Gothic antiquities and Alfredic lore. Carter in particular was wont to proclaim herself a "Goth," and to exalt Gothic patriotic pulchritude, such as that embodied by Ethelred and Alfred, above the conquering prowess of the ancient Greeks and Romans.[7] In the face of the national dangers threatened by the imperial struggles and revolutionary alliances of these decades, Gothicism provided a chronopolitics through which ancient and modern voyages could imaginatively collide, examples of Saxon heroism soothe anxieties over the intensifying militarism of the British state, and the mythologized figure of Alfred provide a wise, learned and courageous monarch – "one of the wisest and best that ever adorned the annals of any nation," as Hume remarked[8] – capable of transforming imperial trauma into noble national triumph through the power of historical surrogation.

Ironically, this surge of interest in ancient Britons and Anglo-Saxons and the origin of the English nation was prodded by the accumulating and ineffable evidence that "England" was the product of its own potent and irreducible ties to a larger world. The routes and commodities of empire, the representations of war and conquest, the epistemologies of exploration and the arts of discovery each revealed that England owed its much-vaunted singularity in no small part to peoples and practices extending beyond the island of Britain or the British archipelago. In this context, the performance of origins, whether of ancient Saxon spirit or modern English cultural and technological superiority, not only exposed the latent racial component in nation-ness, the shift in emphasis from "the continuity of free institutions" as a hallmark of Englishness to the "inherent racial traits which supposedly explained them."[9] It also legitimated ethnicized strategies of rule and difference within the British Isles and the empire, even as it produced the performance of Englishness as a privilege of, and site of resistance for, non-English people in colonial spaces. Indeed, as commentators from Defoe to Burke admitted, the uniqueness of Englishness lay in its compound nature, the product of successful assimilation of waves of invaders. Yet through the performances of origin *as* identity – of nation as a "moral essence," as Burke would have it – the continuing processes of affiliation and transculturation animated by English expansion in the world could be temporarily elided. What was foregrounded instead were the myths of English freedoms and uncontaminated autochthony that deliberately obscured the evidence of their own syncretic pasts – and presents.[10]

The preceding chapters have explored some of the consequences, for cultural production and individual and collective self-consciousness, of divergent articulations of Englishness in eighteenth-century domestic and colonial settings, and of the psychic costs that national identity – indeed, perhaps all national identities? – extracted from their subjects. Clearly national identification provided just one aspect of the complex subjectivities and collectivities through which eighteenth-century people lived their lives. The historical archive permits our access only to limited numbers of these peoples: the privileged, the articulate, the official, or those in whom they had an interest. Nevertheless, the interpretation of archival and literary evidence presented above suggests that the ideologies of English nationhood presented problems of self-location for at least some of their targets, and that understandings of Englishness both shaped, and were shaped by, other realms of social relation and connection. National identity, in other words, like other (gender, class, ethnic, regional, religious and familial) identifications, provided neither a stable and continuous frame of reference nor a full and final recognition. Instead, national identity and its disavowal marked various points on a historical continuum of being and becoming for individuals and groups in many different social and geographical locations. The conditions of possibility for their divergent or collective experiences were firmly rooted in the extended network of communication, diaspora and culture created by the eighteenth-century British empire. In this context, the Island Race was certainly a fiction. But it was a fiction, nonetheless, that illuminated the very real and complicated entanglements of desire, material conditions and imaginative practices promulgated by England's imperial adventures, and the resonant retellings of its histories of peril, glory, aspiration and failure.

NOTES

INTRODUCTION: NATIONS, EMPIRES AND IDENTITIES IN THE EIGHTEENTH CENTURY

1 On the topic of national identity, a few from a very long list would include Tom Nairn, *The Break-Up of Britain* (London: NLB, 1977); Ernest Gellner, *Nations and Nationalism* (Oxford: Blackwell, 1983); Anthony D. Smith, *The Ethnic Origins of Nations* (Oxford: Basil Blackwell, 1986); Etienne Balibar and Immanuel Wallerstein, *Race, Nation, Class: Ambiguous Identities* (London: Verso, 1991); Homi Bhabha, ed., *Nation and Narration* (London: Routledge, 1991); Perry Anderson, *English Questions* (London: Verso, 1992); Liah Greenfeld, *Nationalism: Five Roads to Modernity* (Cambridge, Mass.: Harvard University Press, 1992); Linda Colley, *Britons: Forging the Nation 1707–1837* (New Haven and London: Yale University Press, 1992); Michèle Cohen, *Fashioning Masculinity: National Identity and Language in the Eighteenth Century* (London: Routledge, 1996) Lawrence Brockliss and David Eastwood, eds., *A Union of Mutiple Identities: The British Isles c. 1750–1850* (Manchester: Manchester University Press, 1997); Tony Claydon and Ian MacBride, eds., *Protestantism and the National Identity, 1650–1850* (Cambridge: Cambridge University Press, 1998); John M. MacKenzie, "Empire and National Identities: the Case of Scotland," *TRHS*, 6th ser., VIII (1998), 215–32. On gender, race, politics and class, some examples are: Lyndal Roper, *Oedipus and the Devil: Witchcraft, Sexuality and Religion in Early Modern Europe* (London: Routledge, 1994); Robert Shoemaker, *Gender in English Society 1650–1850* (London: Longman, 1998); Margaret Hunt, *The Middling Sort: Gender, Commerce and the Family in England* (Berkeley and Los Angeles: University of California Press, 1996); and references ahead. My own earlier work, especially *The Sense of the People: Politics, Culture and Imperialism in England 1715–1785* (Cambridge: Cambridge University Press, 1995) is also guilty of not deploying a firm definition of identity, as David Armitage has recently pointed out: *The Ideological Origins of the British Empire* (Cambridge: Cambridge University Press, 2000), 172.

2 Colin Kidd has recently suggested it may be a misnomer to speak of identities before the nineteenth century, but in my view this would be possible only if we erase the imperial frame of eighteenth-century British history: see *British Ethnicities Before Nationalism: Ethnicity and Nationhood in the Atlantic World, 1600–1800* (Cambridge: Cambridge University Press, 1999). Dror Wahrman's forthcoming work on identity also promises to address these questions, and more. Meanwhile, a searching analysis of the production of "national identity," although through the lens of nineteenth-century nationalism, is provided in Geoff Eley and Ronald Grigor Suny, *Becoming National: A Reader* (Oxford: Oxford University Press, 1996). My study aims to do the reverse, by using the problematics of identity as the filter through which ideas about "nation" were produced.

3 Himani Bannerji, *Thinking Through: Essays on Feminism, Marxism and Anti-Racism* (Toronto: Women's Press, 1995), 23; Paul Gilroy, *The Black Atlantic: Modernity and Double Consciousness* (Cambridge, Mass.: Harvard University Press, 1993); Philip Morgan, *Slave Counterpoint: Black Culture in the Eighteenth Century Chesapeake and Low Country* (Chapel Hill: Omunhundro Institute, 1998). As David Eltis has rather dryly remarked, "On board a slave ship with the slaves always black and the crew largely white, skin colour tended to define ethnicity": *The Rise of African Slavery in the Americas* (Cambridge: Cambridge University Press, 2000), 226.

4 David Hume, *A Treatise of Human Nature*, eds. David Fate Norton and Mary Jane Norton (Oxford: Oxford University Press, 2000), 15. Hume believed that the idea of an identical self was a "fiction" of the mind and the way it works, but he nonetheless held that "custom" made it a practicable object of investigation. For a recent review of the debates over identity and individual consciousness in the eighteenth century, see Roy Porter, *The Creation of the Modern World: The Untold Story of the British Enlightenment* (New York and London: Norton, 2000), esp. 156–83. Porter emphasizes the fragmented and intermittent nature of identity in the theories of Locke, Collins and Hutcheson. This discussion of identity in the eighteenth century parts company with that offered by John Tosh, who sees a concern with interior life, divorced from the social "counterfeit of reputation," as the product of evangelicalism late in the century: John Tosh, "The Old Adam and the New Man," in Tim Hitchcock and Michèle Cohen, eds., *English Masculinities, 1660–1830* (London: Longman, 1999), 233.

5 Hume, *Treatise*, 165 (1.4.6.5); Patricia Meyer Spacks, *Imagining a Self: Autobiography and the Novel in Eighteenth-Century England* (Cambridge, Mass.: Harvard University Press, 1976); Jonathan Lamb, *Preserving the Self in the South Seas 1680–1840* (Chicago: University of Chicago Press, 2001).

6 Adam Smith, *A Theory of Moral Sentiments* [2nd edn, 1761], pt. III, esp. chap. 3, in Herbert W. Schneider, ed., *Adam Smith's Moral and Political Philosophy* (New York: Hafner, 1948), 171–3; James Boswell, *Boswell's London Journal 1762–3*, ed. Frederick A. Pottle (New Haven: Yale University Press, 1950), 63; John Dwyer, *Virtuous Discourse: Sensibility and Community in Late Eighteenth Century Scotland* (Edinburgh: John Donald, 1987). This is also one of the most provocative insights of Terry Castle, *Masquerade and Civilization* (Stanford: Stanford University Press, 1986).

7 Mikhail Bakhtin, *Rabelais and His World* trans. Helene Iswolsky (Cambridge, Mass.: MIT Press, 1968), and *The Dialogic Imagination* ed. Michael Holquist (Austin: University of Texas Press, 1981); Kobena Mercer, *Welcome to the Jungle: New Positions in Black Cultural Studies* (London: Routledge, 1994); Dian Fuss, *Identification Papers* (London: Routledge, 1995), and references in n. 8–12 below. Identity should be located between desire – wanting to have – and identification – wanting to be – although clearly the different states of being shade into each other.

8 Stuart Hall, "Cultural Identity and Diaspora," in Nicholas Mirzoeff, ed., *Diaspora and Visual Culture: Representing Africans and Jews* (London: Routledge, 2000), 22–3.

9 Thomas C. Holt, "Marking: Race, Race-Making and the Writing of History," *AHR* (1995), 9, 10; Michel de Certeau, *The Practice of Everyday Life* (Minneapolis: University of Minnesota Press, 1998).

10 Judith Butler, *Gender Trouble: Feminism and the Subversion of Identity* (London: Routledge, 1990). For the productive adaptation of ideas of performance to national, gender and racial identity, see: Joseph Roach, *Cities of the Dead: Circum-Atlantic Performance* (New York: Columbia University Press, 1996); Harry J. Elam, Jr. and David Krasner, eds., *African American Performance and Theater History* (Oxford: Oxford University Press, 2001); and Elin Diamond, *Unmasking Mimesis* (London: Routledge, 1997).

11 Johnson, *A Dictionary of the English Language*, 4th edn (London: W. Strahan, 1773).

12 Butler, *Bodies that Matter: On the Discursive Limits of "Sex"* (London: Routledge, 1993), 105.
13 Balibar, "The Nation-Form: History and Ideology", in Balibar and Wallerstein, *Race, Nation, Class*; Benedict Anderson, *Imagined Communities: Reflections on the Origins and Spread of Nationalism* (London: Verso, 1983). I acknowledge here Anne McClintock's call in *Imperial Leather: Race, Gender and Sexuality in the Colonial Conquest* (London: Routledge, 1995) for historians to take psychoanalysis on board, but I would differ with her interpretation of what that means: I do not agree that social entities can be analyzed in the same way as individuals, even though I see that the collectivity and individual are inextricably bound. I do think that what some are calling the "new biography" affords fresh opportunities to engage with philosophical and psychoanalytic concepts, without invoking the full psychoanalytic hermeneutics. For a convincing use of the Freudian concept of the "family romance" to map the imbrication of national and familial power in historical settings, see Françoise Vergès, *Monsters and Revolutionaries: Colonial Family Romance and Métissage* (Durham: Duke University Press, 1999).
14 Hall, "Cultural Identity and Diaspora," 24; Bhabha, *Nation and Narration*, 1.
15 Butler, *Bodies that Matter*, 191.
16 A point also made by McClintock, *Imperial Leather*, 352.
17 This, and the disregard for gender, have been two of the central planks of criticism of the work of Nairn, Gellner, Hobsbawm and Greenfield as well as Benedict Anderson. See Partha Chatterjee, *The Nation and its Fragments: Colonial and Post-Colonial Histories* (Princeton: Princeton University Press, 1993); Gyan Prakash, ed., *After Colonialism: Imperial Histories and Postcolonial Displacements* (Princeton: Princeton University Press, 1995); Prasenjit Duara, *Rescuing History from the Nation: Questioning Narratives of Modern China* (Chicago: University of Chicago Press, 1995); and Ida Blom, Karen Hagemann, and Catherine Hall, eds., *Gendered Nations: Nationalisms and Gender Order in the Long Nineteenth Century* (Oxford: Berg, 2000).
18 Homi Bhabha, "Signs Taken for Wonders," in *Location of Culture* (London: Routledge, 1994), 108.
19 Oliver Goldsmith, "A Comparative View of Races and Nations" (1760) in *Collected Works of Oliver Goldsmith*, ed. Arthur Friedman (Oxford: Oxford University Press, 1966), III: 85.
20 See Richard Grove, *Green Imperialism: Colonial Expansion, Tropical Island Edens, and the Origins of Environmentalism 1600–1800* (Cambridge: Cambridge University Press, 1995). For a small sample of studies that deal with some aspect of the insularity and singularity of Englishness, see Geoffrey Elton, *The English* (Oxford: Oxford University Press, 1992); Roy Porter, ed., *Myths of the English* (Cambridge: Polity, 1992); Alexander Grant and Keith Stringer, eds., *Uniting the Kingdom? The Making of British History* (London: University of Chicago Press, 1995); Brendan Bradshaw and John Morrill, eds., *The British Problem: State Formation in the Atlantic Archipelago* (Basingstoke: Macmillan, 1996); Keith Robbins, *Great Britain: Identities, Institutions and the Idea of Britishness* (Harlow: Macmillan, 1998); Paul Langford, *Englishness Identified* (Oxford: Oxford University Press, 2000); Kidd, *British Ethnicities*; Jeremy Paxton, *The English: A Portrait of a People* (London: Routledge, 1998); Norman Davies, *The Isles* (Oxford: Papermac, 2000); Linda Colley, "Britishness in the Twenty-First Century," Prime Minister's Millennium Lecture, 1999, http://www.number-10.gov.uk; Raphael Samuel, *Island Stories* (London: Verso, 1998); and Michael Bywater, "Englishness: Who Cares?", *New Statesman*, April 3, 2000. For a polemic against such literature for the modern period, see Peter Mandler, "Against 'Englishness': English Culture and the Limits to Rural Nostalgia, 1850–1940," *TRHS*, 6th ser., VII (1997), 155–75. For the pushing back of chronological boundaries for the emergence of statebuilding and national identity to the Anglo-Saxons (which

medievalists had been pursuing for some time before the investigation of national identity became fashionable), see Elton, *The English*; James Campbell, *The Anglo-Saxons* (Oxford: Praidon, 1982); Patrick Wormald, "Bede, *the Bretwaldas* and the Origins of the *Gens Anglorum*," in Patrick Wormald, Donald Bullogh and Roger Collins, eds., *Ideal and Reality in Frankish and Anglo-Saxon Society* (Oxford: Blackwell, 1983), and *The Making of English Law: King Alfred to the Norman Conquest* (Oxford: Blackwell, 1999). See also J. C. D. Clark, "Protestantism, Nationalism and National Identity, 1660–1832," *HJ*, 43, 1 (2000), 249–76.

21 See, e.g., Antonio Benítez-Rojo, *The Repeating Island* (Durham: Duke University Press, 1996); Eduoardo Glissant, *Caribbean Discourse* (Charlottesville: University of North Carolina Press, 1996).

22 Joseph Addison, *The Freeholder, or Political Essays* (London: D. Midwinter, 1716), 35–7. Addison may have based this anecdote on that relayed in W. Funnell, "Voyage from the West Coast of Mexico to East India," in *A Collection of Voyages*, ed. William Dampier (London: James and John Knapton, 1729), IV: 199, although Funnell sets the scene of action in Holland – a good example of how stories travel and are re-inflected through the telling.

23 *Newcastle General Magazine*, XI (1757), 125; *Boswell's Life of Johnson*, ed. George Birkbeck Hill, 6 vols. (Oxford: Clarendon Press, 1934), 3: 246. Johnson begins his tale by asserting "Now what a wretch must he be, who is content with such conversation as can be had among savages!"

24 In eighteenth-century understanding, the social or the civil provide the opposition to the natural: "culture" had not yet taken on its laden and ethnocentric Victorian meanings, and meant "cultivation" (of the soil or of people) and "the art of improvement and melioration." See Johnson, *Dictionary*, I: 173.

25 The contest between "political" and "organic" concepts of nation, discussed by Eley and Suny, is one legacy of this conundrum: *Becoming National*, 4–5.

26 Joseph Roach, "Body of Law: the Sun King and the Code Noir," in Sara E. Melzer and Kathryn Norberg, eds., *From the Royal to the Republican Body*, (Berkeley and Los Angeles: University of California, 1998), 115.

27 For the term "categories of difference," see Felicity Nussbaum and Laura Brown, eds., *The Politics of Difference*, special issue of *ECS*, 23, 4 (1990); Nussbaum, *The Torrid Zone: Maternity, Sexuality and Empire* (Baltimore: Johns Hopkins, 1996); Roxanne Wheeler, *The Complexion of Race: Categories of Difference in Eighteenth Century British Culture* (Philadelphia: University of Pennsylvania Press, 2000).

28 The existence of ideas about physical difference in the classical period remains in dispute: for a summary, see Martin Bernal, *Black Athena: The Afroasiatic Roots of Classical Civilization*, 2 vols. (London: Free Association Books, 1987–91); and Mary R. Lefkowitz and Guy M. Rogers, eds., *Black Athena Revisited* (Chapel Hill: University of North Carolina Press, 1996). For eighteenth-century debates on this question, see, e.g., James Beattie, *An Essay on the Nature and Immutability of Truth, in Opposition to Sophistry and Skepticism* (London: E. and C. Dilly, 1770), a response to Hume. Interestingly, kinship-ordered societies were not recognized as "nations" in eighteenth-century international law: see Ian K. Steele, "Surrendering Rites: Prisoners on Colonial North American Frontiers," in Stephen Taylor, Richard Connors and Clyve Jones, eds., *Hanoverian Britain and Empire* (Woodbridge: The Boydell Press, 1998), 149.

29 The numbers of periodicals, travel literature, drama and fiction backing up this claim are inventoried by G. R. Crone and R. A. Skelton, "English Collections of Voyages and Travels 1625–1846," in Edward Lynam, ed., *Richard Hakluyt and his Successors*, (London, 1946). Awnsham and John Churchill's *A Collection of Voyages and Travels*, 8 vols. (London: A. & J. Churchill, 1704–47) is a good place to start for the eighteenth century. Periodicals were also full of potted versions of travel accounts:

the *Annual Register*, to take just one example, had a section on "Characters" that was comprised entirely of travel and exploration accounts, within Britain and the world. See, e.g., AR, 16 (1773), 1–33, "A Description of the Island of Otaheite." There was also a heightened interest in describing the differences among European nations: see, e.g., John Andrews, *A Comparative View of the French and English Natives, in their Manners, Politics, and Literature* (Dublin: White, Byrne & Marchbank, 1785); and Brian Dolan, *Exploring European Frontiers: British Travellers in the Age of Enlightenment* (Basingstoke: Macmillan, 2000).

30 John Millar, *The Origin of the Distinction of Ranks*, 4th edn (Edinburgh, 1806), 100; Goldsmith, "Races and Nations," 67–8.

31 Tessie Liu, "Teaching the Differences Among Women from a Historical Perspective: Rethinking Race and Gender as Social Categories," *Women's Studies International Forum*, 14 (1991), 270–1.

32 David Hume, "Of National Characters," in *Essays Moral, Political and Literary*, 2 vols. (London: Longmans, Green and Co., 1875), I: 248; Henry Home, Lord Kames, *Sketches of the History of Man* (London: W. Strahan and T. Cadell, 1778), I: 314.

33 "First Letter on a Regicide Peace" (1796) in *Writings and Speeches of Edmund Burke*, ed. R. B. McDowell (Oxford: Clarendon Press, 1991), IX: 253.

34 Karen O'Brien, *Narratives of Enlightenment* (Cambridge: Cambridge University Press, 1998); J. G. A. Pocock, *Barbarism and Religion*, 2 vols. (Cambridge: Cambridge University Press, 1999–2000); Mary Catherine Moran, "From Rudeness to Refinement: Gender, Genre and Scottish Enlightenment Discourse" (Ph.D. Diss., Johns Hopkins University, 1999); Devoney Looser, *British Women Writers and the Writing of History* (Baltimore: Johns Hopkins University Press, 2000); Mark Salber Phillips, *Society and Sentiment: Genres of Historical Writing in Britain, 1740–1820* (Princeton: Princeton University Press, 2000).

35 Margaret T. Hodgen, *Early Anthropology in the Sixteenth and Seventeenth Centuries* (Philadelphia: University of Pennsylvania Press, 1964), 435.

36 O'Brien, *Narratives*, 4–5. See also Chapters 2 and 3 below. Hume's evolutionary view of History as something that develops through stages over time was very important here: see "Of the Populousness of Ancient Nations" (1748), in *Essays*.

37 William Robertson, *The History of America*, 4 vols. (London: W. Strahan and T. Cadell, 1777), IV: 50–4; for a discussion of Robertson's "enlightened history," see Pocock, *Barbarism and Religion*, II, chaps. 16–19.

38 Grove, *Green Imperialism*, 230–5.

39 Samuel Stanhope Smith, *An Essay on the Causes of the Variety of Complexion and Figure in the Human Species* (Philadelphia and Edinburgh, 1788), v–vi; Johannes Fabian, *Time and the Other: How Anthropology Makes its Objects* (New York: Columbia University Press, 1983).

40 James Cook and James King, *A Voyage to the Pacific Ocean*, 4 vols. (London: John Fielding, 1784), vii–viii.

41 David Doig, *Two Letters on the Savage State* (London, 1792), 152, 155.

42 This essentialism was certainly a topic of debate: Hume argued that the belief in the uniformity of nature was a trick of the mind that could not be proved, but custom led human beings to nevertheless believe in and act upon both the "universality of causes and the uniformity of nature." See *Treatise*, 14–16. Hume's secondary qualification carried the most force, and most philosophers believed they could discern the "natural" propensities of the mind and its changes through time. Lord Kames, for example, controversially believed virtue to be one of these "natural" propensities, which historical circumstances rendered visible: *Sketches*, IV: 22–36.

43 Goldsmith, "Races and Nations," 78; Kames, *Sketches*, IV: 1; Smith, *Theory*, 61.

44 Michael Ignatieff, "John Millar and Individualism," in Istvan Hont and Michael Ignatieff, eds., *Wealth and Virtue: The Shaping of Political Economy* (Cambridge: Cambridge University Press, 1983), 319–20; James Burnet, Lord Monboddo, *The Origin and Progress of Language*, 4 vols. (Edinburgh: James Balfour, 1774), I: 136–44.

45 Wilson, *Sense of the People*, chap. 4; Peter Marshall, "Britain and the World in the Eighteenth Century: ReShaping the Empire," *TRHS*, 6th ser., VIII (1998), 1–18; Eliga H. Gould, *The Persistence of Empire: British Political Culture in the Age of the American Revolution* (Chapel Hill: University of North Carolina Press, 2000). Ignatius Sancho urged Laurence Sterne to turn his pen to antislavery causes in order to "ease the Yoke of many, [and] perhaps occasion a reformation throughout our Islands." *The Letters of Ignatius Sancho*, eds. Paul Edwards and Polly Rewt (Edinburgh: Edinburgh University Press, 1994), 271.

46 Elizabeth Colwell, "Sex, Savagery and Slavery in the Shaping of the French Body Politic," in Melzer and Norberg, eds., *Royal to the Republican Body*, 198–223; Wheeler, *The Complexion of Race*; Robert Dirks, *Black Saturnalia: Conflict and its Ritual expression on British West Indian Slave Plantations* (Gainesville: University of Florida, 1987); Dror Wahrman, "George Washington's False Teeth: the Problem of Identity in the American Revolution," paper given at the North American Conference on British Studies, 1999, panel on "Re-Thinking the American Revolution." Paul Gilroy, *Against Race: Imagining Political Culture Beyond the Color Line* (Cambridge, Mass.: Harvard University Press, 2000), argues that the late eighteenth century constituted "a break point in the development modern thinking about humanity and its nature": 31.

47 For the celebration of exotic others as Europeans in all but outward appearance and origin, see Laura Brown, *Ends of Empire* (Ithaca: Cornell University Press, 1996); Eric Hinderaker, "The Four Indian Kings and the Imaginative Construction of the First British Empire," *WMQ*, 3rd ser., LIII (1996), 487–526; and Chapter 2.

48 Such as Londa Schiebinger, *Nature's Body: Gender in the Making of Modern Science* (Boston: Beacon Press, 1993); Nancy Stepan, *The Idea of Race in Science: Great Britain, 1800–1960* (London: Macmillan, 1982); and Michael Banton, *The Idea of Race* (London: Tavistock Publications, 1977).

49 David Brion Davis, *The Problem of Slavery in the Age of Revolution* (Ithaca: Cornell University Press, 1976); Claire Midgley, *Women Against Slavery: The British Campaigns 1780–1870* (London: Routledge, 1992).

50 Eireann Marshall, "Libyan Portraits and Definitions: Modern Perspectives on Ancient Libyans," unpublished paper, Anglo-American Conference on Race and Ethnicity, July 1, 2000; David Nirenberg, *Communities of Violence: Persecution of Minorities in the Middle Ages* (Princeton: Princeton University Press, 1996) and "Mass Conversion and Miscegenation Anxiety in Medieval Spain," unpublished paper, Dept. of History, SUNY-Stony Brook, 2000; Kim Hall, *Things of Darkness: Economies of Race and Gender in Early Modern England* (Ithaca: Cornell University Press, 1995); Margo Hendricks and Patricia Parker, eds., *Women, "Race," and Writing in the Early Modern Period* (London: Routledge, 1994).

51 Robert Young, *Colonial Desire: Hybridity in Theory, Culture and Race* (London: Routledge, 1995); Catherine Hall, "The Nation Within and Without," in Catherine Hall, Keith McClelland and Jane Rendall, eds., *Defining the Victorian Nation: Class, Race, Gender and the Reform Act of 1867* (Cambridge: Cambridge University Press, 2000), 192–233; Antoinette Burton, *At the Heart of the Empire* (Berkeley and Los Angeles: University of California Press, 2000); Mrinalini Sinha, *Colonial Masculinity: The Manly Englishman and the Effeminate Bengal* (Manchester: Manchester University Press, 1995); Ann Laura Stoler, *Race and the Education of Desire* (Durham: Duke University Press, 1999); McClintock, *Imperial Leather*; Bill Schwarz, ed., *The Expansion of England* (London: Routledge, 1996); Annie Coombes, *Reinventing Africa: Museums, Imperial Culture and Imperial Propaganda* (New Haven and London: Yale

University Press, 1994). Charlotte Sussman and Catherine Hall have both argued that so-called "scientific racism" does not become ascendant until after 1838, when the last slaves were freed from apprenticeship, and the sentimental and evangelical faith in a 'brotherhood of man' was faltering. See Hall, "William Knibb and the Constitution of the New Black Subject," in Martin Daunton and Rick Halpern, eds., *Empire and Others: British Encounters with Indigenous Peoples* (Philadelphia: University of Pennsylvania Press, 1999), 303–24; and Sussman, *Consuming Anxieties: Consumer Protest, Gender and British Slavery 1713–1833* (Stanford: Stanford University Press, 2000), 188–205.

52 Used in their widest senses to denote groups distinguished or connected by common descent or origin, each sought to identify political, religious, social and territorial particularity: see, e.g., Katherine George, "The Civilized West Looks at Primitive Africa 1400–1800," *Isis*, 49 (1958), 67. Nicholas Hudson has argued that, by the later eighteenth century, "race" has come to be used to denote the broader differences among humankind, and "nation" the more particular ones: see his "From 'Nation' to 'Race:' the Origin of Racial Classification in Eighteenth Century Thought," *ECS*, 29 (1996), 247–64. But my research has suggested that these scientific definitions contend with more traditional ones of "race" and "nation," confusingly often in the same document.

53 Henry Louis Gates, Jr., *"Race," Writing and Difference* (Chicago: University of Chicago Press, 1985), 1–15; Dominick LaCapra, ed., *The Bounds of Race: Perspectives on Hegemony and Resistance* (Ithaca: Cornell University Press, 1991); Hendricks and Parker, *Women, "Race" and Writing*; Balibar, "The Nation Form"; Elizabeth Bohls, "Standards of Taste, Discourses of 'Race' and the Aesthetic Education of a Monster: Critique of Empire in *Frankenstein*," *Eighteenth Century Life*, n.s. 18, (November 1994), 23–36; Oliver Goldsmith, *An History of the Earth, and Animated Nature* (London, 1774), I: xxxiii; Adam Smith, *A Theory of Moral Sentiments*, eds. D. D. Raphael and A. L. Macfie (Oxford: Clarendon Press, 1976), 199; Adam Ferguson, *Essay on the History of Civil Society* (Edinburgh, 1767); and references in Chapter 2. "Ethnic" (which was used in the eighteenth century to refer to cultures and humans that were heathen, pagan or otherwise beyond the realm of Judeo-Christendom) and "ethnicity" are used in this book in their modern sense as systems of cultural difference based on shared roots and perspectives, existing within or across national boundaries – a terrain covered by "race" in the eighteenth century. Scare quotes on all of these terms should be taken as implied henceforth.

54 For Jamaica, see Chapter 4; for anti-miscegenation laws in the American colonies, see Alden T. Vaughan, *Roots of American Racism* (Oxford: Oxford University Press, 1995), 18–19.

55 Vaughan, *Roots of American Racism*, 19; James Otis, *Rights of the British Colonies Asserted and Proved* (1764), quoted in Winthrop Jordan, *White Over Black: American Attitudes Toward the Negro 1550–1812* (Chapel Hill: University of North Carolina Press, 1966), 143.

56 Joyce Chaplin, "Natural Philosophy and an Early Racial Idiom in North America: Comparing English and Indian Bodies," *WMQ*, 3rd ser., LIV (1997), 230.

57 Ibid., quoting Wood, *New England's Prospect* (1689), 242.

58 *The Plain Truth, Or Serious Considerations on the Present State of the City of Philadelphia and the Province of Pennsylvania* (Philadelphia: B. Franklin, 1747), 202. For "whiteness" as an English characteristic, see Kathleen Brown, "Native Americans and Early Modern Concepts of Race," in Daunton and Halpern, eds., *Empire and Others*, 79–100; Noel Ignatiev, *How the Irish Became White* (New York: Routledge, 1995).

59 Goldsmith, "A Description of the Manners and Customs of the Native Irish" (1759) in *Works*, 25; see also David Hume, *The History of England*, 7 vols. (London: T. Cadell Jr. and W. Davies, 1802), V: 397–8.

60 Hume, "Of National Characters," in *Essays*, 250.

61 Goldsmith, "Races and Nations," 112–13.

62 Luke Scrafton, *Reflections on the Government of Indostan* (London: G. Kearsley, 1763), 22.

63 Scottish Record Office, Grant papers, GD 248/99/5/24, quoted in A. Karras, *Sojourners in the Sun* (Ithaca: Cornell University Press, 1992), 46.

64 See Chapter 4. For Long's thinking, see BL Add. MS 12,438, "On the Different Races of Mankind"; for his influence, see Grove, *Green Imperialism*, chap. 6. Philip Morgan has suggested that Long was in the vanguard of thinking about race in the eighteenth century, and I think he may be right.

65 Earl of Shaftesbury, "Advice to an Author," *Characteristics of Men, Manners, Opinions, Times, etc.*, 4th edn (London: Thoemmes, 1727), I: 244.

66 Balibar, "The Nation Form," passim. The overlaps between race and nation are also analyzed in Schiebinger, *Nature's Body*; John C. Greene, *The Death of Adam: Evolution and its Impact on Western Thought* (Ames: University of Iowa, 1955); and Emmanuel Chukwudi Eze, ed., *Race and the Enlightenment* (Oxford: Blackwell, 1997). The conceptualization of these terms, outlined above, also muddies the nice distinctions drawn by Victorian scholars between Enlightenment traditions of "Christian universalism" and "permanent physical differences": as in Catherine Hall, ed., *Cultures of Empire: Colonizers in Britain and the Empire in the Nineteenth and Twentieth Centuries* (Manchester: Manchester University Press, 2000), 19.

67 Laurence Sterne, *The Life and Opinions of Tristam Shandy*, [1759–67], ed. Graham Petrie (Harmondsworth: Penguin, 1967), 39, quoted in Porter, *Creation of the Modern World*, 70. Sterne was discussing, in the guise of his hero, his mother's unhappy association of the sound of the clock being wound with her husband. But the point stands.

68 Peter Marshall, one of the leading scholars of British India in the early modern period, has also been one of the more vocal skeptics of the influence of empire on English culture and politics: see, e.g., "No Fatal Impact? The Elusive History of Imperial Britain," *Times Literary Supplement*, March 12 1993, 8–10; *Imperial Britain* (London, Creighton Lecture, University of London, 1994), 17; and "Introduction," in *OHBE*, II: 17. He has been more receptive to this argument in "Britain and the World." Studies investigating, and, in my view, confirming, empire's impact include Gould, *Persistence of Empire*; Wheeler, *Complexion of Race*; Richard Drayton, *Nature's Government: Science, Imperial Britain, and the "Improvement" of the World* (New Haven and London: Yale University Press, 2000); Daunton and Halpern, *Empire and Others*; Susan Thorne, *Congregational Missions and the Making of an Imperial Culture in Nineteenth-Century England* (Stanford: Stanford University Press, 1999); Matthew H. Edney, *Mapping an Empire: The Geographical Construction of British India* (Chicago: University of Chicago Press, 1997); H. V. Bowen, *Elites, Enterprise and the Making of the British Overseas Empire 1688–1775* (Basingstoke: Macmillan, 1996); Nussbaum, *Torrid Zone*; Kate Teltscher, *India Inscribed: European and British Writing on India 1600–1800* (New Delhi: Oxford University Press, 1995); Nancy Koehn, *The Power of Commerce: Economy and Government in the Eighteenth Century British Empire* (Ithaca: Cornell University Press, 1994); Laura Brown, *Ends of Empire*; and Colley, *Britons*. I first made my case for the importance of empire to English culture, politics and consciousness in "The Rejection of Deference: Urban Political Culture in England, 1715–1785" (Ph.D. Diss., Yale University, 1985) and "Empire, Trade and Popular Politics in Mid-Hanoverian England: the Case of Admiral Vernon," *P & P*, No. 126 (1988), 74–109, and developed it in subsequent articles and in *The Sense of the People*.

69 Nicholas Thomas, *Colonialism's Culture* (Durham: Duke University Press, 1994); Ann Stoler and Frederick Cooper eds, *Tensions of Empire: Colonial Subjects in a Bourgeois*

World (Berkeley and Los Angeles: University of California Press, 1997); quote from Marshall, "Imperial Britain," 9. Karen Kupperman has also recently argued for the "complexity, the uncertainty, and the fear" of English colonization of America: *Indians and English: Facing off in Early America* (Ithaca: Cornell University Press, 1999).

70 Some exemplary studies of the flow of peoples, commodities and ideas include Morgan, *Slave Counterpoint*; James Walvin, *Fruits of Empire: Exotic Produce and British Taste, 1660–1800* (Basingstoke: Macmillan, 1997); Kathleen Brown, *Good Wives, Nasty Wenches, and Anxious Patriarchs: Gender, Race and Power in Colonial Virginia* (Chapel Hill: University of North Carolina Press, 1996); Robin Blackburn, *The Making of New World Slavery* (London: Verso, 1997); Sudipta Sen, *Empire of Free Trade: The East India Company and the Making of the Colonial Marketplace* (Philadelphia: University of Pennsylvania Press, 1998); Roach, *Cities of the Dead*; Tim Breen, "An Empire of Goods: the Anglicization of Colonial America, 1690–1776," *JBS*, 25 (1986), 467–99, and "The Baubles of Britain: The American and Consumer Revolutions of the Eighteenth Century," *P & P*, No. 119 (1988), 73–104; and Bernard Bailyn, *Voyagers to the West: A Passage in the Peopling of America on the Eve of the American Revolution* (New York: Knopf, 1986). See also Linda Colley, "Going Native, Telling Tales: Captivity, Collaborations and Empire," *P & P*, No. 168 (2000), 170–93.

71 Teltscher, *India Inscribed*, 62.

72 Wheeler, *Complexion of Race*, 9; *OHBE*, I and II; for the nineteenth century, see, e.g., Catherine Hall, "The Rule of Difference: Gender, Class and Empire in the Making of the 1832 Reform Act," in Blom, Hagemann, and Hall, eds., *Gendered Nations*, 107–36; and Simon Gikandi, *Maps of Englishness: Writing Identity in the Culture of Colonialism* (New York: Columbia University Press, 1996).

73 C. L. R. James, *Black Jacobins: Toussaint L'Ouverture and the San Domingo Revolution* [1938], ed. James Walvin (London: Penguin, 2001); Sidney Mintz, *Sweetness and Power: The Place of Sugar in Modern History* (New York: Viking, 1985); Richard Price, *First Time: The Historical Vision of an Afro-American People* (Baltimore: Johns Hopkins University Press, 1983); and *Maroon Societies: Rebel Slave Communities in the Americas* (New York: Anchor Books, 1973); Robert Farris Thompson, *Flash of the Spirit: African and Afro-American Art and Philosophy* (New York: Random House, 1983), and, with John Mason and Judith McWillie, *Another Face of the Diamond Pathways through the Black Atlantic South* (New York: Intar, 1989); and Robin Law, *The Slave Coast of West Africa 1550–1750: The Impact of the Atlantic Slave Trade on an African Society* (Oxford: Clarendon Press, 1991). Arguably, Gilroy's *The Black Atlantic* owes much to these studies. See also Eltis, *The Rise of African Slavery in the Americas*; Blackburn, *The Making of New World Slavery*; and references in Chapter 4.

74 In one sense, empire as a unit was a phantasm of the metropole: all empire is local. The idea of traveling cultures looks back to James Clifford, *The Predicaments of Culture: Twentieth Century Ethnography Literature and Art* (Cambridge, Mass.: Harvard University Press, 1993) as well as contemporaneously to studies of "Atlantic world(s)." See Chapter 4.

75 Eltis, *Rise of African Slavery*, quoting "Address of the Assembly of Barbadoes to Oliver Cromwell," Sept., 1653, 15; Long, II: 332–3; *Morning Post*, Dec. 22, 1786. For an earlier use of the idea of network in relation to empire, see Peggy K. Liss, *Atlantic Empires: The Network of Trade and Revolution* (Baltimore: Johns Hopkins University Press, 1983).

76 Marshall, "Britain and the World," 10; Bowen, *Elites*, chap. 7; David Hancock, *Citizens of the World: London Merchants and the Integration of the British Atlantic Community 1735–1785* (Cambridge: Cambridge University Press, 1995). See also Chapter 4. Although my remarks here are substantiated in this volume with American

and Pacific case studies, they are also applicable on the subcontinent: as I hope to show in a future study, Calcutta, the most populous and "European"city in India, generated a cosmopolitan and hybridizing cultural and social life in which theater and display, English, Eurasian and indigenous, were central: see my *The Colonial Stage: Theater, Culture and Modernity in the English Provinces 1720–1820* (in progress).

77 Roach, *Cities of the Dead*, 30.

78 Fernando Ortiz, *Cuban Counterpoint: Tobacco and Sugar* [1947], eds. Bronislaw Malinowski and Fernando Coronil (Durham and London: Duke University Press, 1994).

79 Coronil, "Introduction," xiii. The rest of this paragraph is indebted to Coronil's incisive analysis of the import of Ortiz's work.

80 Ortiz, *Cuban Counterpoint*, 69–93; 97–9; the quotation is from Coronil, "Introduction," xiv.

81 Most recent historical studies on gender and empire adopt a metropolitan, as opposed to a colonial, perspective, although historians of the so-called "area studies" of the Caribbean and subcontinent have long been sensitive to these issues. See, e.g., Jennifer Morgan, "'Some Could Suckle Over their Shoulders': Male Travelers, Female Bodies and the Gendering of Racial Ideology," *WMQ*, 3rd ser., LIV (1997), 167–92; Verene Shepherd, Bridget Brereton and Barbara Bailey, eds., *Engendering History: Caribbean Women in Historical Perspective* (Kingston: James Currey, 1995); Edney, *Mapping an Empire*; Sen, *Empire of Free Trade*, and references in Chapter 4.

82 Roy Porter has recently summed up this work by enthusing, "in the guise of consumers, cultivators, and communicators of feeling, women were to the fore in the birth of the Modern." Porter, *Creation of the Modern World*, 338. An overview of recent studies is provided in Chapter 3.

83 See the works by Kim Hall, Parker and Hall, Minnie Sinha and Antoinette Burton, n. 50–1. For the eighteenth century, literary scholars have been more productive in drawing attention to these exchanges. See, e.g., Felicity Nussbaum, *Torrid Zones*; Hans Turley, *Rum, Sodomy and the Lash* (New York: New York University Press, 2000); Jenny Sharpe, *Allegories of Empire: The Figure of the Woman in the Colonial Text* (Minneapolis: University of Minnesota, 1993); Wheeler, *Complexion of Race*; Harriet Guest, "'Curiously Marked': Tattooing, Masculinity and Nationality in Eighteenth Century British Perceptions of the South Pacific," in John Barrell, ed., *Painting and the Politics of Culture* (Oxford: Oxford University Press, 1992), 108–15; Sussman, *Consuming Anxieties*.

84 See, e.g., Catherine Hall, "The Rule of Difference: Gender, Class and Empire in the Making of the 1832 Reform Act," in *Gendered Nations*, 108–9; Claire Midgley, ed., *Gender and Imperialism* (Manchester: Manchester University Press, 1998).

85 Wilson, *Sense of the People*, chap. 3.

86 As evinced by Olaudah Equiano, *The Interesting Narrative of the Life of Olaudah Equiano* [1793], ed. Robert Werkin (New York: St. Martin's Press, 1996); and Chapters 1 and 5.

87 Nancy Armstrong, *Desire and Domestic Fictions: A Political History of the Novel* (Oxford: Oxford University Press, 1987); Harriet Guest, *Small Change: Women, Learning, Patriotism* (Chicago: University of Chicago Press, 2000); Midgley, *Women Against Slavery*; Sussman, *Consuming Anxieties*. William Allen appealed the "*Virtue . . . Honour, and . . . Sympathy*" of the "ladies of England" in his antislavery rhetoric: see *The Duty of Abstaining from West Indian Produce* (London: T. W. Hawkins, 1792).

88 Long, II: 198.

89 See Marietta Morrissey, *Slave Women in the New World* (Lawrence: University Press of Kansas, 1989); Mavis C. Campbell, *The Dynamics of Change in a Slave Society: A Sociopolitical History of the Free Coloreds of Jamaica 1800–1865* (Cranbury, N.J., Associated University Presses, 1976); and Phillip Morgan, "Gender, Sex and Race in

the Caribbean," paper for Huntington Conference, "A New Imperial History: Transculture, Commodities and Identities in the First British Empire," Oct. 2000. See also the references in Chapter 4. Similar patterns are evident in English settlements in India and St. Helena, as my forthcoming study of gender and empire will show.

90 Thomas Laqueur, *Making Sex: Body and Gender from the Greeks to Freud* (Cambridge, Mass.: Harvard University Press, 1990); Dror Warhman, "Percy's Prologue: From Gender Play to Gender Panic in Eighteenth Century England," *P & P*, No. 159 (1998), 113–60; Randolph Trumbach, *Sex and the Gender Revolution* (Chicago: University of Chicago Press, 1998).

91 Butler, *Bodies that Matter*; Eve Kofkosky Sedgwick, *Between Men: English Literature and Male Homosexual Desire* (New York: Columbia University Press, 1985), and *Epistemology of the Closet* (Berkeley: University of California Press, 1990); Lee Edelman, "Homographesis," *Yale Journal of Criticism*, 3 (1993), 185–95.

92 See, e.g., David Hume, "Of the Refinement in the Arts and Sciences" (1752) in *Essays*, where he attributes the effeminacy of the Italians to overweening power of priests, women and aristocrats.

93 Cohen, *Fashioning Masculinity*, 7; see also Dror Wahrman, "Gender in Translation: How the English Wrote their Juvenal, 1644–1815," *Representations*, 65 (1999), 1–41; and Philip Carter, *Men and the Emergence of Polite Society in Britain 1660–1800* (London: Longman, 2001).

94 Tosh, "Old Adam and New Man," 227.

95 Ibid, 217; Anthony Fletcher, *Gender, Sex and Subordination in England 1500–1800* (New Haven and London: Yale University Press, 1995).

96 Robertson, *History of America*, II: 98.

97 William Alexander, *The History of Women, from the Earliest Antiquity to the Present Time* [1779], 2 vols. (London: 3rd edn, C. Dilly and R. Christopher, 1782), I: 151. This observation, among others, is one that becomes codified in Hannah More's directives to women: "The prevailing manners of an age depend . . . on the conduct of the women; this is one of the principal hinges on which the great machine of human society turns." *Essays on Various Subjects, principally Designed for Young Ladies* [1777] (London, 4th edn, T. Cadell, 1785), 8. She also opined that British women were so advanced in learning, liberty, religion and accomplishments that any comparison with women of other nations would be demeaning: see *Strictures on the Modern System of Female Education, with a View of the Principles and Conduct Prevalent Among Women of Rank and Fortune*, 2 vols. (London, 2nd edn, T. Cadell Jr. & W. Davies, 1799), I: xii.

98 Ferguson, *Essay on Civil Society*, 201, 146–7.

99 William Russell, *Essay on the Character, Manners, and Genius of Women in Different Ages. Enlarged from the French of M. Thomas*, 2 vols. (Philadelphia, 1774), II: 112–14.

100 Ignatieff, "John Millar," 321. See also Robertson, *History of America*, II: 96–100; David Milobar, "Aboriginal Peoples and the British Press 1720–1763," in Taylor, Connors and Jones, *Hanoverian Britain and Empire*, 76–7.

101 *Tatler*, 16 May 1710; *Spectator*, 15 May 1711.

102 Kames, *Sketches*, II: 2.

103 More, *Essays on Various Subjects*, 6.

104 Millar, *Ranks*, 32–4.

105 Hence, maternal affection is a constant, but paternal affection must be developed as society progresses: Kames, *Sketches*, II: 1–2. See Moran, "From Rudeness to Refinement," for an arresting discussion of these trends, and Cohen, *Fashioning Masculinity*, 79–85, for the debate over women's nature in the later eighteenth century.

106 Long, II: 330, recommended that women destined for Jamaica be possessed of "a proper education," a "modest demeanor" and a "skill in economy" as bulwarks against local corruption. See also John Stewart, *An Account of Jamaica and its Inhabitants* (London, 1808), 160–1.

107 More, *Strictures*, II: 14–15; see also 22–3.

108 Trumbach, *Sex and the Gender Revolution*. Cf. Emma Donahue, *Passions Between Women: British Lesbian Culture, 1668–1801* (New York: Routledge, 1993).

109 For which, see Tosh, "The Old Adam and the New Man," 233–4.

110 Amanda Vickery, *The Gentleman's Daughter* (New Haven and London: Yale University Press, 1997).

111 Dipesh Chakrabarty, "Trafficking in History and Theory: Subaltern Studies," in K. K. Ruthven, ed., *Beyond the Disciplines: the New Humanities* (Canberra: Australian National University Press, 1992), 106.

112 For the alterity of the past and the impossibility of objectively verifying either one's account of it or one's "right" to speak about it, see David Lowenthal, *The Past Is a Foreign Country* (Cambridge: Cambridge University Press, 1985); and Doug Munro, "Who 'Owns' Pacific History? Reflections on the Insider/Outsider Dichotomy," *Journal of Pacific History*, 29 (1994), 232–7; for the epistemological thicket of interpreting subaltern culture, see Gayatri Chakravorty Spivak, "Can the Subaltern Speak?", in Cary Nelson and Lawrence Grossberg, eds., *Marxism and the Interpretation of Culture* (Urbana: University of Illinois Press, 1988), 271–313.

113 Gyan Prakash, "Subaltern Studies as Postcolonial Criticism," *AHR*, 99 (1994), 1475–90; quotations from 1487, 1489.

1 CITIZENSHIP, EMPIRE AND MODERNITY IN THE ENGLISH PROVINCES

1 *Letters of the Late Ignatius Sancho, an African* (London, 5th edn, 1803), 213–14, quoted in Folarin Shyllon, *Black Slaves in Britain* (London: Institute of Race Relations, 1977), 193.

2 Walter Benjamin, *Illuminations*, ed. Hannah Arendt (New York: Schocken Books, 1969), 263.

3 The "commercialization" thesis was most enthusiastically documented by J. H. Plumb and his students; see Plumb, *The Commercialisation of Leisure in Eighteenth Century England* (Reading: University of Reading, 1973); Neil McKendrick, John Brewer and J. H. Plumb, *The Birth of a Consumer Society: The Commercialisation of Eighteenth Century England* (London: Europa, 1982); John Brewer, *Party Ideology and Popular Politics at the Accession of George III* (Cambridge: Cambridge University Press, 1976); Roy Porter, *English Society in the Eighteenth Century* (London: Allen Lane, 1982); more recently, see Paul Langford, *A Polite and Commercial People: England, 1727–1783* (Oxford: Oxford University Press, 1989). Edward Thompson and his followers countered with the more dyadic, neo-Marxist model of patrician hegemony and plebeian resistance: E. P. Thompson, "Eighteenth Century English Society: Class Struggle without Class?", *Social History*, 3 (1978), 123–65, and *Customs in Common: Studies in Traditional Popular Culture* (New York: Pantheon, 1991); and Douglas Hay, Peter Linebaugh, John G. Rule, E. P. Thompson and Cal Winslow, *Albion's Fatal Tree: Crime and Society in Eighteenth Century England* (New York: Pantheon, 1975). Thompson's hostility to "French" (i.e., non-Marxist) theory is on display in *The Poverty of Theory and Other Essays* (London: Merlin Press, 1978). J. D. C. Clark resurrected the argument that England was an "ancien régime" marked by aristocratic dominance, paternalism and deference (while also excoriating "Whig" history and imported theory alike), and was remarkably effective in drawing up the battle lines: see Clark, *English Society, 1688–1832* (Cambridge: Cambridge University Press,

1985); *Revolution and Rebellion: State and Society in England in the Seventeenth and Eighteenth Centuries* (Cambridge: Cambridge University Press, 1986).

4 Since this essay was written in 1995, a number of studies have appeared which have engaged with a more nuanced reading of "modernity" in eighteenth-century England. See, e.g., in addition to those mentioned in note 8 below, Karen O'Brien, *Narratives of Enlightenment* (Cambridge: Cambridge University Press, 1998); Miles Ogburn, *Spaces of Modernity: London's Geographies, 1680–1780* (New York: Guildford Press, 1998); J. G. A. Pocock, *Barbarism and Religion*, 2 vols. (Cambridge: Cambridge University Press, 1999); and Roy Porter, *The Creation of the Modern World: The Untold Story of the British Enlightenment* (New York: Norton, 2000).

5 E.g., W. W. Rostow, *The Stages of Economic Growth* (Cambridge: Cambridge University Press, 1960); I. Wallerstein, *The Modern World System* (New York: Academic Press, 1974); Paul Johnson, *The Birth of the Modern World: 1815–30* (New York: Harper Collins, 1991). Sociologists such as Emile Durkheim, *The Division of Labor in Society*, trans. George Simpson (New York: Collier-Macmillan, 2nd edn, 1964) and Max Weber, *The Protestant Ethic and the Spirit of Capitalism*, trans. Talcott Parsons (London: Allen and Unwin, 2nd edn, 1976), who stressed the costs and ambiguities as well as benefits of modernization, provide more interesting sociological ruminations on modernity. For the critique of "modernization theory," see John Tomlinson, *Cultural Imperialism: A Critical Introduction* (Baltimore: Pinter, 1991), chaps. 3 and 5.

6 Jürgen Habermas, "Modernity: an Incomplete Project," in Hal Foster, ed., *Postmodern Culture* (London: Pluto Press, 1983), 3–15, and *The Structural Transformation of the Public Sphere*, trans. Thomas Burber and Frederick Lawrence (Cambridge, Mass.: Polity Press, 1989); Marshall Berman, *"All that Is Solid Melts into Air": The Experience of Modernity* (New York: Simon & Schuster, 1982), and *The Politics of Authenticity: Radical Individualism and the Emergence of Modern Society* (London: Allen & Unwin, 1971). Historians of France have been more favorably impressed by the potential of these readings of Enlightenment and modernity, especially Habermas's notion of the eighteenth-century emergence of the "public sphere": see, e.g., Lynn Hunt, *Politics, Culture and Class in the French Revolution* (Berkeley and Los Angeles: University of California Press, 1984) and Lynn Hunt, ed., *The Invention of Pornography: Obscenity and the Origins of Modernity, 1500–1800* (New York: Zone Books, 1993); Tom Crow, *Painters and Public Life in Eighteenth Century Paris* (New Haven and London: Yale University Press, 1985); Joan Landes, *Women and the Public Sphere in the Age of the French Revolution* (Ithaca: Cornell University Press, 1988); Roger Chartier, *The Cultural Origins of the French Revolution* (Durham: Duke University Press, 1991); and Deena Goodman, *The Republic of Letters: A Cultural History of the French Enlightenment* (Ithaca: Cornell University Press, 1994). Exceptions among historians writing on England include Geoff Eley, "Rethinking the Political: Social History and Political Culture in Eighteenth and Nineteenth Century Britain," *Archiv für Sozialgeschichte*, 21 (1981), 427–56; Lawrence Klein, *Shaftesbury and the Culture of Politeness* (Cambridge: Cambridge University Press, 1994), and John Brewer, *The Pleasures of the Imagination: English Culture in the Eighteenth Century* (London: Farrar, Straus and Giroux, 1997). The classic pessimist reading of the modernity inaugurated by the Enlightenment is Theodor Adorno and Max Horkheimer, *Dialectic of Enlightenment* (London: Continuum, 1976).

7 Michel Foucault, *Discipline and Punish: The Birth of the Prison*, trans. Alan Sheridan (New York: Pantheon, 1971), and *The History of Sexuality*, trans. Robert Hurley (New York: Pantheon, 1978); Jacques Derrida, *Of Grammatology*, trans. Gayatri Chakravorty Spivak (Baltimore: Johns Hopkins University Press, 1976), and *Writing and Difference*, trans. Alan Bass (Chicago: University of Chicago Press, 1987); Fredric Jameson, *The Political Unconscious: Narrative as a Socially Symbolic Act* (Ithaca:

Cornell University Press, 1981); and Umberto Eco, *Travels in Hyperreality*, trans. William Weaver (San Diego: Harcourt, Brace Jovanovich, 1986). Thanks to Nick Mirzoeff for the latter reference.

8 C. L. R. James, *The Black Jacobins* (New York: Allison and Busby, 2nd edn, rev., 1989); Eric Williams, *Capitalism and Slavery* (London: André Deutsch, 1964); Paul Gilroy, *The Black Atlantic: Modernity and Double Consciousness* (Cambridge, Mass.: Harvard University Press, 1992); Nicholas Thomas, *Colonialism's Culture* (Durham: Duke University Press, 1994); Nicholas Mirzoeff, *Bodyscape: Art, Modernity and the Ideal Figure* (London: Routledge, 1996); Frederick Cooper and Ann Laura Stoler, *Tensions of Empire: Colonial Cultures in a Bourgeois World* (Berkeley: University of California Press, 1997), Robin Blackburn, *The Making of New World Slavery* (London: Verso, 1997); Antonio Benítez-Rojo, *The Repeating Island* (Durham: Duke University Press, 1992); Joseph Roach, *Cities of the Dead: Circum-Atlantic Performance* (New York: Columbia University Press, 1996).

9 Benjamin, *Illuminations*, 263.

10 A point also made by Thomas, *Colonialism's Culture*, 21.

11 For the structure and efficiency of the British "fiscal-military" state, see John Brewer, *The Sinews of Power: War, Money and the English State, 1688–1783* (London: Unwin Hyman, 1989). For an extended discussion of its ideological significance, see my *The Sense of the People: Politics, Culture and Imperialism in England, 1715–85* (New York and Cambridge: Cambridge University Press, 1995). For a differently conceived, if complementary, view, see Linda Colley, *Britons: Forging the Nation, 1707–1827* (New Haven and London: Yale University Press, 1992).

12 Gilroy, *Black Atlantic*, 17. My formulation of nation-ness here contests the more absolutist definition put forward by Liah Greenfeld in *Nationalism: Five Roads to Modernity* (Cambridge, Mass.: Harvard University Press, 1992), and Eric Hobsbawm, *Nations and Nationalism since 1780: Programme, Myth, Reality* (Cambridge: Cambridge University Press, 1990).

13 Benedict Anderson, *Imagined Communities: Reflections on the Origins and Spread of Nationalism* (London: Verso, 1983), 16.

14 See, e.g., Partha Chatterjee, *The Nation and its Fragments: Colonial and Postcolonial Histories* (Princeton: Princeton University Press, 1993); Gyan Prakash, ed., *After Colonialism: Imperial Histories and Post-Colonial Displacements* (Princeton: Princeton University Press, 1995). As I argue below, Anderson's model of the relationship between newspapers and nation-ness works better for the metropole than for Creole society.

15 Tomlinson, *Cultural Imperialism*, 83–4; Etienne Balibar, "The Nation Form: History and Ideology," in E. Balibar and I. Wallerstein, *Race, Nation, Class: Ambiguous Identities* (London: Verso, 1991), 93.

16 The dominance of metropolitan cultural, economic and political forms in "national" culture is assumed or argued in a number of otherwise excellent studies, among them Gerald Newman, *The Rise of English Nationalism: A Cultural History 1740–1830* (New York: St. Martin's, 1987); Nancy Armstrong, *Desire and Domestic Fiction: A Political History of the Novel* (New York: Oxford University Press, 1987); John Feather, *The Provincial Book Trade in Eighteenth Century England* (Cambridge: Cambridge University Press, 1986) and the studies of "commercialization" (see note 3). Recent work illuminating provincial life includes Joyce Ellis, *The Georgian Town 1680–1840* (Basingstoke: Macmillan, 2000); Peter Clark, *British Clubs and Societies, 1580–1800: The Origins of an Associational World* (Oxford: Clarendon Press, 2000); Carl Estabrook, *Urbane and Rustic: Cultural Ties and Social Spheres in the Provinces 1660–1780* (Manchester: Manchester University Press, 1998); Wilson, *Sense of the People*, passim; James Raven, *Judging New Wealth: Popular Publishing and Responses to Commerce in England 1750–1800* (Oxford: Clarendon, 1992); Peter Borsay, *The English Urban*

Renaissance: Culture and Society in the Provincial Town, 1660–1770 (Oxford: Clarendon Press, 1989); and Jonathan Barry, "The Cultural Life of Bristol, 1640–1775" (D.Phil. thesis, Oxford University, 1985). See also Peter Clark, *The Cambridge Urban History of Britain. Vol. II: 1540–1800* (Cambridge: Cambridge University Press, 2000); and the now classic studies: Leonore Davidoff and Catherine Hall, *Family Fortunes: Men and Women of the English Middle Class 1780–1850* (London: Hutchinson, 1987); John Money, *Experience and Identity: Birmingham and the West Midlands, 1760–1800* (Manchester: Manchester University Press, 1977); Roy Porter, "Science, Provincial Culture, and Public Opinion in Enlightenment England," *British Journal for Eighteenth-Century Studies*, 3 (1980), 20–46.

17 Wilson, "Empire of Virtue: the Imperial Project and Hanoverian Culture," in Lawrence Stone, ed., *An Imperial State at War* (London: Routledge, 1994), 131–5.

18 Such representations were contested, of course, if not undermined, by the growth of abolitionist literature beginning in the 1760s, much of which was also excerpted in periodicals and magazines.

19 See, e.g., *Newcastle Journal*, Jan. 27, June 9, 1750; *Newcastle General Magazine*, VIII (1755), 7–15, 241–4, 405–9; *Liverpool General Advertiser*, Nov. 17, 24, Dec. 8, 15, 1769; June 15, July 6, 27, Aug. 3, 1770; *Lancashire Magazine*, I (1763), 11–12. See also Margaret Hunt, "Racism, Imperialism and the Traveler's Gaze in Eighteenth Century England," *Journal of British Studies*, 32 (1993), 333–57.

20 *Liverpool General Advertiser*, July 27, 1770.

21 *Imagined Communities*, 51–63; T. H. Breen, "An Empire of Goods: the Anglicanization of Colonial America, 1690–1776," *Journal of British Studies*, XXV (1986), 467–99.

22 See Wilson, *Sense of the People*, chaps. 1–5; Margaret Hunt, *The Middling Sort: Commerce, Gender and the Family in England 1680–1780* (Berkeley and Los Angeles: University of California Press, 1996), 172–92; Brewer, *Sinews of Power*, chap. 4; Shyllon, *Black People in Britain*, chaps. 2–5; James Walvin, *Black and White: The Negro and English Society 1655–1945* (London: Allen Lane, 1973), chaps. 4–5; Todd M. Endelman, *The Jews of Georgian England, 1714–1830* (Philadelphia: Jewish Publication Society of America, 1979), chaps. 1, 5; M. D. George, *London Life in the Eighteenth Century* (London: Penguin, 1966), chap. 3. Middle-class women's presence as economic actors and readers was made apparent largely through advertisements, for example.

23 For women's participation in political print culture, see Paula McDowell, *The Women of Grub Street: Press, Politics and Gender in the London Literary Marketplace* (New York: Clarendon Press, 1998); Moira Ferguson, *Subject to Others: British Women Writers and Colonial Slavery, 1670–1834* (London: Routledge, 1992); Laura Brown, *Ends of Empire* (Ithaca: Cornell University Press, 1998); and Hannah Barker, "Women, Work and the Industrial Revolution: Female Involvement in the English Printing Trades, c. 1700–1840," in Hannah Barker and Elaine Chalus, eds., *Gender in Eighteenth Century England* (London: Longman, 1997), 81–100. For travel writing, see Mary Louise Pratt, *Imperial Eyes: Travel Writing and Transculturation* (London: Routledge, 1992); Elizabeth Bohls, *Women Travel Writers and the Language of Aesthetics, 1716–1818* (Cambridge: Cambridge University Press, 1995).

24 G. A. Cranfield, *The Development of the Provincial Newspaper, 1700–60* (Oxford: Clarendon Press, 1962).

25 Ministers tended to endorse an essentially nonresisting, passive version of political subjectivity and patriotism that located political legitimacy and authority solely within a Parliament whose sovereignty was absolute and in a ministry which protected Parliament from domestic and foreign threats. See John Kenyon, *Revolution Principles: The Politics of Party* (Cambridge: Cambridge University Press, 1977); Reed Browning, *Political and Constitutional Ideas of the Court Whigs* (Baton Rouge: Louisiana State University Press, 1982); Kathleen Wilson, "A Dissident Legacy: the Glorious

Revolution and Eighteenth Century Popular Politics," in J. R. Jones, ed., *Liberty Secured? Britain Before and After 1688* (Stanford: Stanford University Press, 1992), 299–326; and Wilson, *Sense of the People*, chaps. 2 and 5.

26 *London Magazine*, VII (1738), 241.

27 Wilson, *Sense of the People*, passim; Hunt, *Middling Sort*, 101–24; Paul Monod, *Jacobitism and the English People* (Cambridge: Cambridge University Press, 1989); H. T. Dickinson, *The Politics of the People in Eighteenth Century England* (Basingstoke: Macmillan, 1995); Nicholas Rogers, *Whigs and Cities* (Oxford: Clarendon Press, 1989).

28 Abel Boyer, *Political State of Great Britain*, 38 vols (1711–29) XXIII: 166; *The Liveryman, or Plain Thoughts on Public Affairs* (London, 1740), 2, 9. See also the *Monitor*, Aug. 9, 1755.

29 *Imagined Communities*, 52.

30 Women and "inferior" races, from Africans to Highland Scots, as well as the English lower classes, were frequently identified in cultural and political discourse with the symbolic feminine, that is, as dependent, irrational and subordinate: see, e.g., Sander Gilman, "Black Bodies, White Bodies," in Gates, Jr., *"Race," Writing and Difference* (Chicago: University of Chicago Press, 1986), 225–35; Vivien Jones, *Women in the Eighteenth Century* (London: Routledge, 1990), 101–24; Nancy Leys Stepan, "Race and Gender: the Role of Analogy in Science," *Isis*, 77 (1986), 261–77; Richard Popkin, "Medicine, Racism, Anti-Semitism: A Dimension of Enlightenment Thought," in G. S. Rousseau, ed., *The Languages of Psyche: Mind and Body in Enlightenment Thought* (Berkeley and Los Angeles: University of California, 1990), 405–42; Londa Schiebinger, "The Anatomy of Difference: Race and Sex in Eighteenth Century Science," *Eighteenth Century Studies*, 23, 4 (1990), 387–405, Marcia Pointon, *Strategies for Showing: Women, Possession and Representation in English Visual Culture* (Oxford: Clarendon Press, 2000); and Harriet Guest, *Small Change: Women, Learning, Patriotism* (Chicago: University of Chicago Press, 2000).

31 Borsay, *English Urban Renaissance*; Brewer, *Sinews of Power*, 184–5; E. A. Wrigley, "Urban Growth and Agricultural Change: England and the Continent in the Early Modern Period," in R. I. Rotberg and T. K. Rabb, eds., *Population History: From the Traditional to the Modern World* (Cambridge: Cambridge University Press, 1986), 123–68; P. K. O'Brien and S. L. Engerman, "Exports and the Growth of the British Economy from the Glorious Revolution to the Peace of Amiens," in B. Solow and S. L Engerman, eds., *Slavery and the Rise of the Atlantic System* (Cambridge: Cambridge University Press, 1991), 177–209.

32 "Masculinist" in this context thus describes values and practices which are meant to uphold "masculine" authority, attributes or hierarchy – it is unrelated to the question of women's presence or absence or to their contributions to its construction. This is important to stress given its recent misinterpretation: as in Margaret Jacob, "The Mental Landscape of the Public Sphere: a European Perspective," *Eighteenth Century Studies*, 28 (1994), 98–9 and n. 13. For the importance of women to polite culture, see G. J. Barker-Benfield, *The Culture of Sensibility: Sex and Society in Eighteenth Century Britain* (Chicago: University of Chicago Press, 1992); Lawrence Klein, "Gender, Conversation and the Public Sphere," in Judith Still and Michael Worton, eds., *Textuality and Sexuality* (Manchester: Manchester University Press, 1993), 100–15; Amanda Vickery, *The Gentleman's Daughter* (London: Yale University Press, 1998).

33 Wilson, *Sense of the People*, chap 1. Most hospitals' managements were in the hands of male subscribers of at least two guineas per year, each of whom had the right to recommend patients and vote; although women made up between 10 and 20 percent of annual hospital contributors, they could vote and sometimes recommend patients only by proxy. See also Adrian Wilson, *The Making of Man-Midwifery: Childbirth in England 1660–1770* (Cambridge, Mass.: Harvard University Press, 1995);

R. B. Outhwaite, "'Objects of Charity': Petitions to the London Foundling Hospital 1768–1772," *ECS*, 32 (1999), 497–510.

34 C. W. Chalkin, "Capital Expenditure on Building for Cultural Purposes in Provincial England, 1730–1800," *Business History*, 22 (1980), 51–70; Gateshead Public Library, Cotesworth MSS, "Meeting of Subscribers for building New Assembly Rooms in Newcastle," 1774; Northumberland Record Office, Blackett (Maften) MSS, ZBL 228, *Rules for Regulating the Assemblies in Newcastle Upon Tyne* [Newcastle, 1776]. The more liberatory pleasures and dangers of the masquerade described by Terry Castle were only infrequently afforded, if at all, in most non-spa provincial towns: *Masquerade and Civilization* (Stanford: Stanford University Press, 1986).

35 See my "Empire of Virtue," 136–43, and "Pacific Modernity: Theater, Englishness and the Arts of Discovery," in Colin Jones and Dror Wahrman, eds., *The Age of Cultural Revolutions* (Berkeley and Los Angeles, University of California Press, 2001); 62–93 Michael Dobson, *The Making of the National Poet: Shakespeare, Adaptation and Authorship, 1660–1769* (Oxford, 1994), esp. 146–64. See also Theophilus Cibber, *Dissertations on Theatrical Subjects* (London: Author, 1756), 75–6, appendix.

36 See John Brewer, "Clubs and Commercialization," in *Birth of a Consumer Society*, 124–80.

37 *Sense of the People*, chaps. 1 and 3; Kathleen Wilson, "Empire, Trade and Popular Politics in Mid-Hanoverian Britain: the Case of Admiral Vernon," *P & P*, No. 121 (1988), 74–109; Colley, *Britons*, 85–96.

38 This claim is substantiated at length in my *Sense of the People*, chaps. 3–5; the reader is referred there for detailed references. For a contending view, see Colley, *Britons*, passim.

39 John Brown, *An Estimate of the Manners and Principles of the Times*, 2 vols. (London: L. Davis and C. Reymers, 1757), II: 40; see also I: 66–7, 78–82, 181–2. For the anxieties about effeminacy in national social and political life of the period, see Barker-Benfield, *Culture of Sensibility*, 37–153; Kristina Straub, *Sexual Suspects: Eighteenth Century Players and Sexual Ideology* (Princeton: Princeton University Press, 1992); Robert Fahrner, "A Reassessment of Garrick's *The Male-Coquette; or, Seventeen-Hundred Fifty-Seven* as Veiled Discourse," *Eighteenth Century Life*, 17 (1993), 1–13; Randolph Trumbach, *Sex and the Gender Revolution*, vol. I (Chicago: University of Chicago Press, 1998); Michèle Cohen, *Fashioning Masculinity: National Identity and Language in the Eighteenth Century* (London: Routledge, 1996); Philip Carter, *Men and the Emergence of Polite Society in Britain 1660–1800* (London: Longman, 2001).

40 Wilson, *Sense of the People*, chaps. 3 and 5; *The Death of the late General Wolfe at the Siege of Quebec*, Manchester Central Library, Playbills, Marsden Street Theatre, Aug. 17, 1763; *Salisbury Journal*, Sept. 22, 29, 1761; *Newcastle Journal*, June 23, Sept. 15, Oct. 27, 1759; *Farley's Bristol Journal*, June 7, 1778; and *Norfolk Chronicle*, July 18, 1778.

41 [Jonas Hanway], *A Letter from a Member of the Marine Society, shewing the Usefulness and Utility of its Design* (London, 1756), 4, 12; *An Account of the Society for the Encouragement of British Troops in Germany and North America* (London, 1760).

42 For a fuller explication of this argument, see Wilson, *Sense of the People*, chap. 4. *Biographical History of Patriots* (London, 1770), advertised in *Liverpool General Advertiser*, July 6, 1770; *North Briton*, April 23, 1763 (No. 45), July 3, 1762 ff.; John Brewer, "The Misfortunes of Lord Bute," *Historical Journal*, 26 (1973), 7–30; *Salisbury Journal*, April 14, 1766.

43 For the masonic clubs, see Margaret Jacob, *The Radical Enlightenment: Pantheists, Freemasons and Republicans* (London: Allen & Unwin, 1981), 206–8; and in France, Goodman, *Republic of Letters*, 233–80. Women were allowed to join the more progressive Wilkite debating societies in the West Midlands, but this seems to have been fairly exceptional: see Money, *Experience and Identity*, 112. In the event, it is not

the empirical presence or absence of women that is at issue here, but the place of the symbolic feminine in the political imaginary of Wilkite radicalism.

44 I owe this point to John Brewer.
45 This argument was first made in a paper presented to the European History seminar at the Center for European Studies, Harvard University, in 1989, and was developed in *Sense of the People*, chap. 4. Since then, other studies have appeared addressing the political significance of Wilkite libertinism; see, e.g., Anna Clark, "The Chevalier d'Eon and Wilkes: Masculinity and Politics in the Eighteenth Century," *ECS*, 32 (1998), 19–48, and Shearer West, "Wilkes's Squint: Synecdochic Physiognomy and Political Identity in Eighteenth Century Print Culture," *ECS*, 33, 1 (1999), 65–84. For Wilkite sexual adventuring, see, e.g., J. E. Ross, ed., *Radical Adventurer: The Diaries of Robert Morris, 1772–4* (Bath: Adams and Dent, 1971), 9–12, 23–6, 34–6; *The Diary of Sylas Neville*, ed. Basil Cozens-Hardy (London: Oxford University Press, 1958) 39–40, 160–1; Horace Walpole, *Memoirs of the Reign of King George III*, 4 vols. (London: R. Bentley, 1845), IV: 156–7n. For attacks on "aristocratic" sodomy, see, e.g., *Interesting Letters Selected from the Political and Patriotic Correspondence of Messrs. Wilkes, Horn, Beckford and Junius* (London, 1769), 35–6, which lampoons Lord George Sackville Germain – called a "buggering hero" by Wilkes and Churchill – through the twinning of his sexual practice with cowardice; see also Piers Mackesy, *The Coward of Minden: The Affair of Lord George Sackville* (London: Allen Lane, 1979), esp. 254–6; Adrian Hamilton, *The Infamous Essay on Women* (London: André Deutsch, 1972); and George Rudé, *Wilkes and Liberty* (Oxford: Clarendon Press, 1969). For the backlash against sodomy in this period, see Randolph Trumbach, "Sodomy Transformed: Aristocratic Libertinage, Public Reputation and the Gender Revolution of the Eighteenth Century," *Journal of Homosexuality*, 19 (1990), 115–16; and Chapter 5.
46 Raymond Postgate, *That Devil Wilkes* (London: Constable & Co., 1930), 140–5; Rudé, *Wilkes and Liberty*, 85–9; quotations from Richard Sennett, *The Fall of Public Man* (New York: Knopf, 1977), 103, and John Brewer, "Theater and Counter Theater in Georgian Politics," *Radical History Review*, 22 (1979–80), 8.
47 For the denigration of such discrepancies between public and private virtue as Wilkes exhibited, see Hall and Davidoff, *Family Fortunes*, 108–18, Barker-Benfield, *Culture of Sensibility*, chaps. 3–4. For women participants, see Wilson, *Sense of the People*, 32–3, 366–8; for the theoretical and practical antagonisms between contractarian politics and women's presence in the political sphere see, ibid., chap. 4; Carol Pateman, *The Sexual Contract* (Cambridge: Polity 1988), 1–16. The penalties for women's over-identification with the prerogatives of "manly patriotism" were illustrated by the life of Catharine Macaulay, who arguably identified herself as a sexual subject by marrying a man twenty-six years her junior: see Bridget Hill, *The Republican Virago: The Life and Times of Catherine Macaulay* (Oxford: Clarendon Press, 1992).
48 For the contending masculinities and femininities at play in eighteenth-century urban society, see Randolph Trumbach, "London's Sapphists: From Three Sexes to Four Genders in the Making of Modern Culture," in Julia Epstein and Kristina Straub, eds., *Body Guards: The Cultural Politics of Gender Ambiguity* (London: Routledge, 1991), 112–41; and Castle, *Masquerade and Civilization*, passim; Tim Hitchcock and Michèle Cohen, *English Masculinities 1680–1830* (London: Longman, 1999); Carter, *Men and the Emergence of Polite Society*.
49 Paul Kaufman, *Libraries and their Users* (London: Library Association, 1969), 223–4; British Library, Arderon MSS, Add. MS 27,966, ff. 241b–2; Peter Clark, *The English Alehouse: A Social History 1200–1830* (London: Longman, 1983), 225.
50 Joseph Addison, *The Freeholder*, ed. James Leheny (Oxford: Clarendon Press, 1979), 182; *The Correspondence of Sir James Clavering*, ed. H. T. Dickinson (*Surtees Society*, CLXXVIII, 1967), 70–5; [Eliza Haywood], *The Female Spectator* (London, 1744–5);

Lois Schwoerer, "Women and the Glorious Revolution," *Albion*, 17 (1986), 195–218; Rachel J. Weil, "Sexual Ideology and Political Propaganda in England, 1680–1714" (Ph.D. Diss., Princeton University, 1991); Michael Harris, *London Newspapers in the Age of Walpole* (London: Associated University Press, 1986), 38–40; R. M. Wiles, *Freshest Advices: Early Provincial Newspapers* (Canton: Ohio State University Press, 1965), 269–302; Ferguson, *Subject to Others*; Mary R. Mahl and Helene Koon, eds., *The Female Spectator: English Women Writers before 1800* (Bloomington: Indiana University Press, 1977); McDowell, *Women of Grub Street*; and Hilda Smith, ed., *Women Writers and the Early Modern British Tradition* (Cambridge: Cambridge University Press, 1998).

51 *Newcastle Chronicle*, April 11, 1766; *Norwich Gazette*, Feb. 9, 1733, Jan. 3, Dec. 19, 1741; HL Montagu MSS, M0 245–6.

52 Frank O'Gorman, *Voters, Patrons and Parties* (Oxford: Oxford University Press, 1990), 93–4; Elaine Chalus, "'That epidemical Madness': Women and Electoral Politics in the Late Eighteenth Century," in Barker and Chalus, *Gender in Eighteenth Century England*, 151–78; Monod, *Jacobitism*, 190–218, 250; Thompson, *Customs in Common*, 306–61; *Newcastle Chronicle*, March 19, 1768; Donna Andrew, ed., *London Debating Societies, 1776–1799* (London Record Society Publications, 30, 1993), viii–ix; Clare Midgley, *Women Against Slavery: The British Campaigns 1780–1870* (London: Routledge, 1992), 15–25; *Female Spectator*, II: 135–68; *Norwich Gazette*, Nov. 16, 1745; *Bonner and Middleton's Bristol Journal*, Jan. 10, 1778; *Freeholder*, 181–4.

53 Wilson, *Sense of the People*, chaps. 1, 3–5; for the 1790s, see Linda Colley, *Britons*, chap. 6, and Midgley, *Women Against Slavery*. For the injunction to "manliness" for women in feminist discourse, see Catharine Macaulay, *Letters on Education* (London: Dilly, 1790), Letters 22 and 24; and Mary Wollstonecraft, *Vindication of the Rights of Woman* (London: J. Johnson, 1792), 80–1, 206–7. The long-hallowed link in Western culture between women's rights and commercial capitalism has been most recently argued by Barker-Benfield, *Culture of Sensibility*, esp. chaps. 4 and 5; for an idealized view of its consequences, see Jacob, "Mental Landscape of the Public Sphere," 95–113.

54 *York Chronicle*, Dec. 25, 1772.

55 Political writers of all stripes, from "civic humanists" to Court Whigs and Tories, identified legitimate political activity with men and the symbolic masculine and subversion, rebellion, supineness and corruption with "feminine" influences. Within civic humanist discourses, women were powerful historical forces, to be sure, but their influence was always in danger of exceeding its proper boundaries; and, because they were seen ultimately as species of property, they could not achieve the independence or civility of true virtue. Even the most "modern" writers of social and political theory, the so-called "conjectural historians" of the Scottish school, saw women as naturally domestic: see Introduction. Contemporary examples include *The History of the Westminster Election* (London, 1785), 102–5, 227–8, 248; *The Female Parliament* (London, 1754); *The Female Patriot* (London, 1779).

56 As Harriet Guest has recently shown: *Small Change*, chap. 5.

57 Georgiana Hill, *Women in English Life*, 2 vols. (London: R. Bentley, 1896), I: 2–20; *Georgiana: Extracts from the Correspondence of Georgiana, Duchess of Devonshire*, ed. Earl of Bessborough (London: John Murray, 1955), 15–16, 25–35, 78–80; HL Montagu MS 6704, 1537; see also Elaine Chalus, "Elite Women, Social Politics, and the Political World of Late Eighteenth-Century England," *Historical Journal*, 43 (2000), 669–97. For the 1739 case, see Hilda Smith, "Women as Sextons and Electors," in Smith, ed., *Women*, 324–42; and Susan Staves, "Investments, Votes and Bribes," in Smith, ed., *Women*, 259–78.

58 For middle- and lower-class women's position in politics, see Gateshead Public Library, Ellison MSS, A54/11, March 15, 1739; *Freeholder*, 182, 52–4, 73–4, 205.

Hunt, *Middling Sort*, chap. 3 and McDowell, *Women of Grub Street*, chap. 2, confirm this assessment.

59 For women's participation in the war efforts, see Chapter 3. Wilson, *Sense of the People*, chap. 3; for its effacement, see [Richard Baldwin], *An Impartial and Succinct History of the Origin and Progress of the Present War*, first published in installments in the *London Magazine*, vols. 28–9 (1759–60). By the 1790s, the acknowledgement of women's contribution became a crucial part of loyalist political culture: Colley, *Britons*, 238–48; Patricia Lin, "Extending her Arms: Military Families and the Transformation of the British State, 1793–1815" (Ph.D. Diss., University of California at Berkeley, 1993).

60 *Freeholder*, 182; see also 52–4, 73–4, 205. For a fuller explication, of these arguments, see Chapter 3.

61 Smith, "Women as Sextons and Electors," 329; *Etherington's York Chronicle*, Nov. 8, 1776, my emphases.

62 Smith, "Women as Sextons and Electors," 331, quoting King's Bench Justice Probyn, 1739; see also Henry Homes, Lord Kames, *Sketches of the History of Man*, 4 vols. (London: W. Strahan & T. Cadell, 1778), II: 4–5. As Carol Pateman has noted, that women were held by virtually all political theorists to be incapable of men's ultimate political obligation – to give up their lives in defense of the state – is part of the notion of (sexual) difference that governed and circumscribed the terms of their inclusion in civil society and continues to bedevil their place there: *The Disorder of Women* (Cambridge: Polity 1989), 4–14; "Women's Writing, Women's Standing: Theory and Politics in the Early Modern Period," in Smith, ed., *Women*, 365–82. For additional reflections on the historical connections between women, politics and political thought, see Linda M. Zerilli, *Signifying Woman: Culture and Chaos in Rousseau, Burke and Mill* (Ithaca: Cornell University Press, 1994); Joan Scott, *Only Paradoxes to Offer* (Ithaca: Cornell University Press, 1997); and M. Jacqui Alexander and Chandra Talpade Mohanty, *Feminist Genealogies, Colonial Legacies, Democratic Futures* (London: Routledge, 1998).

63 See Chapters 3 and 4 below.

64 HL Montagu MS MO 1384, Aug. 6, 1758.; and Chapter 2. Teresa De Lauretis's *Technologies of Gender* (Bloomington: Indiana University Press, 1987) remains a classic in the field in its analysis of the tensions between "woman as representation" and "women as historical beings."

65 Rozina Visram, *Ayahs, Lascars and Princes: Indians in Britain 1700–1947* (London: Pluto, 1986); John Geipel, *The Europeans: An Ethnohistorical Survey* (London: Longmans, 1969), 163–5; V. G. Kiernan, "Britons Old and New," in Colin Holmes, ed., *Immigrants and Minorities in British Society* (London: Allen & Unwin, 1978), 23–43; Edelman, *Jews of Georgian England*, chap. 4; Walvin, *Black and White*, chap. 4; Wilson, *Sense of the People*, chap. 6; John Steegmann, *The Rule of Taste from George I to George IV* (London: Macmillan, 1936), 39; Virginia Berridge, "East End Opium Dens and Narcotic Use in Britain," *London Journal*, IV (1978), n. 3.

66 Colley, *Britons*, passim.

67 English Catholics were objects of penal laws throughout the century, kept under house arrest during the Jacobite rebellions of 1715 and 1745 and the victims of rioters in 1780; Irish Catholics were targets of popular and official animosity at various junctures, such as in 1736, 1745 and 1780; Jews and foreign protestants were harassed during the furor over the naturalization bills of 1751 and 1753 and the objects of exclusionary civic by-laws; Scots were segregated and kept from apprenticeships in several northern towns; and Africans were not only attacked, harassed and kidnapped, but some were also rounded up for "repatriation" in 1786–7. For recent assessments, see Daniel Statt, *Foreigners and Englishmen: The Controversy over Immigration and Population 1660–1760* (Newark: University of Delaware Press, 1995); Colin Haydon,

Anti-Catholicism in Eighteenth Century England (Manchester: Manchester University Press, 1993); and Michael Ragussis, *Figures of Conversion: "The Jewish Question" and English National Identity* (Durham: Duke University Press, 1995).

68 These figures follow the recent re-adjustment by Norma Meyers, in her careful study, *Reconstructing the Black Past: Blacks in Britain 1780–1830* (Oxford: Clarendon Press, 1996), 38. The outports included not only Bristol and Liverpool, but also Chester, Dartmouth, Exeter, Glasgow, Lancaster, Plymouth, Portsmouth, Preston and Whitehaven. David Brion Davis, *The Problem of Slavery in Western Culture* (Ithaca: Cornell University Press, 1976); Nigel Tattersfield, *The Forgotten Trade: Comprising the Log of the Daniel and Henry of 1700 and Accounts of the Slave Trade from the Minor Ports of England, 1698–1725* (London: Cape, 1991); Walvin, *Black and White*, 31–79; Peter Fryer, *Staying Power: The History of Black People in Britain* (London: Pluto, 1984), 58–64; Philip Morgan, *Slave Counterpoint: Black Culture in the Eighteenth Century Chesapeake and Low Country* (Chapel Hill: Omonhundro Institute, 1998).

69 Eighteenth-century Britain was a slave-owning, if not slave, society, and slavery was confirmed as legal by court after court in the name of property rights. The Somerset case of 1772, which rendered illegal slaves' forcible removal from England, increased the freedom of black servants but was ignored or evaded by West Indian planters who tried to have it overturned by Act of Parliament. See Philip Morgan, "British Encounters with Africans and African-Americans," in Bernard Bailey and Philip Morgan, eds., *Strangers within the Realm* (Chapel Hill: University of North Carolina Press, 1991), 158–60; F. O. Shyllon, *Black Slaves in Britain* (London: Oxford University Press, 1974); James Oldham, "New Light on Mansfield and Slavery," *JBS*, 27 (1988), 45–68; Vizam, *Ayahs*, chap. 2.

70 Fryer, *Staying Power*, 72–80; Edwards and Walvin, *Black Personalities*, 31–2.

71 Ukawsaw Gronniosaw, *Wondrous Grace Display'd in the Life and Conversion of James Albert Ukawsaw Gronniosaw* (Leeds: W. Nicholson, 1770), 171. Slave and free black labor was protested against by white artisans in other towns in England and the empire as posing a threat to their livelihoods: Morgan, "British Encounters," 191.

72 Sir John Fielding, *Extracts from such of the Penal Laws, as Particularly Relate to the Peace and Good Order of this Metropolis* (London, 1768), 144.

73 Walvin, *Blacks in Britain*, 64–5. The spiritual imperialism of such organizations as the SPCK, which had been actively converting Africans since the late seventeenth century, aided the process; C. F. Pascoe, *Two Hundred Years of the SPG* (London, 1901), 256–7.

74 *London Chronicle*, Feb. 17, 1764; Shyllon, *Black People in Britain, 1555–1833* (London: Oxford University Press, 1977), 79–81; J. J. Hecht, *Continental and Colonial Servants in Eighteenth Century England* (Cambridge, 1956), 54.

75 See, e.g., the letters of the Sons of Africa in *Memoirs of Granville Sharp* (London, 1828) and those reprinted in Shyllon, *Black People in Britain*, appendix ii. For black radicals in later decades, see Peter Linebaugh, *The London Hanged: Crime and Civil Society in the Eighteenth Century* (Cambridge: Cambridge University Press, 1992), 415–16; Iain McCalman, "Anti-Slavery and Ultra Radicalism in Early 19th century England," *Slavery and Abolition*, 7 (1986); Fryer, *Staying Power*, 214–36.

76 See, e.g., Henry Louis Gates, Jr., "Writing 'Race' and the Difference it Makes," in Gates, ed., *"Race," Writing and Difference*, 11–15; Ferguson, *Subject to Others*, 125–33; Shyllon, *Blacks in Britain*, 169–203; Cugoano, *Thoughts and Sentiments on the Evil and Wicked Traffic of the Slavery and Commerce of the Human Species* (London, 1787), reprinted in Francis D. Adams and Barry Saunders, eds., *Three Black Writers in Eighteenth Century England* (Belmont, CA: Wadsworth, 1971); Olaudah Equiano, *The Interesting Narrative of the Life of Olaudah Equiano, or Gustava Vassa, the African* [1793] (New York: St. Martin's Press, 1996); Adam Potkay and Sandra Burr, eds., *Black Atlantic Writers of the Eighteenth Century* (New York: Macmillan, 1995); Vincent

Caretta, ed., *Unchained Voices: Anthology of Black Authors in the English-Speaking World of the 18th Century* (Lexington: University of Kentucky, 1996); Helena Woodard, *African-British Writings in the Eighteenth Century: The Politics of Race and Reason* (Westport: Greenwood Press, 1999).

77 The most recent and detailed examination is that by Stephen J. Braidwood, *Black Poor and White Philanthropists: London's Blacks and the Foundation of the Sierra Leone Settlement, 1786–1791* (Liverpool: Liverpool University Press, 1994).

78 Belisarius was the Roman general blinded by the Emperor Justinian and forced to wander the world as a beggar for presumed disloyalty – the classic example of the fickleness of princes. The third ship to be commissioned was named the *Vernon*.

79 Shyllon, *Black People in Britain*, 136–46; Cugoano, *Thoughts and Sentiments on the Evils of Slavery*, 139–42; *Morning Herald*, Dec. 15, 1786, Jan. 2, 1787, quoted in Shyllon, *Black People in Britain*, 140–1.

80 *Public Advertiser*, Jan. 1, 1787; *Morning Post*, Dec. 22, 1786, quoted in Shyllon, *Black People*, 142.

81 *Public Advertiser*, Jan. 3, 1787; George, *London Life*, 116–57; James Tobin, *A Short Rejoinder to the Reverend Mr. Ramsay's Reply* (London, 1787); Winthrop Jordan, *White Over Black: American Attitudes toward the Negro 1550–1812* (Baltimore: Johns Hopkins University Press, 1969); *Omiah's Farewell, Inscribed to the Ladies of London* (London: G. Kearsley, 1776); "Song on the Cherokee Chiefs Inscribed to the Ladies of Great Britain" [1763], quoted in Tom Hatley, *The Dividing Paths: Cherokees and South Carolinians through the Era of Revolution* (New York: Oxford University Press, 1993), 151–2 (thanks to Nancy Shoemaker for this reference). The imbalance in the numbers of black men and women – the result of slave recruitment patterns – meant that African men frequently took white wives. See Cobbett's *Weekly Political Register*, June 16, 1804, for disparagement of such intermarriage.

82 *London Chronicle*, Oct. 19–22, 1765, my emphasis. That blacks born in Britain or her colonies may also have been "natives" did not seem to occur to the *Chronicle* writer, who not only thereby exposed the priority of "race" in the national identity but anticipated by almost two hundred years the anti-immigration arguments and legislation of the British right since 1971.

83 Homi K. Bhabha, "Signs Taken for Wonders," in *The Location of Culture* (London: Routledge, 1994), 108.

84 Equiano, *Interesting Narrative*, 132, 340 and passim; Geraldine Murphy, "Olaudah Equiano, Accidental Tourist," *ECS*, 27 (1994), 551–68; *Morning Chronicle*, July 15, 1788 (letter from the Sons of Africa to Sir William Dolben, Bart.); Linebaugh, *London Hanged*, 415. For the hybrid and "radically nonbinary" nature of slave narratives in general and Equiano in particular, see Bhabha, "Signs Taken for Wonders," 102–22, and Susan M. Marren, "Between Slavery and Freedom: the Transgressive Self in Olaudah Equiano's Autobiography," *PMLA* 108 (1993), 95; for Du Bois, see Gilroy, *Black Atlantic*.

85 Quoted in Shyllon, *Black People in Britain*, 193.

86 *Imagined Communities*, 16.

87 As argued by Colley, *Britons*, chap. 3; Richard Helgerson, *Forms of Nationhood: The Elizabethan Writing of England* (Chicago: University of Chicago Press, 1993). For an interpretation which turns these assertions on their head, see Simon Gikandi, *Maps of Englishness: Writing Identity in the Culture of Colonialism* (New York: Columbia University Press, 1996).

88 Quotation from George Lillo, *The London Merchant* (London, 1731), III.i.11–19 – an immensely popular play in London and the provinces in this period. For the retailing of this view of empire, see Wilson, "Empire of Virtue," 141–3.

89 See, e.g., *Gentleman's Magazine*, 28 (1758), 393; *London Chronicle*, June 7/9, 9/11, 1757; *Salisbury Journal*, Jan. 14, 1760; *Newcastle General Magazine*, 11 (1758), 242–5;

A Genuine Narrative of the Deplorable Deaths of the English Gentlemen, and Others, who were Suffocated in the Black-Hole in Fort-William, at Calcutta (London: A. Millar, 1758).

90 Rev. Richard Brewster, *A Sermon on the Thanksgiving Day* (Newcastle, 1759); *Gentleman's Magazine*, 33 (1763), 291.

91 *Parliamentary History*, XVII (1771–4), 857–8 and passim; Samuel Foote, *The Nabob* (London, 1772); Horace Walpole to Sir Horace Mann, Nov. 4, 1772, *The Yale Edition of Horace Walpole's Correspondence*, ed. W. S. Lewis (London: Oxford University Press, 1937), XXIII: 441; *Public Advertiser*, March 14, 1774, July 10, 1769, March 26, 1771; *Lancashire Magazine*, I (1763), 60–2, II (1764), 515–16; Philip Lawson and Jim Phillips, "'Our Execrable Banditti': Perceptions of Nabobs in Mid-Eighteenth-Century Britain," *Albion*, XVI (1984), 225–41; H. V. Bowen, *Revenue and Reform: The Indian Problem in British Politics* (Cambridge: Cambridge University Press, 1991); *The Correspondence of William Pitt, Earl of Chatham*, 4 vols. (London: J. Murray, 1838–40), III: 405.

92 *Parliamentary History*, XVII (1771–4), 567–73, 722–43; *Scots Magazine*, XXXIV (1772), 588; and Peter Hulme, *Colonial Encounters: Europeans and the Caribbean* (London: Methuen, 1986), chap. 6.

93 For the impact of the Cook voyages, see Chapter 2 below. Shyllon, *Black People in Britain*, chap. 4. For the Somerset case, see n. 68.

94 Public Record Office, HO 55/13/2.

95 Peter Marshall, "Empire and Authority in Later Eighteenth Century Britain," *Journal of Imperial and Commonwealth Studies*, 15 (1987), 115. The Zong incident of 1781 added immeasurably to public shock and disillusionment. See Fryer, *Staying Power*, 127–30; and Chapter 2 below.

96 Edward Gibbon, *The History of the Decline and Fall of the Roman Empire*, 6 vols. (London: W. Strahan and T. Cadell, 1776–88); Society for Constitutional Information, *The Second Address to the Public* (London, 1782); see also *Newcastle Chronicle*, Aug. 19, 1786.

97 Benjamin, *Illuminations*, 261.

98 "To the ENGLISH NATION," *Norfolk Chronicle*, Oct. 10, 1778.

99 *Parliamentary History*, XVII (1771–4), 570–5, 735–6.

100 Homi Bhabha, "Of Mimicry and Man: the Ambivalence of Colonial Discourse," *October*, 28 (1984), 125–33. For contemporary recognition of and complaints about this conceptualization of Englishness, see *Gentleman's Magazine*, 25 (1765), 589–90.

2 THE ISLAND RACE:
CAPTAIN COOK AND ENGLISH ETHNICITY

1 Winston Churchill, *A History of the English-Speaking Peoples*, 4 vols. (London: Cassell, 1956–8); a shortened version was also published as *The Island Race* (London: Cassell, 1964). Margaret Thatcher, *The Downing Street Years* (London: Harper Collins, 1994), 183.

2 Diana Loxley, *Problematic Shores: The Literature of Islands* (New York: St. Martin's Press, 1990), 3; see also Michael Seidel, *Robinson Crusoe: Island Myths and the Novel* (Boston: Twayne Publishers, 1987); and Orest Ranum, "Islands and the Self in a Ludovician Fete," in David Rubin, ed., *Sun King* (Washington, D.C.: Folger Books, 1992), 17–34.

3 Oliver Sacks, *The Island of the Colorblind: Cycad Island* (New York: Knopf, 1997); Richard H. Grove, *Green Imperialism: Colonial Expansion, Tropical Island Edens and the Origins of Environmentalism 1600–1860* (Cambridge: Cambridge University Press, 1995), 223–308; Bernard Bailyn, *The Peopling of British North America* (New York: Knopf, 1986); Fernando Ortiz, *Cuban Counterpoint: Tobacco and Sugar*, and the introduction by Fernando Coronil (Durham: Duke University Press, 1994).

4 It thus differed from earlier travelers and explorers' tales that focused on the fantastic, the exotic and the economic. See James Hevia, *Cherishing Men from Afar: Qing Guest Ritual and the Macartney Embassy* (Durham: Duke University Press, 1995), 84–5; Thomas Richards, *The Imperial Archive: Knowledge and the Fantasy of Empire* (London: Verso, 1993); Jonathan Lamb, "Introduction," *Eighteenth Century Life*, 18 (November 1994), 5–6. For another recent analysis of the ethnography of travel writing in this period, see Gordon M. Sayres, *Les Sauvages Américains: Representations of Native Americans in French and English Colonial Literature* (Chapel Hill: University of North Carolina Press, 1997), chap. 4.

5 See Kathleen Wilson, *The Sense of the People: Politics, Culture and Imperialism in England 1715–1785* (Cambridge: Cambridge University Press, 1995), chap. 5.

6 James Walvin, ed., *Slavery and British Society 1776–1846* (London: Macmillan, 1982); F. Shyllon, *Black Slaves in Britain* (London: Institute of Race Relations, 1977); Peter Fryer, *Staying Power: The History of Black People in Britain* (London: Pluto, 1984); Bridget Orr, 'Southern Passions Mix with Northern Art: Miscegenation on the *Endeavour* Voyage,' *Eighteenth Century Life*, 18 (1994), 214–15; Stephen Braidwood, *Black Poor and White Philanthropists* (Liverpool: Liverpool University Press, 1994).

7 Lamb, "Introduction," 5; see also Philip Edwards, *The Story of the Voyage* (Cambridge: Cambridge University Press, 1994), chap. 1.

8 For the scientific accomplishments of the voyages, see Lynn Withey, *Voyages of Discovery* (Berkeley and Los Angeles: University of California Press, 1992); for the political, see David Mackay, *In the Wake of Cook: Exploration, Science and Empire* (London: Croom Helm, 1985); C. A. Bayly, *Imperial Meridian* (London: Longmans, 1989); Derek Howse, ed., *Background to Discovery: Pacific Exploration from Dampier to Cook* (Berkeley: University of California, 1990).

9 Glyndwr Williams, "The Pacific: Exploration and Exploitation," in OHBE, II: 552–575; Alan Frost, "Captain James Cook and the Early Romantic Imagination," in *Captain James Cook: Image and Impact* (Melbourne: Hawthorne Press, 1972), 90–106; for the popularity of voyage literature in general in the eighteenth century and of Cook's voyages in particular, see Edwards, *Story of the Voyage*, chaps. 1, 5 and 6; and Neil Rennie, *Far-Fetched Facts: The Literature of Travel and the Idea of the South Seas* (Oxford: Clarendon Press, 1995).

10 Louis Antoine de Bougainville, *A Voyage Round the World, performed by order of His Most Christian Majesty, in the Years 1766, 1767, 1768 and 1769*, trans. John Reinhold Forster (London: J. Nourse and T. Davies, 1772); John Hawkesworth, *An Account of the Voyages . . . Successively Performed by Commodore Byron, Capt. Wallis, Capt. Carteret and Captain Cook*, 3 vols. (London: W. Strahan and T. Cadell 1773); for excerpts see *Gentlemen's Magazine, London Magazine, Lady's Magazine, Town and Country Magazine, Annual Register*, and *Universal Magazine* for summer–autumn 1773. Other accounts include: Sydney Parkinson's *Journal of a Voyage to the South Seas in His Majesty's Ship the Endeavour* (London: Stanfield Parkinson, 1773); [John Marra], *Journal of the Resolution's Voyage* (London: F. Newbury, 1775); James Cook, *Voyage to the South Pole* (London: W. Strahan and T. Cadell, 1777), Johann Reinhold Forster, *Observations Made during a Voyage Round the World* (London: G. Robinson, 1778); George Forster, *Voyage Round the World during the Years 1772–5*, 2 vols. (London: B. White et al., 1777); and James Cook and James King, *A Voyage to the Pacific Ocean* (London: John Fielding, 1785); all are excerpted and reviewed in the above journals. For the *Annual Register*, see 16 (1773), 1–45, 84–9; 17 (1774), 61–75, 136–7; 20 (1777), 63–7; 87–91, 234–49; 23 (1780), 195–6; 27 (1784–5), 1–13, 473–96. For a more complete print history of the voyage literature, see Beaglehole in Cook, I: ccxlii–cclxiv; Cook, II: cxliii–clvii; Cook, III: clxxi–clxxv.

11 Though "employ'd as a discoverer," Cook explained, he was but "a plain man,

zealously exerting himself in the service of his country," and therefore begs the reader to "excuse the inaccuracies of style." Cook in Cook, I: 380.

12 Andrew Kippis, *The Life of Captain James Cook* (Basil: Tourneissen, 1788), 371; Fanny Burney, *The Early Diary of Fanny Burney* (reprt., Freeport: Books for Libraries Press, 1971), 267; Hannah More, *Slavery, a Poem* (London, 1788); *The Lady's Magazine*, IV (1773), 345–6; Anna Seward, *Elegy on the Death of Captain Cook* (London: J. Dodsley, 1780); William Cowper, *The Task* (London: T. Johnson, 1785); T. M. Curley, *Samuel Johnson and the Age of Travel* (Athens, Ga: University of Georgia Press, 1976), 66, 69; for a more recent endorsement of Cook's upright and strictly nonmiscegenating interactions with native women, see Marshall Sahlins, *Islands of History* (Chicago: University of Chicago Press, 1985), chap. 1. The *AR* of 1784–5, for example, summed up existing sentiment when a reviewer remarked, reviewing the events precipitating Cook's death, that "his humanity . . . proved fatal to him" (154).

13 Kippis, *Life*, 355, 359–60. Many of these encomiums compared Cook to the Spanish conquistadors, rather than to earlier and less "ethical" English explorers and traders, in a strategy meant to erase Britain's less salubrious imperial record, which recent events had done much to drive home.

14 For Fitzgerald, see Bill Pearson, *Rifled Sanctuaries: Some Views of the Pacific Islands in Western Literature to 1900* (Auckland: Auckland University Press, 1984), and Shef Rogers, "The Injured Islanders (1779) and English Sensibility," *Eighteenth Century: Theory and Interpretation* 38 (1997), 256–65; for the debate on Cook's violence, see Gananath Obeyeskere, *The Apotheosis of Captain Cook: European Myth Making in the Pacific* (Princeton: Princeton University Press, 1992); Marshall Sahlins, *How "Natives" Think, About Captain Cook, for Example* (Chicago: University of Chicago Press, 1995).

15 This argument is taken from my *The Colonial Stage: Theater, Culture and Modernity in the English Provinces, 1680–1800* (in progress).

16 Although we arrived at these conclusions independently, Joseph Roach's recent book supports many of the contentions about theater and performance presented here. See Roach, *Cities of the Dead: CircumAtlantic Performance* (New York: Columbia University Press, 1996), quotation from p. 4.

17 This pantomime has been extensively studied. This account is indebted to, but differs significantly from, those by Rüdiger Jöppien, "Phillipe Jacques de Loutherbourg's Pantomime *Omai, or a Trip Round the World* and the Artists of Captain Cook's Voyages," in *Captain Cook and the South Seas* (London: British Museum, 1979), 81–133; Bernard Smith, *European Vision and the South Pacific* (New Haven: Yale University Press, 1985), 115–22; and Greg Dening, *Mr. Bligh's Bad Language: Passion, Power and Theatre on the Bounty* (Cambridge: Cambridge University Press, 1992), 270–6, 293–8; and is based upon John O'Keeffe, *Harlequin Omai* (London, 1785); [William Shields], *A Short Account of the New Pantomime called OMAI, or a Trip Round the World* (London: T. Cadell, 1785); Newberry Library, Microprint of O'Keeffe, Airs, etc. for *Harlequin Omai*, British Library, Add. MS 38622, Plays, Coker Collection, ff. 164–87v; and *Recollections of the Life of John O'Keeffe, Written by Himself*, 2 vols. (London, 1826), II: 113–14.

18 For pantomime, see David Mayer III, *Harlequin in His Element: The English Pantomime 1806–36* (Cambridge, Mass.: Harvard University Press, 1969); and Ralph Allen, "Topical Scenes from Pantomime," *Educational Theatre Journal*, 17 (1965), 289–300; quotation from *Morning Chronicle*, Dec. 21, 1785.

19 See *Early Diary of Burney*, I: 321–37, II: 130–3; George Colman Jr., *Random Records*, 2 vols. (London, Henry Colburn and Richard Bentley, 1830), I: 152–96.

20 See, e.g., K. R. Howe, *Where the Waves Fall: A New South Sea Islands History from the First Settlement to Colonial Rule* (Honolulu: University of Hawaii Press, 1984); Nicholas Thomas, *In Oceania* (Durham: Duke University Press, 1997), 1–7.

21 Michael Taussig, *Shamanism, Colonialism and the Wild Man* (Chicago: University of Chicago Press, 1987), 121.

22 Rüdiger Jöppien, *Phillipe Jacques de Loutherbourg* (London: Westerham Press, 1978), 12.

23 Ibid., 6; *Public Advertiser*, Feb. 21, 1781; Jöppien, "Loutherbourg's Pantomime *Omai*," 111n. The "views" included *A View of London from Greenwich Park*, *The Port of Tangier*, *Rocky Shore on the Coast of Japan* and *Shipwreck of the Haslewell East Indiaman*.

24 *The Times*, Dec. 22, 1785; *Rambler Magazine*, Jan. 1786, 53.

25 Walter Benjamin, "Theses on the Philosophy of History," in *Illuminations*, ed. Hannah Arendt (New York: Schocken Books, 1969); for the "contact zone," see Mary Louis Pratt, *Imperial Eyes: Travel Writing and Transculturation* (London: Routledge, 1992).

26 This idealized notion of history is also discussed by Dening, *Bligh*, 292, and Smith, *European Vision*, 117–18, 121.

27 O'Keeffe, *Recollections*, II: 114; *London Chronicle*, Dec. 22, 1785.

28 As Bridgett Orr has argued for a different but related example, such representations inscribed an "amorous civility" that made miscegenation but an "inevitable condition of discovery." "Southern Passion," 216.

29 This tactic anticipated, as we shall see, English missionaries' use of trans-cultural marriage as the ultimate reward for the conversion, and thus control, of formerly heathen charges.

30 O'Keeffe, *Harlequin Omai*, iv, chorus.

31 O'Keeffe, *Recollections*, II: 114; J. Boaden, *Memoirs of the Life of John Phillip Kemble* (London: Longmans, 1825), I: 311–15. *Omai* was staged fifty times in the 1785–6 season, and eight times in each of the two following ones (1786–7, 1787–8).

32 *The Death of General Wolfe at the Siege of Quebec*, Manchester Central Library, Playbills, Marsden St. Theater, Aug. 17, 1763; *Aris's Birmingham Gazette*, Aug. 30, 1780.

33 Russell Thomas, "Contemporary Taste in the Stage Decorations of London Theaters, 1770–1800," *Modern Philology*, 42 (1944), 73–4; *London Chronicle*, Dec. 25–7, 1781; Dening, *Mr. Bligh's Bad Language*, 287–90; *The Death of Captain Cook* (London: T. Cadell, 1790).

34 For these, see *The Early Journals and Letters of Fanny Burney* ed. Lars E. Troide (Oxford: Clarendon Press, 1988), I: 322–7; Burney, *Early Diary*, 320–33; and numbers of the *Gentleman's Magazine*, *London Magazine*, *Lady's Magazine*, *Town and Country Magazine* for 1773. See also Hoxie Sissy Fairchild, *The Noble Savage: A Study in Romantic Naturalism* (New York: Columbia University Press, 1933); Lois Whitney, *Primitivism and the Idea of Progress* (Baltimore: John Hopkins University Press, 1934).

35 Primitivism could take "hard" and "soft" forms, admiring native peoples for their Spartan courage, fortitude and austerity, or Elysian innocence, luxury and sensuality, respectively. See A. Lovejoy and G. Boas, *Primitivism and Related Ideas in Antiquity* (Baltimore: Johns Hopkins University Press, 1935); Smith, *European Vision*, 5, 42–50 and passim.

36 See, e.g., Nicholas Canny, "The Ideology of English Colonization: From Ireland to America," *WMQ*, 3rd ser., 30 (1973), 575–98; "Identity Formation in Ireland: the Emergence of the Anglo-Irish," in Nicholas Canny and Anthony Pagden, eds., *Colonial Identity in the Atlantic World 1500–1800* (Princeton: Princeton University Press, 1987), 159–212; David Cairns and Shaun Richards, *Writing Ireland: Colonialism, Nationalism and Culture* (Manchester: Manchester University Press, 1988); and John Gillingham, "Foundations of a Disunited Kingdom," in Alexander Grant and Keith J. Stringer, eds., *Uniting the Kingdom? The Making of British History* (London: Routledge, 1995). Thanks to Karl Bottigheimer and Ned Landsman for references.

37 Marsden, *The History of Sumatra* (London, 1783), vii, my emphasis. Adam Ferguson had made much the same point in his *Essay on the History of Civil Society* (Edinburgh, 1767), 3–4. This section on late eighteenth-century anthropology is indebted to the careful and insightful account provided by John Gascoigne in *Joseph Banks and the English Enlightenment: Useful Knowledge and Polite Culture* (Cambridge: Cambridge University Press, 1994), esp. 125–83.

38 Quotation from Samuel Stanhope Smith, *An Essay on the Causes of the Variety of Complexion and Figure in the Human Species* (Philadelphia and Edinburgh, 1788), v–vi; Johannes Fabian, *Time and the Other: How Anthropology Makes its Object* (New York: Columbia University Press, 1983), 11–12. For the contending tenets within the new ethnology, see, e.g., Margaret Jolly, "'Ill-Natured Comparisons': Racism and Relativism in European Representations of ni-Vanuata from Cook's Second Voyage," *History and Anthropology*, V (1992), 3–4, 331–64.

39 Burney in Cook, II: 749–52, quotation from 751; Cook, *A Voyage Towards the South Pole* II: 258. See also J. Forster, *Observations*, 320, 324–5, 557–8; G. Forster, *Voyage*, II: 456–60; AR, 17 (1774), 136–7. For the senior Forster's belief in the greatness of the British imperial project, see *The Resolution Journal of John Reinhold Forster*, ed. Michael Hoare, 4 vols. (London: Hakluyt Society, 1982), where he refers to the "free and spirited Sons of Liberty, who inhabit this Queen of Islands" and lauds the "great impartiality and Justice of the English nation"; he later changed his mind.

40 *The Endeavour Journal of Joseph Banks*, ed. J. C. Beaglehole (Sydney: Angus and Robertson, 1962), I: 351.

41 See Cook in Cook I: 399, where he makes his famous assessment of the Aborigines of New Holland as being "far happier than we Europeans; being wholly unacquainted not only with the superfluous but the necessary Conveniences so much sought after in Europe . . . They live in a Tranquility which is not disturb'd by the Inequality of Condition . . . [and] think themselves provided with all the necessarys of life."

42 For an insightful account, see George Stocking, *Victorian Anthropology* (New York: Free Press, 1992), 18–25.

43 Ronald Meek, *Social Science and the Ignoble Savage* (Cambridge: Cambridge University Press, 1976); David Armitage, "The New World and British Historical Thought: From Richard Hakluyt to William Robertson," in Karen Kupperman, ed., *America in European Consciousness* (Chapel Hill: University of North Carolina Press, 1995), 53–75; J. G. A. Pocock, "Modes of Political and Historical Time in Early 18th-century England," in *Virtue, Commerce and History* (Cambridge: Cambridge University Press, 1992), 95.

44 J. Forster, *Observations*, 576–7.

45 Ibid., 227–8, 342, 342–434, 435. For an extended discussion of the role of women as signs in Pacific societies of progress or degeneration, see Harriet Guest, "Looking at Women: Forster's Observations in the South Pacific," in J. R. Forster, *Observations Made During a Voyage round the World*, eds. Nicholas Thomas, Harriet Guest and Michael Dettenbach (Honolulu: University of Hawaii Press, 1996), l–li.

46 Nicholas Thomas has suggested that, in this, Forster followed Buffon, who also began each section in his *Natural History* with a description of its distinctive physical features. See his discussion in *Observations* [1996], xxvi–xxvii.

47 J. Forster, *Observations*, 226; this is elaborated upon in the chapter entitled "Causes of the Varieties of Races of Man," 252–84.

48 Ibid., 303–4, 320–7, 578–9.

49 Ibid., 578–9, 338–9, 579, 318.

50 Ibid., 608, 322–35.

51 G. Forster, *Voyage*, II:, 324.

52 William Alexander, *The History of Women from the Earliest Antiquity to the Present Time*, [1778] 2 vols. (London: 3rd edn, C. Dilly and R. Christopher, 1782); William

Russell, *Essay on the Character, Manners, and Genius of Women in Different Ages*, 2 vols. (Philadelphia, 1774); William Falconer, *Remarks on the Influence of Climate* (London, 1781), 48, where he notes that "the influence of the fair sex is greatest in moderate climates, where their beauty accompanies their understanding."

53 J. Forster, *Observations*, 421–2. Cf. Felicity Nussbaum, *The Torrid Zone: Maternity, Sexuality and Empire in the Eighteenth Century* (Baltimore: Johns Hopkins University Press, 1995), who argues that women of the torrid zones were represented as "always and everywhere the same" because they occupied "the timeless geographical terrain" (14).

54 National Library of Australia, MS 9/4, Joseph Banks, "Thoughts on the Manners of the Women of Otaheite."

55 Cook in Cook, I: 127–8; [John Courtenay], *Epistle (Moral and Philosophical) from an Officer at Otaheite* (1774); Cook in Cook, II: 238–9; G. Forster, *Voyage*, I: 327–9, II: 83–4, 132–4. For the significance of sexuality in eastern Polynesian cultures, see Chapter 5 below.

56 J. Forster, *Observations*, 422.

57 Ibid., 419–20, 278–9. For the ideological importance of landscape, see Ann Bermingham, *Landscape and Ideology* (Berkeley and Los Angeles: University of California Press, 1993).

58 J. Forster, *Resolution Journal*, 622, 626; J. Forster, *Observations*, 419–20.

59 See, e.g., Sahlins, *Island of History*, chap. 1 and references there. Harriet Guest, "The Great Distinction: Figures of the Exotic in the Work of William Hodges," in Isobel Armstrong, ed., *New Feminist Discourses* (London: Routledge, 1992), 325–6; "Curiously Marked: Tattooing, Masculinity and Nationality in Eighteenth-Century British Perceptions of the South Pacific," in *Painting and the Politics of Culture*, ed. John Barrell (Oxford: Oxford University Press, 1992), 118–19; and "Looking at Women," passim. For other interpretations of Enlightenment thinkers' attempts to arrive at a fixed notion of female nature, see, e.g., Lieselotte Steinbrügge, *The Moral Sex: Woman's Nature in the French Enlightenment*, trans. Pamela E. Selwyn (Oxford: Oxford University Press, 1995); Mary Catherine Moran, "From Rudeness to Refinement: Gender, Genre and Scottish Enlightenment Discourse" (Ph.D. dissertation, Johns Hopkins University, 1999).

60 James Burnett, Lord Monboddo, *Of the Origin and Progress of Language* (Edinburgh, 1773), I: 133, 440, quoted in Peter Marshall and Glyndwr Williams, *The Great Map of Mankind: British Perceptions of the World in the Age of Enlightenment* (London: Dent, 1982), 274. Williams supplies an early and prescient discussion of this point. For Continental scientists, see Schiebinger, *Nature's Body*, 119–200. The popularization of these versions of the stages theory of human development can be seen in the journals of such diverse writers as Elizabeth Robinson Montagu and Lieut. James Hadden, British officer during the American war, and in the assessments of Cook's biographer, Andrew Kippis. For its impact on political economy, see n. 69; for literary versions of the fierceness and coarseness of natural man, see, e.g., Cowper's *The Task*.

61 Henry Home, Lord Kames, *Sketches of the History of Man*, 4 vols. (London: W. Strahan and T. Cadell, 1778), II: 153–219.

62 John Millar, *The Origin of the Distinction of Ranks* (London, 3rd edn, 1779), 45–6, quoted in Meeks, *Social Science*, 171–2; Marsden, *History of Sumatra*, 202–3.

63 James Dunbar, *Essays on the History of Man in Rude and Cultivated Ages* (London, 1780). The description of the Tahitian political system as "feudal" was legion in the published accounts of the voyages: see Beaglehole, *Banks's Endeavour Journal*, I: 384; AR, 16 (1773), 23.

64 Marra, *Journal*, 207–8. This account was excerpted in *Gentleman's Magazine*, 45 (1775), 587–91, 46 (1776) 15–20, 66–70, 118–22. Gibbon noted that "disregard of conjugal honor and female chastity" was alleged by Byzantine historian Chalcondyles

to have been an English custom when the Romans found them: Beaglehole in Cook, I: clxxxvin.

65 Falconer, *Remarks*, 172, 312.

66 Cook in Cook, I: 241; see also G. Forster, *Voyage*, II: 298, 312, 306. It is only fair to point out that Cook was not consistent on this point: when he visited Tahiti in 1774, he had been astonished at the improved houses and canoes which he attributed to the iron tools acquired by the islanders from English ships: *Voyage to the South Pole*, II: 346.

67 See, e.g., accounts of Cook's death in *AR*, 27 (1784–5), 149–63; *London Chronicle*, Jan. 20–23, 1781. The accounts of the deaths of other explorers were also important, like the Frenchman La Perouse, who lost twelve of his crew to a Samoan "massacre" in 1789; news of this did not reach Europe until 1827 however. Smith, *European Vision*, 138–41.

68 Quotation from Ferguson, *Civil Society*, 150. The most famous statement of this position was by the French social scientist Joseph-Marie de Gérando, *The Observation of Savage Peoples* [1800] (London: Routledge and Kegan Paul, 1969).

69 See Thomas Malthus, *An Essay on the Principle of Population*, ed. Patricia James, 2 vols. (Cambridge: Cambridge University Press, 1989), I: bks. 1–3, 21, 47 and passim. Thanks to Ruth Cowan for referring me to this source. See also Stocking, *Victorian Anthropology*, 34–5. Not surprisingly, perhaps, the Abbé Raynal claimed that it was among islanders, and the ancient Britons in particular, that the custom of anthropophagy originated, a theory which Malthus strongly denied: *Population*, 46–59; he quotes Raynal's *Histoire des Indes* (1795), II: 3.

70 Linda Colley, *Britons: Forging the Nation* (New Haven and London: Yale University Press, 1992); Liah Greenfeld, *Nationalism: Five Roads to Modernity* (Cambridge, Mass.: Harvard University Press, 1993), 52.

71 *Journal of Rev. John Wesley*, ed. Nehemiah Curnock (London, repr.: Epworth Press, 1960), VI: 7; *Public Advertiser*, July 3, 1773. Wesley went on to suggest that Hawkesworth's narrative was as fictional as *Robinson Crusoe* – an observation also made by present-day scholars.

72 William Carey, *An Enquiry into the Obligations of Christians, to use means for the Conversion of the Heathen* (Leicester, 1792), quoted in Richard Lovett, *The History of the London Missionary Society 1795–1895*, 2 vols. (London: Henry Frowde, 1899), I: 4; see also I: 18–21, 117–18; John Williams, *A Narrative of Missionary Enterprises in the South Sea Islands* (London, 1835), 2–37; C. Duncan Rice, "The Missionary Context of the British Anti-Slavery Movement," in James Walvin, ed., *Slavery and British Society* (London: Macmillan, 1982), 150–63.

73 Rev. George Burder, *An Address to the serious and zealous Professors of the Gospel, of every denomination respecting an attempt to evangelize the Heathen* (London, 1795), 5; see also Rev. Melville Horne, *Letters on Missions addressed to the Protestant Ministers of the British Churches* (Bristol, 1794), reviewed by Haweis in *Evangelical Magazine*, No. 3 (1794); and Rev. Thomas Haweis, *An Impartial and Succinct History of the Rise, Declension and Revival of the Church of Christ, from the Reformation to the Present Time*, 3 vols. (London, 1803).

74 In the cosmology of evangelicalism, base nations were the younger brothers to the elders of Europe, and non-Christians joined non-Europeans at the bottom of the religious and social hierarchy.

75 See Rice, "Missionary Context," 156–7; Stuart Piggin, "The American and British Contributions to Evangelicalism in Australia," in Mark A. Noll, David W. Bebbington and George A. Rawlyk, eds., *Evangelicalism: Comparative Studies of Popular Protestantism in North America, the British Isles and Beyond, 1700–1990* (New York and Oxford: Oxford University Press, 1994), 292–3.

76 *Gentleman's Magazine*, 112 (1812), 511. See also *Evangelical Magazine*, 8 (1800), 252.

77 Haweis, "The Apostolic Commission," in *Sermons Preached in London* (London, 1795), 12; Captain James Wilson, *A Missionary Voyage to the Southern Pacific Ocean* (London, 1799); Lovett, *History of the LMS*, 117–237, passim; see also the condensed account of the voyage in R. P. Forster, *A Collection of Celebrated Voyages and Travels from the Discovery of America to the Present Time*, 4 vols. (Newcastle upon Tyne: Mackenzie and Dent, 2nd edn, 1817), II: 431–52. Wilson's account became so well known that Malthus only had to refer to it as "the late Missionary Voyage" in his second, extended edition of the *Essay on Population* of 1803. The LMS included Scottish and provincial English as well as London members.

78 Niel Gunson, *Messengers of Grace: Evangelical Missionaries in the South Seas 1797–1860* (Melbourne: Oxford University Press, 1978), 31–106. See also Susan Thorne, *Evangelical Missions and the Making of an Imperial Culture in Nineteenth Century England* (Stanford: Stanford University Press, 1999).

79 See, e.g., *Evangelical Magazine*, 6 (1798), 110–12, 289–91, 471–2; 8 (1800), 1–15; Wilson, *Missionary Voyage*, 5–6, 130–5, 155–7; 350–1; Forster, *Collection*, 447–8.

80 Smith, *European Vision*, 146–7, quoting Haweis. The painting was exhibited at the Royal Academy in 1799 to great acclaim.

81 *Missionary Voyage*, 275–6; 166. See also Lovett, *History of the LMS*, 134–45; and "Journals and Letters of the Missionaries, 1798–1807," in *Transactions of the Missionary Society*, 3 vols. (London 1803–13).

82 Cook was not one for conducting divine services, even aboard ship: Sahlins, *Island of History*, 3n. For the missionary as a new kind of national hero, see William C. Barnhart, "Evangelicalism and National Identity in England, 1790–1830" (Ph.D. dissertation, SUNY-Stony Brook, 1999); for the intended ideological impact of the English family, see *Evangelical Magazine*, 8 (1800), 9.

83 Wilson, *Missionary Voyage*, 157; Lovett, *History of the LMS*, 156–7.

84 Quoted in Smith, *European Vision*, 317.

85 Ibid., 317–18; John Barrow, *Voyages to the Pacific* (London, 1836). These representations segued with the new science of comparative anatomy being developed in the early nineteenth century by Georges Cuvier Lamarck and the British anatomist Sir William Lawrence which treated differences in cranial and nose shapes as signs of deeper differences in biological organization and hence civilization. These scientific "advances" were linked in turn to those medical ones which documented the absolute differences between male and female sexual anatomy: Thomas Laqueur, *Making Sex: Body and Gender from the Greeks to Freud* (Cambridge, Mass.: Harvard University Press, 1990), 155–75.

86 Williams, *Missionary Enterprises in the South Seas*, 29–30, 465, 467; emphasis mine.

87 David Hume, *History of England from the Invasion of Julius Caesar to the Revolution in 1688*, 7 vols. (London: T. Cadell Jr. and W. Davies, 1802), I: 2; see also Hevia, *Cherishing Men from Afar*, 70–1.

88 J. Forster, *Observations*, 608. For his essays, see, e.g., Forster, *Observations on the Geography of King Alfred* (London, 1773) and his notes on Daine Barrington's translation of *The Voyages of Othere and Wulfstan* from the Anglo-Saxon version of Orosious by Alfred.

89 See Hugh MacDougall, *Racial Myth in English History: Trojans, Teutons and Anglo-Saxons* (London: Harvest House, 1982); Samuel Kliger, *The Goths in England: A Study in Seventeenth and Eighteenth Century Thought* (Cambridge, Mass.: Harvard University Press, 1952); Reginald Horsman, "Origins of Racial Anglo-Saxonism in Great Britain before 1850," *Journal of the History of Ideas*, 37 (1976), 387–410. For political uses of Anglo-Saxonism under Walpole, see Christine Gerrard, *The Patriot Opposition to Walpole* (Oxford: Clarendon Press, 1994), 103–49.

90 Kliger, 92; Hume, *History of England*, 13, 15, 424; Edward Gibbon, *The History of the Decline and Fall of the Roman Empire*, 7 vols. (London: Metheun, 1926), I: 63–4.

Gibbon wrote: "the Roman world was indeed peopled by a race of pygmies, when the fierce giants of the north broke in and mended the puny breed." See also *Encyclopedia Britannica*, 2nd edn (Edinburgh, 1778–83), II. For the cosmopolitanism of Hume and other Enlightenment historians, see Karen O'Brien, *Narratives of Enlightenment* (Cambridge: Cambridge University Press, 1998); for the importance of classical history to late eighteenth-century writers, see Philip Ayres, *Classical Culture and the Idea of Rome* (Cambridge: Cambridge University Press, 1997).

91 Paul-Henri Mallet, *Northern Antiquities: or a Description of the Manners, Customs, Religion and Laws of the Ancient Danes, and other Northern Nations, including those of our own Saxon Ancestors*, trans. Thomas Percy, 2 vols. (London, 1770); see also Percy, *Reliques of Ancient English Poetry* (London: J. Dodsley, 1765), which aroused interest in English national origins. For the nationalist historians, see O. Hulme, *An Historical Essay on the English Constitution* (London: Edward and Charles Dilly, 1771); Catharine Macaulay, *History of England* (London: J. Nourse, 1763), XI: 273, II: 1–3, VI: 72; John Pinkerton, *Dissertation on the Origin and Progress of the Scythians or Goths* (London, 1787); for a fuller discussion see Thomas P. Peardon, *The Transition in English Historical Writing 1760–1830* (New York: Columbia University Press, 1933), 114–16, 162–79.

92 See, e.g., AR, 16 (1773), 137–60, which reviewed Grosse's *Antiquities of England and Wales*, Bentham's *Curious Remarks on Saxon Churches*, and *The Voyages of Ohthere and Wulfstan, from the Anglo-Saxon Version by Alfred the Great*; Ian Ousby, *The Englishman's England: Taste, Travel and the Rise of Tourism* (Cambridge: Cambridge University Press, 1990), 92–129; Timothy Clayton, *The English Print, 1688–1802* (London and New Haven: Yale University Press, 1997), 258–9.

93 Linda Colley, "Radical Patriotism in Eighteenth-Century England," in Raphael Samuels, ed., *Patriotism*, I: 173–4; John Cartwright, *Take Your Choice!* (London: J. Almon, 1776); Granville Sharp, *An Account of the Constitutional English Policy of Congregational Courts, and More Particularly of the Great Annual Court of the People called the View of the Frankenpledge* (London, 1786).

94 See, e.g., Christopher Hill, "The Norman Yoke," in C. Hill, *Puritanism and Revolution* (London: Secker & Warburg, 1958); Gerald Newman, *The Rise of English Nationalism* (New York: St. Martin's Press, 1987), 115–19; Léon Poliakov, *The Aryan Myth: A History of Racist and Nationalist Ideas in Europe*, trans. E. Howard (London: Chatto & Windus, 1974).

95 For these, see Peardon, *Transition*, 103–26; Fiona Stafford, *The Sublime Savage: James Macpherson and the Poems of Ossian* (Edinburgh: Edinburgh University Press, 1988); Howard Gaskill, ed., *Ossian Revisited* (Edinburgh: Edinburgh University Press, 1991); Stuart Piggott, *The Druids* (London: Thames & Hudson, 1968), 123–55; Sam Smiles, *Image of Antiquity: Ancient Britain and the Romantic Imagination* (New Haven and London: Yale University Press, 1994); Colin Kidd, *British Identities Before Nationalism: Ethnicity and Nationhood in the Atlantic World 1600–1800* (Cambridge: Cambridge University Press, 1998).

96 Burgess quoted in Gascoigne, *Joseph Banks*, 131; Rev. F. Drake, "Origin of the English Language," reviewed in AR, 23 (1780), 157–63; see also AR, 18 (1775), 157–65.

97 Pearson, "Observations on Some Metallic Arms," 402–3, and Clark to Banks, Jan. 26, 1812, both cited in Gascoigne, *Joseph Banks*, 133; Falconer, *Remarks*, 171–2; Smith, *European Vision*, 131–2; Piggott, *Druids*, 154.

98 Piggott, *Druids*, 109, 155; Lovett, *History of the London Missionary Society*, I: 22–3; Kidd, *British Identities*, chap. 4; Sebastian Mitchell, "James Macpherson's *Ossian* and the Empire of Sentiment," *British Journal for Eighteenth Century Studies*, 22 (1999), 155–71. Interestingly, Scottish conjectural historians liked to insist that, even in their barbaric pasts, northern nations always treated their women well: Kames, *Sketches*, 67–9; Millar, *Origin*, 52–3.

99 See, quoting Sir John Dalrymple's *Memoirs of Great Britain and Ireland*, AR, 14 (1771), 40: G. White, *The Natural History and Antiquities of Selborne*, ed. R. Bowdler Sharpe, 2 vols. (London: S. T. Freemantle, 1900), I: 178. See also "A Description of the Highlands of Scotland, and Remarks on the Second Sight of the Inhabitants," AR, 20 (1777), 83–5.

100 See Peter Womack, *Improvement and Romance: Constructing the Myth of the Highlands* (Basingstoke: Macmillan, 1989); Gwyn Williams, *When Was Wales? A History of the Welsh* (London: Black Raven, 1985); John Brewer, *The Pleasures of the Imagination. English Culture in the Eighteenth Century* (London: Harper Collins, 1997), 658–60.

101 Ralph G. Allen, "The Wonders of Derbyshire: A Spectacular Travelogue," in John Gassner and Allen, *Theater and Drama in the Making* (Boston: Houghton Mifflin, 1964), 1035–47. See also Malcolm Andrews, *The Search for the Picturesque: Landscape, Aesthetics and Tourism in Britain, 1760–1800* (Aldershot: Scolar, 1989); Brewer, *Pleasures of the Imagination*, chap. 16. For the people of the Peak, see William Gilpin in *Observations . . . Made in the Year 1772, Relative to Picturesque Beauty* (London, 1786), II: 216.

102 *Morning Chronicle*, Jan. 30, 1781; *London Chronicle*, Jan. 27–30, 1781; Seidel, *Island Myths*, 36–8; Thomas, "Stage Decorations," 73.

103 For this, see Michael Dobson, *The Making of the National Poet* (Oxford: Clarendon Press, 1994).

104 *Alfred, a Masque* (London, 1773); BL Sir Augustus Harris, A collection of newspaper cuttings relating to London theaters, 1704–79.

105 Sahlins, *How "Natives" Think*, 1.

106 Beaglehole in Cook I: xxii; Seidal, *Island Myths*, 11.

107 Schiebinger, *Nature's Body*, 154–5.

108 Edmund Burke, *Reflections on the Revolution in France* (London: J. M. Dent, 1910), 64–5; Nott, cited in John Brewer, "'This Monstrous Tragi-comic scene': British Reactions to the French Revolution," in David Bindman, ed., *The Shadow of the Guillotine* (London: British Museum, 1989), 21.

3 BRITANNIA INTO BATTLE: WOMEN, WAR AND IDENTITIES IN ENGLAND AND AMERICA

1 HL, Montagu MSS, MP1384, Elizabeth Robinson Montagu to George Lyttelton, Aug. 6, 1758. An abstract of Solís's history was published in A *Compendium of Authentic Voyages*, 7 vols. (London: R. and J. Dodsley, 1756) and the full English translation appeared in 1759: Antonio de Solís, *The History of the Conquest of Mexico by the Celebrated Hernan Cortés*, 2 vols. (London, 1759).

2 Recent work includes: Harriet Guest, *Small Change: Women, Learning and Patriotism, 1750–1810* (Chicago: University of Chicago Press, 2000); Rachael Weil, *Political Passions, Gender, Family and Political Argument in England 1680–1714* (Manchester: Manchester University Press, 1999); Hannah Barker and Elaine Chalus, eds., *Gender in the Eighteenth Century* (London: Longman 1998); Amanda Foreman, *Duchess of Devonshire* (London: Harper Collins, 1998); Paula McDowell, *The Women of Grub Street: Press, Politics and Gender in the London Literary Marketplace 1678–1730* (New York: Oxford University Press, 1998); Sara Mendelson and Patricia Crawford, *Women in Early Modern England 1550–1720* (Oxford: Oxford University Press, 1998); Hilda L. Smith, ed., *Women Writers and the Early Modern British Political Tradition* (Cambridge: Cambridge University Press, 1998); Robert Shoemaker, *Gender in English Society 1650–1850* (London: Longman, 1998); Amanda Vickery, *The Gentleman's Daughter: Women's Lives in Georgian England* (London and New Haven: Yale Univeristy Press, 1998); John Brewer, *The Pleasures of the Imagination: English Culture in the Eighteenth Century* (London: Harper Collins, 1997); Marcia Pointon, *Strategies for Showing:*

Women, Possession and Representation in English Visual Culture (Oxford: Oxford University Press, 1997); Margaret Hunt, *The Middling Sort: Commerce, Gender and the Family in England 1680–1780* (Berkeley and Los Angeles: University of California Press, 1996); Ann B. Shteir, *Cultivating Women, Cultivating Science: Flora's Daughters and Botany in England 1760–1860* (Baltimore: Johns Hopkins University Press, 1996); Kathleen Wilson, *The Sense of the People: Politics, Culture and Imperialism in England 1715–1785* (Cambridge: Cambridge University Press, 1995); Mary Thale, "Women in London Debating Societies," *Gender and History*, 7 (1995), 5–24; Donna Andrew, "Popular Culture and Public Debate: London 1780," *HJ*, 39 (1996), 405–23; Margot Finn, "Women, Consumption and Coverture in England 1760–1860," *HJ*, 39 (1996), 703–22; Catherine Gallagher, *Nobody's Story: The Vanishing Acts of Women Writers in the Marketplace, 1670–1820* (Berkeley and Los Angeles: University of California Press, 1994); Stella Tillyard, *Aristocrats* (London: Chatto & Windus, 1994); Amy L. Erickson, *Women and Property in Early Modern England* (London and New York: Routledge, 1993); Linda Colley, *Britons: Forging the Nation, 1707–1837* (London and New Haven: Yale University Press, 1992).

3   The work of Amanda Foreman and Elaine Chalus, interesting as it is, is susceptible to these criticisms. A more worrying trend has been on display in recent academic conferences, where efforts to discuss women's continuing disadvantages in the expanding commercial society of the period have been decried as attempts to turn them into "victims" or to impose an old-fashioned feminist straitjacket on a presciently postfeminist historical record. Women's relationship to politics and the state has been more evocatively probed and presented in Tillyard, *Aristocrats*, and in Linda Kerber *No Constitutional Right to Be Ladies: Women and the Obligations of Citizenship* (New York: Hill & Wang, 1998). Promising approaches are also evident in the history of masculinity, on scintillating display in Philip Carter, *Men and the Emergence of Polite Society in Britain 1660–1800* (London: Longman, 2001); Tim Hitchcock and Michèle Cohen, eds., *English Masculinities 1660–1800* (London: Longman, 1999); and in John Tosh and Michael Roper, eds., *Manful Assertions: Masculinities in Britain since 1800* (London: Routledge, 1991).

4   Eric Voegelin, "The Growth of the Race Idea," *Review of Politics* (July, 1940), 284, quoted by Paul Gilroy, *Against Race: Imagining Political Culture Beyond the Color Line* (Cambridge, Mass.: Harvard University Press, 2000), 57.

5   The call to attend to "experience" rather than representation is a conceptual double-bind, for it belies the nature of language and "the archive," our own politicized roles in re-presenting representations of the past, and the embedding of all "empirical" events in particular social, cultural and political variables that include representation itself. See Chandra Talpade Mohanty, "Feminist Encounters: Locating the Politics of Experience," in Michèle Barrett and Anne Phillips, eds., *Destabilizing Theory: Contemporary Feminist Debates* (Cambridge: Polity Press, 1992), 74–6; Joan Scott, "On Experience," in *Feminists Theorize the Political* (Stanford: Stanford University Press, 1994); Himani Bannerji, "Politics and the Writing of History," in *Nation, Empire Colony: Historicizing Gender and Race* (Bloomington: Indiana University Press, 1998), 287–90.

6   Quote from Judith Bennett, "Medieval Women, Modern Women: Across the Great Divide," in *Culture and History 1350–1600: Essays on English Communities, Identities and Writing 1350–1600*, ed. David Aers (New York and London: Harvester Wheatsheaf, 1992), 158; a similar case for masculinity is made by John Tosh in "The Old Adam and the New Man: Emerging Themes in the History of English Masculinities," in *English Masculinities*, 217–38; last quotation from Bannerji, "Politics and the Writing of History," 290.

7   Pointon, *Strategies for Showing*, 2–3. As she goes on to argue, such "factual" documents as wills reveal conflicting motivations, obligations, identifications and desires.

8 See, e.g., Alan Bewell, "Constructed Places, Constructed Peoples: Charting the Improvement of the Female Body in the Pacific," *Eighteenth Century Life*, 18 (1994), 37–54; Felicity Nussbaum, *Torrid Zones: Maternity, Sexuality and Empire in Eighteenth Century English Narratives* (Baltimore: Johns Hopkins Univeristy Press, 1995); Londa Schiebinger, *Nature's Body: Gender and the Making of Modern Science* (Boston: Beacon Press, 1993), 127–40; Colley, *Britons*, passim. Quotation from Oriana Baddeley, "Engendering New Worlds: Allegories of Rape and Reconciliation," *Art and Design*, No. 37 (1994), 11–17, 11. For the role of the body in signifying the political nation, see Nicholas Mirzoeff, *Bodyscape: Art, Modernity and the Ideal Figure* (London: Routledge, 1996); and Diana Donald, *The Age of Caricature: Satirical Prints in the Reign of George III* (New Haven and London: Yale University Press, 1996).

9 As I have argued in *The Sense of the People*, in the very period when Britannia comes to prominence as the icon of the nation – a time of both recurrent anxiety about the masculine potency, honor and resolve of the national character in its dealings abroad, and the shift from abstract emblematic to local iconographic visual modes – Britannia is used in political satires to attract and appeal to a gender-conscious audience. She represents the ideal of Georgian femininity: maiden, lover and mother, she is virtuous and beautiful, strong and spirited, yet needing masculine protection and defense. Conversely, although always at the mercy of evil ministers or foreign foes (the Wilkite era inaugurates the most graphic abuse of Britannia at the hands of evil ministers), she manages to incarnate manly resistance, and can be roused – like the Lion – to battle in defense of her children. In both ways – as potentially violated maiden or enraged mother – her representations could mobilize male and female identity, desire, love and emulation. By the American war, by which time the impact of the racial and cultural miscegenation of empire had been made obvious to metropolitan Britons, Britannia is made to represent the racialized tensions between mothers and daughters in the family romance of imperial dissolution. In other words, the evolution of Britannia's image mirrors and shapes the evolution of gendered and racialized notions of the English nation.

10 Benedict Anderson, *Imagined Communities* (London: Verso, 1983), 129.

11 Judith Butler, *Bodies that Matter: on the Discursive Limits of "Sex"* (London: Routledge, 1993), 191, 105. Identification, "a form of violent appropriation in which the Other is deposed and assimilated into the lordly domain of the Self," is itself a colonizing process, according to Diana Fuss, "Interior Colonies: Frantz Fanon and the Politics of Identification," *diacritics*, 24 (1994), 23.

12 As noted by Anne McClintock, *Imperial Leather* (London: Routledge, 1995), 361. For different but complementary treatments of identification and subjectivity in historical contexts, see Lyndal Roper, *Oedipus and the Devil: Witchcraft, Sexuality and the Devil in Early Modern Europe* (London: Routledge, 1994); and Graham Dawson, *Soldier Heros: British Adventure, Empire and the Imagining of Masculinities* (London: Routledge, 1994).

13 I owe this point to James Epstein.

14 As Ania Loomba has argued, "the individual psyche and the social exists in a constitutive, *traumatic*, reciprocity": "Dead Women Tell No Tales: Issues of Female Subjectivity, Subaltern Agency and Tradition in Colonial and Post-colonial Writings on Widow Immolation in India," *History Workshop Journal*, 36 (1993), 221.

15 Colley, *Britons*, 281. In fact by the 1790s the marked advance in the professionalization of the British military establishment was beginning to reduce, if not eliminate, the well-entrenched roles of women in the service. The work of Patricia Lin on the intricate relations between women, military families and the state during the Napoleonic wars must further revise Colley's view: see Lin, "Citizenship, Military Families, and the Creation of a New Definition of 'Deserving Poor' in Britain, 1793–1815," *Social Politics* (Spring 2000), 5–46; and "Extending Her Arms: Military Families and the Transformation of the British State, 1793–1815" (Ph.D. diss.,

University of California at Berkeley, 1997). I would like to thank Professor Lin for making her groundbreaking studies available to me.

16 For women in regimental lists, see, e.g., PRO WO 1–4, 10–16, 44–6 passim; 26/13 (1704–12), 10/123 (1769–70); 10/146 (1776), WO 10/57 (1756–7), 12/3676, passim; for the ubiquity of women and children in armies and prison camps, see: Winthrop Sargent, *The History of an Expedition against Fort Duquesne in 1755 under Major General Edward Braddock* (Philadelphia, Lippincott Grambo, 1855), 331–2, 335–8 and passim; Jeffrey Amherst, *A Journal of the landing of His Majesty's Forces on the Island of Cape Breton* (Boston: 3rd ed., Green and Russell, 1758); F. M. Ray, ed., *Journal of Dr. Caleb Rea* (Salem, 1881); Marvin L. Brown, Jr., ed., *Baroness von Riedesel and the American Revolution: Journal and Correspondence of a Tour of Duty 1776–1783* (Chapel Hill: University of North Carolina Press, 1965); Sergeant R. Lamb, *An Original and Authentic Journal of Occurrences during the Late American War* (Dublin, 1809), 185–7, 193–4, and passim; *Minute Book of a Board of General Officers* (New York Historical Society, *Collections*, 1916), 84–6; Lieut. James Hadden, *A Journal Kept in Canada and upon Burgoyne's Campaign in 1776 and 1777* (Albany: J. Munsell, 1884), 12–15, 298–348; Benjamin F. Stevens, ed., *General Sir William Howe's Orderly Book, at Charlestown, Boston and Halifax 17 June 1775 to 26 May 1776* (London: B. F. Stevens, 1890); "Journal of a Captive, 1745–48," in Isabel M. Calder, *Colonial Captivities, Marches and Journeys* (New York: Macmillan, 1935, repr. Kennikat, 1967), 3–137 passim. Excellent secondary accounts include Edward E. Curtis, *The Organization of the British Army in the American Revolution* (New Haven: Yale University Press, 1926); Sylvia Frey, *The British Soldier in America: A Social History of Military Life in the Revolutionary Period* (Austin: University of Texas Press, 1981); Barton Hacker, "Women and Military Institutions in Early Modern Europe: a Reconnaissance," *Signs*, 6 (1981), 643–71; Myna Tristam, *Women of the Regiment: Marriage and the Victorian Army* (Cambridge: Cambridge University Press, 1984); Paul E. Kopperman, "The British High Command and Soldiers' Wives in America 1755–1783," *Society For Army Historical Research*, 60 (1982), 14–34; and Holly A. Mayer, *Belonging to the Army: Camp Followers and Community during the American Revolution* (Columbia: University of South Carolina Press, 1994).

17 Paul E. Kopperman, "Medical Services in the British Army 1742–83," *Journal of the History of Medicine*, 34 (1979) 19–20, 27; Frey, *British Soldier*, chap. 1.

18 John Burgoyne, *A State of the Expedition from Canada* (London: J. Almon, 1780), 114; *London Chronicle*, Dec. 20–3, 1777; *Journal of Madame von Riedesel*, 59–60. Cf. the estimate in Hadden, *Journal*, 278, 298–9; quotation from 378–9. For the libertinism of Burgoyne and Howe in England, see *Nocturnal Revels: or, the History of King's Place and other Modern Nunneries . . . by a Monk of the Order of St. Francis [Medmenham Priory]* (London: 2nd edn, M. Goadby, 1779). Thanks to John Brewer for this reference.

19 As Margaret Hunt has shown, the free labor of female relatives provided a crucial source of social capital for middling and artisanal men: Hunt, *The Middling Sort*, 151–3.

20 J. R. Hutchinson, *The Press-Gang Afloat and Ashore* (London: E. Nash, 1913); Edward Ward, *The Wooden World Dissected: In the Character of a Ship of War* (London 4th edn, H. Meere, 1707). N. A. M. Rodger, *The Wooden World: An Anatomy of the Georgian Navy* (London: Collins, 1986), 75–9, tends to underplay these difficulties.

21 Eliza Fay, *Original Letters from India*, ed. E. M. Forster (London: L. & V. Woolf, 1925); see also J. K. Stanford, *Ladies in the Sun: The Memsahibs' India 1790–1860* (London: Galley Press, 1962), 18–35; William Hickey, *Memoirs*, ed. Peter Quennell (London: Routledge & Kegan Paul, 1975); Kate Teltscher, *Inscribing India* (Delhi: Oxford University Press, 1998).

22 Stanford, *Ladies in the Sun*; Hickey, *Memoirs*; Hadden, *Journal*.

23 "Journal of a Captive," 9; *The Case of the Distressed Widows of the Commission and Warrant-Officers of the Royal Navy, Most Humbly Represented to the Compassionate Consideration of the Honourable House of Commons* (London, 1751); Hacker, "Women and Military Institutions," 656–8; Margaret Hunt, "Women and the Fiscal-Military State in Late 17th and Early 18th Century London," in Kathleen Wilson, ed., *A New Imperial History: Culture, Identity and Modernity 1660–1836* (forthcoming, Cambridge: Cambridge University Press, 2003); and Margaret S. Creighton and Lisa Norling, *Iron Men, Wooden Women: Gender and Seafaring in the Atlantic World 1700–1920* (Baltimore: Johns Hopkins University Press, 1996).

24 Kopperman, "Medical Services," 36.

25 "The Journal of Charlotte Browne, Matron of the General Hospital with the English Forces in America, 1754–56," in Calder, ed., *Colonial Captivities*, 169–200; quotation from 183–4.

26 Camp wives and female warriors figure in, for example, Sheridan's *The Camp* (1778) as well as Farquhar's *Recruiting Officer* (1709); for other examples see Diane Dugaw, *Warrior Women and Popular Balladry* (Chicago: University of Chicago Press, 1996). Quotation from Kopperman, "Soldier's Wives," 15, quoting from *The Papers of Henry Bousquet* (Harrisburg, 1951), II: 30. See also Roger Norman Buckely, *The British Army in the West Indies: Society and Military in the Revolutionary Age* (Gainesville: University of Florida, 1998), 144–56.

27 Archibald Forbes, *The Black Watch: The Record of an Historic Regiment* (London: Cassell, 1910); Peter Way, "The Cutting Edge of Culture: British Soldiers Encounter Native Americans in the French and Indian War," in *Empire and Others*, eds. Martin Daunton and Rick Halpern (Philadelphia: University of Pennsylvania Press, 1999), 129–30; and Ian K. Steele, "Surrendering Rites: Prisoners on Colonial North American Frontiers," in Stephen Taylor, Richard Connors and Clyve Jones, eds., *Hanoverian Britain and Empire* (Woodbridge: Boydell Press, 1998). Cf. Peter Russell, "Redcoats in the Wilderness: British Officers and Irregular Warfare in Europe and America 1740–60," WMQ, 35 (1978), 629–52.

28 *The Female Soldier: or the Surprising Life and Adventures of Hannah Snell* (London, 1750), reprinted in *Augustan Reprint Society*, ed. Dianne Dugaw, No. 257 (Los Angeles: William Andrews Clark Memorial Library, 1989); for the estimate of American women, see Linda Grant De Pauw, "Women in Combat: the Revolutionary War Experience," *Armed Forces and Society* 7 (1981), 209–34; for other cross-dressed female soldiers, see PRO WO4/23, July 7, 1720; *The Soldier's Companion and Martial Recorder* (London, 1824); Dugaw, *Warrior Women*; Boris Uxkull, *Arms and the Woman: The Intimate Journal of a Baltic Nobleman in the Napoleonic Wars*, ed. Detlev von Uxkull (London: Secker & Warburg, 1966); Julie Wheelwright, *Amazons and Military Maids* (London: Pandora, 1989); and Rudolph M. Dekker and Lotte C. Van de Pol, *The Tradition of Female Transvestism in Early Modern Europe* (Basingstoke: Macmillan, 1989). For other examples, see Hutchinson, *Press-Gang*, 258–65; Rodger, *Wooden World*, 76–7. Accounts of hundreds of these women have been discovered in European and American records.

29 Maggie Craig, *Damn Rebel Bitches* (Edinburgh: Mainstream, 1997), 20–1; Mayer, *Belonging to the Army*, 21, 8; *Rivington's New York Gazetteer*, Sept. 25, 1779.

30 Charles E. Claghorn, *Women Patriots of the American Revolution: A Biographical Dictionary* (Metheun, N.J.: Scarecrow Press, 1991) 235–6; Mayer, *Belonging to the Army*, 37–8, 143–4.

31 *Journal of Madame Riedesel*, 47–8, 66–7 and passim; and references in note 5. For representations of Americans, see Wilson, *Sense of the People*, chaps. 3 and 5.

32 "Journal of a Captive," 71, 95; *Boston Evening Post*, Aug. 18, 1755; Kopperman, "Soldiers' Wives".

33 See Frey, *British Soldiers*, 60–78.

34 Kopperman, "Soldiers' Wives," 17.
35 Mayer, *Belonging to the Army*, 126–7, quoting the diary of Virginia officer Elias Parker.
36 Way, "Cutting Edge," 140.
37 "Hint to the Ladies," *St. James's Chronicle*, Jan. 20–3, 1781; Oliver Goldsmith, "Female Warriors: Containing a humble Proposal for Augmenting the Forces of Great Britain," in *Works*, ed. J. W. M. Gibbs (London: George Bell, 1908), I: 315–20; BM 5629, *Britannia Protect'd from the Terrors of an Invasion* subtitled "A loud crying Woman and a Scold shall be sought out to drive away the Enemies" (1780). Henry Fielding also satirized the image of the warlike woman in his translation of Juvenal: see Laura Brown, *Ends of Empire* (Ithaca: Cornell University Press, 1993), 140–1. See also Wheelwright, *Amazons*; Gillian Russell, *Theatres of War* (Oxford: Clarendon Press, 1995); Wilson, *Sense of the People*, chap. 3.
38 Fanon, *Black Skins, White Masks* (New York: Grove Press, 1991), 141–2; D. A. Kent, "'Gone for a Soldier': Family Breakdown and the Demography of Desertion in a London Parish, 1750–91," *Local Population Studies*, 45 (1990), 27–42.
39 *Etherington's York Chronicle*, Nov. 8, 1776; Hutchinson, *Press Gang*, 188, 272–3. Recruiting and indeed other military officers' fabled sexual voraciousness is represented in drama throughout the century, most famously, perhaps, in Farquhar's *Recruiting Officer*.
40 *London Evening Post*, July 28–31, 1759; and James Gilray, *The Liberty of the Subject*, BM 5609, Oct. 15, 1779, where women attack a press gang with clubs, brooms and mops. Nicholas Rogers, *Crowds, Culture and Politics in Georgian Britain* (Oxford: Oxford University Press, 1998), 95–7, also provides some examples of women resisting the press.
41 Russell, *Theatres of War*, 34. Her argument of the American war as spectacle has been taken up by Elija Gould in his study *The Persistence of Empire* (Baltimore: Johns Hopkins University Press, 2000).
42 "Diary of John Dawson of Brunton," in *North Country Diaries*, Surtees Society, 2nd ser., CXXIV (1914), 260; *Mary Hardy's Diary*, ed. Basil Cozens-Hardy (Norfolk Record Society, XXXVII (1968), 23.
43 *A Series of Letters between Mrs. Elizabeth Carter and Miss Catherine Talbot from the Years 1741–1770*, ed. Montagu Pennington, 4 vols. (London: F. C. and J. Rivington, 1809), I: 222–3. They thus fulfilled a crucial function of "social authorship" as defined by Margaret Ezell in *Social Authorship and the Advent of Print* (Baltimore: Johns Hopkins University Press, 1999), 39–40.
44 Hardy, *Diary*, 20, 23, 43, 33.
45 Ibid., 45. See G. J. Marcus, *A Naval History of England, vol. I: The Formative Centuries* (London: Longmans, 1961), 423; AR, 25 (1782), 218; see also Thomas Rowlandson's sketch of *The Wreck of the Royal George* (1782) in Robert R. Wark, ed., *Drawings by Thomas Rowlandson in the Huntington Collection* (San Marino: Huntington Library, 1975).
46 A good description is provided by Edward Long in his account of his boyhood in Cornwall: see Robert Mowbray Howard, ed., *Records and Letters of the Family of the Longs of Longville, Jamaica, and Hampton Lodge, Surrey* 2 vols. (London: Simpkin, Marshall, Hamilton, Kent and Co., 1925), 93–5.
47 Russell, *Theatres of War*, 35–8; Stephen Conway, "Locality, Metropolis and Nation: the Impact of the Military Camps in England during the American War," *History*, 82 (1997), 547–62; Charles Herbert, "Coxheath Camp, 1778–79," *Journal of the Society for Army Historical Research*, 45 (1967), 129–48. For contemporary accounts, see *Public Advertiser*, June 19, 1777; *London Evening Post*, July 27–30, Aug. 1–4, 27–9, Sept. 15–17, 19–22, 1778; quotation from *Georgiana: Extracts from the Correspondence of Georgiana, the Duchess of Devonshire*, ed. Earl of Bessborough (London: John Murray, 1955), 35–293. For the Duchess of Devonshire see also Anne Stott, "'Female

Patriotism': Georgiana, Duchess of Devonshire, and the Westminster Election of 1784," *Eighteenth Century Life*, 17 (1993), 60–84; Foreman, *Georgiana*, chap. 6.

48 Richard Brinsley Sheridan, *The Camp*, in *Dramatic Works of Richard Brinsley Sheridan*, ed. Cecil Price (Oxford: Oxford University Press, 1973), 707–50; *Morning Post*, Oct. 16, 1778; *Public Advertiser*, Aug. 6, 1778; *London Chronicle*, May 20, 1778.

49 Vere Birdwood, ed., *So Dearly Loved, So Much Admired: Letters to Hester Pitt, Lady Chatham from her Relations and Friends, 1744–1801* (London: H.M.S.O., 1994), 147; HL Montagu MS MO 504 and passim.

50 Cecil Aspinal-Oglander, *Admiral's Wife* (London: Longmans, 1940), 245–6.

51 *St. James's Chronicle*, Jan. 20–3, 1781; More, *Strictures on the Modern System of Female Education* (London: T. Cadell and W. Davies, 1799), 9; see also Joseph Addison, *The Freeholder* [1715–16] ed. James Leheny (Oxford: Clarendon Press, 1979).

52 Eliza Haywood, *The Female Spectator*, II (1746), 117, 121; John Fortescue, *A History of the British Army* 13 vols. (London: Macmillan, 1899–1930), II: 73. As the correspondence of the Duchess of Devonshire makes clear, women admired both the uniforms and the "true soldier's spirit" of bravery and love of conquest: *Georgiana*, 36. See also Hunt, *Middling Sort*, who observes that "self-sacrifice for the benefit of others and obedience to authority remain . . . the central aims of female socialization" (78).

53 *The Female Soldier*, 1–2.

54 Henry Home, Lord Kames, *Sketches in the History of Man* (London: W. Strahan and T. Cadell, 1778), II: 4–5.

55 Colman Sr., *Bonduca* (London, 1778); *Public Advertiser*, July 31, 1778; *London Evening Post*, Aug. 4–6, 1778. Boadicea appears in histories of this period to make the point that northern nations in primitive ages had always treated their women with dignity and thus produced virtuous women – in contrast to contemporary savage and barbarous peoples: Kames, *Sketches*, I: 456–7; William Alexander, *The History of Women, from the Earliest Antiquity to the Present Time*, 2 vols. (London: 3rd edn, C. Dilly and R. Christopher, 1782), I: xv.

56 Nira Yuval-Davis, *Gender and Nation* (London: Sage, 1997), 98.

57 Janet Gurkin Altman, *Epistolarity: Approaches to a Form* (Columbus: Ohio State University Press, 1982); Cynthia Lowenthal, *Lady Mary Wortley Montagu and the Eighteenth Century Letter* (Athens: University of Georgia Press, 1994); Rebecca Earle, ed., *Epistolary Selves: Letters and Letter-Writers 1600–1945* (Aldershot: Ashgate, 1999); Vickery, *Gentleman's Daughter*, 287.

58 HL MO 569, ERM to FB, June 24, 1756; MO 1392, ERM to Lyttelton, Jan. 15, 1760. The anti-war views in the letters provide one of the best documented if least studied sources of nascent pacifism before the Revolutionary and Napoleonic wars.

59 See Sylvia Myers, *The Bluestocking Circle* (Oxford: Clarendon Press, 1990), 29–39. Personal details of Montagu's life come from Myer's fascinating account.

60 HL MO 312 [n.d., 1740]; MO 259; MO 5829, 25 Oct [1765]. A number of affluent women in the bluestocking circle were in unhappy marriages, among them Sarah Scott.

61 Karen O'Brien, *Narratives of Enlightenment* (Cambridge: Cambridge University Press, 1998), 4–5. O'Brien argues that history-writing was conceived of as a *male* occupation in the eighteenth century, since it demanded of its authors "an authorial posture of cultural centrality and spokesmanship unavailable to woman writers" (8) and excludes Catharine Macaulay from consideration on this basis. I would argue instead that "partisan" (as opposed to cosmopolitan) historians like Macaulay contributed to the configuration of a competing kind of national history, aimed at moral reformation that was widely used by radical reformers in the later decades of the century. See also Devoney Looser, *British Women Writers and the Writing of History* (Baltimore: Johns Hopkins University Press, 2000); and Mark Salber Phillips, *Society and Sentiment:*

Genres of Historical Writing in Britain 1740–1820 (Princeton: Princeton University Press, 2000).

62 David Hume, *Philosophical Essays Concerning Human Understanding* (London, 1748), 38–9; see also James Moor, "An Essay on Historical Composition," in *Essays Read to a Literary Society* (Glasgow: R. and A. Foulis, 1759).

63 As Naomi Tadmor has pointed out, this rested on the belief that women were particularly affected by the power of example: "'In the even my wife read to me': Women, Reading and Household Life in the Eighteenth Century," in James Raven, Helen Small, and Naomi Tadmor, eds., *The Practice and Representation of Reading in England* (Cambridge: Cambridge University Press, 1996), 164–5.

64 Hume, *Essays Moral, Political and Literary* (London: Spottiswode, 1903), 558; Samuel Johnson, *The Rambler*, March 31, 1750; George Ballard, *Memoirs of Several Ladies of Great Britain who have been celebrated for their writings or skill in the learned languages, arts and sciences*, ed. Ruth Perry, reprt. (Detroit: Wayne State University Press, 1985); Valentine Green, *Acta Historica Reginarum Angliae* (London: V. and R. Green, 1786); Alexander, *History of Women*. Other examples include *Ladies Magazine*, I (1749); Mary Scott, *The Female Advocate, a Poem* (London: J. Johnson, 1774); William Russell, *Essay on the Character, Manners and Genius of Women in Different Ages, Enlarged from the French of Mr Thomas* (London: S. Bladon, 1773); Charlotte Cowley, *Ladies History of England, From the Descent of Julius Caesar, to the Summer of 1780. Calculated for the Use of the Ladies of Great-Britain and Ireland* (London, 1780); and Mary Hays, *Female Biography*, 2 vols. (London: R. Phillips, 1803). See also S. J. Connolly, "A Woman's Life in Mid-Eighteenth Century Ireland: the Case of Letitia Bushel," *HJ*, 43, 2 (2000), 433–51, esp. 436, for the historical tastes of Bushel and Mrs. Delaney. Wollstonecraft, like Montagu and Carter, read widely in sociology and natural history as well as travelogues: see *Vindication of the Rights of Women* (1792), chap. 4. Historical drama of the period includes Brook's *The Earl of Essex* (1750), Glover's *Boadicea* (1753); Mason's *Elfrida* (1757); Mallet's *Alfred* (1751); Shirley's *Edward the Black Prince* (1750); Shakespeare's history plays, and especially *Henry V*, were also enjoying revivals in this period. For the popularity of historical subject matter in paintings and prints of the day, see Timothy Clayton, *The English Print 1688–1802* (New Haven and London: Yale University Press, 1997), 254–8 and chap. 7 passim. History was also a favorite topic of reading for colonial American women: Kevin J. Hayes, *A Colonial Woman's Bookshelf* (Knoxville: University of Tennessee, 1996). For women and history writing, see Looser, *Women Writers*; Guest, *Small Change*; and Mary Catherine Moran, "From Rudeness to Refinement: Gender, Genre and Scottish Enlightenment Discourse" (Ph.D. Diss., Johns Hopkins University, 1999); for the popularity of history over fiction, see John Feather, "British Publishing in the Eighteenth Century: a Preliminary Subject Analysis," *Library*, 8 (1986), 42–3.

65 Quoted in Clayton, *English Print*, 256.

66 HL MO 6704, Oct. 13, 1753; Myers, *Bluestocking Circle*, 184.

67 HL MO 1537, Nov. 7, 1755. Lady Mary Chudleigh expressed similar sentiments about the practical, moral and imaginative uses of history earlier in the century in her *Essays upon Several Subjects in Prose and Verse* (London: R. Bonwicke, 1710), 258.

68 Gyan Prakash, "Introduction," in Prakash, ed., *After Colonialism: Imperial Histories and Post-Colonial Displacements* (Princeton: Princeton University Press, 1995), 8.

69 Lyttelton was estranged from his wife, and worked together with Montagu on his history of Henry II; he was openly admiring of her intelligence and beauty, and encouraged her intellectual pursuits and development. See Myers, *Bluestocking Circle*, 180–6. If the servants' gossip is to be believed, the two spent quite a lot of time behind closed doors.

70 HL MO 1393, ERM to GL, Jan. 15, 1760.

71 HL MO 1384, ERM to GL, Aug. 6, 1758. Solís's account was a successful attempt to respond to the "black legend" about Spanish imperialism, by presenting Cortés as a benevolent, if resolute, commander, whose just and humane treatment of the Aztecs made him compare favorably to other European nation's exploits in the New World. Montagu, as critical and informed reader, made the political and aesthetic judgments required of her by the author. Dryden's *Indian Emperor* (1667) provided one of the more sympathetic, if tragic accounts of the Cortés epic in English prior to Solís's volume.

72 For Montagu and Lyttelton's propensity for "extravagant flattery," see Myers, *Bluestocking Circle*, 182; HL MO 1393, ERM to GL, Jam. 15, 1760.

73 For these see Wilson, *Sense of the People*, chap. 3.

74 Thanks to Rachael Weil for this point. For the conceptualization of heterosexual intercourse, see Tim Hitchcock, *English Sexualities 1700–1800* (Basingstoke: Macmillan, 1997), 80–1; Hunt, *Middling Sort*, 162–3.

75 See, e.g., BM 3548, *A View of the Assassination of the Lady of John Bull Esq.* (1757); BM 3671, *The Difference* (1758).

76 The alterity at play in Montagu's letter is also a function of the prerogative of mimicry enjoined by the colonizer in an economy of the same: Fuss, "Interior Colonies," 24.

77 Bedfordshire Record Office, MS X67/847, Elizabeth Wheeler's Diary, 1778–1789, unfol., microfilm in *Women's Language and Experience*, Part I (Marlborough: Adam Matthews Publications, 1996), Reel 4; an excerpted version was published as *Some Bedfordshire Diaries*, ed. Joyce Godber (*Publications of the Bedfordshire Historical Record Society*, XL (1959), 110–29. Wheeler's MS diary is comprised of a selection of her daily "memorandums" copied out by her husband, Joshua Wheeler, soon after her death, as a testimony to her piety and salvation; it was probably shared in this form with other Friends in their meetings. For the generic and political significance of Quaker journals, see Howard H. Brinton, *Quaker Journals: Varieties of Religious Experience Among Friends* (Wallingford: Pendleton Hill, 1972); Daniel B. Shea, ed., *Some Account of the Fore Part of the Life of Elizabeth Ashbridge*, in *Journeys in New Worlds: Early American Women's Narratives*, ed. William L. Andrews (Madison: University of Wisconsin, 1990), 117–80; and Leonore Davidoff and Catherine Hall, *Family Fortunes: Men and Women of the English Middle Class 1780–1850* (London: Hutchinson, 1987), 138–48.

78 See Dr. Williams' Library, Evans MS 43.4, Visitation Reports; Michael Watts, *The Dissenters* (Oxford: Clarendon Press, 1978), 284–5, 497, 509; Joyce Godber, *History of Bedfordshire 1066–1888* (Bedford: Bedfordshire County Council, 1969), 347–53.

79 Wheeler exemplified the way in which middling women functioned as a large unpaid labor force for their menfolk as described by Hunt in *Middling Sort*, 152–5.

80 See, e.g., William C. Braithewaite and Henry J. Cadbury, *The Second Period of Quakerism* (Cambridge: Cambridge University Press, 1961); Kenneth Corfield, "Elizabeth Heyrick: Radical Quaker," in Gail Malmgreen, ed., *Religion in the Lives of English Women 1760–1930* (Bloomington: Indiana University Press, 1986), 41–67; Phyllis Mack, *Visionary Women: Ecstatic Prophecy in Seventeenth-Century England* (Berkeley: University of California Press, 1992), 319–50; Adrian Davies, *The Quakers in English Society 1655–1725* (Oxford: Clarendon Press, 2000). For women's meetings, see also Friends Library, London, Box Meeting MSS 1671–1753.

81 The refusal of the American Quakers to join in the military resistance effort, and the harsh sanctions imposed by colonial governments as a result, were well publicized in England: see *Felix Farley's Bristol Journal*, Oct. 11, 18, 1776; *Etherington's York Chronicle*, Nov. 24, 1775.

82 As in other Protestant cultures, reading was part of religious discipline: see, e.g., Thomas Turner's reading list as discussed by Tadmor, "Women, Reading and Household Life," 167. Wheeler's reading was predominantly religious and historical, although she also read the newspapers at soon as they were published; travelogues,

hymns, poems and essays made up the rest of her bibliography recorded in the diary. She had access to all authorized Quaker publications, which were required to be taken in by monthly Meetings.

83 As argued convincingly by Dror Wahrman and James Epstein in their papers at the 1999 NACBS, panel on "Re-Thinking the American Revolution." See also Dror Wahrman, "Percy's Prologue: From Gender Play to Gender Panic in Eighteenth Century England," *P & P*, No. 159 (1998), 113–60.

84 *Victoria County History: Bedfordshire* (London: Constable), II (1972), 109–10; *History of Parliament: The House of Commons*, eds. L. Namier and J. Brooke (London: H.M.S.O., 1964), I: 205.

85 *Public Advertiser*, July 31, 1778.

86 Such sentiments echo those of Elizabeth Carter, among others: a study of anti-war sentiment in Britain prior to the French Revolution is much needed.

87 Joseph Besse, *A Collection of the Sufferings of the People called Quakers, for the Testimony of Good Conscience, from . . . 1650, to . . . the Act of Toleration [1689]*, 2 vols. (London: J. Hinde, 1753).

88 *Etherington's York Chronicle*, Dec. 6, 1776.

89 For this, see the excellent introduction provided by Jennifer D. Thorp to *The Acland Journal: Lady Harriet Acland and the American War* (Winchester: Hampshire County Council, 1993); I am much indebted to her account. My thanks are also due her for helping me to track down the prints of Lady Acland. See also *Gentlemen's Magazine*, 85 (1815), pt. 2, 186–7, and references below. It is interesting to note that here and in some other day books of the period kept by women, such as that of Mary Hardy, other family members and servants would also record family activities and events, pointing to the contemporary use of these records as testimonies of collective experience.

90 *Dictionary of National Biography*, s.n. Acland, 59–60.

91 Thorp, *Acland Journal*, xvii–xix.

92 The travails of the march for the women and children are well captured in *Journal of Madame Riedesel*; see, e.g., 51–61; quotation from 51.

93 Burgoyne, *State of the Expedition*, 171–2.

94 Colonel Malcom Fraser, "The Capture of Quebec: a Manuscript Journal," *Journal of the Society for Army Research* 18 (1939), 142–3; Rozbicki, *Complete Colonial Gentleman*, 89; Way, "Cutting Edge of Culture,", 125–31.

95 Thomas Anburey, *With Burgoyne from Quebec*, ed. Sydney Jackson (Toronto: Macmillan, 1963), 152, 46–7, 10–11. This is a republication of volume one of his *Travels Through the Interior Parts of North America* (London: Wm. Lane, 1789); *Journal of Madame Riedesel*, 66.

96 Through promises of goods and provisions, the British persuaded warriors from Odanak (Abenaki), Caughnawaga, Saint Regis (Akwesasne) and Lake of the Two Mountains (Oka) to join Burgoyne's campaign by June of 1777, but its disastrous ending increased Indian discontent with British policies. For an account of native American political alliances during the revolution, see Colin G. Calloway, *The American Revolution in Indian Country* (Cambridge: Cambridge University Press, 1995), 72 and passim; and *Handbook of North American Indians: vol. 15: Northeast* ed. Bruce G. Trigger (Washington, D.C.: Smithsonian, 1978), 607–20.

97 Anburey, *With Burgoyne*, 141; *Journal of Madame Riedesel*, 63–5; Madame Riedesel also rather tendentiously stressed the gallantry and kindness shown towards women of all ranks by the combatants.

98 James Wilkinson, *Memoirs of My Own Times*, 3 vols. (Philadelphia: A. Small, 1816), I: 267–72.

99 The *laissez-passer* addressed to Major-General Gates, which is among the New York Historical Society Papers, New York Public Library, read: "Sir, Lady Harriot Ackland, a lady of the first distinction by family rank and by personal virtues, is under such

concern on account of Major Ackland her husband, wounded and a prisoner in your hands, that I cannot refuse her request to commit her to your protection. Whatever general impropriety there may be in personas acting in your situation and mine to solicit favours, I cannot see the uncommon perseverance in every female grace and exaltation of character of this Lady and her very hard fortune without testyfying that your attentions to her will lay me under obligation. I am Sir, your obedient servant J. Burgoyne." Oct. 9, 1777, quoted by Thorp, *Acland Journal*, xxvi.

100 The bronze bas-relief commemorating this episode is at the Saratoga memorial; for the painting and engravings, see below.

101 Frederic Kidder, *Military Operations in Eastern Maine and Nova Scotia during the Revolution* (Albany: J. Munsell, 1867), 196, 14–15. For other examples, see Mayer, *Belonging to the Army*.

102 Anburey, *Travels through the Interior Parts of America*, I: 177.

103 Lamb, *Original and Authentic Journal*, 184–5; Thorp, *Acland Journal*, xxiv.

104 *Journal of Madame Riedesel*, 54; *Gentleman's Magazine*, 187; *Dictionary of National Biography*, s.n. Acland, 59–60.

105 The claim by A. Acland, in *A Devon Family* (London: Phillimore, 1981), 36, that Major Acland's death was caused by a fever caught while fighting a duel on Bampton Down with a lieutenant who had made disparaging remarks about the integrity of American officers is not widely accepted by scholars.

4 THE BLACK WIDOW: GENDER, RACE AND PERFORMANCE IN ENGLAND AND JAMAICA

1 See, e.g., A. Karras, *Sojourners in the Sun* (Ithaca: Cornell University Press, 1992); Alison Games, *Migrations and the Origins of the English Atlantic World* (Cambridge, Mass: Harvard University Press, 1999); Richard Sheridan, *Sugar and Slavery: An Economic History of the British West Indies* (Baltimore: Johns Hopkins University Press, 1973); Edward Said, *Culture and Imperialism* (New York: Knopf, 1992), 94–6; Moira Ferguson, *Colonialism and Gender Relations from Mary Wollstonecraft to Jamaica Kincaid* (New York: Routledge, 1988), Antonio Benítez-Rojo, *The Repeating Island* (Durham: Duke University Press, 1996).

2 Edward Said, *Orientalism* (New York: Viking, 1978), 5. Representations of the West Indies' menace and rapaciousness include John Gay's *Polly* (1729), which was printed and widely circulated for decades before being staged by George Colman at the Haymarket in 1777; Richard Cumberland's *The West Indian* (1771), one of several efforts by the playwright to use the generic form of sentimental comedy to change the stage characterization of victims of English "national, professional or religious prejudices," such as Jews, Catholics and West Indian Creoles. Significantly for the present discussion, Cumberland's Belcour vindicates his respectability mainly through his unassailable English parentage, which forces the audience to accept him as one of their own: see Richard Cumberland, *Memoirs* (London: Lackington Allen and Co., 1806–7), I: 274; Joseph Donohue Jr., "*The West Indian*: Cumberland, Goldsmith and the Uses of Comedy," in *Dramatic Character in the English Romantic Age* (Princeton: Princeton University Press, 1970), 101–9.

3 The diverse work of such writers as Fernando Ortiz, Eric Williams, Frantz Fanon, C. L. R. James, Orlando Patterson, Carly Phillips, Peter Hulme, Ian Steele, Derek Walcott, Jean Rhys and Joseph Roach all bears witness to this effort; see also n. 4. See also the special issue of *WMQ*, "African and American Atlantic Worlds," 3rd ser., LVI, 2 (April, 1999). For early modern efforts to grapple with the hybrid nature of Atlantic interculture, see the works by Sir Hans Sloane, Charles Leslie, John Oldmixon and Edward Long, below.

4 Paul Gilroy, *The Black Atlantic: Modernity and Double Consciousness* (Cambridge, Mass.: Harvard University Press, 1993); Joseph Roach, *Cities of the Dead: Circum-Atlantic Performance* (New York: Columbia University Press, 1996), quotation from 5; Ira Berlin, "From Creole to African: Atlantic Creoles and the Origins of African-American Society in Mainland North America," *WMQ*, 3rd ser., LIII (1996) 251–88; Robin Law and Kristin Mann, "West Africa in the Atlantic Community: the Case of the Slave Coast," *WMQ*, LVI (1999), 307–34; Jeffrey Bolster, *Black Jacks: African American Seamen in the Age of Sail* (Cambridge, Mass: Harvard University Press, 1997). Earlier groundbreaking studies of the transracial nature of Atlantic culture include Richard Price and Sidney Mintz, *An Anthropological Approach to the Afro-American Past: A Caribbean Perspective* (Philadelphia: Institute for the Study of Human Issues, 1976); Peter Linebaugh and Marcus Rediker, "The Many-Headed Hydra: Sailors, Slaves and the Atlantic Working Class in the Eighteenth Century," *Journal of Historical Sociology*, 3 (1990), 225–52; and John Thornton, *Africa and Africans in the Making of the Atlantic World, 1440–1680* (Cambridge: Cambridge University Press, 1990; 2nd ed., 1998).

5 This process has been recently described by Ann Stoler in "Rethinking Colonial Categories: European Communities and the Boundaries of Rule," in Nicholas B. Dirks, ed., *Colonialism and Culture* (Ann Arbor: University of Michigan Press, 1992), 321.

6 For the complex commercial, manufacturing and agricultural functions of plantations, see Eric Williams, *Capitalism and Slavery* (London: André Deutsch, 1964), and, more recently, Robin Blackburn, *The Making of New World Slavery: From the Baroque to the Modern* (London: Verso, 1997); for "transculture," see Fernando Ortiz, *Cuban Counterpoint: Tobacco and Sugar* (1947), ed. Fernando Coronil (Durham: Duke University Press, 1994). Although criticized for failing to appreciate the highly developed commercial nature of plantation slavery, Ortiz's dynamic notion of transculture as the destruction, acquisition and syncretic creation of cultural phenomena, and as characteristic of Caribbean islands given over to European monoculture, brilliantly conveys the sense of tentativeness and anxiety that pervaded colonial Jamaican society in the eighteenth century, as well as the hybridities of its animal and human life – a place where the indigenous plants, inhabitants and ways of life had been all but extinguished, and no one could claim to "belong." For the politicized nature of everyday life within the global networks of Atlantic slave societies, see Thomas Holt, "Marking: Race, Race-Making and the Writing of History," *AHR*, C (1995), 1–20.

7 The insufficiencies of these terms to describe black/white social relations and cultures forged in colonial settings have been noted by Gilroy, Robert Young and Françoise Vergès, among others: Paul Gilroy, *Black Atlantic*, 2; Robert Young, *Colonial Desire: Hybridity in Theory, Culture and Race* (London: Routledge, 1995); Françoise Vergès, *Monsters and Revolutionaries* (Durham: Duke University Press, 1999).

8 Felicity Nussbaum, *The Autobiographical Subject: Gender and Ideology in Eighteenth Century England* (Baltimore: Johns Hopkins University Press, 1989); See E. J. Burford, *Wits, Wenchers and Wantons* (London: Hale, 1990); Clare Brant, "Speaking of Women: Scandal and the Law in the Mid-Eighteenth Century," in *Women, Texts and Histories 1575–1760* (London: Routledge, 1992), 242–70; Vivien Jones, "Scandalous Femininity: Prostitution and Eighteenth Century Narrative," in D. Castiglione and L. Sharpe, eds., *Shifting the Boundaries: The Transformation of the Languages of Public and Private in the Eighteenth Century* (Exeter: University of Exeter Press, 1996), 54–70; A. Vincent, ed., *Lives of Twelve Bad Women* (London: Unwin, 1897), 165–85; and Lawrence Stone, *Uncertain Unions: Marriage in England 1660–1753* (Oxford: Oxford University Press, 1992), 236–74.

9 Teresia Constantia Phillips, *An Apology for the Conduct of Mrs. T. C. Phillips*, 3 vols. (London: G. Smith, 4th edn, 1761); *A Letter Humbly Address'd to the Rt. Honourable the Earl of Chesterfield* (London: Author, 1750); "A Collection of Impossibilities," *Columbia Magazine* (Kingston, Jamaica), Feb. 1798, 578–80; and Phillips's article written for the *Kingston Journal* of 1756. For her critics' assessment of her, see Jeremy Bentham, *Works*, ed. John Bowring (Edinburgh: William Tait, 1843), X, 35; Horace Walpole's *Correspondence*, ed. W. S. Lewis, 24 (New Haven: Yale University Press, 1967), 35; Fielding, *Amelia* (London: A. Millar, 1751), 28; Anon., *The Happy Courtezan* (London: J. Roberts, 1735); Richardson Wright, *Revels in Jamaica* (New York: Dodd, Mead and Co., 1937, reprt. 1969); 22; Vincent, *Bad Women*, 136.

10 A more complete narrative of her life can be found in Stone, *Uncertain Unions*, 236–74.

11 *Satires Written by Mr. Whitehead*, ed. V. Carretta, *Augustan Reprint Society*, No. 223 (Los Angeles: William Andrews Clark Memorial Library, 1984), x–xi; Stone, *Uncertain Unions*, 236, 246; *Dictionary of National Biography*, s.n. Paul Whitehead. Phillips dedicated her *Apology* to the 3rd Earl of Scarborough, who was the Prince of Wales's treasurer from 1738 to 1757. That it is her prose that Whitehead edits, and not the reverse, becomes clear on reading her later pieces, from her *Letter to the Earl of Chesterfield* to the "Collection of Impossibilities" written for the *Kingston Journal*.

12 Although her persistent efforts some years later to get him to make the restitution she claimed she was owed came to nothing, the fact that Stanhope's elder brother, the 3rd Earl of Chesterfield, performed some favors for Phillips suggests that his family may have believed her story.

13 Such treatment, evidence suggests, was not uncommon in eighteenth-century marriages at the middling and elite levels, especially when disputes over money were involved. See, e.g., Margaret Hunt, *The Middling Sort: Gender, Commerce and the Family* (Berkeley and Los Angeles: University of California Press, 1996), 160–5; and HL HM 1060–10844, Letters of Charlotte Turner Smith, esp. 10,800–10,809, Oct. 9, 1773.

14 Stone, *Uncertain Unions*, 258.

15 It is summarized with characteristic verve by Stone, *Uncertain Unions*, 247–74. As he points out, her case was used to good effect by the agitators for the abolition of clandestine marriages in 1749–50.

16 Ibid., 239; Bowring, ed., *Works*, X: 47; *Apology*, II: 119–57; 202–13.

17 For Shirley, see John A. Schultz, *William Shirley, King's Governor of Massachusetts* (Chapel Hill: University of North Carolina Press, 1961). Thanks to Ned Landsman for this reference. The account of Phillips's first stay in Jamaica can be found in *Apology*, III: 101–52.

18 This is just one more way in which Phillips and her family were linked with the British empire; her future West Indian countryman, Edward Long, also had East India Company connections through his brothers and uncle.

19 Judith Butler, "Imitation and Gender Insubordination," in *Inside/Out* (London: Routledge, 1994), 24.

20 See, e.g., Julius Scott, "Criss-crossing Empires: Ships, Sailors and Resistance in the Lesser Antilles in the Eighteenth Century," in E. Pacquette and S. Engerman, eds., *The Lesser Antilles in the Age of European Expansion* (Gainesville: University of Florida, 1996), who argues for the importance of highly mobile maritime populations who were the linchpins in transatlantic communications networks, and whose mobility belied images of well-defined national boundaries; David Waldstreicher, "Reading the Runaways: Self-Fashioning, Print Culture and Confidence in Slavery in the Eighteenth-Century Mid-Atlantic World," *WMQ*, 3rd ser., LVI (1999), 243–72, argues, pace Gilroy, that the mobility of a sizeable number of slaves in the course of their everyday duties – as messengers, marketers, shipheavers, etc. – meant that Africans and Creoles could take advantage of the same channels to free themselves.

21 Patricia Meyer Spacks, *Gossip* (New York: Knopf, 1985); Anna Clark, "Whores and Gossips: Sexual Reputation in London 1770–1825," in Arina Angerman et al., *Current Issues in Women's History* (London: Routledge, 1989), 231–48; Laura Gowing, *Domestic Dangers: Women, Words and Sex in Early Modern London* (Oxford: Oxford University Press, 1996).

22 See the excellent account of such channels in Ian Steele, *The English Atlantic, 1675–1740* (Oxford and New York: Oxford University Press, 1986).

23 Brant, "Speaking of Women," 245, 247.

24 The low social class of Defoe's heroines precluded Phillips's using them as examples, keen as she was to stress her relatively high birth, which accords with the tradition of the sentimental heroine. Clearly, however, the picaresque form influenced the presentation of parts of her narrative. Consider, too the figures of the Jew and the fallen young woman in Theophilus Cibber's *The Harlot's Progress, or the Ridotto Al Fresco* (1733), Augustan Reprint Society (Los Angeles: William Andrews Memorial Library, 1977). Thanks to Ned Landsman and Jim Engel for comments here. Cf. Laura Brown, *The Ends of Empire* (Ithaca: Cornell University Press, 1996), who stresses the novelty of the non-aristocratic birth of the heroines of sentimental drama.

25 Indeed, Calista, like Phillips, was condemned by critics for regretting the consequences rather than fact of vice. See, e.g., Theophilus Cibber et al., *The Lives of the Poets of Great Britain and Ireland*, 5 vols. (London: R. Griffiths, 1753), III: 276, where he suggests "The Fair Wanton" would be a better title for the play; Samuel Johnson, *Lives of the English Poets*, ed. George Birkbeck Hill (Oxford: Oxford University Press, 1905), II: 68; *British Theatre*, ed. Elizabeth Inchbald (London: Longmans, 1806), IX (London, 1806), 1. Quotations from Rowe's *Fair Penitent*, ed. Malcolm Goldstein (Lincoln, Nebr.: University of Nebraska Press, 1969), xviii. For criticisms of Phillips, see Catherine Talbot to Elizabeth Carter, July 21, 1752, *A Series of Letters Between Mrs. Elizabeth Carter and Miss Catherine Talbot, from the Year 1741 to 1770*, ed. Montagu Pennington, 4 vols. (London: F. C. & J. Rivington, 1809; repr., 1966), I: 86, and below.

26 Nussbaum, *Autobiographical Subject*, 187.

27 *Pamela* was published in 1740, *Clarissa* in 1747–8, Eliza Haywood's *Female Spectator* in 1744–6, and the scandalous memoirs of Phillips, Laetitia Pilkington, Mrs. Vane and Charlotte Charke in 1748–52.

28 Nussbaum, *Autobiographical Subject*, 187, 155.

29 The public appetite for such tales is revealed in the spate of "memoirs" of compromised ladies that appeared in the wake of Phillips's *Apology*: see, e.g., *London Evening Post*, April 19–21, 1750, advertisement for *Memoirs of the Life of Mrs. A—A W—t*.

30 Eighteenth-century drama and fiction of the period dealing with mistresses include Defoe's *Moll Flanders* and *Roxana* (1726, 1728); Tobias Smollett, *Roderick Random* (1748), and George Lillo, *London Merchant* (1741). T. G. A. Nelson, "Women of Pleasure," *Eighteenth Century Life*, 11 (1987) 181–98; Janet Todd, *Gender, Art and Death* (New York: Continuum, 1993); Nussbaum, *Autobiographical Subject*; Jones, "Scandalous Femininity"; for the canvassing of the careers of some 280 such women whose beauty and poverty led them to take up the careers of mistresses, see H. Bleakley, "Tête à Tête Portraits in the *Town and Country Magazine*," *Notes and Queries*, 10 (1905), 241–3, 342–4, 522.

31 For the riots, see P. Linebaugh, "The Tyburn Riot Against the Surgeons," in Douglas Hay et al., *Albion's Fatal Tree: Crime and Society in Eighteenth-Century England* (New York: Pantheon, 1975), 89–102.

32 Fordyce, *The Folly, Infamy and Misery of UNLAWFUL PLEASURE* (London, 1760); see also his *Sermons to Young Women* (London, 4th edn, 1767) where fallen women get particular attention; and Saunders Welch, *A Proposal to Render Effectual a Plan to*

Remove the Nuisance of Common Prostitutes from the Streets of the Metropolis (London, 1758). For the "swarm" of prostitutes, see Jonas Hanway, *Thoughts on the Plan for a Magdalen House for Repentant Prostitutes* (London: James Waugh, 1758); [Robert Dingley], *Proposals for Establishing a Public Place of Reception for Penitent Prostitutes* (London: W. Faden, 1758), and Martin Madan, *An Account of the Triumphant Death of F.S., A Converted Prostitute* (London and Boston, 1763). For the implication of reforming fervor in sentimentalism, see Jones, "Scandalous Femininity," 55–62. See also Donna Andrew, *Philanthropy and Police* (Princeton: Princeton University Press, 1988).

33 *London Evening Post*, April 19–21, 1750; Martin Madan, *Thelyphthora; or a Treatise on Female Ruin* (London, 1780), 2 vols., cited in Nussbaum, "Polygamy, *Pamela* and Empire," in *The Consumption of Culture: Image, Object, Text*, eds. Ann Bermingham and John Brewer (London: Routledge, 1995), 235n, 219–24; [Caleb Fleming], *The Oeconomy of the Sexes, or the Doctrine of Divorce, the Plurality of Wives, and the Vow of Celibacy Freely Examined* (London, 1751); David Hume, "Of Polygamy and Divorces," in *Essays Moral, Political and Literary* (London: World Library, 1875), I: 231–40; Adam Ferguson, *An Essay on the History of Civil Society* (1766), ed. Fania Oz-Salzberger (Cambridge: Cambridge University Press, 1995), 112–13; and William Robertson, *A History of America*, 4 vols. (London: W. Strahan and T. Cadell, 1777), II: 96–105.

34 *Britain's Remembrancer*, June 11, 1748; *London Magazine*, 17 (1748), 259–60; *London Evening Post*, Aug. 23–5, 1748. For effeminacy, see Introduction.

35 For this, see my *The Sense of the People: Politics, Culture and Imperialism in England, 1715–1785* (New York and Cambridge: Cambridge University Press, 1995) chap. 3; and "The Good, The Bad, and the Impotent: Imperialism and the Politics of Identity in Georgian England," in *Consumption and Culture*, 249–52.

36 *A Letter from Mrs. L—tia Pilk—ton to the celebrated Mrs. T—sia Ph—ps* (London, 1748), 3; *A Defence of the Character of a Noble Lord from the Scandalous Aspersions Contained in a Malicious Apology* (London: W. Webb Jr., 1748), 12; Catherine Talbot to Elizabeth Carter, [Aug., 1752], and Carter to Talbot, Aug. 12, 1752, in *A Series of Letters*, 86, 89; *Gentleman's Magazine*, 18 (1748), 432.

37 *The Parallel, or P–lk—n and Ph–l–ps compared. By An Oxford Scholar* (London: M. Cooper, 1748), 62. See also *Remarks on Mrs. Muilman's Letter to the Right Honourable the Earl of Chesterfield* (London, 1750); John Duncombe, *The Feminiad* (London, 1754), 15; and *A Genuine Copy of the Trial of Thomas Grimes Esq., alias Lord S—, for a Barbarous and Inhuman Rape* (London: E. Anderson, E. Pen, [1748]).

38 *Remembrancer*, June 11, 1748; *To the H—ble Sir J—B—* (London, 1734), 74–5; *Happy Courtezan* (London, 1735), 12.

39 [Edward Ward, *A Trip to Jamaica with a True Character of the People and the Island* (London: E. Ward, 1700), 16; John Oldmixon, *The British Empire in America*, 2 vols. (London: J. Brotherton, 1741), I: 425. These associations also penetrated other imaginative literature besides Defoe: Gay's *Polly*, for example, boasted a character who turned bawd after her transportation to Jamaica on a felony. For an insightful analysis of anticolonial prejudices in this period, see Michal J. Rozbicki, *The Complete Colonial Gentleman* (Charlottesville: University of North Carolina Press, 1998), 76–126.

40 [Charles Leslie], *A New History of Jamaica* (London: I. Hodges, 1740), 35; Long, II: 265, 267. This feature of West Indian life contrasted strikingly with the North American colonies, where mixed-race and illegitimate offspring were a source of shame. See Philip Morgan, *Slave Counterpoint: Black Culture in the Eighteenth Century Chesapeake and Low Country* (Chapel Hill: Omohundro Institute, 1998), 402–3.

41 Hilary McD. Beckles, "White Women and Slavery in the Caribbean," *History Workshop Journal*, 36 (1993), 66–82.

42 *Remarks on Mrs. Muilman's Letter*, 9, 14–15; *A Counter Apology, or genuine confession . . . containing the Secret History, amours, . . . of M—P—., a Famous British Courtezan*

(London: R. Young, 1749), 3; quotation from *Defence of the Character of a Noble Lord*, 7, which referred to her *Apology* as an "uncommon and inimitable Performance."

43 In this respect, she resembles the fictional Millwood in Lillo's *London Merchant* – both masterless women who invert and pervert the natural hierarchy with their sexual talents. See my "Good, Bad, and Impotent," 246–8.

44 In fact, the recourse to infanticide in eighteenth-century England and Scotland has been documented in a number of recent studies: Peter Hoffer and N. E. Hall, *Murdering Mothers: Infanticide in England and New England 1558–1803* (New York: New York University Press, 1981); Thomas Forbes, "Deadly Parents: Child Homicide in 18th and 19th Century England," *Journal of the History of Medicine*, 41 (1986), 175–99; and Deborah A. Symonds, "Reconstructing Rural Infanticide in Eighteenth-Century Scotland," *Journal of Women's History*, 10 (1998), 63–84.

45 W. J. Gardner, *A History of Jamaica from its Discovery by Christopher Columbus to the Year 1872* (New York: T. Fisher Unwin, 1909), 122.

46 There were at least seventy-five slave rebellions in Jamaica over the century, many led by women: see Orlando Patterson, "Slavery and Slave Revolts: A Socio-historical Analysis of the First Maroon War," in Richard Price, ed., *Maroon Societies: Rebel Slave Communities in the Americas* (New York: Anchor Books, 1973), 179–90, and *The Sociology of Slavery* (Rutherford, N.J., University of New Jersey Press, 1967), 268–73; Lucille Mathurin, *The Rebel Woman in the British West Indies During Slavery* (Kingston: African Caribbean Publications, 1975); Barbara Bush, *Slave Women in Caribbean Society 1650–1838* (London and Kingston: Currey, 1988).

47 Leslie, *New History of Jamaica*, 14. Sir Hans Sloane's more positive assessment of Jamaica's climate and topography in *A Voyage to the Islands Madera, Barbados . . . and Jamaica*, 2 vols. (London: Royal Society, 1707, 1725), was geared towards encouraging immigration and investment there.

48 Councilors were appointed from among the local leading landowners by the Board of Trade and governors, but were very prone to "take against" new governors or side with factions in the Assembly. Quotation from Edward Trelawney to Henry Pelham, April 1749, quoted by Jack Greene in "Edward Trelawney's Grand Elixir: Metropolitan Weakness and Constitutional Reform in the Mid-18th-Century British Empire," in Roderick MacDonald, ed., *West Indies Accounts* (Kingston: University of West Indies Press, 1996), 88. The litigiousness of Jamaican colonists was notorious: one Scottish attorney, James Gillespie, observed in 1767 that Jamaica had "more disputes in Equity than all the other North American or Island Colonies put together, belonging to the Crown of Great Britain": quoted by Karras, *Sojourners in the Sun*, 63; Sheridan, *Sugar and Slavery*, 371.

49 Men whose chief education was "that of Pike and Musquet" would serve as governor and chancellor of chancery court, among other roles, "tho' he knows no more of Law than of Gospel", Oldmixon complained, while a soldier in the regiments of foot guards who managed to go to Jamaica on a forged pass was able to marry a planter's widow, and rise to become one of the six assistant judges of the Grand Court: *British Empire*, II: 346–9.

50 Long, IV: 40. There was always at least one regiment on the island, as well as the local militia, comprised of whites and free blacks and people of color. For the fluctuating military presence on the island, see Andrew O'Shaughnessy, "Redcoats and Slaves in the British Caribbean," in Paquette and Engerman, *Lesser Antilles*, 105–27; Roger Norman Buckely, *The British Army in the West Indies* (Gainesville: University of Florida, 1998). By 1800 there were about one thousand sailors and three thousand troops stationed in Jamaica.

51 Sloane, *Voyage*, I: xviii–xx, 198–9, Tab. 235; James Walvin, *Fruits of Empire: Exotic Produce and British Taste 1660–1800* (Basingstoke: Macmillan, 1997), 91–8; Add. MS

30,001, Ricketts Family Correspondence, f. 5, Mary Rickets to her sister, June 23, 1757. Thanks to Sarah Pearsall of Harvard University for referring me to this source.

52 See, for example, the *Journals of the Assembly of Jamaica*, 14 vols. (Kingston, 1812), II, III, IV, passim; Sheridan, *Sugar and Slaves*, 208–332. Interestingly, this anxiety, palpable to residents and visitors alike, was attributed by Edward Long to the "irritable" nervous system produced by the tropical climate that made Jamaican whites "more liable than others to sudden and violent emotions of the mind . . . [that] may actually throw them into acute diseases" as well as to those "slow and durable passions" of "solicitude, grief, stifled resentment, and vexation": II: 267, III: 542–3.

53 Winthrop Jordan, *White Over Black: American Attitudes toward the Negro 1550–1812* (Chapel Hill: University of North Carolina Press, 1966), 176; Long, II: 332–3; Edward Braithwaite, *The Development of Creole Society in Jamaica 1770–1820* (Oxford: Clarendon Press, 1971), 71–81. For the restrictions on mulatto inheritance, see n. 63 below. Laws regarding slaves also reversed the English practice by which children followed the condition of their father, making the condition of slavery inheritable through the mother. Thus the whole plantation system was erected on the basis of gender, sexuality and reproduction.

54 For white society, see Patterson, *Sociology of Slavery*, 49, 50; and Braithwaite, *Creole Society*; for population ratios see Richard B. Sheridan, "Caribbean Plantation Society, 1689–1748," in *OHBE*, II: 400. There were 10,400 whites and 118,100 blacks in Jamaica in 1748.

55 Trevor Burnard, "European Migration to Jamaica 1655–1780," *WMQ*, 3rd ser., LIII (1996): 767–96. Burnard estimates that ninety percent of yearly immigrants to Jamaica were from England. The percentages of absentee owners are in contention. Early estimates of up to 33 percent by 1770 are given in George Metcalf, *Royal Government and Political Conflict in Jamaica, 1729–1783* (London: Longmans, 1965), 6–7, and Blackburn, *New World Slavery*, 406–7.

56 See, e.g., *Assembly Journals*, III (1731–45): 55, 126, 265. Around 142 Jews were naturalized in the decade after the Plantation Act of 1740, which extended naturalization to any Jew or foreign Protestant who had resided in a British colony for seven years. For the Jamaican Jews' campaign to vote see Nicholas Mirzoeff, "Pisarro's Passage: the Sensation of Caribbean Jewishness in Diaspora," in Nicholas Mirzoeff, ed., *Diaspora and Visual Culture: Representing Africans and Jews* (London: Routledge, 2000), 58. For suspicions of Jewish roles in fomenting Tacky's rebellion, see Long, II: 462–3.

57 A disdain for the pleasure-loving lifestyle of the planters and a fierce regard for family and kinship connections were primary. For Scots, see Karras, *Sojourners in the Sun*, 28–9, 54, 138–9; Sheridan, *Sugar and Slavery*, 369–70. For the Irish, see Calendar of State Papers, 1728–9, 1055, quoted in Patterson, *Sociology of Slavery*, 48; Hilary Beckles, "A 'Riotous and Unruly Lot': Irish Indentured Servants and Freemen in the English West Indies, 1644–1713," *WMQ*, 3rd ser., XLVII (1990), 502–33; Burnard, "European Migration," 785. Militia musters to put "the Country in the best Posture of Defence" were recurrent events in local life: See *Jamaica Courant*, April 15, 1719.

58 The Anglophilic cultural identifications of British planters in the Caribbean are also stressed by Michael Craton, "Reluctant Creoles: The Planters' World in the British West Indies," in Bernard Bailyn and Philip D. Morgan, eds., *Strangers within the Realm: Cultural Margins of the First British Empire* (Chapel Hill: University of North Carolina Press, 1991), 346–9; Jack Greene, "Changing Identity in the British Caribbean: Barbados as a Case Study," in Nicholas Canny and Anthony Pagden, eds., *Colonial Identity in the Atlantic World 1500–1800* (Princeton: Princeton University Press, 1987), 231; and Long, II: 254, 275–80. The long-term success of this strategy is evinced by Trollope's remark that Jamaica was "much nearer to England" in customs and culture than "any other of the West Indian islands": *The West Indies and the Spanish Main* (London: Dawsons, repr., 1968), 97–8.

59 As Philip Morgan has recently reminded us, "In sheer number of emigrants, British America was actually more black than white, more an extension of Africa than of Europe": "The Black Experience in the British Empire, 1680–1810," in *OHBE*, II: 465.

60 Robert Robertson, *A Letter to the Bishop of London* (London: J. Wilford, 1730); Sidney Mintz, *Caribbean Transformations* (Chicago: Aldine, 1974); for the "Jamaican Code Noir," see Long, II: 485–92, which was in place in Jamaica, and most American slave-holding British colonies, by the late seventeenth century. Defenders of slavery stressed Jamaican slaves' equal access to "the civil Magistrate . . . alike the Judge of you and your Masters" as well as the easier life they led compared to the "European vulgar" or the "savage Tyrants of your own Complexion" in Africa: *Gentleman's Magazine*, V (1735), 91; see also Sloane, *Voyage*, I: lvii. Yet given that slaves were beyond the reach of common law, denied trial by jury and unable to give evidence against whites, and that their masters were not held accountable for their death by punishment, the chance that brutal masters would ever be charged was very slim: see E. V. Goveia, *The West Indian Slave Laws of the Eighteenth Century* (London and Barbados: Caribbean University Press, 1970). It was widely held by the plantocracy that slavery "reclaimed" Africans "from a savage, intractable" state, as Long put it (I: 271); on this reading, slavery becomes part of the civilizing process itself.

61 New slaves in Jamaica in this period hailed from (in descending numerical order) the Gold Coast (about 40 percent), the Niger Delta, the Windward Coast, Angola and Gambia. Patterson, *Sociology of Slavery*, 134–7; David Richardson, "The Atlantic Slave Trade," in *OHBE*, 456, 459; quotation from Patterson, 275–6. For the case for the "mutual intelligibility" of language among Africans see Morgan, *Slave Counterpoint*, 562.

62 See, e.g., Sloane, *Voyage*, I: lvii, on the "perverse" and cruel nature of Africans justifying their extreme punishments. For the concept of surrogation, see Roach, *Cities of the Dead*. See also Michael Craton, *Searching for the Invisible Man: Slaves and Plantation Life in Jamaica* (Cambridge, Mass.: Harvard University Press, 1978); Richard S. Dunn, "'Dreadful Idlers' in the Cane Fields: the Slave Labor Pattern on a Jamaican Sugar Estate, 1762–1831," in Barbara Solow and Stanley Engerman, eds., *British Capitalism and Caribbean Slavery* (Cambridge: Cambridge University Press, 1984), 163–90; and Douglas Hall, ed., *In Miserable Slavery: Thomas Thistlewood in Jamaica, 1750–86* (London: Macmillan, 1989).

63 See, e.g., *Assembly Journals*, IV (1745/6–1756), 414–15; Gardner, *History*, 116. For the opportunities afforded freed and mulatto women who had relationships with white men, see Mavis Christine Campbell, *The Dynamics of Change in a Slave Society: A Sociopolitical History of the Free Coloureds of Jamaica, 1800–1865* (Cranbury, N.J.: Associated University Presses, 1976); and Philip Morgan, "Sex, Race and Class in Jamaica," unpublished paper given at the Huntington Library Conference, "A New Imperial History: Transculture, Commodities and Identities in the First British Empire," October, 2000. Petitions protesting against black and colored tradesmen's right to apprentice the same was quite common. Freed blacks were usually descendants of white masters or persons rewarded for exceptional loyalty, demonstrated in helping to put down Maroons or slave rebellions. In contrast to other south Atlantic colonies such as South Carolina, the frequency with which masters bequeathed extensive property to their mulatto offspring led the Assembly to outlaw freed people of color and blacks from inheriting more than £2,000 worth of currency or property, but individuals always managed to get around this law: see Braithwaite, *Creole Society*, 170. Thanks to Jennifer Morgan for the information on South Carolina. For the cross, see Long, II: 321; for comparisons with the North American colonies, see Kathleen Brown, *Good Wives, Nasty Wenches and Anxious Patriarchs* (Chapel Hill: University of North Carolina Press, 1998), and Morgan, *Slave Counterpoint*.

64 Gardner, *History*, 117–19; Michael Craton, *Testing the Chains: Resistance to Slavery in the British West Indies* (Ithaca: Cornell University Press, 1982), 75–89; Mavis Christine Campbell, *The Maroons of Jamaica, 1655–1796* (Granby, Mass.: Bergin and Garvey, 1988); Suzanne Miers and Igor Kopytoff, eds., *Slavery in Africa, Historical and Anthropological Perspectives* (Madison: University of Wisconsin Press, 1977); Thornton, *Africa and Africans*, 74–89, 107; Robin Law, *The Slave Coast of West Africa: The Impact of the Slave Trade on African Society* (Oxford: Clarendon Press, 1991), 64–8; Barbara Klamon Kopytoff, "Guerilla Warfare in Eighteenth Century Jamaica," *Expedition*, 19 (1977), 23–4; R. C. Dallas, *History of the Maroons* (London: A. Strahan, 1803), 71–97; *Jamaica Courant*, June 20, 1722.

65 Craton, *Testing the Chains*, 92.

66 The *locus classicus* of this discussion for England of course is Douglas Hay et al., *Albion's Fatal Tree*; and E. P. Thompson, "Patrician Society, Plebian Culture," and "Eighteenth Century English Society: Class Struggle without Class?", in *Whigs and Hunters* (New York: Pantheon, 1983). For the inherent theatricality of "race," see Harry J. Elam, Jr. and David Krasner, eds., *African-American Performance and Theater History* (Oxford: Oxford University Press, 2001).

67 Oldmixon, *British Empire*, II: 412; Braithwaite, *Creole Society*, 117–19 for a detailed description of the visitation. For modern analyses of plantation life that confirm many aspects of Oldmixon's and other eighteenth-century visitors' accounts, see Michel Craton and James Walvin, *A Jamaican Plantation: The History of Worthy Park 1670–1970* (London: W. H. Allen, 1978); J. R. Ward, "A Planter and His Slaves in Eighteenth Century Jamaica," in T. C. Smout, ed., *The Search for Wealth and Stability* (London: Macmillan, 1979), 1–20; and Seymour Drescher, *Econocide* (Pittsburgh: University of Pittsburgh Press, 1977).

68 See, e.g., the description of the gardens of Sir Charles Price in Long, II: 76–7, and Craton and Walvin, *Worthy Park*, 85. The building of grander houses, like the swell of ameliorist slave law in the 1770s, may have been motivated in part by the rise of abolitionist criticism in England – a riposte to accusations that greed only was the springboard of the plantation system.

69 PRO CO 137/30, Gov. Haldane to the Board of Trade, June 2, 1759; Richard Dunn, *Sugar and Slavery*, 285. While planters, merchants and their families wore lavish silks and gold brocades, servants wore "coarse Osnabrug Frocks, buttoning at the Neck and Hands," long trousers, speckled shirts and no stockings: Leslie, *New History of Jamaica*, 34.

70 Metcalf, *Royal Government*, 13, 14.

71 Leslie, *New History of Jamaica*, 39–40, 305; see also *The Interesting Narrative of the Life of Olaudah Equiano*, ed. Robert J. Allison (London: St. Martin's, 1996), 107–8, 144–5, 180–1.

72 Foucault, *Discipline and Punish* (New York, Pantheon, 1977), chap. 1; Roach, *Cities of the Dead*, 41–5; Price and Mintz, *Afro-American Past*, 16.

73 For a detailed analysis of slave law and courts in Jamaica that supports this reading, see Diana Paton, "Punishment, Crime and the Bodies of Slaves in Eighteenth-Century Jamaica," *Journal of Social History*, 34, 4 (2001), 923–54. As Paton demonstrates, slave codes "placed almost no limits on the slaveholder's power to 'correct' his or her slaves"; the slave code's injunction for masters to avoid "wanton" killing was not accompanied by any legal remedy. These regulatory powers of masters could later be ratified by jurists and legislators.

74 See, e.g., Long, II: 459; *London Magazine*, 36 (1767), 258; Bryan Edwards, *The History, Civil and Commercial, of the British Colonies in the West Indies*, 2 vols. (Dublin: Luke White, 1793), 66–7. Such indifference was also attributed by many to Africans' belief that they would return "home" and join their ancestors after death.

75 Morgan, *Slave Counterpoint*, 525–8; Peter Hogg, *Slavery: The Afro-American Experience* (London: British Library, 1979), 47; 48–50; Dunn, "'Dreadful Idlers.'"

76 Peter Marsden, *An Account of the Island of Jamaica* (Newcastle, 1788), 34; Richard D. E. Burton, *Afro-Creole: Power, Opposition and Play in the Caribbean* (Ithaca: Cornell University Press, 1997); Roger D. Abrahams, *The Man-of-Words in the West Indies: Performance and the Emergence of Creole Culture* (Baltimore: Johns Hopkins University Press, 1983), 77–87; James C. Scott, *Domination and the Arts of Resistance* (New Haven: Yale University Press, 1990), 142–4; Robert Dirks, *The Black Saturnalia: Conflict and its Ritual Expression on British West Indian Slave Plantations* (Gainesville: University of Florida, 1987); Craton, *Testing the Chains*, 84. The shared current circumstances and cultural heritage of West Africans, despite ethnic and linguistic differences, is pointed to as a resource by many scholars: Morgan, *Slave Counterpoint*, 559, 562; Robin Horton, "African Conversion," *Africa*, XLI (1971), 85–108; Melville Herskovitz, *The Myth of the Negro Past* (New York: Harper & Bros., 1941), 81. For the overlap and pluralism of African religion see T. O. Ranger, "The Local and the Global in Southern African Religious History," in Robert W. Hefner, ed., *Conversion of Christianity* (Berkeley: University of California Press, 1993), 65–98; and Mintz and Price, *Afro-American Past*, 23–4.

77 The St. Thomas planters thereafter forbade slaves from attending dances, while those in Antigua outlawed nighttime funerals: Mirzoeff, "Pisarro's Passage," 62; Craton, *Testing the Chains*, 121–4.

78 See also *Lady Nugent's Journal*, ed. Frank Cundall (London: Adam & Charles Black, 1907), 72, 103, 131–2 for similar concerns. She writes: "It is extraordinary to witness the immediate effect that the climate and habit of living in this country have upon the minds and manners of the Europeans, particularly of the lower orders. In the upper ranks, they become indolent and inactive, regardless of everything but eating, drinking and indulging themselves, and are almost entirely under the domination of their mulatto favorites. In the lower orders, they are the same, with the addition of conceit and tyranny" (131). Long thought that town ladies, being around other Europeans more, were "better-mannered and more refined": II: 278–9.

79 This "drawl," commented on by all visitors to the island in the late eighteenth and early nineteenth centuries, was in fact an emerging Creole dialect, common to all races and classes, which added African inflection and African and European vocabulary to English. See Craton, "Planters' World," 354–5; Douglas Taylor, "The Origin of West Creole Languages," *American Anthropologist*, n.s., LXV (1963), 800–14.

80 The historical antecedents and successors to the national phenotyping of Long are discussed by Richard Grove in *Green Imperialism: Colonial Expansion, Tropical Island Edens and the Origins of Environmentalism 1600–1800* (Cambridge: Cambridge University Press, 1995), 297–317.

81 Barbara Bush, "White 'Ladies,' Coloured 'Favourites' and Black 'Wenches'; Some Considerations on Sex, Race and Class Factors in Social Relations in White Creole Society in the British Caribbean," *Slavery and Abolition*, 2 (1981), 257.

82 Marietta Morrissey, *Slave Women in the New World: Gender Stratification in the Caribbean* (Lawrence, KS: University of Kansas Press, 1989), chaps. 7 and 8; Beckles, "White Women," 69.

83 As Lucille Mathurin has put it, "the black woman produced, the brown woman served, and the white woman consumed": *Rebel Woman*, 10.

84 See also *Lady's Nugent's Journal*, 72. Long's infamous remarks about lower-class women's fondness for black men was thus just repeating these widely held prejudices.

85 See Beckles, "Sex and Gender in the Historiography of Caribbean Slavery," in Verene Sheperd et al. eds., *Engendering History: Caribbean Women in Historical Perspective* (Kingston and London: Currey, 1995), 134.

NOTES TO PP. 155–8

86 Edwards, *History Civil and Commercial*, 127–8. Charlotte Smith's novel *Letters of a Solitary Wanderer* (reprt., Poole: Woodstock Books, 1995) repeats these remarks almost verbatim: II: 58.

87 Brown, *Good Wives*, 92–3; Wright, *Revels in Jamaica*, 25; Frank Cundall, *The Governors of Jamaica in the First Half of the Eighteenth Century* (London: West India Committee, 1937), 101. Lawes was connected by marriage to the Longs, the two Bishops Godwyn, the Modyfords, Sir Charles and William Henry Lyttelton (afterwards Lord Lyttelton), the Lawleys and Luttrels, and the Earls of Carhampton. Lawes's granddaughter got the gold ring however when she married the Duke of Cumberland, George III's brother. Edmund Morgan has called this pattern for transmission of property in colonial society "widowarchy": *American Freedom, American Slavery* (New Haven: Yale University Press, 1978), 166.

88 Errol Hill, *The Jamaica Stage, 1655–1900: Profile of a Colonial Theatre* (Amherst: University of Massachusetts Press, 1992), 128. See also BL Add. MS 30,001, Ricketts Family Correspondence, f. 7. Mary Ricketts, brought to the island with her husband, considered her time there to be a "purgatory": f. 4b, June 23, 1738.

89 Beckles, "White Women."

90 BL Add. MS 12434, Sugar Plantations in Jamaica, 1739; Add. MS 12436, Landholders in Jamaica, *c.* 1750; and PRO C.O. 142/31 List of the Landowners in the Island of Jamaica (1754) show Henry Needham owning extensive acres, divided among St. Mary, St. Thomas in the Vale and St. George's parishes, as did his uncle and two cousins, Robert and Hampson.

91 Manning divorced his wife for her transgression and Beckford eventually married her. In the shorter term, Beckford's presumptuous remarks about Phillips, calling her Needham's "Girl," a term reserved for colored mistresses, provoked Needham to fight a duel that was resolved with Beckford's injury and apology: *Apology*, III: 109–11.

92 Add. MS 30,001, Mary Ricketts to her sister, f. 4b, June 23, 1738. Significantly, white women owned 25 percent of all Jamaican slaves: Beckles, "Taking Liberties," in Claire Midgley, ed., *Gender and Imperialism* (Manchester: Manchester University Press, 1997). For the assessment of Creole women, see [T. C. Phillips], *Jamaica in Miniature, or a Collection of Impossibilities* [c. 1760] in *Columbian Magazine* (1798), 578–80. Thanks to Russell L. Martin III of the American Antiquarian Society for sending me a photocopy from the Society's holdings. For visiting English women's fears of black and colored slaves, see Sarah Pearsall, "'Nothing but Black Faces All Round Us': the Question of Whiteness in Jamaica, 1780–1812," unpublished paper, Anglo-American Annual Conference, Institute of Historical Research, 1999; for other pejorative assessments of Creole cultural life, see *Lady Nugent's Diary*, 315–18, *Jamaica Magazine*, Aug., 1813, 22.

93 *Apology*, III: 125–8. Needham himself was involved in a lawsuit with a justice of the island over a portion of his deceased father's estate.

94 See, e.g., planter J. Knight's letter to the Duke of Newcastle recommending British colonization of the Darien isthmus, which could be carried out "agreeable to the Laws of Nations, the Principles of Christianity, and the Constant Maxims of the British Nation, whose Possessions [were] founded in Reason and Justice, and not chimerical Grants, Butchery of Millions of Innocent People, and other unjustifiable Means." BL Add. MS 22677, f. 27, Nov. 20, 1739; see also f. 42b, anon. to J. Knight, Dec. 12, 1740; and Oldmixon, *British Empire*, II: 380.

95 See, e.g., *An Essay Concerning Slavery and the Danger Jamaica is expos'd to from the Too great Number of Slaves* (London: Charles Corbett, [1746]). Maroons' example did in fact inspire some rebellions, such as those in 1742, 1745 and 1760.

96 Beckles, "White Women," 68.

97 For the malaria outbreak, see Gardner, *History*, 123–4; and Richard Harding, *Amphibious Warfare in the Eighteenth Century: The British Expedition to the West Indies, 1740–1742* (Woodbridge: Royal Historical Society, 1991), 149.

98 These include: "Letters from a Gentleman in Jamaica," *Gentleman's Magazine* (36) 1766, 83–5; gossip about her Jamaican boarding school shared by Elizabeth Carter and Catherine Talbot in *A Series of Letters*, II: 85–6, 89; *Assembly Journals*, 5 (1757–66), 77, 78, 84; Phillips, "Jamaica in Miniature"; Wright, *Revels in Jamaica*, 23–4.

99 Elizabeth Carter to Catherine Talbot, Aug. 12, 1752, in *Letters*, 89.

100 The "Letter from a Gentleman in Jamaica," 83–5, provides a number of the details about her marriages, but they can be corroborated in local parish records and Council Books; see also Wright, *Revels*, 23–4.

101 "Letter from a Gentleman," 83–4; Wright, *Revels*, 24.

102 PRO CO 137/28, Correspondence on Jamaica, 1754–5, ff. 1–2, 161–6; Metcalf, *Royal Government*, 140–1; Craton and Walvin, *Jamaican Plantation*, 78–9; Robert Mowbray Howard, *Records and Letters of the Family of the Longs of Longville, Jamaica, and Hampton Lodge, Surrey* (London: Simpkin, Marshall, Hamilton, Kent & Co., 1925), 110.

103 *Assembly Journals*, 5 (1757–66), 77–8.

104 *Dictionary of National Biography*, Henry Moore; Howard, *Longs of Longville*, I: 109–10, 184–9, quotation from 188.

105 CO 137/60, Moore to [Fox], March 24, 1757; CO 137/30, Moore to Board of Trade, April 22 and May 21, 1757; Metcalf, *Royal Government*, 140–1; *St. Jago Intelligencer*, May 14, 1757; Sheridan, *Sugar and Slavery*, 448–59; Drescher, *Econocide*, 75.

106 Oldmixon, *British Empire*, 416–17; *Jamaica Courant*, Aug. 5, 1718; Nov. 2, 1726; June 29, 1754; BL Add. MS 30,001, f. 1, Mary Rickets to Mrs. Hester Jervis, Dec. 5, 1757; *Lady Nugent's Journal*, 141.

107 Oldmixon, *British Empire*, 416; Leslie, 27–30; Frank Cundall, *A History of Printing in Jamaica 1717–1834* (Kingston: Institute of Jamaica, 1935). The two papers were the *St. Jago de la Vega Gazette* and the *St Jago Intelligencer*; there are no extant copies of the former until 1791, and only two of the latter, the one cited in n. 105 and one for April 16, 1768.

108 Oldmixon, *British Empire*, 415–16; Leslie, *New History of Jamaica*, 24–6; *Jamaica Courant*, July 30, Aug. 5, Feb. 11, 1718; April 15, 1719; June 17, Sept. 12, 1720; June 28, 1721; June 20, Sept. 12, 1722; Nov. 2, 1726; May 31, 1727; April 24, 1728; June 24, 1730; June 22–9, 1754; *Jamaica Gazette*, Dec. 14, 1745.

109 See, e.g., *Jamaica Courant*, June 22–9, 1754, advertisement for performance of *The Orphan, or Unhappy Marriage*, and *Tom Thumb the Great*; *Jamaica Gazette*, July 1, 1775, advertising performances of *Romeo and Juliet* and *The Wonder! An Honest Yorkshireman*.

110 See Gillian Russell, *The Theatres of War: Performance, Politics and Society 1793–1815* (Oxford: Oxford University Press, 1995), 17; Wilson, "The Good, the Bad, the Impotent," 243; and "A View from the Pit: Theater and the Politics of Culture in Georgian England," in *The Colonial Stage: Theater, Culture and Modernity in the English Provinces 1720–1800* (in progress).

111 Theophilus Cibber, *Dissertations on Theatrical Subjects* (London: Author, 1756), 83; Hill, *Jamaican Stage*, 10. Hill's important work amplifies the insights and corrects the errors of Richardson Wright's earlier study. As Hill notes, theater was priced to prevent laborers of any color from attending; nevertheless, the Jamaican theater was not segregated until the late eighteenth century, and blacks and people of color, slave and free, did attend.

112 Drums had been banned by Jamaican planters because of their association with war in Africa. Sloane, *Voyage*, I: xlix; Long, II: 424–5. See also Dirks, *Black Saturnalia*; Roger D. Abrahams and John F. Szwed, *After Africa: Extracts from British Travel Accounts and Journals of the Seventeenth, Eighteenth and Nineteenth Centuries concerning the Slaves, their Manners and Customs in the British West Indies* (New Haven: Yale University Press, 1983), 138–279; and Judith Bettelheim, "The Jonkonnu Festival in

Jamaica," *Journal of Ethnic Studies*, 13 (1985), 85–106. The overseer Thomas Thistlewood found these "Negro Diversions" "odd" and "strange": *In Miserable Slavery*, 217–18. In the 1760s, myalism appears as a new African-based religious movement, which claimed to be able to counter the sorcery of both obeah men and Europeans; myal dances were held secretly at several estates, causing great unease.

113 See the accounts of Tacky's rebellion in Long, II: 447–70; Hall, ed., *In Miserable Slavery*, 110–11; Craton, *Testing the Chains*, 125–39. Not surprisingly, Tacky's rebellion stimulated the plantocracy and the metropole to place colonial slavery on a more secure footing: laws were passed to "remedy the evils arising from the irregular meetings of slaves" and to outlaw obeah; and public executions, tortures and deportations were carried out on an unprecedented scale: three to four hundred slaves and about sixty whites died in the rebellion; while over six hundred slaves were deported to Belize. This episode also brought out the distrust of the Jews on the island, whose non-white and non-English identifications had long been suspected. For the rationalization of colonial slavery, see Chris Brown, "An Empire Without Slaves," *WMQ*, 3rd ser., LVI (1999), 298; quotation from Long, II: 463.

114 Elin Diamond, *Unmaking Mimesis* (London: Routledge, 1997), 46–7.

115 George Seilhamer, *The History of the American Theatre* (Philadelphia: F. P. Harper, 1888–91), II: 27; Russell, *Theatres of War*, 165. As the correspondence of the Earl of Sandwich indicates, these transatlantic strolling players were suspected by the imperial government of fomenting disloyalty among the Americans in the 1760s and 1770s.

116 Hill, *Jamaican Stage*, 21.

117 See Philip H. Highfill, Jr., Kalman A. Burnim and Edward A. Langhans, *A Biographical Dictionary of Actors, Actresses and Other Stage Personnel in London, 1660–1800*, 10 (Carbondale: University of Southern Illinois Press, 1982), 289; *Thespian Dictionary* (London: T. Hurst, 1805); William Smith Clark, *The Irish Stage in the County Towns 1720–1800* (Oxford: Clarendon Press, 1965), 69–75.

118 A fuller account of the members of the Hallam company can be found in William Dunlap, *History of the American Theatre*, 3 vols. (New York: Burt Franklin, reprt. 1963), I: 7–22; see also Highfill et al., *Biographical Dictionary*, 7, 29–49.

119 See my *The Colonial Stage*, which includes material on English theatre in Cork, Jamaica, St. Helena, Calcutta and Sumatra.

120 The "experiences and amusements" of the enslaved and lower classes may indeed have been intended to be "irrelevant to the cultural ethos of the island" (75) as Errol Hill has asserted, but cross-fertilization and counter-theater clearly occurred.

121 Patterson, *Sociology of Slavery*, 246–7; Bettelheim, "Jonkonnu Festival," 86.

122 Beckles, "White Women," 81.

5 BREASTS, SODOMY AND THE LASH: MASCULINITY AND ENLIGHTENMENT ABOARD THE COOK VOYAGES

1 Ship's log in Cook, II: 23n; Johann Reinhold Forster, *Observations Made During a Voyage Round the World* [1778], eds. Nicholas Thomas, Harriet Guest and Michael Dettelbach (Honolulu: University of Hawaii Press, 1996), 181; subsequent references in this chapter will be to this edition. Marquis de Sade, *Oeuvres complètes du Marquis de Sade*, eds. Annie Le Brun and Jean-Jacques Pauvert (Paris: Pauvert, 1986), III: 472: "A l'abri aigles romaines, il s'étend d'un bout de la terre à l'autre; à la destruction de l'empire, il se réfugie près de la tiare, il suit les arts en Italie, il nous parvient quand nous nous poliçons. Découvrons-nous un hémisphère, nous y trouvons la sodomie. Cook mouille dans un nouveau monde: elle y règne . . . Il sera un scélérat, un monstre, pour avoir voulu jouer le rôle d'un sexe qui n'est pas le sien!" (my translation). Thanks to Nick Mirzoeff for the latter reference.

2 Most notably in Marshall Sahlins, *Historical Metaphors and Mythical Realities: Structure in the Early History of the Sandwich Islands Kingdom* (Ann Arbor: University of Michigan Press, 1981), chap. 3, and *Islands of History* (Chicago: University of Chicago Press, 1985), chap. 1; Greg Dening, *Mr. Bligh's Bad Language* (Cambridge: Cambridge University Press, 1992); Gannath Obeyesekere, *The Apotheosis of Captain Cook* (Princeton: Princeton University Press, 1992); Roy Porter, "The Exotic as Erotic," in G. S. Rousseau and Roy Porter, eds, *Exoticism in the Enlightenment* (Manchester: Manchester University Press, 1986) 117–44; Rod Edmond, *Representing the South Pacific: Colonial Discourse from Cook to Gauguin* (Cambridge: Cambridge University Press, 1997). In what follows, I am not suggesting that sexual and gender relations were the only or even primary means of ranking Pacific islanders and their societies by the Europeans, merely that they were significant ones.

3 See, e.g., David Stoddart, *On Geography* (Oxford: Blackwell, 1986); David N. Livingstone and Charles W. J. Withers, eds., *Geography and Enlightenment* (Chicago: University of Chicago Press, 1999), quotation from 4; and Nicholas Thomas, *In Oceania: Visions, Artifacts, Histories* (Durham, N.C.: Duke University Press, 1997).

4 Charles de Brosses, *Histoire des Navigations aux Terres Australes*, 2 vols. (Paris, 1756); John Callander, *Terra Australis Cognita*, 3 vols. (Edinburgh: A. Donaldson, 1766), I, iii; see also Alexander Dalrymple, *An Account of the Discoveries made in the South Pacifick Ocean to 1764* (London: Author, 1767). The best discussion of the French and English intellectual background remains John Beaglehole, *The Exploration of the Pacific* (Cambridge: Cambridge University Press, 1966), 165–93.

5 [John Marra], *Journal of the Resolution's Voyage in 1772, 1773, 1774 and 1775 on Discovery to the Southern Hemisphere* (London: F. Newberry, 1775), 173. Marra was expressing a view valorized by such luminaries as Edward Gibbon and William Robertson. See, e.g., William Robertson's *History of America*, 4 vols. (London: W. Strahan and T. Cadell, 1777), I: 2–3.

6 See Beaglehole, *Exploration of the Pacific*, 229–315; Richard Sorenson, "The Ship as a Scientific Instrument in the Eighteenth Century," *Osiris*, 2nd ser., 11 (1996), 221–36 (thanks to Elizabeth Garber for this reference), and John Gascoigne, *Science in the Service of Empire: Joseph Banks, the British State and the Uses of Science in the Age of Revolution* (Cambridge: Cambridge University Press, 1998). Quotation from *AR* (1784–5), 140–50.

7 James Hevia, *Cherishing Men from Afar* (Durham, N.C.: Duke University Press, 1996), 85; Kathleen Wilson, "The Island Race: Captain Cook, Evangelicalism and National Identity," in *Protestantism and National Identity*, Tony Claydon and Ian MacBride, eds., (Cambridge: Cambridge University Press, 1998), 265–90. For an allusive reading of the anthropomorphic consequences of travel writing, see Paul Carter, *The Road to Botany Bay* (London: Faber & Faber, 1987).

8 For the broader political context, see my *The Sense of the People: Politics, Culture and Imperialism in England 1715–1785* (Cambridge and New York: Cambridge University Press, 1995), chap. 5, and Chapter 1 above.

9 John Elliott quoted in Anne Salmond, *Between Worlds: Early Exchanges Between Maori and Europeans 1773–1815* (Honolulu: University of Hawaii Press, 1996), 53.

10 For the problems attendant upon eyewitness observation in the scientific culture of the day see Steven Shapin, *A Social of Truth* (Chicago: University of Chicago Press, 1994); Dorinda Outram, "On Being Perseus: New Knowledge, Dislocation and Enlightenment Exploration," in *Geography and Enlightenment*, 280–8; and Jonathan Lamb, "Eye-Witnessing in the South Seas," *The Eighteenth Century: Theory and Interpretation*, 38 (1997), 201–28. For the "naturalist's gaze," see Hevia, *Cherishing Men*, 85; Wilson, "The Island Race"; quotation is from Samuel Johnson, quoted in Peter Marshall and G. Williams, *The Great Map of Mankind* (London: Dent, 1982), 269.

11 Bridget Orr, "Southern Passions Mix with Northern Art: Miscegenation and the *Endeavour* Voyage," *Eighteenth Century Life*, 18 (1994), 220–1; Cook in Cook, II: 685.

12 George Forster, *A Voyage Round the World, in His Britannic Majesty's Sloop, Resolution* [1777], reprt. in *Georg Forsters Werke*, ed. Robert L. Kahn (Berlin: Akademie-Verlag, 1968), 599, 308. Subsequent references will be to this edition.

13 Columbus's crews were also avid collectors of West Indian artifacts and people: see the descriptions in Christopher Columbus, *The Voyage of Christopher Columbus*, ed. John Cummins (New York: St. Martin's Press, 1992), 115–18, 152 and passim; and Stephen Greenblatt, *Marvellous Possessions: The Wonder of the New World* (Chicago: University of Chicago Press, 1991), 52–85. For the role of curiosity in the European appropriation of Oceanic artifacts, see Nicholas Thomas, *Entangled Objects: Exchange, Material Culture, and Colonialism in the Pacific* (Cambridge, Mass.: Harvard University Press, 1991), 125–84. For early eighteenth-century examples of sailors' propensity to exploit the market for voyage narratives, see Jonathan Lamb, "Re-Imagining Juan Fernandez: Probability, Possibility and Pretence in the South Seas," in Nicholas Thomas and Diane Losche, eds., *Double Vision: Art Histories and Colonial Histories in the Pacific* (Cambridge: Cambridge University Press, 1999), 20–2.

14 Marra, *Journal*, 235–6. Marra later immigrated to Port Jackson. By the second voyage, the natives of New Zealand began to sell "artificial curiosities" fabricated just to satisfy the acquisitive impulses of British crews: see G. Forster, *Voyage*, 289.

15 Foucault, "Of Other Spaces," in N. Mirzoeff, *The Visual Culture Reader* (London: Routledge, 1999), 244; Paul Gilroy, *The Black Atlantic: Modernity and Double Consciousness* (Cambridge, Mass.: Harvard University Press, 1992), 12; Marcus Rediker, *Between the Devil and the Deep Blue Sea* (Cambridge: Cambridge University Press, 1987); Peter Linebaugh, *The London Hanged* (Cambridge: Cambridge University Press, 1992); Marcus Rediker and Peter Linebaugh, *The Many-Headed Hydra: Sailors, Slaves, Commoners and the Hidden History of the Revolutionary Atlantic* (Boston: Beacon Press, 2000); and Greg Dening, *Mr. Bligh's Bad Language* (Cambridge: Cambridge University Press, 1992); see also his *Islands and Beaches* (Chicago: University of Chicago Press, 1980). For the concept of the chronotope, see Mikhail Bakhtin, *The Dialogic Imagination*, ed. Michael Holquist (Austin: University of Texas Press, 1981), 84–5. Other recent accounts of shipboard life include Phillip Edwards, *The Story of the Voyage* (Cambridge: Cambridge University Press, 1994); W. Jeffrey Bolster, *Black Jacks: African American Seamen in the Age of Sail* (Cambridge, Mass.: Harvard University Press, 1997); and N. A. M. Rodger, *The Wooden World* (London: Collins, 1986). Two classic eighteenth-century accounts are Edward Ward, *The Wooden World Dissected: In the Character of a Ship of War* (London: H. Meere, 1707); and Woodes Rogers, *A Cruising Voyage round the World* (London: A. Bell & B. Lintot, 1712).

16 The journals and accounts of the voyages give palpable form to the conflict of wills that riveted the ships' companies: see, e.g., Cook II: 313n; Salmond, *Between Worlds*, 40–1. For the clashes aboard navy and merchant ships, see Rediker, *Devil and the Deep Blue Sea*, 205–53.

17 These figures are for those whose backgrounds can be traced, and exclude the dozen or so marines that were on every vessel. The figures are: on the second voyage: 96 English, 15 Scots, 12 Irish, 2 Americans, 2 "East Indians," 2 Germans, and 1 Bengali, Dutchman, Swede and Azorean; on the third, 110 English, 11 Scots, 7 Irish, 5 Welsh, 7 Americans, 2 Germans, 1 Guernsey and 1 Bengali: calculated from Cook, I: 588–601; III: 872–95, and III: 1457–80; Joseph Banks, *Endeavour Journal*, ed. J. C. Beaglehole, 2 vols. (Sydney: Angus Robertson, Ltd., 1962), I: 220–1.

18 "In the naval context," N. A. M. Rodger has assured us, "the word 'punishment' was virtually synonymous with flogging": *Wooden World*, 218–19. This could take the form of a single whip or colt, but more frequently was executed formally with the cat. For a striking account of the potential for violence aboard eighteenth-century vessels,

see Hans Turley, *Rum, Sodomy and the Lash* (New York: New York University Press, 1999), 10–28.

19 Rediker, *Between the Devil and the Deep Blue Sea*, chap. 5; cf. the more benign view of sea-going life is provided by Rodger in *Wooden World*. More in keeping with Rediker's perspective is Henry Marshall, *Military Miscellany* (London, 1846), who notes that five hundred lashes were a not uncommon naval punishment ordered by court martial in this period. Indeed, in 1812 a law was passed limiting the number of lashes imposed by court martial to three hundred (354, 185). Thanks to Barbara Donagan for this reference.

20 Marra, *Journal*, 43, 133–4; Dening, *Bligh*, 63.

21 Thanks to Philip Morgan for making this comparison. Indeed, parliamentary debates over the use of the lash and the maintenance of shipboard morale often stressed the need to keep the sailors from believing *they* were slaves, by avoiding excessively harsh disciplinary measures. See the Earl Egmont's discussion, quoted in Marshall, *Military Miscellany*, 140–1.

22 For the proportionately greater likelihood of different ethnic groups being punished, see Dening, *Bligh*, 63.

23 Beaglehole, II: 313n. Nevertheless, "it was not unusual for three or four of them one day with another to be punished for going on shore, and one day in particular no less than ten of them were punished for the same offence," Marra recalled (43).

24 Dening, *Bligh*, 384, 116.

25 R. Reynall Bellamy, *Ramblin' Jack: The Journal of Captain John Cremer* (London: J. Cape, 1936), 35–46; Sir Evan Cotton, *East Indiamen: The East India Company's Maritime Service*, ed. Sir Charles Fawcett (London: Batchworth Press, 1949); Rediker, *Devil*, 212–17.

26 Cook, II: 227n; see also ibid., 271–2, 389; Cook, III: 515, 530–2, 1000. Quote from R. McNab, ed., *Historical Records of New Zealand* [1908], vol. II (Wellington: A. R. Sheearer, 1973), 79–80, Cook to Capt. James Walker, Whitby, Yorkshire. For British press accounts of the Maori following the first voyage, see *Critical Review*, 31 (1771), 256; *London Chronicle*, 27–30 July 1771. The *Endeavour*'s crew had found chewed human bones beside an earth oven at Queen Charlotte Sound, thereby inaugurating the crew's trade in heads, bones and hair – all very *tapu*, as embodiments of ancestral power whether of an enemy or kinsman. See Salmond, *Between Worlds*, 68–9, and references there. For a skeptical re-assessment of the Maori "anthropophagi associated with human sacrifice," see Gananath Obeyesekere, "'British Cannibals': Contemplation of an Event in the Death and Resurrection of James Cook, Explorer," in *Identities*, eds. Kwame Anthony Appiah and Henry Louis Gates, Jr. (Chicago: University of Chicago Press, 1995), 7–31.

27 Cook in Cook, II: 413–14; Samwell in Cook, III: 1218–22.

28 For women on other navy vessels, see Chapter 3, and Margaret S. Creighton and Lisa Norling, eds., *Iron Men, Wooden Women: Gender and Seafaring in the Atlantic World 1700–1920* (Baltimore: Johns Hopkins University Press, 1996). A female botanist and friend of Joseph Banks attempted to board the *Resolution* in disguise as a man at Madeira, but was detected: Cook, II: 685.

29 Rodger, *Wooden World*, 80–1, 226–7. In one case, Rodger notes, sodomy received the extraordinary punishment of a thousand lashes.

30 Cook, II: 313, 361, 393; III: 495, 582, 1505, 534. Dening has read the charge of "uncleanliness" to be a euphemism for sodomy, but I am not convinced: *Bligh*, 117.

31 Harriet Guest, "'Curiously Marked': Tattooing, Masculinity and Nationality in Eighteenth-Century British Perceptions of the South Pacific," in John Barrell, ed., *Painting and the Politics of Culture* (Oxford: Oxford University Press, 1992), 112.

32 J. R. Forster, *Observations*, 181.

33 Joseph Banks, "Thoughts on the Manners of the Women of Otaheite," National Library of Australia, MS 94; Marra, *Journal*, 54; Wales in Cook, II: 796.

34 Londa Schiebinger, *Nature's Body: Gender in the Making of Modern Science* (Boston: Beacon Press, 1993), 62.

35 See Barbara Charlesworth Gelpi, *Shelly's Goddess: Maternity, Language, Subjectivity* (Oxford: Oxford University Press, 1992), 47–9; Ruth Perry, "Colonizing the Breast: Sexuality and Maternity in Eighteenth-Century England," *Eighteenth Century Life*, 16 (1992), 185–213.

36 Schiebinger, *Nature's Body*, 52–74; 155–8. For a typical eighteenth-century assessment of the "large and languid" nature of African genitalia and breasts, see Oliver Goldsmith, *A History of the Earth, and Animated Nature*, 8 vols. (London: J. Nourse, 1774), I: 372–3. Pendulous breasts in the later eighteenth and early nineteenth centuries become signs of class deprivation, attributed to hardships of the laboring poor: see, e.g., Samuel Stanhope Smith, *Essay on the Causes of the Variety of Complexion and Figure in the Human Species* (Edinburgh: C. Elliott, 1788), 82–4.

37 G. Forster, *Voyage*, 520; J. Forster, *Observations*, 260.

38 See, e.g., Sander Gilman, "Black Bodies, White Bodies: Toward an Iconography of Female Sexuality in Late 19th Century Art," in *"Race," Writing and Difference*, ed. Henry Louis Gates Jr. (Chicago: University of Chicago Press, 1986), 223–61; Anne Fausto-Sterling, "Gender, Race and Nation: the Comparative Anatomy of 'Hottentot' Women in Europe, 1815–1817," in Jennifer Terry and Jacqueline Urla, eds., *Deviant Bodies* (Bloomington: Indiana University Press, 1995), 19–48; Schiebinger, *Nature's Body*, 53–74; Jennifer L. Morgan, "'Some Could Sucke over Their Shoulder': Male Travelers, Female Bodies, and the Gendering of Racial Ideology," *WMQ*, 3rd ser., LIV (1997), 167–92.

39 For a lucid discussion of this gap between visual and textual description – and of eighteenth-century belief that graphic media "displace[d] the unavoidable subjectivity of the written word" – see Bronwen Douglas, "Art as Ethno-Historical Text: Science, Representation and Indigenous Presence in Eighteenth and Nineteenth Century Oceanic Voyage Literature," in Thomas and Losche, eds., *Double Vision*, 65–99; quotation from 69.

40 J. Forster, *Observations*, 421; G. Forster, *Voyage*, 161. Such a sight, George Forster goes on, "was perhaps more than sufficient entirely to subvert the little reason which a mariner might have left to govern his passions."

41 Bernard Smith, *Imagining the Pacific: In the Wake of the Cook Voyages* (New York and Melbourne: Melbourne University Press, 1992), 132.

42 G. Forster, *Voyage*, 496; Johann Reinhold Forster, *Resolution Journals*, ed. Michael Hoare, 4 vols. (London: Hakluyt Society, 1982), IV: 622, 626; Rüdiger Jöppien and Bernard Smith, eds., *The Art of Captain Cook's Voyages*, 4 vols. (New Haven: Yale University Press, 1988), II: 90–1, 100–1, 231; Cook in Beaglehole, II: 464, 462.

43 As scholars have pointed out, this painting masks the violence done in its name: on the third voyage, Poedua was taken hostage, with her father, Orio, by Cook to find out the whereabouts of two British deserters. Most recently, see Margaret Jolly, "From Point Venus to Bali Ha'I: Eroticism and Exoticism in Representations of the Pacific," in Lenore Manderson and Margaret Jolly, eds., *Sites of Desire, Economies of Pleasure: Sexualities in Asia and the Pacific* (Chicago: University of Chicago Press, 1997), 104–5.

44 Sydney Parkinson, *Journal of a Voyage to the South Seas in His Majesty's Ship, The Endeavour* (London, 1773), pl. xxvii; Cook in Cook, I: 399; see also Banks, *Endeavour Journal*, II: 122–31.

45 Dampier described them as "the miserablest People in the World" who "differ little from Brutes." See [William] Dampier, *A Collection of Voyages* (London: James and John Knapton, 1729), I: 463–6; III: 101–3.

46 Oceanic anthropologists and historians have been at some pains in recent years to emphasize that Judeo-Christian concepts of gender, the family, the "sacred" and the "profane" cannot be mapped onto Oceanic societies in this period. See, for example, Caroline Ralston, "Introduction," in "Sanctity and Power: Gender in Polynesian History," *Journal of Pacific History*, 22 (1987), 115–22; "Polyandry, 'Pollution,' 'Prostitution': the Problems of Eurocentrism and Androcentrism in Polynesian Studies," in B. Caine, E. A. Grosz and M. de Lepervanche, eds., *Crossing Boundaries: Feminism and the Critique of Knowledge* (Sydney: Allen and Unwin, 1988), 71–80; "Deceptive Dichotomies, Private/Public and Nature/Culture: Gender Relations in Tonga in the Early Contact Period," *Australian Feminist Studies* 12 (1990), 65–82; Phyllis Herda, "Gender, Rank and Power in 18th Century Tonga," *Journal of Pacific History*, 22 (1987), 195–207; J. Linnekin, *Sacred Queens and Women of Consequence: Rank, Gender and Colonialism in the Hawaiian Islands* (Ann Arbor: University of Michigan, 1990); and Jolly, "From Point Venus to Bali Ha'I."
47 Nicholas Thomas has made this point eloquently and at length: see his "Gender and Social Relations in Polynesia: a Critical Note," *Canberra Anthropology*, 9 (1986), 78–89; "Unstable Categories: Tapu and Gender in the Marquesas," *Journal of Pacific History*, 22 (1987), 123–38; and "Complementarity and History: Misrecognizing Gender in the Pacific," *Oceania*, 57 (1987), 261–70; and In Oceania. See also Annette Weiner, "Dominant Kings and Forgotten Queens," *Oceania*, 57 (1988), 157–60.
48 Samwell in Cook, III: 1149.
49 Sahlins, *Islands of History*, 6.
50 Jolly, "From Point Venus to Bali Ha'I," 303 n.2.
51 Sahlins, *Islands of History* 26, 7–8; Ralston, "Polyandry, 'Pollution,' 'Prostitution,'" 76–7.
52 "Young chiefs were sexually initiated by older women, preparing them thus for the sexual conquests that singularly mark a political career: the capture of a senior ancestry," Sahlins has argued of the Hawaiians (*Islands of History*, 10), and it seems a reasonable generalization of other eastern Polynesian cultures. On the other hand, having too many lovers before marriage was frowned upon, and adultery after marriage, except for the *arioi* and upper chiefs, was severely chastised.
53 Ralston, "Polyandry," 79 and "Introduction," 116.
54 See, e.g., Cook in Cook, II: xcii–xciii, 207–36; Douglas Oliver, *Ancient Tahitian Society*, 3 vols. (Honolulu: Hawaii University Press, 1974), II: 890–912; H. A. H. Driessen, "Outriggerless Canoes and Glorious Beings: Pre-contact Prophecies in the Society Islands," *Journal of Pacific History*, 17 (1982), 4–17; Meredith Filihia, "'Oro-Dedicated *maro'una* in Tahiti: Their Rise and Decline in the Early post-European Contact Period," *Journal of Pacific History*, 31 (1996), 127–43.
55 Samwell in Cook, III: 1085, 1159; Henry Homes, Lord Kames, *Sketches in the History of Man*, 4 vols. (Edinburgh: W. Creech; London: W. Strahan and T. Cadell, 1778) II: 80–1.
56 Sahlins, *Islands*, 28, 27.
57 Caroline Ralston, "Changes in the Lives of Ordinary Women in Early Post-contact Hawaii," in *Family and Gender in the Pacific*, eds. Margaret Jolly and Martha Macintyre (Cambridge: Cambridge University Press, 1989), 45–8. For the Pacific women's role as investigators of European alterity, see David A. Chappell, "Shipboard Relations between Pacific Island Women and Euroamerican Men 1767–1887," *Journal of Pacific History*, 27 (1992), 131–5. W. H. Pearson first formulated the theory that chiefs' offering of women was an attempt to manipulate sex-starved Europeans, in "European Intimidation and the Myth of Tahiti," *Journal of Pacific History*, 4 (1969), 199–217.
58 I owe this point to Greg Dening.
59 Andrew Kippis, *Biographia Britannica*, 4 vols., 2nd edn (London: C. Bathurst, 1789), "James Cook," 237n.

60 Cook in Cook, II: 444. Cook went on to say that although he could "withstand" the girl's beauty, "the abuse of the old Woman I could not, and therefore hastened into the Boat." – without the young girl however. Greg Dening has suggested to me that this sort of denunciation by Maohi women was a tactic designed to draw attention to themselves; if so it seemed to work. Elliott reported that Cook's celibacy earned him the frequent taunts of the locals: "I have often seen them [the women] jeer and laugh at him, calling him Old, and good for nothing." Quoted in Cook, II: 444n.

61 Marra, *Journal*, 45; Cook in Cook, II: 174–5; G. Forster, *Voyage*, 218.

62 G. Forster, *Voyage*, 133.

63 E.g., Salmond, *Between Worlds*, 76–80; Thomas, *In Oceania*, chap. 4. For the performative nature of Enlightenment science, see Adrian Johns, *The Nature of the Book* (Chicago, 1999).

64 Cook in Cook, III: 56. For an introduction to the complexity of Aboriginal society, see W. H. Edwards, ed., *Traditional Aboriginal Society: A Reader* (Melbourne: Macmillan, 1987).

65 Orr, "Southern Passions," 226–7; Cook, I: 589–99 indicates how many sailors and marines deserted for love.

66 G. Forster, *Voyage*, 290.

67 See Chapter 2. Malthus would elaborate on this view in his *Essay on Population* [4th edn, 1806], ed. Geoffrey Gilbert (Oxford: Oxford University Press, 1993).

68 J.R. Forster, *Resolution Journal*, ed. Michael Hoare, 4 vols. (London Hakluyt Society, 1982), II: 303, 309; see also G. Forster, *Voyage*, 132–3.

69 Clerke in Cook, II: 123n.

70 Harriet Guest, "Looking at Women: Forster's Observations in the South Pacific," in Forster, *Observations*, xlv.

71 Ibid.

72 Wales in Cook, II: 858–9; 790, 819. For a fuller analysis of European–Tannese encounter, see Ron Adams, *In the Land of Strangers: A Century of European Contact with Tanna, 1774–1874* (Canberra: Australian National University, 1984).

73 Wales in Cook, II: 791. For the role of gender within the complex gradations and ranks of Vanuatu society, see Margaret Jolly, "Soaring Hawks and Grounded Persons: the Politics of Rank and Gender in North Vanuatu," in *Big Men and Great Men: Personifications of Power in Melanesia* (Cambridge: Cambridge University Press, 1991), 48–80; Joel Bonnemaison, *The Tree and the Canoe: History and Ethnography of Tanna*, trans. Josée Pérot-Demetry (Honolulu: University of Hawaii Press, 1994). Quotation from *The Phoenix of Sodom or the Vere Street Coterie* (London: J. Cook, 1813), 12.

74 Obeyesekere, "'British Cannibals,'" 7–31; Lee Edelman, "Homographesis," *Yale Journal of Criticism*, 3 (1993), 192.

75 Wales in Cook, II: 791. See also Lee Wallace, "'Too Darn Hot': Sexual Contact in the Sandwich Islands on Cook's Third Voyage," *Eighteenth Century Life*, 18 (1994), 232–42. For the role of sodomy in the "civilizing process" of the conquistadors, see Jonathan Goldberg, *Sodometries: Renaissance Texts, Modern Sexualities* (Baltimore: Johns Hopkins University Press, 1992), part iii. For sodomy as an act of violent conquest, see Richard C. Trexler, *Sex and Conquest: Gendered Violence, Political Order and the European Conquests of the Americas* (Cambridge: Polity Press, 1995); and for the culturally transgressive nature of sodomy, see Turley, *Rum, Sodomy and the Lash*.

76 The complexities of this melding of practice and identity has been addressed by a number of scholars. See Wilson, *Sense of the People*, 219–26; Tim Hitchcock and Michèle Cohen, eds., *English Masculinities: 1660–1800* (London: Longman, 1999), 11–17, 226–8; Randolph Trumbach, *Sex and the Gender Revolution: Heterosexuality and the Third Gender in Enlightenment London* (Chicago: University of Chicago Press, 1998); Tim Hitchcock, *English Sexualities* (Basingstoke: Macmillan, 1997), 72. G. J. Barker-Benfield, *The Culture of Sensibility: Sex and Society in Eighteenth Century Britain*

(Chicago: University of Chicago Press, 1992); Polly Morris, "Sodomy and Male Honour: the Case of Somerset, 1740–1850," in Kent Gerard and Gert Hekma, eds., *The Pursuit of Sodomy: Male Homosexuality in Renaissance and Enlightenment Europe* (New York and London: Harrington Park Press, 1989), 383–406; Louis Crompton, *Byron and Greek Love* (Berkeley and Los Angeles: University of California Press, 1985), 12–62 and "Homosexuals and the Death Penalty in Colonial America," *Journal of Homosexuality*, 1 (1974–6), 277–93; G. S. Rousseau, "The Sorrows of Priapus: Anticlericalism, Homosocial Desire and Richard Payne Knight," in *Sexual Underworlds of the Enlightenment*, eds. G.S. Rousseau and Roy Porter (Manchester: Manchester University Press, 1987), 102–30; Laurence Senelick, "Mollies or Men of Mode? Sodomy and the Eighteenth-Century London Stage," *Journal of the History of Sexuality*, 1 (1974–6), 33–67. For mollyhouse culture, see Netta Goldsmith, *The Worst of Crimes: Homosexuality and the Law in Eighteenth Century London* (Aldershot: Ashgate, 1998); and Rictor Norton, *Mother Clap's Molly House: The Gay Subculture in England 1700–1830* (London: GMP, 1992).

77 Patrick Wald Lasowski, *La Science pratique de l'amour: manuels révolutionnaires érotiques* (Arles: Picquier, 1998); thanks very much to the author for this reference and the French euphemisms for sodomy. Thanks also to Peter Cryle for comments on this portion of my essay. For more fulsome thoughts on the transgressiveness of sodomy, see Marquis de Sade, *Les 120 journées de Sodome, ou, L'Ecole du libertinage* (Paris: Cercle du Livre Précieux, 1964); for the longstanding association of sodomy with disorder, see Cynthia Herrup, *A House in Gross Disorder* (Oxford: Oxford University Press, 2000).

78 Kames, *Sketches*, I: 400–1; ii, 90–1; John Millar, *The Origin of the Distinction of Ranks*, 4th edn (Edinburgh, 1806) 100–5, 180, 191, first quotation from 102; Robertson, *History of America*, I: 102–3, 104–5.

79 Barker-Benfield, *Culture of Sensibility*; Philip Carter, *Men and the Emergence of Polite Society in Britain 1660–1800* (Basingstoke: Macmillan, 2001); Dorothée Sturkenboom, "Historicizing the Gender of Emotions: Changing Perceptions in Dutch Enlightenment Thought," *Journal of Social History*, vol. 34 (1999), 55–75; for the concept of "failed gender," see Judith Butler, *Bodies that Matter* (London: Routledge, 1993) 238.

80 Marra, *Journal*, 54.

81 W. D. Ellis, *An authentic narrative of a voyage performed by Captain Cook*, 2 vols. (London: G. Robinson, 1782), II: 153.

82 These incidents also provide cogent historical examples of how sexual practice could be "regulated through the policing and shaming of gender," as Butler has contended: *Bodies that Matter*, 238.

83 I owe this witty formulation to Richard Drayton.

84 Banks, *Endeavour Journal*, I: 461–2. Aboriginal women of Van Diemen's Land also thought some of the British tars were women: see Cook, III: 55n.

85 *Captain Cook's Second Voyage: The Journals of Lieutenants Elliott and Pickersgill* (Dover, N.H.: Caliban Books, 1984), 69; Wales in Cook, II: 780; see also Forster, *Resolution Journal*, II: 254.

86 Cook in Cook, II: 464, 466.

87 See, e.g., Laura Ann Stoler, *Race and the Education of Desire* (Durham: Duke University Press, 1995), and "Educating Desire in Colonial Southeast Asia: Foucault, Freud and Imperial Sexualities," in *Sites of Desire*, 27–47.

88 James Cook and James King, *A Voyage to the Pacific Ocean*, 4 vols., 2nd edn (London: T. Cadell, 1785), III: 26. Thanks to Burton Edwards of the John Carter Brown Library for sending me a crucial photocopy from this volume. Similarly, Cook's suggestion that New Zealand tribes would make a "musical pipe" from the penis of the men they killed in battle did not find its way into the printed voyage account (Cook in Cook, III: 815).

89 Ellis, *Authentic Narrative*, II: 153.

90 Neil Gunson, *Messengers of Grace* (Oxford: Oxford University Press, 1978), 155.

91 Wales, in Cook, II: 859–60; 791; Forster, *Resolution Journal*, V, 595. Wales later changed his mind.

92 Certainly, as Philip Carter has recently argued, "effeminacy" referred to a range of behaviors that were not sexual: *Men and the Emergence of Polite Society*. But I am arguing that effeminate manners and behavior are *becoming* identified with same-sex desire and practice in the 1770s and 1780s, although not with the abruptness that Trumbach suggests.

93 For the first, see Michèle Cohen, *Fashioning Masculinity* (London: Routledge, 1998); for the second, Millar, *Origin*, 52–5.

94 Senelick, "Mollies or Men of Mode?", 60. Pamphlets throughout the century can be found identifying effeminacy with same-sex desire: see, e.g., the excerpts from *Reasons for the Growth of Sodomy* (1742) and *The Destruction of Sodom Improved* (1756) in Ian McCormick, *Secret Sexualities: A Sourcebook of 17th and 18th Century Writing* (London: Routledge, 1994), 135–42, 160–1; James Burgh, *Britain's Remembrancer* (London: M. Cooper, 1746), 18, 43; and John Brown, *An Estimate of the Manners and Principles of the Time* (London: L. Davis & C. Reymens, 1757).

95 This idea, scarcely remarked upon by scholars, is present in the stadial theory of Millar, Robertson and Kames, all of whom argue that same-sex desire was the product of luxury and excess in advanced societies (where appetites are unrestrained and free to focus on new desires); *and* that restraint is necessary to inflame the men's passions and regard for women.

96 For this see Nicholas Mirzoeff, *Silent Poetry: Deafness, Sign and Visual Culture in Modern France* (Princeton: Princeton University Press, 1995), 30–5 and passim; and "Framed: The Deaf in the Harem," in *Deviant Bodies*, 49–77. The quotation from Rousseau's *Essays on the Origins of Language* (1749) is on 53. As Mirzoeff demonstrates, by the 1830s and 1840s sign language was demoted to being a symptom of the deaf community's pathology. Paul Carter, "Making Contact: History and Performance," in *Living in a New Country: History, Travelling and Language* (London: Faber, 1992), 163.

97 For the British identification of Muslims in general and Turks in particular with the vice of sodomy throughout the early modern period, see Nabil Matar, *Turks, Moors and Englishmen in the Age of Discovery* (New York: Columbia University Press, 1999). It is only fair to note that by the time of the British departure from Tanna, after a stay of a fortnight, Cook remarked upon the "Civil and good Natured" conduct of the Tannese, especially given that the British appeared bearing arms, "as invaders of their Country": Cook in Cook, II: 493.

98 See Michael R. Allen, "Homosexuality, Male Power and Political Organization in North Vanuatu," in *Ritualized Homosexuality in Melanesia* (Berkeley and Los Angeles: University of California Press, 1984), 83–127.

99 See Douglas L. Oliver, *Oceania: The Native Cultures of Australia and the Pacific Islands* (Honolulu: University of Hawaii Press, 1989), 635–8; and *Ancient Tahiti Society*, I: 370; Bengt and Marie Therese Danielsson, "Polynesia's Third Sex: The Gay Life Starts in the Kitchen," and Robert I. Levy, "The Community Function of Tahitian Male Transvestism," in Walter Dynes and Stephen Donaldson, eds., *Ethnographic Studies of Homosexuality* (New York: Garland Press, 1992), 132–3, 316–21; Niel Gunson, "Sacred Women Chiefs and Female Headmen in Polynesian History," *Journal of Pacific History*, XXIII (1987), 58–9, and *Messengers of Grace*; Ben R. Finney, "Notes on Bond-Friendship in Tahiti," *Journal of Polyneisian Society*, 73 (1964), 434; Samuel Manaiakalani Kamakau, *Ruling Chiefs of Hawaii* (Honolulu: University of Hawaii Press, 1961), 234–40; David F. Greenberg, *The Construction of Homosexuality* (Chicago, 1988) 56–65.

100 Wales in Cook, II: 839; Forster, *Observations*, 254. The first *published* account of the *mahu* occurs in George Mortimer, *Observations and Remarks Made During a Voyage to the Islands* (London: T. Cadell, 1792), which describes the infatuation of a sailor with a *mahu* performing in a *heiva* show, whom he had mistaken for a woman.

101 Goldsmith, *Worst of Crimes*, 7 and chap. 1 passim. At the mollyhouses, some men were said to dress in women's clothing and mime pregnancy and childbirth.

102 William Bligh, *The Log of the Bounty* (London: Golden Cockerel Press, 1935), 25, 16–17; James Wilson, *A Missionary Voyage to the Southern Pacific Ocean 1796–98* (London: T. Chapman, 1799), 156–7; see also 200–1, and the description of the *mahu* in 1789 by another *Bounty* sailor, in *The Journal of James Morrison* (London: Golden Cockerel Press, 1935), 238. It was "not to be wondered at," one LMS missionary recorded in his journal, that such chiefs "seem to favour Antinomian principles": quoted by Oliver, *Ancient Tahitian Society*, I: 372. A great deal more work needs to be done on the missionary descriptions of Polynesian sexuality, in which denunciation, titillation and incoherence contend. Consider, for example, Wilson's description of the *arioi* women: "'many of the arreoy women pride themselves on the number of their admirers, and live in a fearfully promiscuous intercourse. Few children can be the consequence, and these are universally murdered the moment they are born. Yet, with all this, many are true and tender wives; their large families prove their sacred attachment to the individual with whom they are united; and our European sailors who have cohabited with them have declared, that more faithful and affectionate creatures to them and their children could no where be found." Ibid., 360.

103 Interestingly, sodomy was alleged by *mahu* in the 1960s to be an "unclean perversion introduced by Europeans": Levy, "Tahitian Male Transvestism," 16.

104 Ralston, "Polyandry," 78.

105 Gunson, "Sacred Women." Gunson argues that in both cases, the long delay in gender identification for Polynesian children probably contributed to reverse gender roles in adult life. Children were named for events and places, not by gender, and, before puberty, domestic chores and childcare were allocated to children on basis of size rather than sex. See also "Great Women and friendship Contract Rites in Pre-Christian Tahiti," *Journal of the Polynesian Society*, 73 (1964), 58–9.

106 Thomas, "Unstable Categories," 134–5.

107 For the *āikane* in Hawaiian society, see Robert Morris, "Āikane: Accounts of Same-Sex Relationships in the Journals of Captain Cook's Third Voyage (1776–1780)," *Journal of Homosexuality*, 19 (1990), 21–54; and "Same-Sex Friendships in Hawaiian Lore: Constructing the Canon," in *Oceanic Homosexualities*, ed. Stephen O. Murray (New York: Garland, 1992), 71–102. While my discussion is much indebted to Morris's important articles and to that by Lee Wallace in "Too Darn Hot," the interpretation is my own.

108 Samwell in Cook, III: 1171–2.

109 Ibid., 1184, 1226.

110 Millar, *Origin*, 100–2; Robertson, *History of America*, I: 92–5; Malthus, *Essay on Population*.

111 John Ledyard, *John Ledyard's Journal*, ed. James Kenneth Munford (Corvallis: Oregon State, 1963), 131–2, also quoted in Morris, "Āikane," 32–3.

112 King in Cook, III: 624.

113 Ibid., 518–19.

114 King in *Voyage to the Pacific*, iii, 26, 30.

115 Wallace, "Too Darn Hot," 237.

116 Samwell in Cook, III: 1185. Here I would cavil with Margaret Jolly's recent contention (in "From Point Venus," 103) that male bodies were not eroticized in the visual images generated by the voyages. This seems to me to be an overly literal

definition of the erotic and the male, as the paintings and drawings of eastern Polynesian phallic statues suggest.

117 Beaglehole in Cook, III: lxxviii; Wallace also makes this point in "Too Darn Hot," 236.

118 For liminality, see Victor Turner, *The Forest of Symbols* (Ithaca: Cornell University Press, 1967), 94–7 and *Dramas, Fields and Metaphors* (Ithaca: Cornell University Press, 1974), 274. In a description of Omai, the tattoos on his hands were interpreted as Tahitian signs of marriage: "Omiah . . . has been honoured with eight or ten sets of these marks, having already had as many wives." *Annual Register*, 17 (1774), 61.

119 Heywood's letter is included in Sir John Barrow, *A Description of Pitcairn's Island and Its Inhabitants with an Authentic Account of the Mutiny* (New York: Harper and Bros., 1845), 131, and is also quoted at greater length in Edmond, *Representing the South Pacific*, 70.

120 As Millar wrote, one of "the great expedients of nature" was to convert a "simple desire or appetite . . . into a violent passion" by restraint or prohibition: Millar, *Origin*, 58, 61.

121 Michael Taussig, *Shamanism, Colonialism and the Wild Man: A Story in Terror and Healing* (Chicago: University of Chicago Press, 1987), 121.

EPILOGUE: "SAVE THE STONES!" KING ALFRED AND THE PERFORMANCE OF ORIGINS

1 Upper Deverill Parish Council and Upper Deverill Village Hall Committee, *Save the Stones!* [June 4, 2000]; Ethandun Memorial Committee, *Removal of One of the Sarsen Stones from Kingston Deverill Village* [June 2000], Chris Ralph, *The Kingston Deverill Sarsen Stones* [June 2000]. Thanks to Sacha Mirzoeff for this material.

2 *New York Times*, July 4, 2001.

3 Joseph Roach, *Cities of the Dead* (New York: Columbia University Press, 1996), 6.

4 Christopher Hill, "The Norman Yoke," in *Puritanism and Revolution*, reprt. (Harmondsworth: Penguin, 1990), 58–125; Iain McCalman, *Radical Underworld* (Cambridge: Cambridge University Press, 1989); James Watt, *Contesting the Gothic: Fiction, Genre and Cultural Conflict 1764–1832* (Cambridge: Cambridge University Press, 1999), 49–55, quotation from 51.

5 Kenneth Woodbridge, *Landscape and Antiquity: Aspects of English Culture at Stourhead 1718–1838* (Oxford: Clarendon Press, 1970), 54–5. The Tower was completed in 1772.

6 See David Garrick and David Mallet, *Alfred, a Masque* (London: T. Cadell, 1773); Alexander Bicknell, *The Life of Alfred the Great, King of the Anglo-Saxons* (London: J. Bew, 1777); and *The Patriot King: or Alfred and Elvida: An Historical Tragedy* (London: Author, 1788); John Ryland, *The Life and Character of Alfred the Great* (London, 1784); and Chapter 2. For contending political positions adopted through invocation of Gothic identities, see Colin Kidd, *British Ethnicities Before Nationalism* (Cambridge: Cambridge University Press, 1998). The eighty-nine entries brought up by the Eighteenth Century Short Title Catalogue under the keyword Alfred include poems, plays, ballads instructors, histories, political pamphlets and Alfred's translation into Anglo-Saxon of Orosius.

7 For Forster, see Chapter 2 above and his *Observations on the Geography of King Alfred* (London, 1773); for Carter, see *A Series of Letters Between Mrs. Elizabeth Carter and Miss Catherine Talbot*, ed. Montagu Pennington, 4 vols. (London: F. C. and J. Rivington, 1809), 148–9. See also Harriet Guest, *Small Change: Women, Learning and Patriotism* (Chicago: University of Chicago Press, 2000), chap. 5.

8 David Hume, *The History of England*, 7 vols. (London, T. Cadell, 1802), I: 99.

9 Reginald Horsman, "Origins of Racial Anglo-Saxonism in Great Britain Before 1850," *Journal of the History of Ideas*, 37 (1976), 390.

10 The importance of this aspect of English performance history is discussed by Roach, *Cities of the Dead*, 103–10.

INDEX

Gilray, James: *Sale of English Beauties* 98, 100*illus*
Gilroy, Paul 31, 173, 210n
Goldsmith, Oliver 5, 7, 8, 10, 13
gossip: in colonial world 136–7, 137–8, 156, 161; as slave resistance 153, 164
Gothic inheritance 85, 86, 203
Grant, Lewis 14
Green, Valentine 111–12
Greenfeld, Liah 80
Gronniosaw, Ukawsaw 44, 45
Guest, Harriet 177
Gunson, Neil 267n

Hadden, Lieut. James 232n
Hall, Catherine 211n
Hall, Stuart 3
Hallam, Lewis 166
Hallam, William 166, 167
Happy Courtezan, The (pamphlet) 144
Hardwicke, Philip Yorke, Earl of 137; Marriage Act 143
Hardy, Mary 106, 107
Harnage, Mrs 121, 124
Hau Fa'naui 185
Hawaiian people: *āikane* 196–9; doubt virility of Europeans 192–3; as ignoble savages 78; impact of European expeditions on 185; sexual practices 184, 186, 263n; tattoos 180
Haweis, Thomas 81
Hawkesworth, John: *Voyages* 58, 59, 80
Hay, Michael 162
Hayman, Francis: *Triumph of Britannia* 20*illus*
Hays, Mary Ludwig (Molly Pitcher) 102
Haywood, Eliza 108–9, 249n
headmen, female 196
heathenism 81, 82; sanctification of sexuality 184–6, 196
Henry, John 155
Herd, Leonard 33
heritage politics 201–4
"hermeneutics of suspicion" 190
Hevia, James 171
Heywood, Peter 199
Highlanders: subject of ethnographic study 87
Highmore, John: T. C. Phillips portrait 133*illus*, 145
Hill, Errol 257n, 258n
H/history: analysis of modernity 29–31; ancient history of Britain 84–91, 112,

203–4; heritage politics 201–4; identity as historical process 3; and national identity 8–10, 84–9, 111, 117–18; as popular feminine pursuit 111–12; subaltern sources 26–7; theatrical representations 88–9, 201, 203
Hitihiti (Mahine)(mediator) 65, 187
Hoare, Henry 203
Hodges, William 66; *Tahiti Revisited* 75, 76*illus*, 180
Hogarth, William 97
Holt, Thomas 3
Home, John 89
homoeroticism of Polynesian culture 199
homophobia on Cook voyages 177, 190
homosexuality *see* same-sex desire
homosociality: same-sex island groups 195–9
Horne, Rev. Melville 87
hospitals: army hospitals 101; Lock and Magdalene hospitals for fallen women 141–2; subscriptions to 36
Hottentot Venus (Saartje Bartman) 179
Howe, General William 97
Hudson, Nicholas 211n
Hulme, Obadiah 85
human development, study of: breasts as metonym 169, 177–84, 188–9; discovery voyages extend 58, 71–80, 171; North American example 122–3; physical markers of 178–9, 180, 183; requirements for progress 77–80; social evolutionism 72–3, 74–5, 78; stadial theory 8–10, 72–3, 77–8, 80, 187; treatment of women indicator 23–4, 74–5, 77, 179, 198, 242n; *see also* race
human nature: degenerative tendencies of female nature 25–6; gender differences 24–5; influences on 10
human sacrifice 72, 81, 84, 87
Hume, David: on Alfred the Great 203; on history of nations 84–5; on identity 2; on national character 7–8, 13; on study of History 111; and uniformity of nature 209n
Hunter, Robert 149

identity: concept in premodern society 1–3; as historical process 3; sexual identity 22–3, 199–200; *see also* gender, national identity
imagined communities 49; print culture reinforces 31–6

moral difference between races 10; *see also* sexual practices
More, Hannah 24, 25, 60, 108, 215*n*
Morgan, Edward 256*n*
Morgan, Philip 253*n*
Morris, Robert 196
Mughal warriors 14
Muilman, Henry 134–5, 137
mulattos in Jamaica 148, 150, 155
myalism 258*n*

Nanny (obeah priestess) 150
nation: concept in History 8–10; as racial concept 7, 11–12, 15
national character 7–8; degenerates out of context 13–14, 154; effect of climate in Jamaica 154; effeminacy undermines 37, 191; and History 13; immutability of 91; impact of empire on 16, 27; morality as formative feature 10
national identity 3–15, 205*n*; absolutist view of 8–9; Caribbean ambivalence 130–1; as category of difference 7; as changing continuum 204; concept of 3–4; of English *see* Englishness; essentialist view of 8, 10; and gender 18–27, 42–3, 93–6, 199–200; heritage politics 202–3; and History 8–10, 84–9, 111, 117–18; impact of empire on 6, 10–11, 16, 27–8, 49–53, 203–4; "island race" 54–6, 84–91, 203–4; legal conditions in Jamaica 148; moral difference 10; and otherness 43–8, 58, 67, 177; print culture reinforces 31–6; and race 7, 9–12, 15; in stadial theory 8–9; and theater 63, 164, 165–6
Native Americans 17, 112, 122, 123, 150
natural history/sciences: classification of human societies 55, 171, 178; "deep time" 9; voyages enhance knowledge 71–80, 171; *see also* race, science
nature: and nurture form national identity 6, 10; *see also* human nature, state of nature
Needham, Hampson 156
Needham, Henry 136–7, 156, 160
Needham, William 156
network of empire 16–18
Neville, Sylas 39
"new biography" 207*n*
New Caledonia: women of 77, 180
New Hebrides *see* Vanuatu

New Holland Aborigines 72, 180, 182*illus*, 183, 231*n*
New Zealand peoples *see* Maori people
Newcastle General Magazine 1
newspapers: in colonial Jamaica 162; debate on Sierra Leone repatriation project 45–6; provincial 32–6
ni-Vanuatu *see* Vanuatu
"noble savage": ancient Britons as 85, 112; Omai as 63, 64*illus*, 65–70; as primitivist construction 70–1, 72
Nott, Job 90
Nugent, Lady 255*n*
Nussbaum, Felicity 141

obeah magic 150, 153, 164
Oberea ("queen" Purea) 65
Obeyesekere, Gananath 190
O'Brien, Karen 111
Oceania *see* Pacific peoples
O'Flaherty, Major 166
Ogle, Rear-Admiral Sir Chaloner 157, 158
O'Halloran, Sylvester 87
O'Keefe, John *see* Omai, or a Trip around the World
Oldmixon, John 144, 151, 251*n*
Omai (noble savage) 63, 65–70, 78, 90; Reynolds portrait 64*illus*, 65; tattoos 268*n*
Omai, or a Trip around the World (O'Keefe and Shields) 54, 62–70, 83, 89; critical reception 66, 67
Oro (Tahitian god) 75, 185
Orr, Bridget 187, 230*n*
Ortiz, Fernando 17–18, 247*n*
Ossian (James Macpherson) 87
other/otherness: and national identity 43–8, 58, 67, 177; projected desires 192
Ottawa Indians 123
Otway, Thomas 142, 166
Oxford History of the British Empire 16

"Pacific craze" 59, 70, 85
Pacific peoples: artistic representations 75, 76*illus*, 77, 84; assessments of breasts 177–84, 188–9; classification of 9, 67, 73–4, 75, 77, 90–1, 171, 178; comparison with ancient Britons 86–7; dynastic rivalries 185; effeminacy of 191; European corruption and exploitation of women 187, 188, 200; flogging as discipline for 175, 200;

homoeroticism in culture of 199; and
identity 17, 199–200; "Indian"
designation 67; interpretations and
misinterpretations of Cook voyages
169–200; moral turpitude 81–2;
sanctification through sexual
intercourse 184–6, 196; sexual
practices misrecognized 169, 184–6,
189–200; sodomy attributed to 23,
189–90, 191–2, 193–200; study of
9–10, 70–80, 90–1; theatrical
representations 66–7, 70; theories on
origins of 73–4, 194
Pakington, Sir Herbert 135–6
pantomime 63
Parkinson, Sydney 79*illus*, 180
Pateman, Carol 224*n*
Paton, Diana 254*n*
patriotism: Britannia as embodiment of
93–4, 95*illus*; as manly virtue 37, 38–9,
41, 109; of women on home front
108–9, 126
Pearson, George 86
pekio 196
penis sheaths 192
Penlez brothel riots 141
Percy, Thomas 85
performance: of difference 63, 67, 151; and
national identity 17, 164, 165–6,
213–14*n*; Phillips's *Apology* as 137,
140–1; of plantocracy in Jamaica
151–3; as resistance in Jamaica 153,
164; sexual custom in Pacific islands
186; theater in Jamaica 131, 163–7; *see
also* display, theater
periodicals: travel accounts in 208–9*n*
Phillips, Teresia Constantia 131–46;
Apology 129, 131, 132, 134, 135, 137,
138–44; *Apology* reception and
reactions to 142–4; background and
family 132–4; bigamous marriages 131,
134–5; "black widow" epithet 160, 168;
in Boston society 136–7; as career
widow 158–9; character 140, 143; on
Creole character 156–7; death 167;
debt 135, 137, 158, 167; early liaisons
134, 135–7; on England 145–6;
Englishness 157–8, 168; exotic
depiction 133*illus*, 145; in Jamaica
136–7, 146, 156–68; as Mistress of the
Revels 131, 160–1, 162–3, 166–7;
notoriety 132, 135, 136–7, 137–8, 140,
142–5, 156; opinions on Jamaican

issues 157, 159–60; servants fidelity to
158
philology 86
Phipps, Captain Constantine 48, 58
physical features: environmental
adaptation 14, 154; as marker of
human development 178–9, 180, 183;
see also breasts
Pickersgill, Lieut. Richard 58
Pilkington, Laetitia 249*n*
Pinkerton, John 85
Pitcher, Molly 102
plantation societies: in West Indies 130,
146–7, 151–3, 156–8, 160–1, 164–6;
women in 21–2
Poedooa (chief's daughter) 180, 181*illus*
Poetata (servant) 65
politics: heritage politics 201–4; of
identity 2; opposition use of print
culture 34–6; women's role in 40–3
Pollard, Robert 126, 127*illus*
polygamy 141, 142
polygeneticism 77
Polynesia *see* Hawaiian people, Maori
people, Marquesas people, Society
Islands, Tahitian people, Vanuatu
Poor Blacks Going to their Settlement, The
(satirical print) 46, 47*illus*, 48
Porter, Roy 206*n*, 214*n*
postmodernism 30
Prakash, Gyan 27, 114
press gangs 105–6
primitivism 70–2, 73; antiprimitivism 71,
72, 78–80; *see also* savages
print culture: accounts of voyages 58,
59–60, 78, 80; in colonial Jamaica 162;
denigration of Phillips 142–5; and
national identity 31–6; travel accounts
208–9*n*; Wilkite journalism 38–9;
women's role in 40; *see also* newspapers
progress in human development 77–80
promiscuity: European corruption of
Pacific islanders 187; "free love" of
Tahitians 75, 78, 81, 83, 184; misrecognition 184; in stadial theory 142
prostitution 141–2
Protestantism 44–5; evangelical
missionaries 80–4, 87
provincial culture: clubs and societies 37;
newspapers 32–6; theater 36–7
psychoanalysis and identity 207*n*
punishment: slave punishments in Jamaica
152–3

Wilkinson, Colonel James 124, 126
Williams, John 84
Wilson, Captain James 234n, 267n
Windward Maroons 150
Woffington, Peg 108&*illus*
Wollstonecraft, Mary 243n
women: breasts as metonym for human
 development 169, 177–84, 188–9;
 Britannia as symbol of empire 19,
 20*illus*, 38*illus*, 39; as citizens 40–3; as
 civilizing influence 19, 21, 24–5, 75,
 77; degenerative tendencies 6, 19,
 25–6, 103, 105, 142–3, 155;
 destabilizing influence 22, 39, 223n;
 effeminacy attributed to 194; European
 corruption and exploitation of native
 women 187, 188, 200; "fallen women"

138, 141–5; histories of 111–12;
patriotic endeavors 108–9, 126;
reputation 137–8; role in 18C society
92–6; sanctification through sexual
intercourse 184–6, 196; as spies 102–3;
status in colonial societies 21–2;
Tahitian women 75, 77, 178, 179–80,
191; treatment of women as
development indicator 23–4, 74–5, 77,
179, 198, 242n; and warfare 94,
96–128; *see also* body, gender, marriage,
sexual practices
Woolhead, Thomas 160
Woollett, William 112, 113*illus*
Wright, Richardson 257n

Zong incident (1781) 56, 227n